LITERARY NAMES

Literary Names

Personal Names
in English Literature

ALASTAIR FOWLER

OXFORD
UNIVERSITY PRESS

Great Clarendon Street, Oxford, OX2 6DP,
United Kingdom

Oxford University Press is a department of the University of Oxford.
It furthers the University's objective of excellence in research, scholarship,
and education by publishing worldwide. Oxford is a registered trade mark of
Oxford University Press in the UK and in certain other countries

© Alastair Fowler 2012

The moral rights of the author have been asserted

First published 2012

Impression: 1

British Library Cataloguing in Publication Data
Data available

Library of Congress Cataloging in Publication Data
Data available

ISBN 978-0-19-959222-7

Printed in Great Britain by
Clays Ltd, St Ives plc

For my daughter Alison

Preface

My title *Literary Names* calls for explanation. The subtitle "Personal Names in English Literature" provides some of this but not quite enough. It gives no hint that while the main focus is on English I have made sorties into Latin, Greek, French, and Italian.

This book is an expansion of my 1974 Witter Bynner lecture at Harvard and my 2008 F. W. Bateson lecture at Oxford. Discussion after the Bateson lecture suggested the subject of literary names was far larger than I had grasped, and deserved treatment at book length. Subsequent work confirmed this: indeed, it now seems that a single book is hardly enough.

The following pages do not amount to a definitive or systematic treatise. I have rather aimed at a series of interrelated essays exploring how names have functioned in literature. The broader chapters (1, 2, 4, 7, and 9) are mixed with others on individual authors who use names in specially interesting ways: Spenser, Shakespeare, Milton, Dickens, Joyce, and Nabokov. I hope these case studies may be found less superficial.

Emphasis has fallen on earlier literature, partly because I am less ignorant about it and partly because names mattered more in Renaissance literature, and more diversely. In pre-Enlightenment literature names loomed large, not least in its hidden levels, in acrostics and anagrams.

A book of this sort incurs a mountain of indebtedness—more, probably, than I am aware of, and certainly more than can be adequately acknowledged here. Perhaps the greatest intellectual debt of scholars is to educative conversation with colleagues and friends. In my case this means colleagues at Oxford, Edinburgh, Princeton, Charlottesville, and elsewhere—many of them now gone: F. W. Bateson, Irvin Ehrenpreis, C. S. Lewis, Wallace Robson. Among living colleagues at Edinburgh University, it is a pleasure to acknowledge what I have learned from Michael Bury, Owen Dudley Edwards, Liz Elliott, R. D. S. Jack, Roger Savage, and Susan Shatto (the last almost a collaborator).

Others, elsewhere, have corresponded generously: William Bellamy, Eleanor Cook, Jerry Leath Mills, James Nohrnberg, Bernard Richards, Tom Roche, Roger Swearingen, David Vander Meulen, Sir Christopher Ricks, and Jack Levenson (who after more than thirty years of contestation has finally persuaded me that *Finnegans Wake* is immensely enjoyable). On heraldry, I consulted Robin Orr Blair (formerly Lord Lyon King of Arms) and Katy Lumsden of the Genealogical Office, Dublin.

Former pupils too have instructed me, especially Christopher Butler, Anne Coldiron, Tom Corns, Peter Field, and Misako Himuro. But debts to pupils remain unknowably vast.

Some friends or acquaintances made the sacrifice of reading individual chapters or part chapters in draft: Howard Erskine-Hill, Robert Cummings, Denis Feeney, Juan Pellicer, and Peter Davidson. Others helped on particular points: John Burrow, Martin Dodsworth, Peter France, Christopher de Hamel, Emrys Jones, Aleta Konkol, Norman Kreitman, Michael Lurie, Mark Scowcroft, Karen Thompson, and Robbert Wetselaar. And always the staff of the National Library of Scotland have been unfailingly helpful.

It is a particular pleasure to acknowledge the contribution of Professor John Considine of the University of Alberta, who made many learned and valuable suggestions.

What I owe to my wife Jenny may be imagined from the fact that she had to talk names every single day for three years.

Alastair Fowler
Edinburgh, 2011

Contents

Abbreviations

12N	*Twelfth Night*
a.	*adjective*
Aen.	*Aeneid*
AYLI	*As You Like It*
BL	British Library
c.	approximately
CCCHA	*Colin Clouts Come Home Againe*
EETS	The Early English Text Society
e.s.	extra series
FQ	*The Faerie Queene*
HTOED	*Historical Thesaurus of the Oxford English Dictionary*
MND	*A Midsummer Night's Dream*
MWW	*Merry Wives of Windsor*
n.s.	new series
N&Q	*Notes and Queries*
o.s.	original series
OCD	*Oxford Classical Dictionary*
ODECN	*Oxford Dictionary of English Christian Names*
ODN	*Oxford Dictionary of Nicknames*
ODNB	*Oxford Dictionary of National Biography*
OED	*Oxford English Dictionary*
OLD	*Oxford Latin Dictionary*
ONC	*Oxford Names Companion*
PMLA	*Publications of the Modern Language Association*
SC	*The Shepheardes Calender*
SEnc	*The Spenser Encyclopedia*
STS	The Scottish Text Society
TLS	*The Times Literary Supplement*
Var. Spenser	*Variorum Spenser*
wr.	written

Is not my name Sir Bounteous, am I not exprest there?
(Thomas Middleton, A Mad World, My Masters 4.3.44)

Introduction

What is it we call a proper name? and how do proper names differ from common nouns? Such questions have long been wrangled over by philosophers. Some of them consider proper names meaningless, crediting them with unique specificity of reference, so that "Napoleon's barber" denotes one man only—as if there were only one Napoleon and he never changed his barber. And how are we to reconcile uniqueness with the thousand George Washingtons in the USA? The comparative uniqueness of proper names goes with the untranslatability W. H. Auden draws attention to.[1] Other philosophers regard names as condensed descriptions, the most meaningful of nouns.[2] Can one even be sure that proper names are a "subdivision" or "subset of language", as Laurie Maguire assumes?[3] Her view becomes problematic when one reflects that any proper name can become a common noun ("a Judas", "a Hitler"), and conversely that all words— grammatical words as well as nouns—can be names. The Who perhaps thought it would be original to call themselves after a relative pronoun; but grammatical words have often been used as names: for example From, Thus, How, and And.[4] Paul Ziff tries to get out of these thickets by saying that proper names ordinarily are not part of language at all, and so escape grammatical and linguistic constraints.[5] But Ziff's extreme measure is unnecessary. One need only be aware of the confusion that easily arises from the ambiguity in Latin *nomen* ("name", "noun"), particularly among writers like Thomas Sprat, who identified names with words and paired words with things.[6]

The question whether names are meaningful received a classic statement in Plato's *Cratylus*. This seminal but often misunderstood dialogue opposes the onomastic theories of the stylist Hermogenes and the Heraclitean philosopher Cratylus. Hermogenes argues that names are arbitrarily assigned; Cratylus thinks them natural and meaningful. Socrates, represented as more of a linguist than either, speaks of names as correct "at the time of utterance". He overthrows both their positions; which should discourage any simple contrast. But this conclusion has seldom been drawn: the un-Platonic dichotomy is too convenient. And many suppose the so-called "essentialists" of the early modern period preferred Cratylus' view (wrongly identified with Socrates').[7] Nevertheless, Anne Barton has shown the usefulness of the terms Cratylic and Hermogenean. They serve as clear labels for contrasting sorts of name: the ordinary, meaningless name and the meaningful, often moral, name, as in Morality plays.[8] "Magnificence" is a Cratylic name, "Kermode" is Hermogenean. Thomas Docherty holds that significant names restrict the freedom of fiction by determining character development.[9] But the wide variation in names' explicitness and plausibility makes this thesis highly debatable.

Useful as the terms have proved to be, they are not without difficulties. A name may, for example, be hard to place within either category exclusively. After all, every word in literature is supposed to be in some sense apt and meaningful. Not that all literary names need be explicit charactonyms: they can be meaningful in different ways. When Humpty-Dumpty demands what Alice's name means, she wonders "*must* a name mean something?" "Of course it must," says Humpty positively: "my name means the shape I am—and a good handsome shape it is, too. With a name like yours, you might be any shape, almost."[10] "Humpty-Dumpty" was then still descriptive of "a short, dumpy, hump-shouldered person".[11] Alice recognizes Humpty at sight because she has just recited the riddling nursery rhyme and knows, or thinks she knows, the answer is an egg.[12] Lewis Carroll, that is, C. L. Dodgson the mathematical logician (two names for two distinct identities), knew that names cannot easily be categorized as meaningful or meaningless. "Alice" and "Humpty-Dumpty" had their histories and meant different things at different times.

As we shall see, Victorian writers knew that names like Alice formerly had meanings. Besides, the most Hermogenean of names may have allusive potential. The original meaning of "Hitler" has become obscure; yet a writer could hardly name a character "Hitler" without intending an allusive type-name. Allusion being a relatively recent device in vernacular literatures, early discussions of naming overlooked it. But when Sir Philip Sidney writes of "the Terentian Gnatho and our Chaucer's Pandar so expressed [represented] that we now use their names to signify their trades", he shows some awareness of how proper names can become allusive common names.[13] More recently, Ludwig Wittgenstein (1889–1951) in his attempt to purify the language of the philosophical tribe, subjected naming to determined analysis. But he was not much aware of the historical entanglement of names, the "complex human circumstances under which the naming of persons becomes charged with meaning and power".[14] As Frank Kermode notes, "names can have power, but not always",[15] citing *Tempest* 1.1: "What cares these roarers for the name of king?" and *Coriolanus* 5.6.100, where Coriolanus is disallowed the name Martius. Every word, to some degree, retains associations, both individual and communal, which give it meaning. Possessed as he was by his quest for the chimeric, fundamental particle of reference—the irreducible name— Wittgenstein did not see that associations are ineradicable. A word's sense, even its sound, adheres to it, whatever its referential function.

Philosophers innocent of linguistics tend in their discourse to rely implicitly on the generalizing present tense. Doing so simplifies many philosophical problems wonderfully. It took an Egyptologist, Sir Alan Gardiner (1879–1963), to detect the error of this synchronic approach. Gardiner thought it deplorable that logicians should say "here the word *smith* ... is used as a proper name ... as if the name 'Smith' were a fortuitous momentary application, and had not belonged to its owner from the very day of his birth"—or, to put it a little more exactly, from the registration of his birth.[16] Few philosophers have joined Saul Kripke in discussing how names are arrived at; and fewer still consider how they change with context. Kripke shows flaws in the simple cluster-of-descriptions theory of names. How, for example, are ambiguous references to be explained? (Is "Cicero" a Roman orator or a German spy?).[17] But even Kripke cannot be said to explore the temporal dimension very far. Every name changes its meaning over time. The ambiguity of "Cicero" did not antedate World War II. Nicknames are particularly mutable. As a medical student I was called Slasher; but few call me that now. Much depends on historical context: "Kevin", the name of a seventh-century saint of noble Leinster ancestry, became a 1980s type-name for a flashy, lower-class youth. In discussing names, diachronic factors always need to be kept in mind.

Fictional names

In real life, first names are usually chosen by parents or godparents or—in the case of some nineteenth-century servants—imposed by employers. Births are by statute registered by name at a Registry, and the Registrar may disallow the proposed given name if it seems outrageously foolish or cruel. Surnames, however, are in Britain part of the inheritance of a child, who bears the name passed on from paternal ancestors, either directly or according to a patronymic rule. But names in literature are not inherited like this: a fictional character's name must be found or invented—if, that is, the character is to be named at all. The novelist Joyce Cary once told Wallace Robson he thought it a good working rule that characters should not be named unless they play a part in the story.

    This is a point of some importance: many writers find it impossibly difficult to select the right name for a character. For the "true name" must perfectly suit a character who as yet does not fully, or even definitely, exist. To arrive at this right name the writer must relinquish shadowy alternatives—between which there has up till now been secret hesitation—and must embrace one, newly definite, character. Naming a fictional character thus calls for more knowledge than the writer had when earlier, vaguer drafts were sketched. Yet many writers cannot get started until they have names, however provisional these may be. Kingsley Amis agonized over using "Margaret" (Philip Larkin's friend's name) in *Lucky Jim*.[18] He seems to have wanted a real name with associations he knew. J. R. R. Tolkien had similar difficulties with *The Hobbit*; at one stage Bilbo Baggins ran a serious risk of being called "Bingo". It is understandable, then, that a character's name may need to be changed. Often such changes are put down to oversight; but they may be the result of deliberate decisions.[19] George Bernard Shaw seems to have had an unusual writing practice, in that he drafted dialogue for anonymous characters.[20]

    To overcome such difficulties, many writers select names from some sort of real-life list. Shakespeare drew on William Camden's essays on names in *Remains*; Henry Fielding used a subscription list; Henry James collected names from *The Times* newspaper for future use; Émile Zola studied the *Paris Directory*; and Irvine Welsh gets his names from the Edinburgh phonebook.[21] Charles Dickens has been imagined finding names by chance on posters or vehicles. In fact, as we shall see, he too kept lists of possible names, with many alternatives for the same character.[22] Such lists sometimes merit more attention than they have usually received from critics.

Another route a writer may follow is to take over a name already selected by an earlier writer. Again, this possibility has not apparently been much explored. Yet it is probably commoner and more significant than we realize, if only because the name then comes trailing clouds of associations, good or bad, from previous literary incumbents. In short, it may be an allusive name. Think how often romance heroes have been called Arthur, or Gawain. Samuel Butler's Hudibras alludes to Spenser's unwise Hudibras in *The Faerie Queene*, who in turn alludes to the legendary king in Geoffrey of Monmouth. Similarly, Soames in Galsworthy's *Forsyte Saga* may be named after the business manager of Trollope's Lord Lufton.

A sort of literary name almost invariably allusive is the mythological. The names of deities in particular already had rich implications in classical times, and were among the first to acquire a similar potency of reference in vernacular literature. They will require separate treatment in discussing literary periods when mythology tended for one reason or another to be taken seriously, as for example with Spenser and Shakespeare. In the Middle Ages, when pagan mythology had to be accommodated through moral or spiritual allegory, the names of deities often served as moral type-names. The Renaissance mythographers still laboured to discover philosophical significances in the pagan gods. Thus Natale Conti (c. 1520–82) divides his explanations under the heads *historice*, *physice*, *ethice*, and the like: euhemeristic, scientific, and moral.[23] In popular handbooks these meanings could become starkly simple: in *Parnassus Illustratus* Diana is said to be "the goddess of hunting and virginity; and she is the moon". Julius Caesar Scaliger's *Poetice* (1561) distinguishes two kinds of *numina*: one group of powers divine and the other expressing internal experience.[24]

The habit of finding moral meanings in all sorts of names led to their being regarded as ideals of behaviour, especially for the bearer of the name. One's name was to be lived up to, and valued because embodying reputation: it might therefore be of ultimate importance. According to Joseph Addison, "every honest Man sets as high a Value upon a good Name, as upon Life it self".[25] In an early essay Robert Louis Stevenson focuses on the formative effect of a person's name, which "makes itself felt from the very cradle". Such views on what is sometimes called nominative determinism have been statistically validated: study of American dental rolls, for example, show a significant correlation between men called Dennis and men becoming dentists.

Stevenson remembers the pride "with which [he] hailed Robin Hood, Robert Bruce, and Robert le Diable as [...] name-fellows", and considers those who have triumphed over the dire influence of unfortunately anticlimactic names such as William Shakespeare Cockerill and John Milton Hengler.[26] Notable among these is Dante Gabriel Rossetti, who "dared to translate from his mighty name-father".[27] Stevenson leaves conspicuously unmentioned here the heavy burden of the name of a famous family of engineers on someone with no vocation for engineering. Dickens seems to have been oblivious to such considerations: he named most of his sons (not, significantly, his daughters) after writers who were his friends or heroes. He called his first son Charles, after himself; his second, Walter Landor after Walter Savage Landor; his third, Francis Jeffery after the "critic laureate"; his fourth, Alfred D'Orsay Tennyson; his fifth, Sydney Smith Haldimand; his sixth, Henry Fielding; and his seventh, Edward Bulwer Lytton ("Plorn").

Because literature is by definition reread, names from literature are invariably familiar, or potentially familiar, and have a content of associations, resembling in this London names for anyone who has visited the places denoted. Peter Lamarque and Stein Olsen make the interesting point that names in fiction can never be purely denotative, since they cannot be replaced by another formulation of equal truth-value.[28] The London in a story is not all London, but only certain aspects of it selected by the author. And one might add that for similar reasons this applies also to mythological names. A mythological name in a literary work does not imply all that the name can mean.

Written names

When proper names came to be written down, they often presented special difficulties of spelling. Except for biblical and classical names, texts or reference books could not be relied on for authoritative precedents. While the culture was still oral, or largely oral, names were given whatever spelling seemed best to represent their sound. In Chaucer, Arcturus appears also as Arcture and Arctour; Semiramis might be Semyram,

Semyrame, Semyramis, or Semyramus.[29] With printed Bibles, and printed lists of names such as those in William Camden's *Remains* (1605), standardization gradually advanced; but at first printers' arbitrary spellings increased the chaos.[30] Surnames in particular continued to give trouble, as we shall see in chapter 3. The diarist Samuel Pepys (1633–1703) still often spelt surnames as he heard them, putting "Martin" for Merton; "Kerneguy" for Carnegie; "Dancre" for Danckerts; "Harlow" for Harley; "Chevins" for Chaffinch; and "Hogsden" for Hoxton. Indeed, he wrote his own name in shorthand as *Peps*, indicating a monosyllable that might be pronounced *Peeps*, *Peps*, or *Payps*. But he also wrote it in a book, in Greek letters, spelling it Πῆπυς; so he probably pronounced it *Peeps*.[31] In *No Bed for Bacon*, Caryl Brahms and S. J. Simon make a running joke of the problem, picturing Shakespeare as hopelessly undecided how to spell his own name. Their Shakespeare tries out *Shakesper, Shakspere*, and *Shekspar, Shakspaw*, and *Shakeshpeare*. "He crossed out *Shakespere* and wrote *Shakspur*"; "*Shakespur Shakspire Shikspar*. He crossed them out. *Shacspore* he wrote."[32] In real life Shakespeare probably did not use many variants of his name.[33] But Anne Hathaway was registered as Anna Hatherrewaye. And Queen Elizabeth herself misspelled Leicester's name "Leycesterre". English spelling was relatively fluid during the Renaissance compared with that of the Romance languages, where Latin orthography was more often a reliable guide. The possibilities for ludic variation were endless, foreshadowing the freedoms taken in *Finnegans Wake*.

Proper names have continued to present orthographic problems. How, for example, are foreign and classical names to be translated? Elizabethan authors boldly anglicized, as even George Chapman did, writing *Biron* as "Byron". By comparison Victorian writers tried to be more consistent and more correct. Thomas de Quincey (1785–1859) thundered against Walter Savage Landor (1775–1864) for his method of anglicizing classical names: "he insists on our saying—not *Heracleidae* and *Pelopidae*, as we all used to do,—but *Heracleids* and *Pelopides*".[34] But Landor's worst "caprice" showed in his treatment of Greek names:

Nous autres say "Aristotle", and are quite content with it until we migrate into some extra-superfine world; but this title will not do for *him*: "Aristoteles" it must be. And why so? Because, answers the Landor, if once I consent to say Aristotle, then I am pledged to go the whole hog; and perhaps the next man I meet is Empedocles,—whom in that case, I must call Empedocle. Well, do so. *Call* him Empedocle; it will not break his back, which seems broad enough. But, now, mark the contradictions in which Mr Landor is soon landed. He says, as everybody says, Terence and not Terentius; Horace and not Horatius; but he must leave off such horrid practices, because he dare not call Lucretius by the analogous name of Lucrece, since that would be putting a she instead of a he; nor Propertius by the name of Properce, because *that* would be speaking French instead of English.

In the face of custom and history, both writers were pursuing an impossible ideal of consistency.

Sometimes the problem resolves itself into one of relative authority. As Walter de la Mare notes, Lewis Carroll "was so little known to the public in his later years that a 'special correspondent' in Oxford spelt his name *Dogson* throughout an obituary article which appeared in a leading London newspaper".[35] It would not have been difficult for an Oxford correspondent to discover the correct spelling. More recently, reference books such as *Who's Who* has made spelling of personal names much easier. But journalists, thinking they have no time to consult these, and imagining websites will be quicker, still often spell names wrongly. My own name, for example, more often than not appears misspelled.

This is not a theoretical book, although occasionally it touches on philosophy or narratology. For a more abstract treatment of names, readers may be referred to such works as Willy Van Langedonck's *Theory and Typology of Proper Names* (2008).

Historical changes in naming customs and in the function of naming in literature have determined the arrangement of this book. Chapters 1 and 2 survey the history of real-life names and the function of names in various literary genres. Chapters 3, 5, and 6 are more detailed case studies of Spenser, Shakespeare, and Milton. Chapter 4 surveys the history of hidden names, an important feature of much pre-Enlightenment literature. Chapter 7 treats temporary names such as nicknames and servant names. Chapter 8 focuses on how Thackeray and Dickens varied the naming of characters. Arrays—ordered groups of names from Homer to Pope—are the subject of chapter 9. Finally, chapter 10 studies Joyce and Nabokov, perhaps the two most eminent namers in our literature.[36]

Notes

1. Auden 1971: 267.
2. See Jesperson 1924: 64–71, esp. 66.
3. Maguire 2007: 4, 58.

4. White 1857: 525–8. Cf., too, Rudyard Kipling's poem in "The Elephant's Child": "I keep six honest serving-men | (They taught me all I knew); | Their names are What and Why and When | And How and Where and Who."
5. Ziff 1960: 85–9, perhaps supported by Crystal 1995: 122, where proper names are considered to be on the edge of the lexicon. For a critique of Ziff's position, see Kripke 1980: 32–3.
6. See Ferry 1988: 65; Maguire 2007: 22; Sprat 1667.
7. On this error, see Screech 1979: 388; Barton 1984: 356; Vickers 1984: 95–163; Marks 1988: 212, 231 n.1.
8. Barton 1990.
9. Docherty 1983: 45, 49.
10. Carroll 2000: 208.
11. OED 2. "Dumpty", a by-form of "dumpy", meant "a very short person"; see Halliwell-Phillipps 1847. "Humpty-Dumpty" may echo "Dump" and "Dumphry", pet-forms of "Humphrey". Before the eponymous nursery rhyme, the name had been applied to a cannon used by Royalist defenders at the siege of Colchester, which fell from the wall; whereupon "All the king's horses and all the king's men | Couldn't put Humpty together again." See Jack 2008: 80–3.
12. Humpty reverses the situation where proper names usually have no obvious meaning, whereas other words usually have generally shared meanings: see Alexander 1951: 551–66; Mare 1932: 57–8.
13. Sidney 1973: 86.
14. Ragussis 1986: 222.
15. Kermode 2001: 195, 197.
16. Gardiner 1954: 6–7.
17. Kripke 1980: 92–4.
18. See Amis 2000: 262, 292. Cf. Lodge 1992: 7–8.
19. See, e.g., Jack 1991: 102.
20. See Watt 1957: 20; Barton 1990: 91–2.
21. James 1987: 57.
22. See Stone 1985: 191–204, and ch. 8 passim.
23. See Seznec 1953: 248.
24. Scaliger 1964: 163 column 2.
25. Spectator 451.
26. Stevenson 1922–3: 25.92. Robert the Devil murdered his schoolmaster; see De Quincey 1896–7: 11.437.
27. Ibid. 95.
28. Lamarque and Olsen 1994: 80–1.
29. See David et al. 1979.
30. See Crystal 1995: 66–7.
31. See Pepys 1970–83: 6.173 n. 1.
32. Brahms and Simon 1941: 13, 19, 22, 42, 226.
33. Only Shakespeare, Shakspeare, and Shakspere; see Schoenbaum 1970: 227.
34. Quincey 1896–7: 11.441.
35. Mare 1932: 28.
36. Ibid. 11. 336.

I

Naming in History

In the course of history, the aptness of names has in general diminished. Sound changes and changes of social circumstances have tended to reduce it. D'Urbervilles have become Durbeyfields: tradesmen's sons do not always follow their father's trade.[1] Besides, successive bearers of a family name are liable to have different occupations and personal characteristics. The limitations of historical knowledge make it impossible to determine quite how far early names were meaningful. Nevertheless, many names originated in nicknames. And there can be no doubt children used often to be given names that might inspire them, names with "good signification" that might be "as a thread tyed about the finger, to make us mindful of the errand we came into the world to do for our Master".[2] As we shall see, recent writers have had to find new ways of apt naming.

Full names

The need to disambiguate reference supposedly led to the development of fuller names with a particularizing addition: among many Edmunds, Edmund Ironside would stand out, and among Swein, Swein Forkbeard. With the higher population densities of towns and eventually cities it took more than a single name or patronymic to specify individuals. In the centuries after the Conquest, the Normans gradually superimposed a system of surnames that individuated by specifying hierarchical places and functions. But this model needs to be modified to some degree. As Scott Smith-Bannister has shown, the choice of names came to have other functions besides disambiguation. Perhaps equally important, for example, they belonged to changing patterns of baptismal sponsorship.[3]

Looking back through history, the hypothetical age when single names were universal tends to recede.[4] "Mister" before surnames only came in about 1550; but "Master" with surnames goes back to at least 1297,[5] and was still used for ancient writers in the seventeenth century. The accounts for London Bridge list full names, not only for artificers but even for labourers: William Sporiour, John Archer, Henry Tomson, Thomas Richard, John Crowcheman, John Rowland, and many more.[6] These are from the accounts for 1501–2; but already the 1381–2 accounts list John Hoo and Henry Yevele as Keepers of the Bridge, James Rameseye as fishmonger, and Matilda Bray and Richard Albon (tenement holders).[7]

In literature, Shakespeare gives even the rebel Jack Cade his surname. Jean Froissart (and Lord Berners his translator[8]) already use many full names (Francis Ackerman, Hugh Spencer). And although *Orlando Furioso* (1532) has some single romance names (Alcina; Marfisa), Ariosto often acknowledges family connections: Astolfo son of King Otto of England is cousin to Orlando and Rinaldo. Ariosto makes sure that real-life contemporaries (Bernardo Cappello; Pietro Bembo) receive their full, two-part names.[9] Among the Scottish paladins, many are given Latinized or Italianized forms of their full titles: "Il Conte d'Ottonlei" (Earl of Athol); "Lurcanio Conte, ch'in Angoscia regna" (Earl of Angus); Ariodante, "Duca d'Albania" (Duke of Albany); "Arimano, Signoreggia Forbesse" (Lord of Forbes)—perhaps examples of the untranslatability of proper names. Earlier, Dante already had many full names, for example Sassol Mascheroni and Camicion de' Pazzi (*Inferno* 32.66). But his Francesca and Paolo are appropriately the single names of romance.

Chaucer uses full names for writers—William Seynt Amour, Thomas Bradwardyn—and (prudently) for Harry Bailly. As for Chaucer's Roman names, they imply the full *tria nomina*: praenomen, gens name, and cognomen: his "Fabricius" implies Caius Fabricius Luscinus; and his "Affricanus", a cognomen recalling achievement, implies Cornelius Scipio Africanus. In short, naming practices have been extremely variable.

Early surnames might be descriptive in four ways, or a combination of these.[10] Many surnames derived from a place or region, like Calder (or Cawdor); Blair (Gaelic *blár*, "plain, field, battlefield"); and Waleys ("foreigner") as in Thomas Waleys, the fourteenth-century Oxford Dominican commentator on Ovid. Secondly, surnames might derive from a craft: Mason; Cook; Fowler; Smith; and Gow (Gaelic *gobha*, "smith"); although an occupation might also indicate rank. Occupation and location might coincide, as in Ackerman ("acre-man"), either a topographic name or a mark of status (a feudal tenant employed as a ploughman).

A third group of surnames conveyed kinship, the particular relationship being fixed by a prefix (Mac) or a word ending (-son, -daughter). Hence Johnson; Anderson ("Andrew's son"); MacNab ("son of the abbot"); Macpherson ("son of the parson"). Where such a patronymic practice was established (as in the west Highlands and Shetland), "surnames" changed from generation to generation. The son of a John Robertson might be Andrew John-son or Andrew Robertson (if he adopted his father's patronymic as a fixed surname). Indeed, when patronymic practice interacted with occupational names the range of choice was wider still. In Ireland, patronymic names were forbidden by the 1366 Statutes of Kilkenny, but continued in practice until the nineteenth century (as indeed they did locally in England and Scotland).[11] Such names abound in the historical fiction of George Mackay Brown, for example: "Magnus Erlendson" and "Hakon son of Paul" in *Magnus* (1973); and "Ronald Sigmundson" in *Vinland* (1992).

A fourth group of surnames are evidently from nicknames, like Meikle and Grant (or Grand), "big". Some of these are insulting, as Anne Barton notices. But apparently descriptive names can be deceptive. Forward, for example, which may seem descriptive in much the same way as Froward, probably derives from Anglo-Saxon *forweard* ("swineherd"), an occupational name.[12]

Meanings became less overt with changes of pronunciation and spelling: the name Mainwaring had more than 130 distinct forms in a single family archive.[13] In consequence, Tudor and Stuart orthography offered ample opportunities to stress Cratylic aptness or conceal it.

In the Middle Ages the first or given name was often that of a saint, although not necessarily the saint celebrated on a person's natal day. After the Reformation, non-scriptural saints' names became less popular, perhaps because associated with superstition. Instead, sectarians often supplemented the stock of biblical names with pious inventions. William Camden disapproves of these invented names as "vanitie":

If that any among us have named their children *Remedium amoris, Imago saeculi,* or with such like names, I knowe some will thinke it more then a vanitie, as they do but little better of the new names, *Free-gift, Reformation, Earth, Dust, Ashes, Delivery, More fruite, Tribulation, The Lord is neare, More triall, Discipline, Joy againe, From above*: which have lately beene given by some to their children with no evill meaning, but upon some singular and precise [Puritan] conceit.[14]

Similar examples in baptismal registers led the Victorian Charles Bardsley to make the exaggerated claim that "Puritan names were widespread from 1560 to 1650 south of the Trent"; only a local prevalence, however, is now accepted.[15] And sometimes the invention was not out of whole cloth. "Praisegod Barebone", the name of a real Puritan (c. 1598–1679 or 1680), seems to extend invention to the family name. But Barebone only modifies his real surname Barbon.[16] Nevertheless, almost every Puritan name in Ben Jonson's *Alchemist* (1610) came from real life. Zeal of the Land is close to Bardsley's Zeal for God (with "God" replaced to placate the censors).[17] Such names have been regarded as allegorical inventions; but much of life was then allegorical. Camden lists Mauger and Original, besides Faith, Fortitude, Grace, and Temperance, as actually used in the seventeenth century—and some still were, in the nineteenth.[18]

First names had long been used as surnames, for example Nicholas, and Mitchell (from Michael). But in the sixteenth century, surnames began to be used as first names: "in late yeres Surnames have beene given for Christian names among us".[19] Camden approves of this practice as springing from the godfathers' affection and a wish to propagate the family name. At first the practice was mostly confined to the peerage and upper gentry:[20] Bulstrode Whitelocke, for example, was the son of Sir James Whitelocke and Elizabeth Bulstrode. Camden's examples include "Pickering Wotton, Grevill Varney, Bassingburne Gawdy, Calthorp Parker, Pecsall Brocas, and Fitz-Raulfe Chamberlaine, who are the heires of Pickering". He may have been wrong in saying such first names were found "no where else in Christendom"; a Napoleonic edict later forbade the practice in the Netherlands. This use of surnames as forenames has literary significance, since it lent plausibility to double-barrelled charactonyms like Politic Persuasion and Sir Politic Would-Be. Surname-forenames have flourished in the modern novel, as in real-life social pretension. Somerset Maugham's *The Razor's Edge* (1944) provides an example: it seems almost inevitable that the exquisite snob who lives for social advantage should bear the name Elliott

Templeton.[21] Sometimes, too, a forename is chosen because it is an element of the surname (Aulay Macaulay, Dru Drury).

A shortage of first names also seems to have led to the wide use of variants: short forms, pet forms, and regional and foreign variants. A popular riddle makes fun of the number of diminutives of Elizabeth:

> Elizabeth, Elspeth, Betsy, and Bess,
> They all went together to seek a bird's nest;
> They found a bird's nest with five eggs in,
> They all took one, and left four in.[22]

The riddle does not exaggerate: there were as many as forty-four forms of Elizabeth.[23] Paucity of Welsh first names in the seventeenth century led to frequent addition of middle names.[24] In England, by contrast, middle names were rare, except in the peerage, before 1700.[25] By then "full names" (two, three, or more) were usual. Yet single names have continued to the present day in special contexts, such as art (Massin), couture (Prada), and celebrity (Madonna).

As Derwent May observes, the use of surnames has in recent decades declined.[26] From the 1850s to the 1950s, surnames could be used between male friends, even by a wife addressing her husband. And Trollope's Mrs Proudie is invariably "Mrs Proudie": the reader is never told whether she had a Christian name. Such factors as relative seniority, relative status, and degree of intimacy make the use of surnames between friends a complex matter.

Vernacular names in literature

The introduction of realistic names into literature was an important threshold. In this the great innovator was Geoffrey Chaucer (early 1340s–1400), who used something like 2,000 names, far more than any of his contemporaries. William Langland's names are largely personifications; Piers the Plowman (not quite a full name) being the only prominent exception. John Gower (c. 1330–1408) mingles antique and romance names with charactonyms (Nessus; Fals-Semblent), but often makes do without any ("the Kinges moder"; "his Chamberlein"). Chaucer draws his names at will from the Bible, the ancient classics, and from modern romances. But he also introduces vernacular names, probably influenced in this by his fabliau sources and by Boccaccio (almost a Renaissance author already). In some ways, however, Chaucer was slow to realize the literary possibilities of naming. His Wyf of Bath is a great character, yet she shares her name Alison with her close friend, not to speak of the Miller's wife. Similarly with the Wyf of Bath's fifth husband Jankin (Jenkin, diminutive of John): he has to share this name with his apprentice. The idea of a fully individual name seems hardly yet established.

Drama was even slower to introduce vernacular names. For the most part, the liturgical and cycle plays use exclusively biblical names. But there are a few glorious exceptions, such as Noah's feisty wife in the Wakefield *Noah*. In the speech prefixes she is merely *Uxor*. But Noah addresses her as Gil (line 219). *Secunda Pastorum* ("The Second Shepherds' Play"), with its famous comic episode of the sheep-stealer Mak (Gaelic, "son") and his wife Gyl or Jelott, has long been regarded as a medieval Mystery Play; but the manuscript is of the Marian period, and many now think the play more consistent with a mid-sixteenth-century date.[27]

Characters in the Morality plays naturally have abstract names such as "Mankind"; although individual character begins with the Vice.[28] A full cast of realistic vernacular names did not arrive until the academic comedies of the sixteenth century, such as William Stevenson's *Gammer Gurton's Needle* (1553).

Formal realism

Ian Watt's theory of the novel's "formal realism" implies the model of philosophical realism and progressive individuation.[29] He links the "particularizing approach to character" with a circumstantial realism in which full names imply complete identity and a social context. In earlier fictional genres, he argues, authors did not try to establish fully individualized characters, preferring types with typic or legendary names—names associated with previous literature rather than contemporary life. The individuating function of proper names supposedly "was first fully established in the novel".[30] On this view, early novelists like Henry Fielding (1707–54) and Samuel Richardson (1689–1761) broke with literary tradition in giving their characters the full names of real life.

Until recently Watt's influential theory has not been questioned very vigorously.[31] But it is now objected that real-life naming was far more heterogeneous than he assumed.[32] He exaggerated early novelists' consistency, explaining away Defoe's single or descriptive names (Roxana; Moll Flanders) as belonging to the underworld milieu. But Fielding too has Cratylic names, such as Allworthy and Sophia, and even Richardson is liable to assign names "subtly appropriate and suggestive": in other words imperfectly Hermogenean.[33] Thus the heroine of *Pamela* is named after the proud prisoner in Sidney's *Arcadia*, while in *Clarissa* Lovelace's name not only suggests the bold love poet Richard Lovelace but also hints at "loveless" and deficiency of true love. As for Watt's historical contrasts, they call for endless qualifications. Greek tragedy's single names, for example, were just as circumstantially realistic as the names in modern novels. Ancient Athenians usually had only one name, such as Alcibiades, unless it was qualified by a patronymic. Again, a century before Defoe, Elizabethan fiction quite commonly used full names; while two-part names were possible from the thirteenth century.

Watt's position has been further eroded on another front. For no firm line can be drawn between "ordinary" names and moral charactonyms like Jonson's Morose, a name hinting broadly enough at his personality. Anne Barton has found numerous Cratylisms in archival records.[34] As her excellent books on literary naming show, Aristophanes' descriptive names can be matched in real life, and the same is true of medieval names, even derogatory ones. In the fourteenth century a single English county had six people called Ribald.[35] Barton asks whether audiences would have registered such names as fictive. But that may be an inappropriate question, in view of the alterity of medieval realism. Fiction was not then a fully separate category. Any name—real or invented made no difference—might be meaningful. On the other hand, names such as Patience need not always, or primarily, communicate a descriptive meaning. However, caution is needed with early names: Ribald may be from *Ribault*, and Forward, as we saw, may be from OE *for* ("hog") and *weard* ("guardian").

Cratylic names are not entirely a thing of the past: there are Goodmans in the phone book. But their literary application now calls for tactful negotiation between realism and thematic aptness. And the negotiation has continually to be renewed. Anthony Trollope's Quiverful in *Barchester Towers* (1857) would have been perfectly acceptable in a Fielding novel; but it seemed heavy-handed to Henry James. The conventions of circumstantial realism have narrowed the options for writers: they have had to find new ways to convey meaning through the names of their characters.

Social pressures

Watt's formalist theory has also lost ground to Michael Ragussis' idea of a "family plot". By this term Ragussis means the effacing of independent identity, typically the identity of a daughter, by assimilation to her family's or her husband's identity. This theory has great explanatory power when applied to early novels such as Richardson's *Clarissa* (1748), where naming and un-naming are thematic. Clarissa is judged as to whether she is "worthy of the name of daughter"; and when she is found to be "none of our child" she becomes a "helpless orphan".[36] With genders switched, the Family Plot can easily be seen to operate in Dickens' *Bleak House* (1852–3), where Turveydrop allows his son no independent life: "he wouldn't let his son have any name, if he could take it away from him" (ch. 14). Ragussis shows the Family Plot to be central to the inner structures of *Clarissa*, *Tess of the Durbervilles* (1891), and (through "parodic exaggeration") in *Lolita* (1955). It is a prominent feature of Wilkie Collins' *No Name* (1862). But in approaching Proust, Ragussis has to modify his method drastically. The fact is, family names lost much of their authority in the centuries after Richardson. Family was already of secondary importance in the fiction of Tobias Smollett (1721–71); and by 1883 Trollope could blandly generalize that "when a young girl is determined to be married nothing can prevent it".[37] It is no accident that for a modern example of the family plot Ragussis turns to the special case of underage Lolita.

By the end of the seventeenth century, as Smith-Bannister's statistics show, male children of the peerage showed a high incidence of surnames as given names (30 per cent) and of double given names (9 per cent).[38] This pattern is explained by obvious motivations: a wish for the prestige of the family name and (by bonding with godparents) for inheritance of wealth.

But class and other social structures have now largely displaced family as determining factors in naming. The names of poor children especially have long been governed by class considerations. The very poor have even had names directly assigned by institutions other than the family. Nineteenth-century foundlings were often named after the streets where they were found;[39] immigrants through Ellis Island lost their own names to the melting pot of American spelling preferences; and in the twentieth century, newborn poor often got their names, for good or ill, from a medical attendant. If a mischievous student attended the delivery, twins might be burdened with the names Ethyl and Methyl. A story is told of an embarrassed stevedore Duke U. Smith trying to hide his middle name, "University". Such names are touching, amusing, or shameful, according to one's social perspective. They can also be deceptive. U. T. Miller Summers (wife of the scholar Joseph Summers) was the child of poor parents from the rural south of the USA. Her parents had both at last succeeded in enrolling as mature students in the University of Texas, and gave their daughter (to her subsequent disappointment) the name U. T. "as a reflection of how far they had come".[40] A new twist in the Family Plot?

The pressures of organizational structures have naturally found reflection in novels. A striking instance is Joseph Heller's *Catch-22* with its grotesque satiric names such as Major Major Major Major. In a way, the family name exerts here some of its old force: Major Senior's secret switching of his newborn son's first name from Caleb to Major is a practical joke played on the family:

A lesser man might have wavered that day in the hospital corridor, a weaker man might have compromised on such excellent substitutes as Drum Major, Minor Major, Sergeant Major, or C. Sharp Major, but Major Major's father had waited fourteen years for just such an opportunity, and he was not a person to waste it.[41]

But in the event an IBM machine promotes the hapless Major Major Major to be Major Major Major Major. That is not so much the father's plot as Heller's own—to highlight the absurdities of military hierarchy. The vaudeville routines of outranked COs saying "Yes sir" to a subordinate show poor Major Major Major Major to be an "organization man". He is oppressed not so much by family as by the army.[42]

Fashions

Besides changes in naming conventions, fashion has probably always worked to refresh the stock of available names. This gradual, elusive, yet universal process has striking statistical results. A third of boys and a fifth of girls are given one of the top ten names for the year of their birth.[43] Thus Nicola, Joanne, Helen, Lisa, and Karen, all among the top ten girls' names of the mid 1970s, gave way by the mid 1980s to Laura, Gemma, Kelly, Victoria, and Katherine.

Names are chosen for a variety of conflicting reasons: as fashionable; as ordinary; as unusual; as traditional; or for their patriotic or regional associations. They may be avoided, or chosen, as "old-fashioned" (currently Percival; Albert; Maggie; May). Other choices reflect the influence of royalty (William; George). Fashions of naming are not just a matter of liking but of class affiliation or aspiration. Smith-Bannister's statistics put the decisiveness of class associations beyond dispute. Even the annual lists of most popular names show this class bias, since their data are derived from birth announcements in national papers. To be freer from bias the lists would have to take into account wider data such as registers of birth, university records, and voters' rolls.

Fashions for particular sources of names have often been influential. In the sixteenth century Old Testament names enjoyed great popularity, and this partly continued in later centuries, especially in the USA. In the late sixteenth century romance names came into vogue, simultaneously with a taste for chivalry, neo-Gothic houses, and toy fortifications. Some may think of romance as medieval or ancient Greek; but in fact it reached the height of its popularity in the early seventeenth century.[44] Many romance names, particularly those of Greek or Persian origin, were too exotic to be much used outside the genre; but the nuclear group at least became fashionable. Names from Italian romantic epic were familiar and imitable, especially feminine names in -a and -ia (Sophrosina; Lydia). Romance names such as those listed by Camden[45] were actually used in real life, as contemporary sources make clear—Bulstrode Whitelocke's *Diary* and the correspondence of Dudley Carleton and John Chamberlain, for example.[46]

The Victorian novelist Charlotte Yonge commented on a fashion of forming feminine names by changing the termination of a masculine name; and Thomas Colley Grattan wrote about American names ending -ia "under the inspiration of the last sixpenny novel", instancing Sophronia, Amelia, and Phidelia.[47] Class aspiration probably informed the preference for romance names. Yonge ridicules Aspasia (Greek, "welcome"), the name of a character in *The Maid's Tragedy* (1610): "it has even been heard as a Christian name in a cottage. 'Her name's Aspasia, but us calls her Spash.'" Isaac Disraeli deplores all such naming:

"The practice of romantic names among persons, even of the lowest orders of society, has become a very general evil."[48]

The fashion for romance names has importance for literature because it introduced a new range of associations and allusions, unlike the comparatively fixed meanings of biblical names. In the seventeenth century romance names were so fashionable that they affected English literary naming in a way not possible for Catholic Italians and French, for whom saints' names were privileged. In England nicknames and pseudonyms such as Orinda and Ephelia derived from actual romance names such as Mabilia and Melicia, Mellicent and Elisena. The romantic origin of the English novel can thus be discerned in its naming. In the absence of much English classical tragedy, romance was the best recourse for naming characters of high seriousness. The protagonist of Defoe's *Roxana* (1724) may bear a name proximately drawn from Racine's tragic heroine Roxane, but it derives ultimately from the romances of Alexander, where she is the daughter of the Bactrian Oxyartes and wife of Alexander the Great. (Yonge explains the name as Persian: "Dawn of Day".)

Literary names have always enjoyed prestige. In Ludlow two boys were christened "Tamberlaine" in 1620.[49] "Joyce" became popular in the 1860s after Mrs Henry Wood's *East Lynne* (1861); "Alice", following Lewis Carroll's *Alice in Wonderland* (1865), reached the top ten by 1900; and "Wendy" quickly gained currency after *Peter Pan* (1904). (It derived from Barrie's own early nickname Fwendy-Wendy, used by a child acquaintance Margaret Henley.[50]) Margaret Mitchell's *Gone with the Wind* (1936) made several names popular: not only Rhett (from a Dutch surname) but also Ashley and Scarlett.[51] Similarly Justine, a feminine form of Justin, has been current in Britain since the 1960s—prompted by Lawrence Durrell's novel *Justine* rather than Sade's.

In the twentieth century a new pattern for naming emerged: stage, film, and television celebrity. Not unknown before, it became more salient, and generated the flimsier fame of those known merely for being "icons" or celebrities. Darren, in the top ten in the 1970s, was the name of a character in *Bewitched* (a 1960s TV series). Julie (a French form of Julia) became popular in the 1960s through the prominence of two film stars, Julie Harris (b. 1925) and Julie Andrews (b. 1935).[52] And in the 1980s Kylie (Australian, from Kyle or Kelly) gained currency from the fame of Kylie Minogue (b. 1969). Similarly with Marlon

(Brando), Marilyn (Monroe), Cary (Grant), and Elvis (Aaron Presley).
Such celebrity-associated fashions, although they can be transatlantic
or even global, are by their nature evanescent.

In our own time, naming seems to have reached a new depth of
irresponsibility. Nothing is too trivial now to be a name. It is easy to
suppose the British have become a nation of cruel practical jokers,
when a Mr and Mrs Walls call their boy Stone; when the Waters name
a daughter Mineral; and when the Castles name a son Windsor. But
eccentric, jocular, or merely silly names have always been given, when-
ever the registrar or officiating clergyman has allowed it, or made a
mistake (as with James Augustine Aloysius Joyce, christened Augusta).
John Ward tells of a drunken mother who persuaded the parson to
name her child Incombob instead of Ichabod; while, according to
Thomas Beard, a Jacobean atheist who was a witness at a baptism
"wished for the infant to be named Beelzebub".[53] Another miserable
child was given twenty-six names. Russell Ash has compiled a list of
more than 5,000 grotesque names from five centuries.[54] Many of these
may seem hilarious; but they also imply culpable insensitivity to the
plight of the child burdened with such names as Pervert or Botty. Of
course, Ash maximizes the grotesquerie: some of his examples are the
result of sound changes. "Fucker", for example, may have been a variant of "Fugger" (occupational: "shearer").[55]

In the late twentieth century a new naming practice has emerged.
Apparently as a gesture of political protest or affirmation of ethnic alle-
giance, conventional forms and spellings are deliberately transgressed:
Malcolm X; Deshawn; Latisha.

Histories and glossaries

So far we have looked at broad trends and social patterns, naming
practices and the pressures on them. But names can also be a subject
of enquiry. The thoughtful have probably always reflected on whether
names have meaning as well as denotative function. As we have seen,
Plato's *Cratylus*, a seminal text for the history of names, addresses the
issue of the correctness or rightness (ὀρθότης) of names. Plato's Socrates moderates between Cratylus' idea that names have an inherent
correctness and Hermogenes' contrary view of arbitrary names applied
by social convention. Socrates qualifies Hermogenes' scepticism by

adducing circumstances that account for many inappropriate names. In the case of the impious son of Theophilus ("Beloved of God") the patronymic principle explains his continuing to bear his father's pious name (394). Names originally apt are liable in such ways to lose their former correctness (433–6). In a word, they are subject to change. Nevertheless it is right to give "faire and happie names", since these influence the bearer's life.[56]

The substantial *De Mutatione Nominum* of Philo Judaeus (c. 20 BC– AD 50), a Hellenistic Jewish exegete, dominated the theory of naming throughout the Middle Ages and up to the sixteenth century. Philo analyses naming on the basis of Genesis 17: 1–22. To explain the renaming of "Abram" as "Abraham" he relates it to divine agency and the Covenant. Pursuing the theme of multiple naming, Philo explains the significance of many other biblical names in terms of Hebrew derivation.

From St Jerome onward, Philo's method continued to be systemati- cally applied to names in the Bible. From about 1230 a standard feature of Latin Bibles was an alphabetical list of over 5,500 place and personal names, with translations of their Hebrew meanings into Latin. This "Interpretation of Hebrew Names" began about 1180–1200 as a sepa- rate compilation, possibly by Stephen Langton (d. 1228), but it proved useful enough to be fairly regularly appended to the Latin Bible.[57] For centuries it was a common feature, even surviving the Reformation. The Calvinist Geneva version included "A Brief Table of the Interpre- tation of the proper names [...] chiefly found in the olde Testament [...]". This was the version often used by Milton, and in its glossary he may have found some of the names of *Paradise Lost*. Extremely popular too was Robert Estienne's separate dictionary of names published in 1537, presenting the fruits of his combined biblical and lexicographical studies.

Wider exploration of names, ranging beyond their biblical mean- ings, began in the sixteenth century. The decisive figure was the histo- rian William Camden (1551–1623), whose three highly original essays on names, gathered in *Remaines concerning Britaine* (1605, 1614) and anonymously published as by M. N., put the study of names on a new footing. Camden starts from the "granted veritie, that names ... are sig- nificative".[58] But this does not mean he believes all names Cratylic. He understands the need to discover the earlier meanings frequently obscured by "daily alteration of our tongue"—a view of linguistic decay shared, as we shall see, by Edmund Spenser. Camden grasped the need for a historical approach to names; distinguishing the ancient "hopeful luckie names" (as in Cicero's *bona nomina* and in the proverb *bonum nomen, bonum omen*) from their later forms as falsified by events or obfuscated by linguistic change. He had learned from St Jerome how nicknames can become regular names. And, in his own age, he observed the distinctively English custom of using surnames as first names, as well as the use of double given names.[59]

Etymological inferences were often sound in the Renaissance: surprisingly so in view of the ignorance of sound changes. The great divide in etymology was between medieval and post-medieval periods. Camden, who has been called the father of English lexicography, devoted much of his attention to personal names. Franciscus Junius' *Etymologicum Anglicanum* (posthumously edited by Edward Lye) was not published until 1743; but he had many English contacts through his place in the Earl of Arundel's household, and later lived in Oxford. He knew Gothic and Old English and some Danish and Icelandic. As for Cornelis Kiliaan and even John Minsheu, they belong with modern linguistics far more than with the glossators of the Middle Ages.[60]

Camden's lists of "Usuall Christian Names" are glossaries of obvious service to writers. Edgar and Oswald in *King Lear* are Cratylic names whose interpretation may well have been drawn from Camden.[61] And so, possibly, may Ben Jonson's understanding of "Benjamin", the name of his first son ("Farewell, thou child of my right hand").[62] Camden's explanations are largely etymological, tracing the "diversity of names, from the originall in divers languages" (53). He argues with some care, multiplying authorities and comparing explanations. On Hebrew names he cites not only St Jerome but Philo's *De Mutatione Nominum* and "the common tables of the Bible". He is particularly impressive on German and Anglo-Saxon origins; bringing to bear—besides his own scholarship—Martin Luther, Petrus Dasypodius (d. 1559), Cornelis Kiliaan (1528–1607), and the humanist Beatus Rhenanus (1485–1547).[63] Often he compares alternative etymologies and theories. In any case, his linguistic shortcomings are from the present viewpoint irrelevant: what matters is that writers may have assimilated his glosses in their own naming.[64]

For centuries after Camden no great advances were made in the study of proper names. Surnames in particular seem to have been a neglected field in the English-speaking scholarly world.[65] Indeed,

Patrick Hanks roundly affirms that "between Camden and the Victorians, no name dictionaries were compiled" (127). This is not the case, however: there were quite a few. Among them may be mentioned Richard Rowlands or Verstegan, *A restitution of decayed intelligence in antiquities*, in the same year as Camden's *Remains*. There soon followed John Penkethman, *Onomatophylacium; or, the Christian names of men and women, now used within this realme of Great Britaine* (1626). Then in 1655 came Edward Lyford's *The True Interpretation and Etymologie of Christian Names*, mostly on biblical names. Stephen Skinner's *Etymologicon Linguae Anglicanum* (1671) has an appendix of names, and so has the anonymously published (pirated) abridgement and English translation by Richard Hogarth, *Gazophylacium Anglicanum* (1689).[66]

These seventeenth-century dictionaries add to Camden's explanations many new etymologies, often unconvincing. Lyford's Preface emphasizes the social value of good names: "As for the knowing the Etymologies of names, I think it... usefull." "Would it not be a great encouragement and enducement to all youth when they know the sweet... etymologies of their happy and hopeful names, to make them walk answerable thereunto." With all their shortcomings, such special dictionaries would have been useful to writers wishing to find apt names for their characters. And even general dictionaries such as Henry Cockeram's and Edward Phillips' included proper names, particularly mythological ones.[67] As we shall see in chapter 8, it was left to Charlotte Yonge and Charles Bardsley to break new ground, if not always with very scholarly precision.

By the twentieth century, advances in linguistics had put etymology on a sounder footing, so that it was possible to compile scholarly dictionaries of names.[68] Literary critics contributed studies of the functions of naming in particular works or even passages. These in turn have been organized in bibliographies.[69] And full-length studies of naming in a genre or particular author have begun to appear.[70]

Notes

1. On "Durbeyfield", see Weekley 1912: 162.
2. Jenkyn 1652: 7, cit. Smith-Bannister 1997: 11.
3. Smith-Bannister 1997: 17. On the growth of surnames, see Ostler 2007: 43; Crystal 2010: 177.

4. See Camden 1984: 45; Barton 1984.
5. *ONC* xi.
6. Harding and Wright 1995: 160.
7. Harding and Wright 1995: 1–2.
8. Froissart 1545.
9. *Orlando Furioso* 46.15.
10. See Crystal 1995: 148–9; Donaldson 1996; Smith-Bannister 1997: 1–21.
11. See Ostler 2007: 136. On English insistence on surnames and opposition to Irish naming practices, see Spenser, *A View of the Present State of Ireland* 4852–64, *Var. Spenser* 10.215, 419–20.
12. Barton 1984: 40 n. 11; *ONC* 224.
13. Crystal 1995: 148.
14. Camden 1984: 49; cf. Whitelocke, *Diary*, e.g. Elias Ashmole, Dorcas Byshop, Elisha Crisp, Tobias Crisp, Hezekiah Haynes, Theophilus Bidollphe, Prudence Mostyn, Prudence Lumley, Thankful Owen, Theodosia Thynne, Rebecca Whitelocke. See also Barton 1984: 62, 65, noticing "Christian" as common in the Middle Ages and still occurring in the sixteenth century. Cf. *OCD*, and Yonge 1884: 468 on "Ehrenpreis".
15. Bardsley 1996: 118; Smith-Bannister 1997: 3–5. Between 1583 and 1589 a Puritan minister called his children Much-Mercy, Increased, Sin-deny, and Fear-not; see *ODECN* xxix–xxx.
16. See *ODNB*. Praisegod's son, Nicholas If-Jesus-Christ-Had-Not-Died-For-Thee-Thou-Hadst-Been-Damned, used only the name Nicholas.
17. Bardsley 1996: 200.
18. Grattan 1856: 435. Cf. Kilvert, *Diary* 27 Feb. 1870: Mrs Jones the Jockey's baby is christened "Mahalah" ("tenderness") after one of Cain's wives.
19. Camden 1984: 48; cf. Weekley 1912: 159.
20. Smith-Bannister 1997: 7–8; *ODECN* xxxii–xxxiii. Not only knights, *pace* Levin 1976: 56. Examples in Whitelocke's *Diary* include Marchmont Needham, Sir Dudley North, Sir Seymour Pile, Grindall Sheafe, Sir Burbeck Temple, Willoughby Whitelocke, Heneage Finch, Knollys Kitson, Carnsen Helmes, and Hansard Knowles.
21. Surnames as forenames are now commoner in the USA; see *ODECN* xxxiii.
22. Opie and Opie 1952: 158.
23. Crystal 1995: 148.
24. Crystal 1995: 148.
25. See Smith-Bannister 1997: 124–5.
26. "Rise and Fall of the Surname", *The Times* (3 Feb. 1997) 20.
27. McGavin 2010: 203.
28. See Barton 1984: 61–2.
29. See Watt 1949; Watt 1957: 19.
30. Watt 1957: 18.
31. See, however, Duncan-Jones and Chapman 1950.
32. See Spacks 2006: 3–4.
33. As Watt 1957: 19 concedes.
34. E.g. Barton 1990: 40, 52.
35. Barton 1990: 43. Other instances include Sturdy, Smalfeyth, Drydust, Milkgos, Lytylworth, Crakebone, even Cuttepurse, Small-behynd, Fillecupe, Forward, and Froward.
36. Ragussis 1986: 20.
37. Trollope 1946: ch. 45.
38. Smith-Bannister 1997: 126–8.
39. Smith-Bannister 1997: 9, 31.
40. Summers 2007: 20.
41. Heller 1962: 83. On the doubling of the name, see Dexter 2007: 193.

42. William Hollingsworth Whyte's *Organization Man* (1956) was published a year after the first chapter of *Catch-22* appeared in *New World Writing*, and five years before the American publication of the complete novel.
43. Crystal 1995: 150.
44. See Spufford 1981: 72–3, 233, Index s.v. *Amadis de Gaul, Palmerin*; Febvre and Martin 1990: 285–7; Hellinga and Trapp 1999: 237; Cooper 2004: 1–44; Hamilton 1982. Despite the conclusive statistics refuting Frederic Jameson in Hamilton 1984, Sharpe and Zwicker 2003: 13 repeat the shibboleth: "the romance, until its full novelization in the eighteenth century (and even then) remained a suspect mode".
45. Camden 1984: 78, "Tristram, I knowe not whether the first of this name was christned by king Arthurs fabler." Among Camden's romance names are Guy, Roland, Baldwin, Bevis, Percival, and Polyxena, Sophronia, Sophia.
46. Whitelocke has Sir Launcelot Lake MP; Sir Orlando Bridgeman; Baldwin Hamey; Sophia. Carlteton has Sir Bevis Bulmer.
47. Yonge 1884: 60; Grattan 1856: 434. Although Amelia originated with Fielding's novel it seems to have been the result of a cross between Latin Emilia and Germanic Amalia. In Louisiana, romance names were especially numerous; including such rarities as Odalia and Odelia. See Kane 1943: 173.
48. Disraeli 1881: 2.71.
49. See Gurr 2009: 75.
50. Hanks 2002: 885.
51. Hanks 2002: 853.
52. Hanks 2002: 797.
53. See Smith-Bannister 1997: 11 and 16.
54. Ash 2007; cf. Ash 2010.
55. See *ONC*.
56. Camden 1984: 47.
57. De Hamel 2001: 112–13, 123.
58. Camden 1984: 52.
59. Camden 1984: 46, 48.
60. See Liberman 2009: 273–4. On Junius, see Considine 2008, Index, s.v. *Junius, Franciscus*.
61. So Levith 1978: 21.
62. Jonson, Epigram 45; Camden 1984: 60. Camden, Jonson's teacher at Westminster School, was with him when he heard of the child's death. Camden's *Remains* was not published for another two years, however: Jonson probably learned the meaning at school, or from the Geneva Bible glossary.
63. Camden 1984: 53, 54, 384. Luther, *Aliquot Nomina Propria Germanorum* (1570); Dasypodius, *Dictionarium Latino–Germanicum* (?1570); Killianus, *Etymologicum Teutonicae Linguae* (1599).
64. Cf. Cowie 2009: 1.128 on folk etymologies.
65. See Hanks 2009: 125–6.
66. See Smith-Bannister 1997: 10–12; Maguire 2007: 10, 22–3; Lyford 1655: Preface.
67. Henry Cockeram, *The English Dictionarie*, 1623; Edward Phillips, *New World of English Words*, 1658.
68. E.g. Chandler 1992; Weever 1988.
69. E.g. Rajec 1978.
70. E.g. Levith 1978; Barton 1984; Maguire 2007; Bliss 2008.

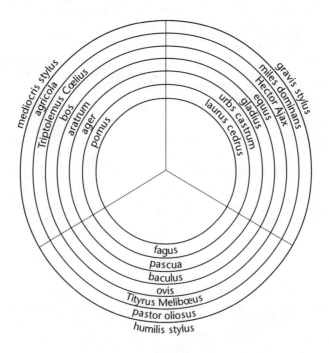

Figure 1. The Wheel of Virgil from Edmond Faral *Les Arts poétiques du 12ᵉ et du 13ᵉ siècle* (Paris 1962) 87.

2

Modes of Naming

Literary names were already correlated with genres in the earlier thirteenth-century *rota Vergiliana*, "the Wheel of Virgil", associated with John of Garland. This diagrammatic scheme distributes typical features of literature among three social divisions, modes, and styles.[1] To the three style heights *gravis, mediocris,* and *humilis* it assigns characteristic occupations, animals, tools, places, trees—and names (Diagram 1). In the high style, paradigmatic names are Hector and Ajax: Trojan and Greek heroes in the Troy cycle. Such legendary or historical names characterize ancient epic (Homer's *Iliad*, Vergil's *Aeneid*). They also appear in tragedies,[2] but would not be appropriate in pastoral.

Georgic names

The georgic names in the *rota* are Triptolemus and Coelius. Of these, Coelius (often confused with Caelius) was an ordinary *gens* name, as in Lucius Coelius Antipater the historian or Lucius Cae(ci)lius Firmianus Lactantius.[3] Triptolemus,[4] who received the art of agriculture from the goddess in the Homeric *Hymn to Demeter*, may seem legendary; but he was an actual hero of Eleusis. So both the georgic names belong to the ordinary historical world, whatever legendary associations they may also have possessed.

Georgic poets use place names freely, particularly in the exotic digressions characteristic of the genre. But they seldom use personal names, since they speak *in propria persona*. (One might compare lyric, another genre said to be nameless.[5]) Among the very few names associated with georgic may be mentioned Hodge. Hodge (earlier Hogge, Hog), a by-form of Roger, seems to have been the early modern type-name for a rustic or agricultural labourer. Thus Robert Greene (1560?–92) contrasts simple rustics with the pastoral Arcadians, who "are given to take the benefit of everie Hodge".[6] In John Pikering's *Interlude of Vice* (1567), Hodge appears in dialogue with Rusticus; and in William Rowley's *A New Wonder* (1631), Hodge is a "clown".[7] But in realistic drama of the sixteenth and seventeenth centuries Hodges tended to be urbanized as household servants or drunks or bruisers. One might instance William Stevenson's *Gammer Gurton's Needle* (1553); Thomas Dekker's *The Shoemakers' Holiday* (1599); Henry Porter's *Two Angry Women of Abington* (1588); and Ben Jonson's *The New Inn* (1631). Robert Herrick's Hog is probably rustic as well as drunken; and Peter Pinder's Hodge is certainly georgic ("No more shall Hodge's prong and shovel start").[8] B. E.'s *A New Dictionary of the Terms Ancient and Modern of the Canting Crew* (c. 1698) offers the definition "*Hodge*, a Country Clown".

As a name usually implying downgraded rusticity, Hodge was not much used in georgic itself. Indeed, in the nineteenth century protests began at the contemptuous associations of what Paul Alpers calls a "stock name" (instancing Thomas Hardy's "Drummer Hodge").[9] In *Tess of the d'Urbervilles*, Hardy goes so far as to deny altogether the very existence of the type in real life. When Angel Clare lodges with a dairyman he finds no Hodge: "The conventional farm-folk of his imagination—personified by the pitiable dummy known as Hodge—were obliterated after a few days' residence. At close quarters no Hodge was to be seen."[10] A decade earlier, Hardy had written against the stereotype in "The Dorsetshire Labourer": "we find [the farm-labouring community] to be seriously personified by the pitiable picture known as Hodge [...]. This supposed real but highly conventional Hodge is a degraded being of uncouth manner and aspect, stolid understanding, and snail-like movement. His speech is [...] a chaotic corruption of regular language."[11] With this genre history behind him, Tom Stoppard modernizes and finesses the type-name in *Arcadia* (1993) when he gives Thomasina Coverly's tutor the name Septimus Hodge. Is this a conventional georgic name? Septimus certainly labours, and in the country; but his work is intellectual, and the country is a country house estate.

Another georgic name is Giles. "Farmer Giles" is the stereotypic, commonsensical English farmer, probably derived from Isaac Bickerstaff's comic opera *The Maid of the Mill* (1765).[12] Somewhat different is "Farmer George", the derisive nickname of George III (1738–1820), who took an enthusiastic interest in the improvement of farming, and contributed pseudonymously to Arthur Young's *Annals of Agriculture*.

Pastoral names

The two pastoral names in the *rota*, Tityrus and Meliboeus, are from Vergil's first Eclogue. Tityrus (Greek Τίτυρος), a shepherd in Theocritus, has sometimes been considered Vergil's persona (his own father was ejected from his farm near Mantua), while Meliboeus' location name also suggests dispossession.[13] Other Vergilian pastoral names are Alphesiboeus, Corydon, Damoetas, Damon, Lycidas, Menalcas, Moeris, Mopsus, Palaemon, and Thyrsis.[14] Subsequently, several hundred names accrued to the dramatis personae of pastoral, contributed by Calpurnius, Petrarch, Boccaccio, Mantuan, and others, notably the Neapolitan Jacopo Sannazaro (c. 1458–1530). Sannazaro—*magnus vir Sanasarus* as J. C. Scaliger calls him—re-emphasized fishing as one of the principal *pastoralia*. His piscatorial eclogues greatly extended the register of recognizable pastoral names;[15] but a nucleus (including Amaryllis, Corydon, Damoetas, Damon, Lycidas, Menalcas, Moeris, Mopsus, Palaemon, and Thyrsis) remained salient. From the early Renaissance onward, these nuclear names were reused repeatedly and came to have fairly stable assocations. Corydon, for example, is generally a rustic, ineffectual in love. Such is his role in writers as various as Theocritus, Thackeray, and Noel Coward.[16] The nuclear group of recognizably pastoral names constitute the personae of "pure" or Vergilian pastoral.[17]

Borderline and anomalous instances have troubled the taxonomists. Vergil's Galathea is not a shepherdess but a sea nymph (*Eclogue* 9). And in Theocritus, her uncouth lover Polyphemus is a Cyclops despised as lacking the arts of agriculture[18]—a one-eyed giant who cuts his beard with a georgic pruning-hook and is human only by virtue of suffering unrequited passion. Renato Poggioli sees him as foreshadowing the uncouth swains of much later pastoral.[19] However, Ovid's Polyphemus goes well beyond mere awkwardness: he is savage enough to crush Acis with a rock, much as Homer's Polyphemus tries to do to Odysseus.[20] In fact, Theocritus' *Idylls* often overstep the bounds of what has

become the narrower pale of pastoral. Generic names are seldom distributed neatly.

Within the core personnel of Vergilian pastoral, allusion can be
richly communicative. When Alexander Pope in his *Pastorals* gives
"Alexis" the flute "which Colin's tuneful Breath | Inspir'd when living,
and bequeath'd in Death", he is announcing an implicit claim to be
Spenser's successor, with all that entails for his poem. And in *Lycidas*,
when the mourning shepherd doubts

> Were it not better done as others use,
> To sport with Amaryllis in the shade
> Or with the tangles of Neaera's hair...

Milton alludes, as John Carey explains, to Vergil's *Eclogue* 2.14–15 ("was
it not better to put up with Amaryllis' sullen rage and scornful dis-
dain"). Carey further notes Vergil's debt to Theocritus' *Idylls* 3 and 4.[21]
And the name conveys even more. In *Idyll* 4 it is Corydon's tactless
reference to Amaryllis that renews Battus' grief. All Theocritus tells
about Amaryllis, in fact, is her death.[22] So even the thought of earthly
diversions—sporting with Amaryllis—leads the poet back to prema-
ture death and inescapable mortality. Similarly, Milton's choice of the
pastoral name Lycidas is not a random one. If we recall its association
with Theocritus 7.52–60 it implies hopes for the well-being of Edward
King, "safe and sound" like Lycidas and Ageanax.[23] The pastoral names
were almost inexhaustibly allusive—so long as the canon remained
familiar.

Enlargement of pastoral

Whatever the advantages of its familiar names, Vergilian pastoral has
from time to time seemed too idealized, too far removed from real life.
Dr Johnson, famously attempting to dislodge *Lycidas*, declares "there is
no art, for there is nothing new. Its form is that of a pastoral, easy, vulgar, and therefore disgusting: whatever images it can supply, are long
ago exhausted".[24] Johnson deplores

the artificial accommodation of shepherdly speakers to the heightened senti-
ments appropriate to poetry. He found preposterous the expedient of setting
them in a Golden Age unreality [...]. The Golden Age expedient had the
absurd consequence of leaving only the rump of a pastoral canon: about a third of

Theocritus (the rest being too rustic) and two-thirds of Virgil (the rest being too political).[25]

Various means of renewal have been adopted. First, as we have seen, diversifying the pastoral occupations by returning to the Theocritean model—and sometimes to Theocritean names. The *Idylls* have a maritime setting: their world is populated not only with shepherds and cowherds like Menalcas and Daphnis (*Idylls* 8, 9, 20) but with reapers (Milon and Bucaeus) and fishermen (Asphalion, 21; Cyclopes, 11). Farming is combined with fishing and shepherding with herding of goats and cows (only subsequently to be thought "unpastoral"). Theocritus' *Idyll* 7 is a "harvest home", *Idyll* 13 is maritime, and throughout references appear to the Nereides and to Proteus as "shepherd" of Poseidon's flocks of seals.[26]

Sannazaro, Phineas Fletcher in *Sicelides* (1631) and *Piscatorie Eclogs* (1633), William Diaper in *Nereides* (1712): all returned to Theocritus' original variety, developing it into new modalities with pastoral settings distinct from Virgil's land-bound *mise-en-scène*. Diaper found four recruits among the thirty-three Nereides in Homer's *Iliad* 18;[27] his nature is presided over not by Pan but Nereus, Thetis, Phorcys, and Proteus. He drew on Theocritus and Spenser; although he might not have succeeded without Sannazaro's example.[28] In all such neoclassic pastoral a special pleasure is taken in the multiple, often literary, aptness of names. Thus, Melanthius in Sannazaro's *Eclogue* 4 is the name of a Tyrrhenian pirate metamorphosed into a dolphin in Ovid;[29] while *Muraena* (lamprey) is the family name of a Roman notoriously fond of this fish.

Piscatory eclogue occasioned the use of many river names. From the ancients Sannazaro took over Tanais (R. Don), Achelous, and Alphaeus; and he originated others, such as "Varus" (R. Var) and "Avar" (R. Saone).[30] Ovidian mythologizing of rivers readily took its place as a distinct variant of pastoral alongside Theocritus' maritime piscatorial. A familiar example is Spenser's etiological legend of Molanna and Faunus in the *Cantos of Mutabilitie*, together with its Italian analogues.[31]

Increasingly, though, rivers came to belong with the topics of georgic rather than pastoral. Michael Drayton's *Poly-olbion* (1612, 1622), which abounds in mythological personifications of rivers, is clearly georgic, even if it teaches history and geography rather than husbandry. Drayton's River Camel, for example, derives from Camelot: its associations are with history and romance, not pastoral. Besides, his teeming names seldom have the innocent imprecision of pastoral: they follow a well-informed geographical plan. In his enlargement of Vergilian pastoral by this second, georgic turn, Drayton learned from Spenser's river procession in *The Faerie Queene*, 4.11, in effect a survey of Britain's material and cultural resources.[32] Spenser's "Dart, nigh chockt with sands of tinny mines" (4.11.31) implies a background of economic geography: the success of Dartmoor tin mining, for example, and its threatened decline when access to ports diminished because of silting. Conveying concentrated factual information, Spenser's *mise-en-scène* departs from the "cartographic fiction" of pastoral Arcadias: his names are as much from the map as from literature. In this realistic development, insular pastoral differed from the continental equivalent. Perhaps this was because of Britain's dominance in the wool trade. For the British, herding sheep and exporting wool were big business.

Vernacular pastoral names

For a third escape from remote artificiality, some pastoral poets turned to the vernacular names of real-life shepherds. Spenser makes this innovation in a consistent, thoroughgoing way: of the eleven speakers in *The Shepheardes Calender* (1579), not one has a classical name;[33] although a few classical names (Pan, Syrinx, Dido) are referred to in passing, or slip into the inset songs.[34] This roster strikingly departs from tradition: the shepherds of Alexander Barclay (1475?–1552), however rustic otherwise, all have conventionally pastoral, or at least classical, names: Coridon, Cornix, Codrus, Menalcas, Amintas, Faustus, Fulica.[35]

For support in this new departure, Spenser turned to the French pastoralists, who (whether from nationalistic or religious motives) had freed themselves from the strict convention of Latin naming.[36] Spenser's Colin and Thenot had been shepherds in pastorals by the Protestant Clément Marot (c. 1497–1544); Perigot recalls the French spelling of Marot's Margot, Ronsard's Perrot, or Du Bellay's Bellot.[37] E. K. confirms this: Thenot is "the name of a shepherd in Marot his Aeglogues".[38] Spenser gave even Vergilian names vernacular associations. His Tityrus (February 92), like Skelton's, disguises Chaucer rather than Vergil. Piers (a form of Peter) may now suggest Langland's Piers Plowman; but Spenser's earliest readers would probably associate it with the Piers of

Pierce the Plowman's Crede (1561)—the satiric voice of the people.[39] Equally indigenous is Cuddie, a northern shortening of Cuthbert. Others of Spenser's key names, however, are made up, as we shall see in chapter 3.

Spenser's indigenous naming was imitated by some, disliked by others. Almost all Drayton's speakers in *The Shepherd's Garland* (1593) have English names: Batte, Borrill, Perkin, Rowland, Winken. Some of them, however, have special associations. Beta, from Elisabeta, is Drayton's name for the Queen. Batte or Bat, short for Bartholemew (Hebrew, "Son of furrows"), recalls Battus in Theocritus.[40] Gorbo and Motto are probably invented, the former on the pattern of Theocritus' Gorgo.[41] And Borrill ("rustic") is a tag name.[42] But Winken once referred to a real person: Wynkyn de Worde, the printer and bookseller.[43] And Perkin (Peter) is also a real-life name, as in Perkin Warbeck. This emergent idiom of indigenous names was notably followed by Ambrose Philips (1674–1749). Philips had various English models: his Colinet and Cuddie, Hobbinol and Lobbin are Spenserian, but Geron (γέρων, "old", "old man") and Lanquet derive from Sidney's *Arcadia*.

Some of Philips' rustic names are impossibly awkward: it was not difficult for John Gay (1685–1732) to draw out their bumpkin possibilities in *The Shepherd's Week* (1714). But Philips was a dangerous opponent, so that any criticism had to be carefully disguised. Gay and Pope managed this in part by scrupulously sustained ironies, in part by singling out for ridicule names Philips had taken over from Spenser: Hobbinol, Lobbin, Cuddy, Colin Clout.[44] Pope's ironies in *Guardian* 40 (1713) were devious enough to deceive even the editor of that Whiggish journal.[45] Gay's burlesque travesties are broader. He either combines incompatible Spenserian names ("Lobbin Clout") or constructs ludicrous portmanteaus out of innocent materials from Spenser or Philips. "Bowsybeus" is from *bowsy* ("boozy", "corpulent") and *ibeus* (a Latin location marker, as in Melibeus).[46] "Bumkin-et" similarly follows the pattern of Philips' Colin-et. "Hobnelia", aimed at Hobbinol, suggests the hobnails of rustic boots combined with the romance ending -*elia*. And "Sparabella" is made up of *bella* and *sparable* ("a sort of small Iron nail, which some Country-People wear in their Shooes"[47]). As for Cuddie, it needed no alteration to trigger anti-Scottish prejudice.

The preference for realistic, vernacular names was deplored by neoclassical critics like Nicolas Boileau (1636–1711) and Bernard Le Bovier de Fontenelle (1657–1757). They preferred courtly, idealized shepherds.

Pastoral poetry was to strike a "middle note between the high and the low, *éclater sans pompe*". Boileau probably also disliked the higher strain of *The Shepheardes Calender* October; but mostly he feared the dangers of decline to the language of the village. He opposed any poet "low in style" who

> Makes shepherds speak a language base and vile:
> His writings flat and heavy, without sound,
> Kissing the earth, and creeping on the ground;
> You'd swear that Randal in his rustic strains
> Again was quav'ring to the country swains,
> And changing, without care of sound or dress,
> Strephon and Phyllis into Tom and Bess.[48]

Boileau disapproved of Ronsard and other vernacular pastoralists who replaced classical poetic names with ordinary ones: "Et changer, sans respect de l'oreille et du son, | Lycidas en Pierrot, et Philis en Toinon".[49] Translating this passage, Dryden substituted for Ronsard the English name Randal, which Walter Scott read as referring to Thomas Randolph. This has puzzled editors, for Randolph's eclogues are conventionally Latinate. But Scott's conjecture makes sense if one thinks of Randolph's pastoral tragicomedy *Amyntas* (1638), which clearly belongs to the vernacular movement. Its names are un-classical, even if some can boast Italian pedigrees: Laurinda, Silvio, Amarilli, Mirtillo, and Mopsus (from Sannazaro).[50] Randolph's Claius is from Sidney, his Oberon from Greene, Shakespeare, or indigenous romance.

Pope's *Pastorals* (1709), although indebted to Spenser, return in the main to the classical roster. His speakers (Aegon, Damon, Daphne, Daphnis, Lycidas, Thyrsis) are all Vergilian except for the Ovidian Daphnis—and even Daphnis, like Aegon and Thyrsis, is Theocritean. Yet Pope's roster is not without native admixtures: Strephon, though Greek, comes directly from Sidney's *Arcadia*; while Alexis, firmly in the tradition of Vergil and Sannazaro, nevertheless glances as we have seen at his own name Alexander.

English pastoral rarely attained the purity of Pope's youthful work. Theocritus might authorize mixed farming and Vergil admit woodland figures like Silvanus, but English pastoral eclogue mostly steered much further than that in the direction of georgic. With wool production a major industry, the complete innocence of pure pastoral must have seemed inaccessible.[51]

So too with pastoral drama. Indeed, *As You Like It* has often been discussed as an example of *genera mista*.[52] Renato Poggioli distinguishes three "levels" in it, roughly corresponding to heroic romance, pure pastoral, and georgic-pastoral: "The first level includes the exiled Duke, his retinue, Orlando, Celia, and Rosalind; the second, the shepherds Corin, Silvius, and Phebe; the third, two peasants, Audrey and William." What Poggioli calls "peasants" are georgic characters doing active work rather than watching sheep in pastoral *otium*. His three worlds are epitomized by the names: Orlando is from Ariostan romance, just as Silvius ("forest dweller") recalls Petrarch's Silvius or Sannazaro's athletic Silvio. Corin derives from conventional pastoral[53]—although, as Murray Levith notes, in Elizabethan pronunciation it would have suggested "corn" and farming. Silvius and Phebe were from Lodge; Audrey was a name favoured by the English poor; and William, of course, was Shakespeare's own name.

Of all the play's names, Celia is the most neglected. Regarded merely as translating Latin *Caelia* ("heavenly"), it has been identified as an amorous type-name common in love poetry, for example Carew's "The Rapture", or in satire such as Swift's "The Progress of Beauty". But Shakespeare's names seldom work so simply. Originally *Caelia* was the feminine of *Coelius*, the Roman family name associated with farming in the *rota Vergiliana*. Shakespeare's Celia takes the name Aliena ("Outsider"), acknowledging her exile; but she remains true to her given, georgic name when—more practical than her companion—she buys "the cottage, pasture, and the flock" (2.4.90). She happily adjusts to country life: it is her alias Aliena that "hath a reference to my state [dignity]" (1.3.123). In fact, her names go beyond the decorum of indicating inextricably mixed genres. The representative Celia gestures towards an idealized gentry ready to farm their own estates.

Satiric names

In satire names are often determined by the satiric vehicle. Thus, mock-heroic needs heroic or at least burlesque heroic names. In *The Rape of the Lock* Thalestris is named after the Amazonian Queen in Strabo, or else comes from a more proximate source in Butler's *Hudibras* ("stout Armida, bold Thalestris").[54] And Ariel, associated with magic in *The Tempest* and in Rosicrucian literature, may also allude to the heroic angel in *Paradise Lost*. Alternatively, satires may exploit extra-literary facts about their targets. Then, the real-life names of the targeted group will be useful. But here one must be cautious. In Aristophanes' *Clouds*, for example, the real target is not Socrates but sophists in general: Socrates is only a representative figure.

Aristotle's *Poetics*, stressing the generality and philosophic truth of fiction, on the basis of the New Comedy distinguishes comic type-names (invented, general) from satire's individual names.[55] But the Old Comedy, in Aristotle's terms satiric comedy, initiated the more enduring tradition. It was Aristophanes, father of comic naming, who devised the sort of Cratylic names now especially linked with satire. The Old Comedy abounds with these type-names drawn from life: Lysistrata ("Demobilizer") and Strepsiades ("Deceitful") in *Clouds*. Such descriptive names, personifications, and cod etymologies were a dependable source of wit.[56] Later, the Roman satirists made moral naming almost routine. Martial, who withheld true names *parcere personis, dicere de vitiis*, has Classicus ("Upper class"), for example, and Fidentinus (an assured plagiarist).[57] Ambiguous referential status makes these charactonyms interestingly anomalous. They are simultaneously singular and universal, individual and typic, proper and common.

Moral naming merged with a strong tradition of allegorizing in late antiquity.[58] Later, abstract names of various sorts—moral, psychological, philosophical—abound in medieval drama, satiric sermons, and secular dream visions. And crossover between genres was quite acceptable, so long as it served a didactic purpose. William Langland's Glottoun and Sloth, for example, soon found their way into homiletic preaching.[59]

Renaissance satire recovered the pungency of classical naming. So Jonson's satiric epigrams emulate Martial's for concision—matched in this, and sometimes overgone, by Herrick.[60] Simple instances include Jonson's Guilty and Surly ("Surly's old whore in her new silks doth swim").[61] Other Jonsonian names are more tropic, like the lascivious Colt (39) or Cheverel (37, 54), the lawyer as pliant as kid leather. Or Chuff (44), implying "churl", "miser", and "chough", a carrion-eating bird supposed to have a sour disposition. Social types include Playwright (68), Luckless Woo-all (46), and Sir Voluptuous Beast (25). Jonson sometimes names so directly that he risks breaking satire's fictive illusion.

Several of his encomiastic epigrams focus on the addressee in a way almost peculiar to Jonson. "To Sir Horace Vere" opens with the names that epitomize Jonson's vision of *vera nobilitas*:

> Which of thy names I take, not onely beares
> A *romane* sound, but *romane* virtue weares:
> Illustrious VERE, or HORACE; fit to be
> Sung by a HORACE, or a *Muse* as free...
> > (*Epigrams* 91, lines 1–4)

And "To William, Earl of Pembroke" shows awareness of names as a feature of genre: "I doe but name thee, PEMBROKE, and I find | It is an *epigramme*, on all man-kind" (*Epigram* 102. 1–2).

Herrick's tag names compress and miniaturize even more extremely. Characteristic are Gut; Hog (shortened from Hodge?); and Chub, a type of rustic simpleton.[62] Sometimes Herrick's naming approaches a reductive extreme: Cob and Bice, Buggins and Spokes recall the abstract minimalism of legal fiction. In law the names John Doe, John (or Tom) Stiles, Richard Roe, and Richard Miles were used for (fictitious) parties in an action. John Doe was often the lessee of the plaintiff; John Stiles (originally John-a-stiles, "John who lives at the stile") paired with John-a-nokes ("John who lives at the oak"); and Richard Roe and Richard Miles were defendants. Such names referred to anyone in the situation specified: they lacked the full referentiality of real-life names. Sir Philip Sidney asks "doth the lawyer lie then, when under the names of 'John a Stile' and 'John a Noakes' he puts his case? But that is easily answered. Their naming of men is but to make their picture the more lively, and not to build any history: painting men, they cannot leave men nameless."[63] It is much the same with Herrick's briefest epigrams. Buggins and Spokes hardly qualify as tag names, they have so little descriptive content.

> *Upon Buggins*
> Buggins is Drunke all night, all day he sleepes;
> This is the Levell-coyle that Buggins keeps.[64]

(In level-coil the unseated player remained passive until his turn came round again.) "Buggins's turn" is allotted regardless of character and qualification: anyone, Herrick implies, may become a drunkard.

No poet was a more important link between Jacobean and Augustan satire than John Oldham (1653–83).[65] His work shows how problematic Aristotle's contrast of "comic" and "satiric" can be. From the start he uses real names, both historical and contemporary (Loyola, Hobbes, Gadbury). Sometimes these swarm in considerable numbers, as with the slighted poetry of "ancient time":

As Pordidg, Fleckno, or the British Prince? [by Edward Howard]
Quarles, Chapman, Heywood, Withers had Applause,
And Wild, and Ogilby in former days....
                                    (*Spencer's Ghost*, lines 98–100)

But these mix with type-names, some of them simultaneously literary
like "Butler's Sir Sydrophil" from *Hudibras*. And some of the real names
are representative types: "What Scipio, what Maecenas would'st thou
find, | What Sidney now to thy great Project kind?" (127–8). Oldham
strives for generality, sometimes taking this as far as personification:

> Others Ambition, that imperious Dame,
> Exposes cruelly, like Gladiators, here
> Upon the World's Great Theatre.
> (*Counterpart to the Satyr Against Vertue*, lines 78–80)

Pope in "The Fourth Satire of Donne Versified" (1733) shows himself
to have learned much from Oldham in these matters. Free to mod-
ernize at will, he uses a range of names different from and wider than
Donne's. Where Donne has real names, Pope sometimes leaves them
almost untouched: "More than ten Hollensheads, or Halls, or Stows
| Of trivial household trash" becomes "Meer Houshold Trash! . . . More
than ten Holingsheds, or Halls, or Stows".[66] Sometimes he substi-
tutes more recent names: Donne's "outlie either | Jovius, or Surius, or
both together" (lines 47–8) becomes "And Oldmixon and Burnet
both out-lie" (line 61). And for Donne's "linguists" Calepine and
Beza (lines 53–9), Pope puts Onslow, Swift, and Ho——y [Bishop
Hoadly] (lines 71–3). This is not mere updating. Pope has learned to
work towards generality, leaving Donne's personifications, but replacing "Calepine's Dictionary" (line 54) with "the Dictionary" (line 69).
He implies Walpole, but leaves him unnamed, as "the Great Man"
(line 159). With the real names he juxtaposes literary names such as
Panurge (Donne's Panurgus, line 59, from Rabelais) and Sir Fopling
Flutter from Etherege (line 233); key names such as Naso, later Fan-
nius (Lord Harvey, line 178); and charactonyms such as Umbra (line
177), often from mythology, like Circe (line 166).[67] In *To Cobham*,
similarly, Pope has Helluo (234, Latin "glutton") and Narcissa (243, a
character in Cibber's *Love's Last Shift*). Narcissa was a favourite stage
role of Anne Oldfield's, and so functions simultaneously as a key
name. "An Ascapart" makes the allusion to the romance Giant into a
general type.

The Renaissance charactonym, sometimes muted and made less implausible in Restoration comedy, was to be subtilized still further. After centuries of realistic fiction and ludic name-play by Thackeray and Dickens, it survived, variously disguised, in the modern novel of satiric social observation. Evelyn Waugh relies on it, and occasionally abandons disguise altogether. In *Decline and Fall* (1928) he uses moral names (the Hon. Miles Malpractice, Margot Beste-Chetwynde),[68] together with others, like Fagan, that are openly allusive. Waugh's most characteristic names have multiple references, as when the large Lady Circumference "wanders from the point". The relevance of a name may be unobvious and so need highlighting. Waugh achieves this by deliberate error (Pennyfoot for Pennyfeather) or by explicit announcement ("'Viscountess Metroland,' said Peter. 'What a name.'").[69] Surnames with two or more barrels imply negative judgements in Waugh: Alastair Digby-Vane-Trumpington, for example, or Sir Wilfred Lucas-Dochery, or Freddy French-Wise.[70] Paul Pennyfeather, the protagonist unburdened with wealth, is a Simplicissimus figure who discovers the hard way that colleges are liable to collude with moneyed members who behave badly, like the Bollinger (Bullingdon) Club.

John Mullan has drawn attention to the brilliance of Martin Amis' satiric naming:[71] "At Fielding Goodney's exclusive New York tennis club, Self spots the leading players Chip Fournaki and Nick Karebenkian, as well as the women's world champion Sissy Skolimowsky. Even the names are muscled. His business partners are Terry Lines and Keith Carburton: matey yet threatening; oikish yet upwardly mobile." Occasionally Mullan overstates: "John Self? He of course has the name of the very era." Amis' success, like Thackeray's, depends on a scintillating variety of jokes, sharp observation of type, and wild exaggeration of vulgarity: the restaurateur Krud, the ageing porn star Caduta ("Sagging"). His clever use of non-standard, sloppy pronunciation opens up possibilities of multiple association: Wayno ("Wino"), Lorne Guyland ("Long Island"). When Amis gives a dentist the name "Frift", he uses transferred association to suggest a patient trying to speak through mouthfuls of water.

Satire has long been given to grotesque names. In the sixteenth-century controversy over Talmudic literature, Dominican attempts at suppression were opposed by Johann Reuchlin in his collection of *Letters of Distinguished Men* (1514). Promptly, the anonymous *Letters of Obscure Men* (1515–17), probably by Crotus Rubianus and Ulrich von Hutton,[72] countered with devastating parodies in the mode of confessional satire. The correspondents have cumbersome Germanic names such as Lyra Bunts-chuchmacherius, Mammotrectus Buntemantellus ('Breast-Feeler Fancy-Cloak'), and Magister Bartholomaeus Kuckuk. (The last was to return as Professor Kuckuk in Thomas Mann's *Felix Krull*.) A similarly bizarre quality can be found in Fielding's Princess Hunca Munca.[73]

The grotesque name was a favourite device of Charles Dickens (Quilp, Podsnap, Pumblechook). But with Dickens grotesquerie need not serve any ostensible satiric purpose: as we shall see in chapter 8, he collected such names simply for their quiddity. In the twentieth century, considerations of plausibility tended to constrain grotesque naming. Nevertheless, Nat West has a Miss Lonelyhearts, and Joseph Heller a Major Major Major Major—not to speak of insulting names such as Mudd and Scheisskopf. The distinguished fantasist Mervyn Peake seems to have mastered what may be called Dickensian naming. Yet Anthony Burgess faults *Titus Groan* (1946) on just this feature:

we seem to be given clues directing us towards the daylight of a literary category, but all the keys change into red herrings. Take the names of the characters, for instance—Nettel ("the octogenarian who lived in the tower above the rusting armoury"); Rottcodd, curator of the Hall of the Bright Carvings; Flay, Swelter, Steerpike, Mrs Slagg, Prunesquallor. These are fitting for a Peacock novel, for Dickens or for a comic children's story. They are farcical, but the mood is not one of easy laughter or even of airy fantasy: the ponderous architectural quality holds everything down, and we have to take the characters very seriously, despite their names.[74]

In Burgess' view, Peake's names fail to fulfil the genre expectations they arouse.

Romance

Great names play an important part in romances. What would the Matter of Britain be without such names as Arthur, Lancelot, and Guinevere, Tristram, King Lot, and Iseult? But the vast body of ancient, medieval, and Renaissance romances called for a numerous cast of characters and corresponding variety of names. Not all of these were famous. Many of the names of Italian romantic epic, however, soon became familiar and were to prove easily imitable. Indeed, some of them resemble each other so closely as to be almost mutual anagrams—Orlando:

Rinaldo; Bradamante: Bradimarte: Britomart. The masculine romance
names often end in -*o*, and feminine ones, as we have seen, in -*a* and -*ia*.
So it was not difficult to invent convincing romance names, both in
fiction and in real life. Almost any exotic legendary name would do,
however implausible—although Dryden's "Aureng-Zebe" was a real
person. Nicknames and pseudonyms like Orinda and Ephelia, which
had the authority of the romances, were soon fashionable. The heroines
of Daniel Defoe and even of Samuel Richardson, as we saw, were often
given romance names.

One of the most striking features of romance names is the way in
which they are introduced: their delay by the author and their concealment by the characters. For it is not only the selection of names
that alters with genre but their deployment.

Deployment

Satire tends to introduce names abruptly, without preamble. As Antonio Sebastiano Minturno (d. 1579) notes, in satire "the opening is sud-
den".[75] Thus, in Pope's *Epistle to Dr Arbuthnot* the very first line is
"Shut, shut the door, good John". Pastoral names are brought in infor-
mally too, but less abruptly. In the ideal community, informal and intimate, shepherds all know each other already: introductions are
unnecessary.[76] As in the bar in *Cheers*, where all is fixed in a Golden
Age stasis, "everybody knows your name".

The name of a romance protagonist, however, is likely to be deployed
in a very distinctive way. Often it will be withheld, perhaps for some
considerable time, while the narrative continues anonymously. Chrét-
ien de Troyes delays naming Perceval in the *Conte del Graal*;[77] and in
Amadis of Gaul, King Perion is nameless until he has fought and killed
two vassals of King Garinter and heard the latter's name. In *The Faerie
Queene* St George goes under the *nom de guerre* "Red Cross" until book
1 is almost over.[78] Similarly Priscilla, who appears at *FQ* 6.2.16–21, is
not named until 6.3.10. Sometimes a knight's name is unknown even
to himself, and his adventure amounts to a search for identity.[79] The
withholding of a protagonist's name in romance is of such far-reaching
importance that we shall return to it in chapter 7. As a literary device,
the withheld name continued in late modulations of romance: it is
used to strong effect, for example, in the first chapters of Anthony

Trollope's *The American Senator* (1877) and George Meredith's *The Adventures of Harry Richmond* (1897).

Very short genres, even those with no special personnel, nevertheless use names in a characteristic way. Thus, epitaphs and funeral elegies have real names, often those of the deceased. The Earl of Surrey's epitaph on Thomas Clere is packed and patterned with place and personal names:

> Norfolk sprang thee, Lambeth holds thee dead,
> Clere of the County of Cleremont though hight;
> Within the womb of Ormondes race thou bread,
> And sawest thy cosine crowned in thy sight.
> Shelton for love, Surrey for Lord thou chase...

An even more extreme case of elegiac naming comes in the latter part of "The Lament for the Makars", William Dunbar's meditation on death. After surveying categories of the dead, Dunbar increases the poem's intensity with a catalogue of twenty-four fellow-poets who have been taken:

> He had done petuously devour
> The noble Chaucer, of makaris flour,
> The monk of Bery and Gower, all thre:
> *Timor mortis conturbat me.*

Alternatively, epitaphs in epigrammatic versions may use "punnable" names that offer opportunities for wit—"Who kill'd Kildare? Who dar'd Kildare to kill? | Death kill'd Kildare, who dare kill whom he will."[80]

Lyric, notably love lyric, may dispense with personal names— although Shakespeare's *Sonnets* do so deceptively, as we shall see in chapter 4. More usually, however, a sonnet mistress is prominently named. A Renaissance sonneteer may refer to several loves, drawing their names from ancient or neo-Latin love poetry or from romance (Parthenope, Corinna). Such names impart idealization through mythological associations (Diana) or by exaltation to the starry heavens (Caelia, Stella).[81] Recycling frequently occurs: Delia, for example, a name of Diana occurring in Tibullus, is reused by Maurice Scève (1510–64), Samuel Daniel (1562–1619), and several others, for its implication of purity, and perhaps also as a near anagram of *l'idée*.[82] Caelia ("heavenly") is a clear favourite, appearing in Hieronymus Angerianus' *Erotopaegnion* (1512), William Percy's *Coelia* (1594), Sir David Murray's *Coelia* (1611), and Thomas Carew's *Poems* (1640).[83]

These "fained" names shared by several poets (Stella, Celia, Rosalind) have naturally provoked speculation about the relation of poetry to life, name to mistress—speculation not always discouraged by the poets themselves.[84] The name of a sonnet mistress may be introduced in various special ways: dwelt on with wordplay, insisted on by repetition, or covertly conveyed through anagrams and acrostics. These possibilities are explored in chapter 4.

Abstract names

In the *Hesperides* of Robert Herrick (1591–1674), names relate to genre in a different way. His mistresses number fourteen, like the lines of a sonnet: some are directly addressed, others named obliquely in poem titles. Victorian critics debated which of them were the most important women in Herrick's life. But the severe Victorian Edmund Gosse, thinking badly of the seventeenth century's "false Anacreontic spirit", is ready to "dismiss Perilla, Silvia, Anthea, and the rest at once, as airy nothings, whom the poet created for the sake of hanging pretty amorous fancies on their names".[85] He takes Julia seriously, however, as having "ruled [Herrick's] youth" before he took holy orders. On the basis of literalistic interpretation Gosse is able to describe Julia's physical appearance and character and sartorial taste. More recently, Achsah Guibbory and John Shawcross, rightly in my view, have rejected such biographical fallacies.[86] Only by keeping speculation on a tight rein can one hope to be receptive to intimations of the "airy" ideals that sometimes excite Elizabethan poets.

That Renaissance love poetry amounts to more than chronicles of philandering seems obvious enough when one considers such documents as Giles Fletcher's preface to *Licia* (1593):

> If thou muse what my LICIA is, take her to be some Diana, at the least chaste, or some Minerva, no Venus, fairer farre. It may be shee is Learnings image, or some heavenlie wonder: which the precisest may not mislike. Perhaps under that name I have shadowed Discipline. It may be, I meane that kinde courtesie which I found at the Patronesse of these Poems, it may bee some Colledge. It may bee my conceit, and portende nothing.[87]

The possibility that Licia may shadow "Discipline" is interesting in connection with Herrick's "The Changes to Corinna", for he advises Corinna to incline "to Discipline".[88] Similar idealization—not necessarily Neoplatonic—may inform George Chapman's Mistress Philosophy, Drayton's *Idea*, and other sonnet Muses.

So, when Guibbory identifies Herrick's mistresses as personifications of the poems themselves, she may be very near the mark. "The bad season makes the Poet sad", for instance, laments the difficulty of writing in a hostile political climate:

> Dull to my selfe, and almost dead to these
> My many fresh and fragrant Mistresses:
> Lost to all Musick now.[89]

Even the attractions of Julia may not be altogether sexual: "I must confesse, mine eye and heart | Dotes less on Nature, then on Art." Gordon Braden's censure of "voyeuristic preference of perception to action"[90] is beside the point if Herrick's passion is for poetry, and necessarily contemplative.

The names of Herrick's "mistresses" may perhaps offer a useful guide. Thus, Dianeme is a simple tag name, made up from the Greek elements Δί, *Di,* and 'άνεμος, *anemos*: "Breath of Zeus", "divine inspiration". Hardly less explicitly, Lucia, from *lucis* (Latin, "light"), means illumination.[91] At least three of the fourteen names specifically identify Muses. Sappho and Corinna of Tanagra were both among the "nine lyric Muses",[92] unless Sappho, by an alternative reckoning, should count as a tenth Muse.[93] And Perilla, Ovid's stepdaughter, was the Muse of Herrick's special genre, epigram: Ovid tells a poem it will find her sitting "among books and her Pierian maidens [Muses]".[94]

Julia, the most often addressed of Herrick's mistresses, was a great name in erotic poetry after the Julia Monobiblos of Janus Secundus (Jan Everaertes, 1511–36), the Netherlandish love poet. In the first book (hence Monobiblos) of his love elegies, *Amores*, Janus' Julia had emulated Propertius' Cynthia and incidentally made famous his own youthful affair with Julia of Mechlin in 1531.[95] Herrick's Julia, however, takes a more ceremonial turn. She is "Flaminica Dialis, or Queen-Priest" and "Pious-Priestesse",[96] wife of the Priest of Jupiter. Herrick's Silvia, similarly, has religious associations. She is "the patient saint" who makes him holy "circumcrost by her hand",[97] besides being another royal priestess. For, as Rhea Silvia or Ilia, she was anciently *regina sacerdos*, Vestal Virgin yet also mother of Romulus and Remus.[98]

Several of Herrick's names evoke the mistresses of other poets. As Julia was Janus Secundus', so Corinna was Ovid's[99] and Perilla that of Giovanni Gioviano Pontano (1426–1503) the author of a didactic neo-Latin *De Hortis Hesperidum*.[100] These and others of Herrick's loves are beneficiaries of the advice to Corinna to learn from Ovid's fate and write purely.

Others suffer metamorphosis into trees or stars. Ovid's incestuous Myrrha is metamorphosed to a tree exuding myrrh, and exhorted to be "like a Virgin full of ruth, | For the lost sweet-heart of her youth".[101] All stellifications idealize, but these are specifically Hesperidean. "Heaven-like Chrystalline" Anthea (Ἄνθεια) and "dark-eyed" Electra (Ἠλέκτρη, "shining, brilliant"), mother of Harmonia, joined the constellation Pleiades or Hesperides, here multiply relevant.[102] First, the gardens of the Hesperides lie far in the west, mythologizing Herrick's own Devon. Then, as a grove, they befit the genre of *Hesperides* itself—a *silva*, or collection of apparently miscellaneous poems.[103] Thirdly, the grove contained the tree of golden apples, the object of Hercules' quest, symbolizing the philosopher's stone.[104]

Herrick's other names need less explanation. Anna Perenna, another Atlantid, personifies the ancient year and so qualifies as Muse of the many calendrical poems.[105] Like Oenone (Paris' first, innocent love), she is associated with wine, and so with the poems of intoxication.[106] Biancha, "White", refers to the white of innocence (as in "The white Island: or place of the Blest") and to the whitened spiritualized body of alchemy.[107] In a time of civil war, one might expect a martial Muse; but Herrick instead has Irene (εἰρήνη, "peace").[108]

In "Upon the losse of his Mistresses",[109] Herrick mourns the loss of seven mistresses corresponding to the genres celebrated in *Hesperides*. They are only half of his fourteen; yet the poem contrives to seem comprehensive. It deplores the loss, under the Commonwealth, of Julia (religious verse), Sappho (lyric), Anthea, Electra, and Myrrha (metamorphoses and stellification), together with "witty" Corinna and Perilla (epigram). The loss of all these closes portals to a world of poetic imagination where he had once found the joy in life's beauty that made life worth living. Now,

> All are gone;
> Onely Herrick's left alone,
> For to number sorrow by
> Their departures hence, and die.

Notes

1. See Faral 1962: 87; Fowler 1997: 240.
2. See Aristotle *Poetics* 9.5–6: "tragic poets keep to real names" (ὀνομάτων). But this is soon qualified: "in some tragedies one or two of the names are familiar (γνωρίμων) but others invented" (9.7). And he goes further: "in some the names are all invented, as in Agathon's *Antheus*". He might have added that Cratylic names also occur in tragedy: the name Creon ("ruler") is given to more than one tragic character.
3. See *OLD*; Ostler 2007: 18n.
4. A name familiar to Spenser, e.g. from Vergil, *Georgics* 1.19 and *Culex* 136 (which he imitated as *Vergil's Gnat* 207–8: "That Ceres seede of mortall men were knowne, | Which first Triptoleme taught how to be sowne").
5. See Oliver 1970.
6. *Menaphon* (1589).
7. *OED* s.v. *Clown*, 1: "countryman".
8. Wolcott 1794–1801: 3.350.
9. See Alpers 1996: 301–3; Jefferies 1880.
10. Ch. 18, Hardy 1978: 173. Cf. Jefferies 1880.
11. Cit. Skilton, Hardy 1978: 527.
12. Giles is also the name of the orphan labourer in "The Farmer's Boy" (1800), a poem by Robert Bloomfield (1766–1823).
13. See *Enciclopedia Virgiliana* 3.458.
14. On the personal names in Vergil's *Eclogues*, see Volk 2008: 73–7; Grant 1965: 67. Vergil shares with Theocritus the names Corydon, Menalcas, and Thyrsis.
15. See *Poetice* 3.99, Scaliger 1964: 150. Mopsus and Chromis, shepherds in Vergil, are fishermen in Sannazaro. See further Jones 1925; Sannazaro 1966; Hubbard 2007; Cummings 2006; Pellicer 2010.
16. Corydon first appears in Theocritus, *Idylls* 4 and 5, herding cows for a friend, Aegon, against the background of mixed farming and fishing usual on islands such as Cos. Subsequent Corydons/Coridons, shepherds or undifferentiated rustics, reappear in Vergil, *Eclogue* 2; Calpurnius, *Eclogues* 1.8; 4; 7; Propertius 2.34.73; Columella 10.298; Juvenal 9.102; Petrarch, *Eclogue* 6.144; Barclay, *Eclogues* 1–3; Googe, *Eclogues* 3, 8; Thomas Greene, *Ciceronis Amor*; Thomas Lodge, *Rosalinde*; Sidney, *Arcadia* (1593); Francis Sabbie, *Pan's Pipe* (1595) "To the Reader"; Spenser, *FQ* 6.9 (the jealous shepherd Coridon, whom Chaudhuri 1989 unnecessarily sees as betraying Spenser's dissatisfaction with conventional pastoral); *CCCHA*, 200, 282; Shakespeare, *AYLI*; Milton, *L'Allegro* 83; Thackeray, *Vanity Fair* 2.12; Jackie Coryton in *Hay Fever*. For eight examples of Coridons in Elizabethan drama, see Berger, Bradford, and Sondergard 1998: 34.
17. See Fowler 1997: 78–81. On pastoral in general, see Greg 1959; Rosenmeyer 1969; Sambrook 1983; Chauduri 1989.
18. *Idylls* 6.6, 11.31–2; see Finley 1999: 60, 78.
19. Poggioli 1975: 26, 48, 288.
20. *Metamorphoses* 13.884; *Odyssey* 9.537–600.
21. Milton 1997: 248.
22. Neaera may have had similar associations for Milton, in view of G. G. Pontano's funeral elegy for her in his *Amores*. But Neaera was also Janus Secundus' second love, *urbana Neaera*; Marullus' Neaera; and before that the faithless Neaera of Horace's *Epode* 15. Cf. Fletcher, *Licia*, 17–19, Fletcher 1964: 90–1, 421, and see Schoolfield 1980: 61–2, 102. See Revard 1997: 182 n. 34.
23. Theocritus 7.55, discussed Cairns 1972: 27–8.
24. Johnson 2006: 1.278–9.

25. Cummings 2006: 197.
26. *Idylls* 7.59; 8.52; cf. *Georgics* 4.388; Sannazaro 1966: 175.
27. Diaper 1952: xxvii.
28. Diaper's Cymothoe, e.g., appears in *Iliad* 18 and *FQ* 4.11. On Sannazaro, see Hubbard 2007.
29. *Metamorphoses* 3.617.
30. *Eclogue* 5.114–15.
31. *FQ* 7.6.40–53; see Gottfried 1937: 107–25.
32. See Fowler 1989: 42–4; Fowler 1986: 105–25.
33. Colin, Cuddie, Thenot, Willye, Thomalin, Hobinoll, Palinode, Piers, Morrell, Perigot, Diggon Davie. Morrell or Morel was a diminutive of More or Moore, "dark".
34. Cf. Harrison 2007: 59 finding "confrontation between the literary genres of pastoral and love-elegy".
35. Coridon and Menalcas are from Theocritus and Virgil, Cornix and Fulica from Phaedrus, and Amyntas from Theocritus and Sannazaro. Codrus was an exemplary king of Athens, and Faustus was the son of Sulla. See Cooper 1977: 118.
36. Cf. Cooper 1977: 111.
37. See Chaudhuri 1989: 37–8; Margot shadowed Marguerite d'Angoulême. Colin is a diminutive of medieval Col(le), itself a short form of Nicholas.
38. *SC* February, 25 gloss.
39. On polemical pastoral, see Jones 2011.
40. *Idylls*, 4.10.
41. Motto was sometimes spelt Motho; it may hint at Shakespeare's Moth, also a juvenile.
42. Cf. Spenser, *SC* July 95, "I am but rude and borrell": E. K. glosses this as "plain fellow".
43. See Tillotson and Newdigate's note to *Shepherd's Garland* 4.25, Drayton 1931–41: 5.8.
44. Ibid. 522.
45. See Gay 1974: 2.513–4.
46. Ibid. 532.
47. Philips, cit *OED* s.v. *sparable*. Gay mentions the nails again in *Trivia* 1.263, Gay 1974: 2.528, 555.
48. Boileau, "The Art of Poetry", tr. Dryden, 248–54, Dryden 1995: 162.
49. Poggioli 1975: 35; Cooper 1977: 134–5.
50. See Greg 1959: 287, 291.
51. See Fowler 1986: 105–25; Fowler 1992: 83–7.
52. E.g. Colie 1974: 245–6; Poggioli 1975: 37–8; Fowler 1984: 1–14. In this connection the motif of names on trees could well be the topic of a separate chapter; see, e.g., Grant 1965; Lee 1977.
53. Cf. *MND* 2.1.66, from Tottel, "Harpalus' Complaint". Lodge's *Rosalynde* (1590), a source for *AYLI*, has a Corydon, drawn in turn from Corin in *Sir Clyomon and Sir Clamydes* (1570).
54. Strabo 11; *Hudibras* 1.2.393, Butler 1967: 40.
55. 51 b 11–15; b 29–32.
56. See Barton 1990: 20–7.
57. *Epigrams* 7.72; 2.69.
58. See Whitman 1987.
59. See Owst 1961: 430, 436 on *Piers Plowman* A-text *passus* 5.212–33. Cf. Barton 1990 on examples in drama.
60. Barton 1990: 75.
61. Jonson, *Epigrams* 30, 38, 82. For bibliography on names in Jonson's poetry see Donaldson's note in Jonson 1985: 647.

62. Herrick 1956: 327; 326; 327, Herrick 1968: 432; 430; 432.
63. Sidney 2002: 103.
64. *Hesperides*, no. 1011, Herrick 1956: 311, Herrick 1968: 412.
65. See Hammond 1983.
66. Donne, Satyre 4.97–8; Pope, "The Fourth Satire of Donne Versified" 130–1, Pope 1961: 34–5.
67. See Erskine-Hill 1983: 93.
68. Highet 1962: 193 suggests "Beast-Cheating".
69. Waugh 1937: 214.
70. Waugh 1937: 69, 215.
71. Mullan 2006: 275–8.
72. Moss 2003: 242; Highet 1962: 140; Stokes 1925: 72–6.
73. *Tom Thumb* (1730) Act 2, scene 4; see Highet 1962: 121, 265 n. 69. Hunca Munca is remembered by Beatrix Potter in *The Roly-Poly Pudding*.
74. Peake 1968: 11.
75. Minturno 1564: 276; see Fowler 1985: 99, 295 n. 28.
76. Cf. Rosenmeyer 1969: 107.
77. See Stevens 1973: 117; Parker 1979: Index s.v. Naming; Fowler 1985: 82.
78. At *FQ* 1.10.61, although hinted earlier at 1.2.12. See Marks and Gross, *SEnc* 494 col. 2.
79. See Cooper 2004: 333–4.
80. Grigson 1977: 3.
81. See further in Fowler 1982: 76–7. For Parthenopeus, see Pontanus 1531: 1.31.
82. See Scève 1966: 14–16. Other instances include Marcantonio Flaminio (1498–1550) and Agostino Ricchi (1512–64).
83. See Klein 1984: 2.242. Angerianus was well known in the 1590s, perhaps from *Poetae Tres Elegantissimi* (Paris, 1582); see, e.g., Fletcher 1964: 418–23 *passim*.
84. See Hadfield 2008: 13–14.
85. Gosse 1897: 136.
86. Guibbory 1978: 79–87; Shawcross 1978: 89.
87. "To the Reader", Fletcher 1964: 79–80.
88. Herrick 1956: 96, Herrick 1968: 135.
89. Herrick 1956: 214, Herrick 1968: 284–5.
90. Braden 1978: 223.
91. A further association may be Lucy (patron saint of sight) who was miraculously saved from exposure in a brothel.
92. *Greek Anthology* 9.26 and 184 (accessible to Herrick in the *Planudean Anthology*); also Propertius 2.3.21; Stephanus, *Dictionarium Historicum* s.v. *Corinna* "quae Lyricorum principem Pindarum quinquies vicisse, et epigrammatum 50 libros edidissse fertur".
93. *Greek Anthology* 9.571.
94. *Tristia* 3.7.1–4: "inter libros Pieridasque suas". Aulus Ticidas, contemporary with Catullus, wrote love poems to Perilla; see Poliziano, *Nutricia* 708, Poliziano 2004: 154.
95. The name Monobiblos was given by Janus' first editor, Filippo Beroaldo (1453–1505). See Schoolfield 1980: 41 and Index s.v. *Julia*.
96. Herrick 1956: 196; Herrick 1968: 262. In ancient Rome, the Flaminica Dialis was the wife of the Flamen Dialis, the priest performing the ritual of Jupiter. See Ovid, *Fasti* 6.226, *coniunx sancta Dialis*.
97. Herrick 1956: 204, 227; Herrick 1968: 272, 300.
98. Ennius, *Annales* 55; Vergil, *Aen.* 1.273; Horace, *Odes* 4.8.22; Tibullus 2.5.52; Statius, *Silvae* 1.2.243; Dio Chrysostom 354.23.
99. *Amores* 1.5.9 *et passim*.

100. Pontano, *Parthenopeus* 1.31, Pontano 1948: 97. "Ad Perillam Puellam" appears in the *Amores* 1.

101. *Metamorphoses* 10.489–518; Herrick 1956: 47, Herrick 1968: 66. George Sandys interprets her as "love melancholy".

102. For Anthea, see Herrick 1956: 11, 34, 59, Herrick 1968: 19, 49, 88; for Electra, Herrick 1956: 34, 154, Herrick 1968: 49, 209. See e.g. Hesiod, *Astronomia* 1; Apollodorus 3.10.1; Ovid, *Fasti* 4.31–2; Middleton 1596: sig. D1b.

103. On the Hesperides as gardens, see Moore Smith 1914. On the *silva* genre, established by Statius and revived by Poliziano, Jonson, and Dryden, see Fowler 1982: 163–80, and cf. Poliziano 2004: ix.

104. See Abraham 2000: 101; Maier 1989. Musgrove 1976: 240–65 traces many alchemic motifs in *Hesperides*, e.g. 260 "level-coyle", the alchemist's horizontal *canale serpentium*.

105. E.g. Herrick 1956: 67–9, 101, 103, 126, 285, 304, Herrick 1968: 98, 140, 143, 172–3, 376, 400. See Ovid, *Fasti* 3.654–9.

106. At Anna Perenna's feast, wassailers were supposed to live as many years as they drank cups of wine: see Ovid, *Fasti* 3.523ff. For Oenone, see Herrick 1956: 168, Herrick 1968: 226. In Oenone's case the association was etymological.

107. Herrick 1956: 32, 376, Herrick 1968: 47–8, 497. In the seventeenth century "white" was rich in associations: see *OED* s.v. *White* 6–8. On its alchemic senses, see Abraham 2000: 215–17.

108. Herrick 1956: 32, 376, Herrick 1968: 271. See Hesiod, *Theogony* 902.

109. Herrick 1956: 15–16, Herrick 1968: 25.

3

The Faerie Queene

One of the first British poets to give full attention to fictional names was Edmund Spenser (1552–99). Much of his effort must have gone into discovering and selecting names, and enriching them with multiple implications. Very often, indeed, interpreting *The Faerie Queene* depends on understanding its names. Spenser is brilliant at naming: more so even than Shakespeare, who had commonly to reuse names within theatrical tradition and convention. Among sixteenth-century works *The Faerie Queene* is unusual in the extent to which it mixes names of different sorts: only the *Orlando Furioso* stands comparison.[1]

Variety of types

Adonis, Arthur, Britomart, Burbon, Celeno, Coridon, Cymothoe, Florimell, Matilda, Night, Numa, Perissa, Red Cross: these all mingle without discordance, so that the reader easily runs on without stopping to reflect that some are ordinary real-life names, others allegorical, or exotic. They are simply fictional, the names of Spenser's world. Thus, the first Canto introduces Gloriana, Errour, Morpheus, Hecate, and Archimago: a sequence with its own logic. Spenser's first editor, John Upton (1707–60), well recognized this variety in naming: "Spenser varies his names from history, mythology, or romance, agreeable to his own scheme." The variety has to do with genre. Renaissance theorists regularly dwelt on epic's all-embracing, encyclopedic character, claiming it included other genres. So the heterogeneous names of *The Faerie Queene* show Spenser attempting to fulfil this inclusive aim. Throughout the poem, shifts of mode and mood are signalled, and partly effected, through grouping of generically similar names. Thus, names in the pastoral romance of book VI (Calidore, Corydon) differ from those in the historical chronicles (Brennus, Bellinus) or in the erotic mythology of Busyrane's tapestry (Cupid, Europa). Overriding such modulations, however, a drive towards synthesis can be sensed: towards a single fiction, comprehensive and diverse, like the world itself.

More than a dozen types of names can be distinguished.[2] Most obvious, personifications: either English or foreign-language abstractions, sometimes complicated by archaistic or significant spellings (Shame, Errour, Slowth). Whether in one or more languages, the names may be simple or compound (Una, Corceca, Maleger, Ruddymane). Components may be of classical or biblical or romance origin, or several of these combined (Furor, Mammon, Amidas, Timias). Different provenances mix freely (Mercilla, Corflambo). And mythological names (Proserpina, Proteus) mingle with those from more recent literature (Arthur, Colin, Calidore). Some have a chivalric ring (Red Cross Knight, Squire of Low Degree); others suggest a locally appropriate genre such as pastoral (Corydon, Meliboe). A structurally significant type is the family of names, all formed in the same way or with a common pattern of sound (Priamond, Diamond, Triamond). Key names—another type—abound. Some of these were announced by Spenser (Gloriana, Belphoebe); others, recently discovered, are discussed in chapter 4. Of the key names, some are anagrams, others rebuses (Dumarin, Lansack). The last line of the poem as we have it ("O that great Sabbaoth God, graunt me that Sabaoths sight"), playing on different interpretations of the biblical name, depends on another, sacred type.[3]

Real romance

The real-life world has more presence in *The Faerie Queene* than may at first appear. Some of its names, it may naturally be assumed, are invented, while others are not. But determining which are fictional and which extra-fictional proves to be surprisingly tricky, for allegorical names were common in Elizabethan times. Scudamour ("Shield of love") seems obviously made up; yet it was a familiar surname in the sixteenth century. Camden, as we have seen, was critical of precisians who named their children with abstractions such as "Reformation"; Bulstrode Whitelocke's *Diary* is full of names like "Prudence" and "Thankful"; and many similar examples have been collected from early baptismal records.[4] When moral names were part of real life, Spenser's Maleffort and Despetto, charactonyms as they are, may well have seemed plausibly realistic. To complicate matters further, proper names were still spelt variably enough for meaningful variants to be introduced at will.

As for classical and mythological names, these were commoner still in everyday life. Sir Julius Caesar (1538–1636) was Queen Elizabeth's physician; Troilus Atkinson kept the Brazen George at Cambridge;[5] and Spenser and Mulcaster each had a son called Sylvanus. Romance names, too, invaded ordinary life, as we have seen. The modern reader may associate Spenser's Amyas with *Amadis de Gaul* (as Charlotte Yonge did); but Amyas Paulet was Mary Queen of Scots' gaoler, Amyas Hill founded Michael Drayton's school, and the name kept figuring in Curia Regis rolls. Drummond of Hawthornden (1585–1649) so hankered after romance that he inscribed some of his own books "Don Murmidumilla".[6] Such overlaps between the realm of romance and the quotidian world delighted Spenser: his naming spans that uncertain border even more often than Ariosto's.

Cratylic names, especially personifications, are sometimes said to limit character development in fiction. But to criticize Spenser's names as "short-circuiting" ignores their complex purposes. Even after centuries of criticism, new implications of his names keep emerging. This started as early as Upton's great edition of 1758. On Timon (*FQ* 1.9.3–5), Upton comments: "by saying that Arthur was nurtured by Timon, allegorically he [Spenser] means, that he was brought up in the ways of *honour*: for so his tutor's name signifies" in Greek. But already this is sensed to oversimplify, for "in the romance history [...] Uther Pendragon by the counsel of Merlin delivers the young prince to be nurtured by Sir Ector". Behind Spenser's "old Timon" stands not only Malory's Ector (the "Faery knight" of *FQ* 1.9.3 who brought the unweaned Arthur to Timon to be trained in "virtuous lore") but also Merlin, charged to oversee Arthur's upbringing and his "discipline to frame" (*FQ* 1.9.5). The names imply complex issues of nature, nurture, and grace. Occasionally Spenser explicitly acknowledges the Cratylic relevance of an abstract name; as with Ignaro: "His name Ignaro did his nature right aread".[7] He had learned from his schoolmaster Richard Mulcaster (who expounded both the Cratylic and the Hermogenean theories) "what a cunning thing it is to give right names".[8]

Moreover, even the simplest personifications may be more than bare abstractions. Like emblems, they often come with imagery that contributes detailed realization. Spenser's Gluttony, for example, has a crane's neck because his name derives from *gluttire* (Latin, "swallow"). The long narrow neck of the crane was thought to prolong the pleasure of swallowing.[9]

Constructed names

Spenser's charactonyms are often constructed from foreign-language components—generally Latin, Greek, Italian, French, and Irish.[10] Latin was the language of academic discourse, quite as familiar to many intellectuals as the vernacular. But this was less true of Greek, which provided the basis of naming in medieval learned allegories by Alanus de Insulis, Bernardus Silvestris, and other Platonic authors.[11] Similarly with the humanists: Thomas More drew on Greek for the names in his *Utopia* (Hythlodaeus, Ademus).[12] An important factor here is the competitiveness of Renaissance etymological theories. Guillaume Budé, Cornelis Kiel, and others constructed Greek derivations for vernacular words to show them more ancient and biblical than those merely derived from Latin.[13]

It was the same with Spenser's most congenial source, the *Hypnerotomachia Polifili* (1499) of Francesco Colonna. This long-neglected work, translated into French by Jean Martin in 1546 and into English by Sir Robert Dallington in 1592,[14] provided naming models for both Sidney and Spenser.[15] Colonna's compound Greek names, such as Eleuterilyda, "Free-will" (from ἐλευθερία, *eleutheria*, freedom, generosity) and Erotomoride (ἔρωτος, *erotos* + τιμωρέω, *timoreo* "Avenger of passion")—and indeed Polifilo itself—inspired many of Spenser's, such as Perissa "who in excess exceeded" (περισσή, *perisse*, "excessive"). Colonna's bizarre style, coupling Italian syntax with Latin and Greek vocabulary, must have been difficult in an almost modernistic way. His allegory of erotic initiation has never been fully explicated, partly because the names are so richly suggestive. Even Polifilo might mean "Lover of Polia" or "Lover of many things". (For the *Hypn-erotomachia* abounds with attractive things: gardens, clothes, and sensu-ous architecture.) Scores of Colonna's minor characters—Cinosia the portress, Algerea ("Sorrow-bearer")—have abstract names shrouded in ambiguity; while others are mythological or allude to Latin erotic poetry: Corinna, Lesbia, Delia, Neaera. Spenser studied Colonna's names, and directly appropriated "Amorous Phaon" (*FQ* 2.4).[16]

The Faerie Queene has more than a thousand names, some of them loaded with implications even richer and subtler than Colonna's or Sidney's. As a guide to help readers through this onomastic labyrinth, Spenser often uses a grammar whereby names related in meaning have similar components. Doublets and trios (Marks and Gross' "serial names") share a word segment to show their relationship: the sisters Perissa and Elissa; the brothers Bracidas and Amidas; Sansfoy, Sansloy, and Sansjoy; Priamond, Dyamond, and Triamond; and Despetto, Decetto, and Defetto. These formal resemblances, while recalling medieval romance pairs such as Balin and Balan, here indicate sibling relationships, and imply membership of a particular category, moral or psychological, that partly defines the character's content. Usually the siblings contrast with each other, or at least are clearly distinct. Thus Perissa ("Excess") contrasts with Elissa ("Deficiency"), and Pyrochles with Cymochles. A parent–child relationship, however, implies causa-tion. Thus Mortdant and Amavia *cause* the blood-guiltiness of Ruddy-mane. And Night is "Mother of annoyance sad" (*FQ* 3.4.55) and "mother of dread darknesse (*FQ* 1.5.44).[17]

The kindred components in doublets and trios are not put there only for euphony but for meaning. Take the example of Perissa and Elissa sharing the component -*issa*. Upton regarded Elissa as Italianate: "ἔλλειψις [*elleipsis*] which the Italians (and Spenser Italianizes many of his words) would call Elissa [*elisa*, past participle of *elidere*]; so that we have Spenser's Elissa. She is deficient and wanting in all good man-ners".[18] Upton here explains more than William Nelson or A. C. Ham-ilton is able to do, by deriving "Elissa" from ἐλάσσων, *elasson*, "too little [pleasure]".[19] Modern etymologists derive the suffix -*ess* (denoting a female person) from Greek -ισσα (-issa) through late Latin -*issa* and Romanic -*essa*. But Spenser may have thought of "Perissa" as com-posed of *Peri* (Greek, "beyond measure") and -*issa* (a colloquial Latin form of *ipse*),[20] making Perissa "Excess in itself". Elissa, by analogy, is "Deficiency in itself" (alluding to Aristotle, *hyperbole kai elleipsis kai to meson*, "excess and deficiency and the mean").[21] Members of doublets and trios are partly defined by their relations with others in the group, whether of alliance or opposition. Perissa is the opposite "Extremitie" to Elissa, and Medina represents the mean between them. So too with their champions Sansloy, Guyon, and Hudibras. Sansloy ("Lawless") intelligibly supports Perissa ("Excess, Beyond measure"), whereas the puritanical Hudibras takes Deficiency's side. Guyon tries to maintain a temperate control of appetite for pleasure.

"Elissa" also plays on the Phoenician name of Dido in *Aeneid* book 4.[22] "Medina" may simply be constructed from Latin *mediana*, "situated in the middle". But in the context of sieges and fortifications ("the face of golden Meane" is a curtain wall[23]), "Medina" would suggest the ancient capital of Malta, famously besieged in 1565 by the Saracens. No accident, then, that Perissa's champion Sansloy is a Saracen.[24] The primary implications of Spenser's names are often supplemented by secondary associations, in a kind of wide-ranging wit that Joyce will later develop in *Finnegans Wake*.

The component *-essa* seems in *The Faerie Queene* to have a different implication from *-issa*. It has usually been linked with *esse* (Latin, "being").[25] This fits "Duessa" (combining *esse* with Latin *duo* or Italian *due*—"double being"); but it hardly suits "Fidessa" or "Abessa". Perhaps instead Spenser means us to connect *-essa* with ἕσσα, *hessa* (from ἕννυμι, *hennumi*, "clothe oneself, wear"). Then Fidessa (Latin *fides* + *esse*) will mean "apparent faith", "seeming faith" rather than "being faith".[26] If so, the component *-essa* would belong to the evil world of appearances and disguises, as befits Abessa (*FQ* 2.3.18). "Abessa" could also be construed as *Abbess* + *a* ("Abbess"), or even as *Ab-esse*, "Being absent"—a hit at non-resident clergy. Moreover, the component *-essa* might suggest a grand Italian title like *principessa*. The names of *The Faerie Queene* are not simple.

Spenser's abstract names usually include at least three elements: (1) an English, Latin, or Greek component conveying the primary meaning; (2) a romance association, often an Italianate form or an archaic spelling; and (3) further wordplay, contributing supplementary meanings. Critics like to disambiguate the names, forcing choices between univocal alternatives so as to reduce Spenser's names to "mere allegory". But *The Faerie Queene* is not to be read in the same way as the single-minded pilgrimages of Guillaume de Deguileville or Jean Cartigny or William Baspoole.[27] We should expect Spenser's personifications to present complex associations. Even the simple scheme underlying the Saracen trio Sansfoy, Sansloy, and Sansjoy proves to have complications. At first the Saracens seem to represent categories of sin corresponding to Neoplatonic triads such as *mens, voluntas, voluptas* and *illuminari, purgari, perfici*.[28] In Elizabethan spelling and pronunciation, however, the shared component *sans* fell together with *saint*.[29] Thus the Red Cross Knight has to deal with the disguised trio, St Foy, St Loy, and St Joy. And these had romance associations, both with *The Passion of Ste Foy* and the "Bryan sance foy" in the romantic play *Sir Clyomon and Sir Clamydes* (1570).[30]

Such poetic patterns cannot, of course, be strictly regular. "Braggadocchio", for example, has the Italianate form (*occio* or *ochio*), but no Greek or Latin component. Instead, the name has several vernacular associations, almost amounting to a personal portrait. "Braggadocchio" is usually related to English *brag, braggart*, and French *bragard*. But in his description "avaunting in great bravery | As Peacocke" (*FQ* 2.3.6), "bravery" means "finery". In view of the the Elizabethan swaggerer's wide slops, commonly satirized, "Braggadocchio" may also hint at *braga(s)* (Spanish and Italian, "breeches").[31] And the apt *bragado* (Spanish, "vicious") can hardly be excluded. Such wit lies in multiplying the name's resonances, without obscuring the primary meaning. As James Nohrnberg observes, Braggadocchio's henchman *Trompart* means not only "Art of the boastful trump" but also "Art of deception" (*tromper*).[32]

Cultural associations

In the less abstract names of *The Faerie Queene*, certain preoccupations stand out. Harry Berger wonders "what the poet had in mind when he picked those good humanist names, Calepine and Aldus".[33] and Nohrnberg suggests book 6 introduces "the book-as-subject", with the hermit tracing the lineage of the Blatant Beast "as in books is taught"; and adds that books "may also appear in some of the characters' names". Indeed they may. Ambrogio Calepino (c. 1435–1511) compiled a standard Latin dictionary and Aldus "is the name of the great printer of classical texts whom Erasmus made proverbial for the laborious scholar".[34] Pursuing similar literary associations, Berger and Nohrnberg notice that "Pastorella" calls to mind *pastourelle*, a subgenre of erotic pastoral. And they have seized on what turns out to be a very long clue. For throughout *The Faerie Queene* real-life authors keep appearing. This probably escaped the early commentators because allusion was then a relatively new and problematic device.

Some of the allusions, however, are beyond reasonable doubt. Enias (who accompanies Arthur at 6.8.4–30) has been identified as Aeneas the founder of the Roman dynasty. But in a poem often concerned with origins, "Enias" surely alludes to Ennius (239–169 BC), father of Latin poetry.[35] Similarly, the name of Pastorella's father, Meliboe, alludes to Chaucer, the father of English poetry, who in his own person tells the Canterbury Tale of Melibeus. Other real-life authors include Tryphon the sea-gods' physician (*FQ* 3.4.43; 4.11.6); Turpine the Castellan of the Ford (5.4.26); Bonfont, Malfont's original name (5.9.26); Dony, Florimell's dwarf (5.2.3); Aladine son of Aldus (6.3.3); Priscilla, Aladine's mistress (6.3.10); and the Acidalian mount (6.10). Of these, Tryphon was an important first-century BC grammarian from Alexandria";[36] Turpin (d. c. 800), Charlemagne's Archbishop in the *Chanson de Roland*, allegedly wrote the *Chronicle of Pseudo-Turpin*;[37] Bonfont was Joannes Bonefonius, a prominent neo-Latin poet;[38] Dony suggests Antonio Francesco Doni (1513–74), whose *Morall Philosophie* was translated by Thomas North (1570); Aladine and Aldus allude to Aldo Manuzio (?1450–1515), the humanist printer of the 1499 *Hypnerotomachia*; Priscilla, diminutive of *prisca*, "ancient", may recall Priscian the grammarian (5th–6th century AD, author of a common school textbook); and Acidalia, besides its mythological associations, gave its name to the Rudolfine poet Valens Acidalius (1568–95).[39] In short, Spenser's "fierce warres" are largely culture wars, and his paladins are poets and scholars and patrons. If Red Cross is "the Patron of true Holinesse", Meliboe is a patron in a more literal sense, being traditionally linked with Sir Francis Walsingham on the strength of Thomas Watson's Latin elegy *Meliboeus* (1590). Watson's preface calls Walsingham "chief patron of virtue, learning, and chivalrie".[40]

The *Orlando Furioso* similarly introduces writers' names, as we have seen. But Spenser goes much further than Ariosto, treating poets and patrons as chivalric heroes and even elevating them to be the saints of a new secular calendar foreshadowing Herrick's "greeny calendar". In Spenser's vision, a gentleman was to be fashioned "in vertuous and gentle discipline"[41] as much by reading as by fighting. Besides, the age was one of ideological controversy, when writers fought as paladins, heroes, or villains.

Ancient fame

Several of Spenser's heroes are inaugurators; which relates them to the
poem's broader concern with origins. It reflects the early modern fascination with discoverers and founders of arts, languages, and institutions. Polydore Vergil's *De Inventoribus Rerum* (1499) went through
thirty Latin editions by 1555 and over a hundred versions in eight languages by the early eighteenth century. An abridged English translation had no fewer than five editions beween 1546 and 1560. First
beginners of all, the father and mother of mankind were thought of as
inaugurators of language; interest in the Adamic language before the
Fall continued well into the seventeenth century.[42]

In making their new beginnings, the Elizabethans naturally drew strength
from earlier originators, ancient and modern. Similar reasons, in part, stirred
their genealogical passions—as witness their search for validating roots and
the authority of heralds. A common mural decoration was a family tree,
sometimes with its roots planted in enthusiastic fictions. Sir Thomas Urquhart traced his descent back to the red earth from which Adam was formed.
And a similar aspiration informs Spenser's "rolles of Elfin Emperours" tell-
ing Gloriana's lineage "Which though from earth it be derived right, | Yet
doth it selfe stretch forth to heavens hight" (2.10.2). Throughout the poem
priority is honoured: that of Dumarin the first conqueror of Munster,[43] for
example, and that of Numa the lawgiver ruling "without policy", who
"first wore crowne of gold for dignitie" (2.10.39).

The theme of antiquity is naturally expressed through stylistic archaisms, a prominent feature of the poem. In an important article, Martha
Craig describes Spenser's archaism and opaque, foregrounded diction
as the outcome of a visionary struggle with language.[44] Behind a sustained etymological effort she discerns the doctrine that words have
degenerated throughout history. Spenser's archaism is thus more than
gothic quaintness: it offered a way to rediscover better, truer forms.
Spenser's names thus belong to a "secret wit of reality",[45] their wealth
of associations and allusions opening large historical perspectives.
Many evoke the world of romance. The feminine names ending in -*a*
or -*ia* (Mercilla, Phaedria) resemble those of the *Amadis* (Elisena, Oriana, Mabilia, Melicia). Sometimes Spenser reuses an actual romance
name. Medina appears in *Orlando Innamorato*, where Valibruno, Count
of Medina, is a Saracen; but Spenser appropriates his location name for

the Christian sister's charactonym.[46] Spenser's masculine names are
often those of ancient kings or heroes such as Arthur (also in Ariosto)
and the British king Hudibras (from Geoffrey of Monmouth).[47]
Argante (*FQ* 3.7) is Barbante's father in Boiardo; Brunell (*FQ* 5.3.5) is
a thief in Ariosto.[48] Mortdant (*FQ* 2.2.45) recalls Boiardo's Mordante
(*Orlando Innamorato* 2.19.17); and Burbon (*FQ* 5.11) figures in *Orlando
Furioso* 33–44. Even abstractions can have romance antecedents: Dis-
cord (*FQ* 4.2.1) is prominent in *Orlando Furioso* 14.76; while Sophy
(*FQ* 2.9.6) is both a personification (σοφία, "wisdom") and the son of
King Gurlicke of north Wales.[49]

"Red Cross" is characteristically many-faceted.[50] At first (*FQ*
1.1.2) "Red Cross Knight" may seem simply to refer to the "bloudie
Crosse" he wears "on his brest"—the red cross on a white ground
actually displayed in the Irish wars by the English; although the
Fitzgeralds were entitled to bear *Argent a Saltire Gules*.[51] But later
he will become "a Saint, and thine owne nations frend | And
Patrone: thou Saint George shalt called bee"—the martial saint
familiar as the protector of England,[52] whose attribute is a red cross
on a white or silver ground. Red Cross' paradoxical arms, bearing
"old dints of deep wounds" yet never wielded, are also, however,
the "glorious badge" of Christ put on by the believer. Moreover,
John Lydgate, long before Spenser, had taken "George" to signify
holiness or knighthood and renown.[53] And John Selden, retelling in
1612 how St George delivered a king's daughter from a dragon,
adds that in consequence "some account him an allegory of our
saviour Christ", and that Spenser "hath made him an embleme of
Religion".[54] The legends of St George, together with the tradition
of patriotic pageants, generate several episodes, such as the battle
with the old dragon. At the House of Holiness, Red Cross learns his
true name to be Georgos, "farmer, husbandman": "thee a Ploughman all unweeting fond [...] brought thee up in ploughmans state
to byde, | Whereof *Georgos* he thee gave to name" (*FQ* 1.10.66).
The derivation of γεωργός, *georgos* (from γῆ, *ge* ("earth") and ἔργω,
ergo ("work"), known from the *Legenda Aurea*, implied that Georgos
cultivated the earth of his own flesh in spiritual improvement—or,
in another metaphor, edification.[55] This agricultural trope recurs in
a strand of georgic imagery running throughout the poem, for
example in figures of writing as ploughing and allusions to the par-
able of sowing the seed of the gospel.[56]

"Guyon" is no less complex. As a romance name it recalls Guy of
Warwick and Guy (Gyoun) of Burgundy. A Guyon was Ogier the
Dane's brother, and Gwion was an Arthurian knight.[57] But Spenser
interweaves religious allusions belonging to a distinct, homonymous
name. For the patron of temperance bears the name of a river held to
symbolize temperance. From the time of St Ambrose (c. 339–97)—who
drew on the first-century Philo Judaeus—the four rivers of paradise in
Genesis 2: 10–14 were allegorized as the four cardinal virtues. Pison
corresponded to Prudence, Tigris to Fortitude, Euphrates to Justice,
and Nile or Gihon (Gaeon, Geon, Gyon) to Temperance.[58] Guyon's
name generates the plot of book 2, for emblems of temperance are
worked into his adventure. Thus, he uses the set-square or "norm of
temperance", a "golden squire [square]" to "measure out a mean"
between Mortdant's fleshly indulgence and Amavia's self-accusing
death.[59] Another emblem of temperance was the bridle of restraint,[60]
realized in the name of Guyon's horse, "Brigador", recalling Ariosto's
and Boiardo's *Brigliadoro*. But the most fully developed emblem of
temperance is the mingling of wine and water. The temperate river
Guyon, Gihon, or Geon (Genesis 2: 13) runs from the Fountain of Life
to the Bower of Bliss, to enact the mixing of water of baptism with
Acrasia's wine. Acrasia—like Acratia in the *Italia Liberata da' Goti*
(1547–8) by Giangiorgio Trissino (1478–1550)—is from medieval Latin
acrasia ("bad mixture, intemperance"), anglicized to "acrasy" (*FQ* 22.12
motto).[61] Acrasia's wine is the wine of excess, of the concupiscent
human will.[62]

Mythological names

The literary taxonomist J. C. Scaliger (1484–1558) distinguishes
between human fictions (Jealousy, Rumour), given allegorical names,[63]
and cosmic *numina* like elements or seasons, "explained" through
mythology. To the second group presumably belong the natural features mythologized in the spousals of Thames and Medway (*FQ* 4.11).
As Gordon Braden shows, the epithets qualifying Spenser's Nereids
improve on those in a translation of Hesiod's *Theogony* by the humanist
Boninus Mombritius (1424–82), revitalizing meanings inherent in
their Hesiodic names.[64] Spenser finds meaning even in a name's sound:
"Maeander intricate" (4.11.21) has itself a convoluted texture, the *ntr*

of *intricate* being a near echo of the *ndr* of *Meander*.[65] Throughout the
canto names rise from meanings and give rise to others in happy
exchanges between nature and its fictions. The river catalogue
approaches pure poetry when it sets aside propositional communication and *"thesis* yields back all its ground to *taxis"*.[66]

The names are listed, Spenser tells us, "in order as they came"; and
the ordering is sometimes more interesting than the rivers themselves.
There are too many for the modern taste: the demand to encompass
so much information can be daunting. Yet such verse gazetteers were
once popular. English Renaissance poets were belatedly emulating
Continental georgic models: before long Drayton would begin his vast
Poly-Olbion (1612, written ?1598–1612).

However assiduous it may seem, Spenser's catalogue is by no means
exhaustive. It includes "only what needeth". Various considerations guide
the selection. One is degree of renown: some are "famous rivers"
(4.11.20), items on the short list of fame, not the long list of "endlesse
memorie". Another consideration is economic value, as with the fish of
the Darent (4.11.29) and the adamant of the Avon (4.11.31). The Dart is
"nigh chockt with sands of tinny mines," while all "water [...] the [...]
soile" (4.11.30). A third consideration tends now to be overlooked. We
think of rivers as symbols of mutability, but forget how much they once
counted for stability and order. In Tudor times waterways were preferred
routes for travel, trade, and communication: they brought civilization.
Hence Spenser's choice of settlements on the rivers, notably the four
academic cities.[67] He reviews the national resources built up through
peaceful communication and Cambina's historical alliances.[68]

During the Renaissance great interest was taken in mythological
names. Mythographers such as Lilio Gregorio Giraldi (1479–1552)
compiled vast catalogues of pagan gods—notably, hundreds of the cult
names of Venus. Names and cognomens seemed to offer a key to
mythology. Even on a popular level, the mythographer Natale Conti
(c. 1520–82) listed names of Diana. One of these is Luna, another Lucifera—a connection underlying the solar pretensions of Spenser's Lucifera.[69] Phoebe, another name of Diana, appears in Spenser's Bel-phoebe,
the Diana-like huntress of *The Faerie Queene* 2.3.

The divine names of classical mythology are appropriately reserved
for principal characters in the poem. Queen Elizabeth's various personas, for example, bear the names used in her mythological cults.[70] As
Spenser tells us in the Letter to Ralegh,

In that Faery Queene I meane glory in my generall intention, but in my particular I conceive the most excellent and glorious person of our soveraine the Queene, [...]. And yet in some places els, I doe otherwise shadow her. For considering she beareth two persons, the one of a most royall Queene or Empresse, the other of a most vertuous and beautifull Lady, this latter part in some places I doe expresse in Belphœbe, fashioning the name according to your owne excellent conceipt of Cynthia (Phœbe and Cynthia being both names of Diana).

Similarly, "Britomart" expresses Elizabeth's regal persona as well as her mythological persona, Minerva or *Venus Armata*.

Spenser's Britomart also calls up Ariosto's and Boiardo's Bradamante and Brandimarte.[71] But "Britomart" primarily suggests "Brito-Mart", the British Mars or martial Briton. And besides these associations "Britomart" can be construed as a shortened form of "Britomartis" (whom King Minos attempted to ravish), a name of Diana in the pseudo-Vergilian *Ciris*.[72] British antiquarians claimed that Diana was anciently worshipped in England under this name of Britomartis: a chaste anti-type to Scylla and Myrrha.[73] Through Britomartis, Britomart's story relates to a group of mythological narratives of chastity under attack, that include the adventures of Belphoebe and of Florimell.[74] "Britomartis" became *Brictona Martis...filia* in Boccaccio; hence in *The Faerie Queene* the "martiall Mayd", "mayd Martiall", "Briton Maid", and "bold Britonesse" (Spenser's coinage).[75] The ramifying allusions in "Britomart" find reflection in John Selden's *Illustrations* to Drayton's *Poly-Olbion* Song 1, where he speculates that "Βρύτον [Bryton] may be had from ordinary primitive, or else from Βρίθυ [Brithu], 'sweet' (as Solinus teaches, making *Britomart* signify as much as sweet Virgin) in the Cretique tongue". Selden was too serious a scholar to take such *figurae etymologicae* as historical evidence: he adds "but this is to play with syllables, and abuse precious time".[76] The name of Britomart's nurse, Glauce, is not only the name of the mother of Diana (according to Cicero) but also leads back to Minerva, since Pallas Athene was *Glaucopis* ("owl-eyed").[77] No English poet before Spenser practised such interweaving of mythological names.

Conflicting genealogies

Most of Spenser's mythological names occur in genealogical passages, which tend to be read too cursorily—for the genealogies of *The Faerie*

Queene, like those of Hesiod or Boccaccio, provide the basis of authority. The more ancient the ancestor, the stronger the claim. This is made clear enough in Lucifera's family tree:

> Of grisly Pluto she the daughter was,
> And sad Proserpina the Queene of hell;
> Yet did she thinke her pearelesse worth to pas
> That parentage, with pride so did she swell,
> And thundering Jove, that high in heaven doth dwell,
> And wield the world, she claymed for her syre,
> Or if that any else did Jove excell:
> For to the highest she did still aspyre,
> Or if ought higher were then that, did it desire.   (*FQ* 1.4.11)

Lucifera claims, here, that Jupiter is her father. But this claim is immediately undermined by an alternative possibility: "Or if that any else did Jove excel". She vaguely desires to be descended from whoever has the highest authority.

Nohrnberg, exploring the deep structure of Spenser's mythology, draws on *The Faerie Queene* and other poems by Spenser, together with works by Plato, Claudian, Boccaccio, Cartari, Calvin, Thomas Cooper, and others, to assemble a single pantheon of cosmic powers. It is very doubtful, however, that such a single, coherent system of mythology ever existed. Mythological names belong to myths. And every myth exists as a variety of narratives, each embodied in a text that is more or less discrepant from the others.[78]

The mythic genealogies in *The Faerie Queene* are no exception. They present distinct, often incompatible, variants, some of them in Spenser's view false, others true. It is the reader's task to distinguish between them, not regard every character as a truth-teller. For example, Duessa, "faire falsehood", has to be treated as an unreliable witness. She should never be trusted, least of all when she tells her own family history. Spenser includes at least two versions of each cosmogonic myth: one told (with variants) by Archimago, Duessa, Mutabilitie, and their like; the other by Nature and the narrator. These two groups are mutually contradictory.

In the very first canto, Archimago (yet unnamed) boldly utters words so evil they must not be repeated ("let none them read"): a spell to raise dark spirits. He speaks, that is, the name "Great Gorgon [...] | At which Cocytus quakes, and Styx is put to flight" (*FQ* 1.1.37). It is fatally easy to take these last words as authorial. But they are not: they express Archimago's own expectation of the power of the forbidden name, and the consequences of uttering it. So they imply a false myth. After all, Styx, the "granddame of the Gods" (FQ 4.11.4) would hardly be "put to flight" by the name of her own descendant Demogorgon. Similarly, when Duessa addresses Night—

> O thou most auncient Grandmother of all,
> More old then Jove, whom thou at first didst breede,
> Or that great house of Gods cælestiall,
> Which wast begot in Demogorgons hall [...]   (FQ 1.5.22)

—it would be thoughtless to accept her attribution of seniority to Night, or her account of Night as coexisting with Demogorgon.[79] For if Night was "begot in Demogorgons hall" then Demogorgon must belong to an older generation than hers. Instead of being coeval with Night, he is much older, coeval with Night's parent Eternity. Again, Duessa claims Night is senior (and superior) to Jupiter, whom she (Night) "at first didst breede". But this claim is later undercut when the repentant Aesculapius fears "The wrath of thundering Jove, that rules both night and day" (1.5.42). Aesculapius' rhetorical question "Can Night defray [bear the charge of] | The wrath of Jove?" implies a negative answer. Duessa has overestimated Night's authority: Jupiter is senior to Night and has authority over her.

Similar issues underlie Mutabilitie's genealogy. She says that Titan (Saturn) is her "great Grandsire" and that on her mother's side she is a "daughter" ("descendant") of Earth, "grandmother of all the gods".[80] On this lineage depends her case against Nature. Moreover, Mutabilitie claims that "Earth (great mother of us all)" is "thrall" ("subject") to her. But these claims are patently false: Nature, not Earth, is "grandmother of all creatures" (this we have on the authority of the poet himself)[81] and "far greater [...] than any of the gods or Powers on high" (7.7.5). Nature is senior to all the gods and powers she bred, including Earth and Saturn and their offspring—and Mutabilitie. Nature makes this explicit when she calls Mutabilitie "daughter" at 7.7.59. So Nohrnberg's idea that "Nature and Mutabilitie are differentiations out of a single theogonic principle" cannot be right—far less that "Nature and Mutabilitie are related to each other dialectically".[82] Nature and her daughter belong to different generations—the one on a more fundamental level of reality than the other.

Some of the most interesting discrepancies concern Demogorgon, in Spenser a chthonic power accompanying Eternity and Chaos.[83] Nohrnberg, following Boccaccio and the mythographers, identifies Demogorgon either with Eternity or with Chaos—as if the identification might go either way.[84] But Spenser surely means us to think Agape ("Christian love") more trustworthy than any mythographer. And when Agape goes to visit the Fates "downe in the bottome of the deepe Abysse" she finds them, she says, sitting

> Where Demogorgon in dull darkenesse pent,
> Farre from the view of Gods and heavens blis,
> The hideous Chaos keepes [...]   (FQ 4.2.47)

Certainly Demogorgon is shrouded here in ambiguity as well as darkness. Does Demogorgon, pent, keep ("entertain") Chaos? Or does Demogorgon keep Chaos pent in darkness? Or is it Chaos who keeps Demogorgon? Spenser evokes in masterly fashion the dubious state of Demogorgon. Nevertheless, Agape in her descent into hell finds that not even Jupiter can affect the Fates' spinning of mortal threads, the cosmogonic process. "Not all the gods can change, nor Jove him selfe can free" (4.2.51).

Nohrnberg improves on his earlier position in a recent essay, "Supplementing Spenser's Supplement",[85] where he acknowledges that "Nature as a deity is brought to resemble or participate in [God] alone", and affirms that the *Cantos of Mutabilitie* forecast the disappearance of Nature and "the incipience of Eternity": "However constant, Nature will ultimately mutate into Eternity".[86] Anything else is only an appearance, "as if Nature were disappearing into the demogorgonical yet maternal cave". But "mutate" is not an Elizabethan word: Nohrnberg is still in thrall to Mutabilitie, and credits her claims. The beauty of the *Cantos of Mutabilitie* is indeed sublime; but that does not make Mutabilitie win her case against Nature.

Demogorgon

The name Demogorgon seems to have originated, appropriately, from the chaos of scribal transmission. In Statius and Lucan he is a powerful god invoked to threaten others. Statius' Tiresias conjures spirits by the name they dread, the name of "the high lord of the triple world, which it is forbidden to know" (*triplicis mundi summum, quem scire nefastum*).[87] The name itself—from γοργός, "terrible", or γοργώ, Gorgon—is first given by a commentator, Lactantius Placidus (fifth or sixth century AD), who may have confused a general magical formula with the name of a specific deity. Demogorgon is also mentioned by a scholiast on Lucan, *Pharsalia* 6.742, as the name of one able to look on Gorgon. Probably, then, "Demogorgon" had no original connection with δημιουργός, *demiourgos* ("magistrate, authority, or creative principle").

In time poets and mythographers such as Boccaccio and Conrad de Mure made Demogorgon a primordial deity, father of the other gods.[88] "Demogorgon" was explained as *daemonibus terror* ("terror to demons") or *terribilis daemon* ("terrible demon") or derived from δαίμων (*daimon*) + γεωργός (*georgos*, "demon of the earth"). From Boccaccio the name came to Boiardo, whose Orlando makes Morgana swear by Demogorgon the *segnore* of all fairies, who at dawn drives them from the upper earth.[89] Giraldi, who disapproved of the name as a mere textual corruption, was by now in a minority.

By introducing the name Demogorgon into English, Spenser raised a spirit that would not soon be exorcised. Subsequently, the unutterable name was much uttered and among lesser poets lost some of its mystery. Abraham Fraunce might claim priority over Spenser on the strength of *The third part of the countesse of Pembrokes Ivychurch. Entitled, Amintas dale* (1592).[90] But his Demogorgon is still in the late medieval tradition of Boccacio, Boiardo, and the dictionaries. In Fraunce the elements cannot function until "sov'raigne God Demogorgon | Ends these broyles, brings peace" (p. 2).[91]

When Drayton took up the matter, he imagined only a susceptible earth god, who could be disturbed by a deity so junior as Apollo:

> Great Demogorgon feeles thy might,
> His Mynes about him heating:
> Who through his bosome dart'st thy light,
> Within the Center sweating.
> (*The Muses Elizium* (1630), 9.45–8)

Drayton's chthonic power is not indistinct enough to be credibly metaphysical: Spenser achieves more by defining his Demogorgon less. Later, Milton also makes his description too definite, locating Demogorgon next the thrones of Chaos and Night: "by them stood [. . .] the dreaded name | Of Demogorgon".[92] It must be unwise to have

Demogorgon do anything so visually explicit as *stand*. But Milton, seldom one to countenance alternative cosmogonic possibilities, was sure of the fated destiny.

Not until Percy Bysshe Shelley (1792–1822) was Demogorgon again treated by a poet with a political imagination open enough to reassert the god's authentic mystery. *Prometheus Unbound* (1820) recovers the terror of undetermined form—"Awful shape, what art thou?" Shelley drew heavily on Spenser for his conception of Demogorgon's power, as well as for the rhetoric needed to adumbrate abstraction. Shelley, however, now makes for the name a new etymology. He derives "Demogorgon" from *demos*, "the people": the god is now a popular, political movement—a historical process—fated to dislodge the divinely ordained establishment represented by Jupiter. When Demogorgon descends from the Car of the Hour and moves on Jupiter's throne, the tyrant having done his worst gives way. They sink down, "the conqueror and the conquered", to the "bottomless void" of hell.[93]

Spenser's successors have perpetually echoed and transformed his naming inventions. But they owe him much more than that. Their debt is nothing less than the whole idea that names can serve complex associative purposes. *The Faerie Queene* can be a profoundly elusive fiction; so that its names (which are not always equally elusive) offer invaluable assistance to the reader. Before Spenser, characters were named casually, often without much deliberation. But with him the names of English literature came to be used with new sophistication: even his charactonyms are more than mere labels. Without Spenser's achievement it would be hard to imagine the great names of Dickens and Joyce and Nabokov, far less the ironies whereby the greatness is questioned.

Notes

1. On Spenser's names, see the highly informative entry by Marks and Gross in *SEnc* 494a–496b with bibliography; Upton 1758; *Variorum Spenser*; Nohrnberg 1976; Spenser 2001.
2. See Marks and Gross 1990, *SE* 494a–496b, with different examples.
3. See Spenser 1758: 2.665; Spenser 2001: 712; Camden 1984: 83 interpreting "Elizabeth" as "Quiet rest of the Lord".
4. Camden 1984: 49; Bardsley 1996: 200.
5. Parker 1968: 24.

6. E.g. his copy of *The Faerie Queene*, Macdonald 1971: 201 item 922; see Fowler and Leslie 1981: 821.

7. *FQ* 1.8.31; see *SEnc* 495c–496a.

8. Mulcaster 1970: 168–9; see *SEnc* 495c.

9. *FQ* 1.4.21–3; cf. Aristotle, *Nicomachean Ethics* 3.10.10, the gourmand who wished his throat were longer than a crane's.

10. See Borris 2000: 102.

11. E.g. Alanus, *De Planctu Naturae*, referred to at *FQ* 7.7.9; Bernardus, *Cosmographia*, chs. 3 and 12 (Pantomorphos, Urania, Physis), Bernardus 1973: 96, 118.

12. More 1961: 8.

13. See Considine 2008: 279 *et passim*; Index s.v. Greek language.

14. As *The Strife of Love in a Dreame.*

15. See Colonna 1999: viii. Sidney's *Arcadia* has many names of Greek derivation, e.g. Strephon (στρέφω, "evade, turn aside"), Klaius (κλαίω, "lament"), Basilius (βασιλεύς, "king"), and Gynecia (γυνή, "woman"). Dallington had meant to dedicate his translation to Sidney.

16. But see Spenser 2001: 193. In the *Dictionarium Historicum Poeticum* appended to Thomas Cooper's *Thesaurus* (1565), Phaon is merely "the name of a fayre yonge man".

17. Cf. Russell 2010: 291 citing Bacon, "every cause is as a parent to its effect".

18. Upton 1758: 2.440.

19. Spenser 2001: 177 on *FQ* 2.2.35, citing Nelson 1963.

20. As in Martial 1.109.1.

21. *Nicomachean Ethics* 1106 b 17: ὑπερβολή και ἔλλειψις και τό μέσον.

22. See Hamilton in Spenser 2001: 177; Nelson 1963: 181. Cooper's entry ("one of the names of Dido") shows the familiarity of Dido's Tyrian name.

23. *FQ* 2.2 Argument.

24. *FQ* 1.6.2, 8; 2.2.18; see Bull 1997: 471–2. The lifting of the Siege of Malta was one of the most important events of the sixteenth century.

25. Doubtless on the authority of *Cratylus* 401C, where οὐσία (reality, essence) is linked with Doric ἐσσία.

26. See, however, Craig 1972: 321.

27. Deguileville 1899–1904; Cartigny 1951; Baspoole 2008.

28. See Fowler 1973: 53–82. Smith 1985: 65 finds the same triad in St Bonaventura.

29. See Fleming 1918, cit. *Variorum Spenser* 1.201. The Christian "St George" was pronounced "San George", like the deceptively similar "Sansfoy" the "faithless Sarazin" (1.2.12), "Sansloy" the "proud Paynim" (1.3.35), and "Sansjoy" who carries a "heathenish shield" (1.4.38). On the triads, see Wind 1968: Index, s.v. *Triad*; Fowler 1973.

30. See Sheingorn 1955. On romance connections generally, see Barton 1990: 144–5.

31. Cf. Thomas Nashe's *braccahadocheos*, from Latin *bracca*: Nashe 1966: 226; *OED* s.v. *braggadoccio*.

32. On multiple derivation of Spenser's names, see *SEnc* 494c–495a.

33. "A Secret Discipline", in Nelson 1961: 171 n. 6, rpt in Berger 1988: 218 n. 5. For Greek derivations of Calepine as "gracious speech" (M. Parker) or "difficulty" (Nohrnberg) see Spenser 2001: 622.

34. Nohrnberg 1976: 683 n. 52.

35. Spenser refers to Ennius in Dedicatory Sonnet 1, Spenser 2001: 727.

36. *OCD*; Cooper 1977; Cook 2006: 36.

37. *De Vita et Gestis Caroli Magni*. On Turpine as distinct from Terpine, see *SEnc*, 495a.

38. Jean Bonnefons (1554–1614) of Clermont, author of *Pancharis* (1592). Jonson told Drummond that Bonefonius' "*Vigilium Veneris* was excellent" and that "he imitated the description of a night from it"; see Jonson 1925–52: 1.134, 143.

39. Evans 1973: 148.

40. Epistle to Lady Frances Sidney (Walsingham's daughter), Watson 1895: 145. Spenser calls him "the great Mecenas" in Dedicatory Sonnet 12, Spenser 2001: 732.
41. Letter to Ralegh, Spenser 2001: 714.
42. See Fraser 1977; Donawerth 1984.
43. See ch. 4.
44. Craig 1972.
45. Craig 1972: 316, 319.
46. *Orlando Innamorato* 2.1.14; 2.24.58.
47. *Orlando Furioso* 45.2; *Historia Regum* 2.9; *FQ* 2.10.25. The resemblance to the name of Sir Hugh de Bras, knight of the Round Table, may be coincidental.
48. *Orlando Innamorato* 2.1.10; *Orlando Furioso* 3.69.
49. See *Poly-Olbion* 24.219, Drayton 1931–41: 4.482.
50. Marks and Gross, however, rightly describe the polysemy of the Middle Ages as very different; see *SEnc* 495a.
51. See Woodcock and Robinson 1988: 66.
52. *FQ* 1.10.61. See Weatherby 1987.
53. See Hamilton on *FQ* 1.1.1–6, Spenser 2001: 31.
54. Drayton 1931–41: 4.85.
55. The allegory was based on meanings of the verb γεωργέω, "cultivate, improve".
56. *FQ* 3.12.47; 6.9.1; 1.4.42; 1.6.45. See Sessions 1980.
57. See Yonge 1884: 228. Such romance analogues, however, offer no connection with the virtue of temperance.
58. See further in Fowler 1960; 1960a; 1989: 39–41; Nohrnberg 1976: 304; Scafi 2006: Index s.v. Gihon.
59. Fowler 1960: 143.
60. See Ripa 1976: 509.
61. See *OED*, prose examples from 1617; Hamilton 2001: 282.
62. *FQ* 2.2; 2.12; see Fowler 1960a.
63. Scaliger 1964: 163.
64. Mombritius' translation, first printed in Ferrara in 1474, was included in Basel editions of Hesiod's works. See Braden 1975: 32–3; *Var. Spenser* 4.274–5; Herendeen 1986.
65. Thomas Thomas (1587) explains the river name Maeander as "a turning or winding: [...] a winding in and out of the threds... after the manner of a Labyrinth".
66. Nohrnberg 1976: 683. Cf. Fowler 1964: 182–91 on the catalogue's numerical ordering.
67. Oxford, Cambridge, London (Inns of Court), and Stamford. The Carmelite houses at Stamford formed a rival university in all but name. Camden records the founding of a university at Stamford in 1333: northern students seceded there until forbidden by royal proclamation. Before 1827 Oxford graduates took an oath not to deliver or attend lectures there. See *Var. Spenser* 4.459–60.
68. See further in Fowler 1989: 43.
69. See Fowler 1964: 73.
70. On these cults see Wilson 1966; Yates 1975.
71. Ariosto, *Orlando Furioso* 1.60 *et passim*; 8.86 *et passim;* Boiardo, *Orlando Innamorato* 2.6.23; 1.9.49–64.
72. *Ciris* 254ff. For narrative connections with Florimell, see *Variorum Spenser* 3.332–3; Nohrnberg 1976: 446. See also Hamilton in Spenser 2001, on *FQ* 3.1.8.
73. See Fowler 1964: 162 n.
74. See further in Nohrnberg 1976: 446–7.
75. *FQ* 3.2.9; 3.3.53; 3.2.4; 3.12.2. See French 1972: 192 and ch. 8 *passim* on the patriotic antiquarian theories of John Dee, Henry Lyte, and others.

76. Drayton 1931–41: 4.25. Cf. SEnc 495c. On etymological interpretation of mythology see Morales 2007: 60.

77. Fowler 1964: 126 n., citing Giraldi 1548.

78. Cf. the approach of Morales 2007.

79. Nohrnberg 1976: 739.

80. *FQ* 7.7.16 ; 7.6.26.

81. *FQ* 7. 7. 13.

82. Nohrnberg 1976: 741.

83. *FQ* 2 4.41; 4.2.47. See Russell 2010: 288.

84. Nohrnberg 1976: 739.

85. Nohrnberg 2009.

86. Nohrnberg 2009: 122,123.

87. Statius, *Thebaid* 4. 516.

88. Boccaccio, *Genealogia Deorum Gentilium* (?1350–75); Conrad de Mure, *Repertorium* (1273); see *OED* s.v. *Demogorgon*; Starnes and Talbert 1955: 357, 359; Seznec 1953: 312 n. 96. The mythographers made Demogorgon father of the Fates (who were thus almost coeval with the beginning of things, and lived in the cave of Chaos).

89. *Orlando Innamorato* 2.13.26–9.

90. The passage in Fraunce appeared earlier than the Demogorgon of *FQ* 4.2.47 but not earlier than the "great Gorgon" of *FQ* 1.1.37 and 1.5.22. In any case, Fraunce had access as early as 1588 to some of *FQ* in manuscript; see Ethel Seaton in Fraunce 1950: xl.

91. Cf. Cooper, *Thesaurus*: "Demogorgus, An inchaunter, which was supposed to bee of such excellencie, that he had authoritie over all spirites that made men afearde".

92. *Paradise Lost* 2.963–5.

93. *Prometheus Unbound* 3.1.

4

Hidden Names

Before title pages came in, writers affirming authorship had to name themselves within the text, openly or in disguise. The usual means of disguise was to disorder their names by anagram; distribute the letters among salient positions by acrostic; separate the syllables; or represent them by rebus. According to Cicero, Ennius used the initial acrostic QUINTUS ENNIUS FECIT.[1] Cynewulf (c. 900 AD), perhaps the earliest poet in English, gives his name in anagram, putting the runes in reverse order. Laȝamon, however, begins *Brut* (c. 1200–20) with his name and address and next of kin: "An preost wes onleoden: Laȝamon wes ihoten [called] | He wes Leouenaðes sone: Liðe him beo Drihten. | He wonede at Ernleȝe." Like many such affirmations of authorship, this is formally a petition.[2] But casting it as a third-person account of the poem's genesis gives it a fictive quality. By poetic convention the dreamer of a medieval dream vision might share the poet's own name.[3] In *The Owl and the Nightingale* (thirteeenth century), similarly, the poet Nicholas is named inside the fiction and his responsible maturity certified by both the birds. The wren later adds Nicholas' address, Portesham in Dorset, calling it a shame that a man of his calibre should be left to live in the obscurity of a remote country parish.

Naming himself in *Piers Plowman* (B-text, c. 1377–79), William Langland supplies an autobiographical statement which is simultaneously a rebus or syllabic anagram of his signature: "I have lyved in londe [...] my name is longe wille" (i.e. Will Lang Land).[4] Almost as plain is the embedded signature of Sir Richard Roos (c. 1410–82): "And up I roos, three houres after twelve."[5]

Signatures and rebuses

Chaucer names himself several times.[6] To the eagle in *The House of
Fame* he is "Geffrey", and to the disgruntled Man of Law he is "That
Chaucer", who has used up all the good stories.[7] John Gower's *Confessio Amantis* (wr. 1390s) has a similar self-deprecation in his interview
with the goddess-patroness:

> as it were halvinge a game
> Sche axeth me what is mi name.
> "Ma dame", I seide, "John Gower".
> "Now John", quod sche, "in my pouer [power]
> Thou most as of thi love stonde".

Although "half in jest", Venus implies Gower has been "halving", that
is, giving only half the service he owes.[8]

But names could also be conveyed by picturing the syllables of
rebuses (*non verba sed rebus*). In *The Book of the Duchess* Chaucer refers
to several names in this way: "ryche hil" suggests Richmond; "long
castel", Lancaster or Longcastel; "walles white", Blanche; and "seynt
Johan", John of Gaunt.[9] Heraldry made the rebus an extremely familiar genre. In the seventeenth century the arms of the poet Charles
Cotton (1630–87) included three cotton hanks, and to this day the
needle-and-thread ceremony at The Queen's College, Oxford, com-
memorates Robert de Eglesfield (*aigle* and *fils*). Early title pages often
included printers' devices in the form of such punning rebuses. Thus
Sebastian Gryphius' device was a frisky griffin, Richard Grafton's a
graft and a tun.[10] In the same vein the Scottish Renaissance poet Gavin
Douglas (1474?–1522) signs his translation of Virgil with a rebus:

> To knaw the naym of the translatour
> The *Gaw* onbrokyn mydlyt with the *Wyne*
> The *Dow* jonyt with the *Glas* richt in a lyne:
> Quha knawis nocht the Translatouris name,
> Seyk na forthar, for lo with lytill pane
> Spy weill this verse; men clepis him swa at haym.[11]

The unbroken GAW, or gall, mixed with WYNE makes GAWIN; the DOW
or dove joined with GLAS makes DOUGLAS—"As thai war simple as a
dow but [without] gall". (Gall was associated with wine in several biblical texts.)[12] Douglas' rebus seems plain enough; but it was lost on a

reviewer in *The Times Literary Supplement* who attributed Douglas' translation to David Lindsay.[13]

Authorship might also be affirmed through an acrostic. The ancient rage for ordering letters in acrostics (initial letters of lines or other units), telestichs (final letters) or mesostichs (caesural letters) was at first a religious convention, ranging from the simple *IXΘΥΣ* (*Iesus CHristos THeos Uios Soter*, "Jesus Christ: God, Son, Saviour") and the divine monogram IHS[14] to the intricate mazes and carpet pages of Publilius Optatianus Porfyrius (third–fourth century AD), the *Aenigmata* of St Boniface (c. 680–c. 784), and Hrabanus Maurus (c. 780–856). In the seventeenth century various meditations on the name of Jesus continued the tradition, notably George Herbert's "Jesu":[15]

> JESU is in my heart, his sacred name
> Is deeply carved there: but th'other week
> A great affliction broke the little frame,
> E'vn all to pieces: which I went to seek:
> And first I found the corner, where was *J*,
> After, where *ES*, and next where *U* was graved.
> When I had got these parcels, instantly
> I sat me down to spell them, and perceived
> That to my broken heart he was *I ease you*,
>
> > And to my whole is *JESU*.

Gillian Wright traces these pictorially based meditations in imitations by William Browne and Edward Benlowes.[16]

In the later Middle Ages and Renaissance, acrostics were so common that educated readers seem to have traced them almost at sight. Writers such as François Villon (1431–after 1463), Francesco Colonna (1433/4–1527), and Palingenius (Pier Angelo Manzoli)(c. 1500–c. 1543) still signed their works acrostically.[17] A prominent English example is John Gower, who gives his acrostic signature in a prologue to book 1 of *Vox Clamantis*.[18] Perhaps they meant by this to perpetuate their fame: authorities on the art of memory sometimes recommended using acrostics.[19] Printers too used the device for self-advertisement, as with the initial acrostic ROBERT COPELAND.[20] A more elaborate instance is *The Testament of Love* by Thomas Usk (c. 1354–88). Here the initial letters of the chapters form the acrostic MARGARETE OF VIRTW HAVE MERCI ON THIN VSK.[21] Even allowing for different reading habits this must have been a fairly demanding acrostic. But it is a trifle by comparison with Boccaccio's profoundly concealed 1,501-letter acrostic in

the *Amorosa Visione* with its doubly secret inner acrostic MARIA.[22] Both
these examples suggest something like the secrecy of prayer.

Complimentary acrostics

More often, acrostics were used to compliment a patron, mistress, or
friend. The social verse of Sir Richard Roos is full of acrostic compli-
ments to Elizabeth Beaumont (née Phelip) and others: acrostics simple,
double, or triple; downward or upward; initial, caesural, or final; and
anagrammatic (complete or incomplete). The dazzling variety must
have presented enough difficulty to limit uptake to an in-group.[23]
Roos' complex acrostics would be hard to parallel, although the later
Denbighshire poet Robert Parry (1564–after 12 February 1613)
attempted something similar. Parry's Posie 4 contains acrostics on JOHN
SALESBURY (1566–1612) his patron (initial letters of the seventh lines of
each stanza); on DOROTHI HALSALL, Salesbury's sister-in-law (initial letters of each stanza); on FRANSIS WILOWBI (initial letters of the second
lines of each stanza); and on ELIZABETH WOLFRESTONE ROBERT PARRYE
(initial letters of lines 3–6 in the first eight stanzas).[24] More simply,
Parry's Sonetti 16, 17, and 18 have initial acrostics in reverse order:
reading up, they spell HELENA OWEN, the name of his beautiful patroness.
   Acrostics of the late sixteenth and early seventeenth centuries are
made more obvious. Each of Sir John Davies' twenty-six *Hymns of
Astraea* has the same initial acrostic, ELIZABETHA REGINA,[25] and this is
signalled in the first edition (1599) by typographic separation of the
initial capitals. Similarly with Andrew Willett's figure poems in *Sacro-
rum Emblematum Centuria Una* (Cambridge 1592), such as the piously
patriotic double acrostic ELISABETHAM REGINAM DIU NOBIS SERVET IESUS
INCOLVMEM: AMEN ("May Jesus keep Queen Elizabeth safe, long to
reign over us") and the Puritan compliment to Essex: COMITI NOBILI
ESSEXIO LITERATO ("To the noble and learned Earl of Essex").[26]
   Printed acrostics were easier to read, but ran the risk of being too
obvious and seeming trivial. As the pace of life quickened, too, the
pleasure of tracing loved names through acrostic mazes may have
diminished. Samuel Butler (1612–80) deprecates the "Small Poet" who
"uses to lay the Outsides of his Verses even (like a Bricklayer) by a Line
of Rhime and Acrostic, and fill the Middle with Rubbish".[27] Before
long Joseph Addison will categorize acrostics as "false wit", and Rich-

ard Cambridge ridicule them at length.[28] The Enlightenment was
turning against the hidden or non-semantic element of literature.

Anagrams

This was especially true of anagrams. Close study of classical texts in
the Renaissance had led to recovery of the embedded anagrams in
Virgil, Ovid, and others.[29] The ancient practice was understood and
emulated by Renaissance poets, and recommended by theorists such as
Joachim du Bellay (c. 1522–60). In consequence, a heightened awareness developed of texts as precise letter sequences. Nevertheless, anagram always belonged in part to the unspoken element of the poet's
craft: it was never assimilated to Renaissance rhetoric. Rhetoricians
and theorists in particular passed over embedded anagrams, or sub-
sumed them under the head of figures such as *traductio, exergasia,* and
expolitio.[30] The convention was to forbid explicit mention of them.
A partial exception to the general obedience to this prohibition is the
Delle Rime Volgari Trattato of Antonio da Tempo (d. 1336) with the com-
pendium of it by Francesco Baratella. Remarkably, Baratella explains
the early Renaissance type of syllabic anagram acrostic. In this, syllables
rather than letters are rearranged: DO.MI.NE. MAR.GA.RI.TE. AN.TO.NI.US.
DA. TEM.PO ("Antonio da Tempo to Lady Margarita").[31]

The anagram was especially popular in France, where it attracted
royal patronage. Du Bellay's *La Défense et Illustration de la Langue
Françoise* (1549) became a seminal text for the anagrammateur. Unlike
da Tempo, du Bellay has no truck with syllabic anagrams. He defines
the anagram as "transposition of letters in a proper name, which bears
some device apt to the person"—as in FRANÇOYS DE VALOYS: DE FAÇON
SUYS ROYAL ("Royal in his style").[32] Du Bellay cites ancient precedents:
the anagrams of Lycophron (early third century BC) for Ptolemy II
Philadelphus (PTOLEMAIUS: APO MELITOS, "of honey") and his queen
Arsinoë (ARSINOE: HERAS-ION, "Violet of Hera") as well as the Eryth-
rean Sibyl's prophecy IESUS CHRISTUS: SERVATOR, CRUX, supposed to have
been used by Cicero to show the Sibyls worked by diligence, not
divine inspiration.[33] In Britain the anagram had an almost equal vogue.
Among Elizabethan and Stuart writers there are many references to
the device.[34] Anagrams would have been easier to find in an age when
spelling of proper names was subject to wide variation. Later, when the

spelling of names had become less variable, Addison tells in *Spectator* 60, a lover spent months on an anagram of his mistress' name, only to find he had the spelling wrong (*Bohun*, not *Boon*).

Most of what George Puttenham has to say about anagram is in an unpaginated insertion of four leaves after quire N of *The Arte of English Poesie* (1589).[35] Puttenham paraphrases du Bellay, taking over (inaccurately) his Lycophron and Valois anecdotes. He thus appeals to French validation of the panegyric anagram. Only then does he add Tudor examples such as ELISSABET ANGLORUM REGINA: MULTA REGNABIS ENSE GLORIA ("By thy sword shalt thou reign in great renown").[36] Puttenham (like du Bellay) has nothing to say about the function of anagram, beyond suggesting that transposition of letters may reveal a name's destiny ("fatality"). He concedes anagrams are "courtly trifles" but at once takes this back: they are no more vanity than "the most serious studies of man".[37]

The Elizabethan writer with most to say about anagram is the historian William Camden (1551–1623). Camden benefits from his predecessors: he repeats Lycophron's anagrams (adding new errors),[38] and adds biblical examples of "alphabetary revolution".[39] (This phrase may hint at gematria, the cabbalistic method of interpreting Hebrew scripture by interchanging "equivalent" words whose letters add to the same numerical total.) He attempts to put the anagram fashion into perspective, blaming its excesses on French influence: "the French exceedingly admire and celebrate this facultie, for the deepe and farre fetched antiquitie, the piked fines [*fins piquées*, pointed conclusions] and the mysticall significations thereby". This last property prompts an affirmation of his own: "names are divine notes [signs], and divine notes do notifie future events; so that events consequently must lurke in names, which only can be pried into by this mystery".[40] Camden by no means aligns himself with the "sour sort" who condemn the anagram as "nothing but a troublous toy", but rather with those "more mild" who grant it to be a "daintie devise", and allow that "as good names may be ominous [auspicious] so also good Anagrames". The difficulty of anagrams seems to him a point in their favour: *difficilia quae pulchra* ("difficult things are beautiful"). Above all, the point of a "good anagram" lies in aptness of meaning.

In the same essay Camden sets out—perhaps for the first time in English—the rules of anagram. He lists all the standard licences: doubling of letters; omission of a letter; and substitution of *E* and *AE*,

V and *W, S* and *Z, C* and *K*. Retention or omission of *H* is sanctioned on the authority of Lycophron—for whom [h] was indicated only by a breathing, not a letter.[41] Drummond of Hawthornden, writing about 1615, added a few other licences.[42] One or two repeated letters may be omitted (as with two of the *R*s in the famous ROSE DE PINDARE anagram for PIERRE DE RONSARD). Then, a letter may be repeated; diphthongs may be separated; a letter may be changed for another similar letter, as *D* and *T*; and a composite letter may be resolved, as *Z* into *S* or *DS*. Drummond thinks an embedded anagram in a sonnet or epigram "fitly cometh in mostly in the Conclusion": it should not be signalled typographically but appear "of it self naturally".

Camden gives over sixty Latin and Greek panegyric anagrams, sacred, royal, and noble.[43] Several praise Queen Elizabeth, such as ELIZABETHA REGINA: ANGLIAE HERA, BEASTI ("Mistress of England, you have blessed it") and ELIZABETHA REGINA ANGLORUM: GLORIA REGNI SALVA MANEBIT ("the glory of her rule will remain intact").[44] Others are of Mary Queen of Scots, such as MARIA STEUARTA: VERITAS ARMATA.[45] Aristocratic names include the Earl of Southampton (HENRICUS WRIOTHESLEIUS: HEROICUS, LAETUS, VI VIRENS, "noble, happy, growing in power").[46] The surname of the Earl of Essex yields DEVEREUX: VERE DUX , that of Sir Fulke Greville GREVILIUS: VERGILIUS.[47]

The anagram for Lord Mountjoy, the Earl of Devon, is embedded in a distich—

> Carolus Blountus
> BONUS UT SOL CLARUS
> Tu BONUS UT SOL CLARUS, Nil clarius illo
> Caelo, te melior Carole nemo solo.[48]
>
> ("You are good, shining like the sun. Nothing is brighter than that sky, and no one, O Charles, is better than you alone.")

—and so are those on Sir Robert Sidney:

> ROBERT VISCOUNT LISLE: LO, I BORN, VERTUES SELECT
> He that was borne vertues select, hath got
> A rare choice gemme; divinest lovers lot.

As Camden alerts his reader, the last line here is an anagram of DOR-OTHY VICOUNTESSE LISLE.[49] Camden was apparently the first to print the famous anagram of James I, later used, as we shall see, by Jonson: CHARLES JAMES STEUART: CLAIMES ARTHURS SEATE.[50]

The vogue for political anagrams was so widespread that whole books of them were published, some "nude" and some embedded in epigrams. Such are William Cheeke's *Anagrammata... Regia* (1613) and Mary Fage's *Fames Roule* (1637). The level of achievement cannot be called impressive: a fair example is Cheeke's IACOBVS PRIMVS: MUSA, CHARI, PHOIBVS. Besides such books there were many broadsheets, often anonymous, like *Upon the King's most excellent majesty*: ARTS, CHASTE, RULE (1660) and the embedded *Anagram of his Excellency the Lord General Monck* in the same year:

> You Divine Cabalists who raise your Fame
> By your expounding ev'ry Word and Name;
> See here's a Name, makes all the world to Ring!
> GEORGE MONCK interpreted is come ore king.
>   COME ORE KING Charles, receive your triple Crown...

The number of such publications suggests that anagram was a habitual mode of reading and writing.

Not all were complimentary: Gaspar Scioppius found that his adversary SCALIGER was an anagram of SACRILEGE. Calvin anagrammatized RABELAESIUS as RABIE LAESUS ("Afflicted with madness"); Immanuele Tesauro made CALVINUS into ANI ULCUS ("Haemorrhoid"); and a 1653 broadsheet made JOHN LILBURNE exclaim O: I BURN IN HELL. The satiric examples anticipate more recent anagrams, such as WILLIAM EWART GLADSTONE: WILD AGITATOR! MEANS WELL; DISRAELI: I LEAD, SIR; TONY BLAIR MP: I'M TORY, PLAN B; MARGARET THATCHER: THAT GREAT CHARMER or MEG, THE ARCH TARTAR; and SHIRLEY WILLIAMS: I WHIRL AIMLESSLY.[51] The cryptogrammic book title RANCID PANSIES, concealing PRINCESS DIANA, may seem original.[52] But the idea of anagram titles was anticipated in the seventeenth century: Joshua Sylvester's *Anagrammata Regia* before his 1641 Du Bartas are set in large type, although subsequently embedded:

> My Liege JAMES STUART A just Master is.
> And A just Master could my Worke deserve,
> Such A just Master would I justly serve,...

Embedded anagrams

The practice of embedding names received renewed stimulus from the seminal example of Petrarch's *Canzoniere* (wr. before 1374). Petrarch

introduces Laura's name in *Canzoniere* 5 as a syllabic anagram embodying central themes of the sequence:

> Quando io movo i sospiri a chiamar voi
> E 'l nome che nel cor mi scrisse Amore,
> LAUdando s' incomincia udir di fore
> Il suon de' primi dolci accenti suoi.
> Vostro stato REAl, ch' encontro poi,
> Raddoppia a l' alta impresa il mio valore:
> Ma, TAci, grida il fin, ché farle onore
> È d'altri ómeri soma che da' tuoi.
>
> (When I move my sighs to call you and the name that
> Love wrote in my heart, the sound of its first sweet accents
> is heard without in LAUds.
> Your REgal state, which I meet next, redoubles my strength
> for the high enterprise; but "TAlk no more!" cries the
> ending, "for to do her honour is a burden for other
> shoulders than yours.")[53]

The name device here alludes to Ovid's myth of Apollo and Daphne,
and to the Christian interpretation of it by Petrarch's friend Pierre
Bersuire. In this, "Laureta" is associated with the symbolic laurel wreath
of victory. To bring home the blasphemousness of associating Laura
and Christ, the "discrepancies between Petrarch's love for Laura and
his love of God" are amplified.[54] Petrarch explores "Laureta" (Laura's
name in Latin) syllable by syllable, dwelling on each in turn to expound
its meaning as if divine. The name written in his heart sounds out-
wardly in praise (LAUdando); her regal (REale) state redoubles his cour-
age for love's high enterprise; but the last syllable tells him to speak no
more (TAci).

The early commentaries on the *Canzoniere* all trace the embedded
anagram LAU-RE-TA. The earliest and most independent Petrarch commentator, the humanist Francesco Filelfo (1398–1481), laboriously spells
out each syllable ("interpretando la prima syllaba LAU...per laude").
Others—Alessandro Vellutello (1525), Bernardino Daniello (1549), and
Ludovico Castelvetro (1582), for example—take more for granted. All
explain that the anagram is repeated with variations in the sestet. Each
syllable of Laureta begins the word it is embedded in, and forms a dispersed anagram's correctly ordered sequence of letters (LAU-, RE-, TA-).

Petrarch's institutive sonnet did much to establish the practice of
embedding anagrams in sonnets. Du Bellay, for example, took it up in

his Petrarchan sequence *L'Olive* (1549), where Sonnet 4 recalls Petrarch's meditation on the name his love shared with the bay tree or laurel (*laurea*). Du Bellay's love, too, bears the *doulx nom* of a tree, this time "L'heureuse branche à Pallas consacrée, | Branche de paix", the olive.[55] "Olive" anagrams the name of du Bellay's mistress, Mlle Viole.[56]

In English, Petrarch's sonnet was anonymously imitated in the anthology *Phoenix Nest* (1593). And the Scottish poet Sir David Murray of Gorthy (1567–1629) embedded letter anagrams of his mistress' name in *Cælia* (1611), Sonnet 3. One of Murray's anagrams, with letters dispersed but in correct order, is

> For beauty now faire [Cælia she is cal'd,
> Whose sight sometimes, as *it* the gods *a*]ll thralled [...]
> (Murray, *Cælia*, 1611)

Another, in the first of these lines, is compressed within four words, with the letters scrambled (AEICAL): "For beauty now faire Cæli[A she is CAL']d, ..."[57] In such letter anagrams only initial and final letters or letter groups in words or word-parts are admissible.

Between Petrarch and Murray, four influential poets practised embedding of name anagrams: Sidney, Spenser, Shakespeare, and the Scottish court poet William Fowler (1560–1612).[58] Fowler, Secretary to Queen Anne and a friend of the King, was the uncle of Drummond of Hawthornden: he studied at St Andrews University, at Padua, and at Paris, where he was infected (as English Camden might have put it) with the French passion for anagram. His papers are full of draft anagrams, and he published accomplished letter anagrams in Latin distichs, such as:

> *Anagrame*
> Anna Britannorum Regina.
> In anna regnantium arbor.
>
> *Perpetuo vernans* arbor regnantium in anna
> Fert fructum et frondes, germine laeta novo.[59]

Fowler was fond of plays on his own name, such as "then cruell shee sal see | A FLOUER to perrishe and a FOULER dee".[60] He wrote poems to Arabella Stuart ("Belissa"), using embedded anagrams: "My hart her Bell on which Disdayne assayes".[61] He also wrote love sonnets with similar syllabic anagrams to Mary Middlemore, a Maid of Honour to Queen Anne: "My harte as Aetna burnes, and suffers MORE | Paines in my MIDDLE then ever MARY proved".[62]

But it was Sir Philip Sidney (1554–86), "our English Petrarke" as Sir John Harington called him, who best empathized with Petrarch's confession of his love's impiety—and followed him too in troping the beloved name. His own pseudonym Astrophil implies he is the lover of "Stella", and he introduces the poetic name Stella no fewer than eighty-nine times in his sequence *Astrophil and Stella* (1591), besides referring to "my star". In the Eighth Song she is "Stella starre of heavenly fier". Her eyes are "two starres", "morning starres."[63] Even the stars in Astrophil's tournament device praise her name: "If I but stars upon my armour beare" (Sonnet 104). Morpheus ana-grammatizes her name, claiming "Sweet STELLA's image I do STEALE to me" (Sonnet 32).

Sidney's Stella married Robert, Baron Rich, occasioning as many as fifteen allusions to her married name. Thus, Sonnet 24 considers the folly of misers in general ("Rich fooles there be") but dwells on one in particular, "that rich foole, who by blind Fortune's lot | The richest gemme of Love and life enjoyes". And in Sonnet 35, "Fame | Doth even grow rich, naming my Stella's name". Most explicitly,[64] Sonnet 37 tells a "riddle" of Astrophil's life, how "a Nymph doth dwell: | Rich in all beauties":

> Rich in the treasure of deserved renowne,
> Rich in the riches of a royall hart,
> Rich in those gifts which give th'eternall crowne;
> Who though most rich in these and everie part,
> Which make the patents of true worldly blisse,
> Hath no misfortune, but that Rich she is.
>
> (*Astrophil and Stella*, Sonnet 37)

The riddle was solved by Harington, for his manuscript of *Astrophil and Stella* is titled "Sonnettes of Sir Phillip Sidneys to the Lady Ritch".[65]

Before her marriage in 1581, Stella had been Penelope Devereux, a name that suggested further wordplays. In *Certain Sonnets* 10 (dated before 1581), Sidney wonders that his heart "Fear'st not a face that oft whole harts DEVOWRES"—an anagram of DEVEREUX.[66] The wordplays on "star", "Rich", and "Devereux" raise expectation of similar play on "Penelope", so that the closing couplet of *Astrophil* Sonnet 1 attracts attention: "Biting my trewand PEN, beating my selfe for spite, | FOOLE": an anagram of PENELOPE, given the licence of reusing "P" and "E". The same name is hidden more elaborately in the "Penelope game" shaping

the sequence, for its 108 sonnets correspond to the stones thrown by
Penelope's suitors in the *Odyssey*.[67]

Lesser poets "concealed" names with less subtlety. Typical are Sir
John Davies' acrostic *Hymns to Astraea* (1599) and his Latin anagrams
on the name of his daughter Lucy Davis:

> LUCIDA VIS oculos teneri perstrinxit amantis,
> Nec tamen erravit, nam VIA DULCIS erat.[68]

Here, the anagram outline is [Lucida . . . dulciS]. The anagrams include
"[LUCIda DA vis oculos teneri perstrinxit amantis]"; "LUCIDA VIS: LUCI
DAVIS"; and, more condensed, [DA VIS OCUL]. The medial letters *-cul-* are
available since *ocul-* and *-os* are distinct word-parts.

Spenser's sonnet "Harvey, the happy above happiest man" to his
friend Gabriel Harvey has an unusual anagram acrostic on HOBBINOL,
Harvey's poetic name.[69] In this sonnet, simply to list the initial letters
of the lines may at once suggest that the initial letters of lines 1, 3, 9, . . .
form a series in which each term, multiplied by three, gives the next
term. The initials form an acrostic beginning HOB:

$$H \quad i \quad O \quad t \quad a \quad n \quad n \quad o \quad B \quad l \quad l \quad a \quad f \quad s$$
$$1 \quad 2 \quad 3 \quad 4 \quad 5 \quad 6 \quad 7 \quad 8 \quad 9 \quad 10 \quad 11 \quad 12 \quad 13 \, 14$$

The next term, 27, is too large for a sonnet line number; but its digits,
2 and 7, indicate the line initials I and N, bringing the acrostic to
HOBIN. The next term again is 81, whose first digit, 8, indicates O. This
promisingly brings the acrostic to HOBINO, but meets a new obstacle:
the second digit of 81 is already assigned. But we can substitute 10,
on the basis of the arithmological doctrine[70] that 10 is equivalent to
1. Making this substitution gives L, and makes the completed acrostic
HOBINOL.

Confirming factors are the aptness of Harvey's poetic name Hobinol; the fact that the acrostic begins with the sonnet's first letter; that it
observes a rule; and that the rule is the odd-number series, appropriate
to Harvey's interest in Platonic mathematics. Few will regard this
acrostic as having occurred by chance, yet it is just the sort of anagram
acrostic to arouse the scepticism of critics impressed by the arguments
of W. F. and E. S. Friedman.[71]

Elsewhere Spenser, like Sidney, plays on his lover's name—most
directly in *Amoretti* 75, where Elizabeth mocks his writing her name
on the sand:

> For I my selve shall lyke to this decay,
> And eek my name bee wyped out lykewize.
> Not so, (quod I) let baser things devize...

The words that assert her name will be wiped out are the same words that count against the assertion by anagrammatizing her name. An anagram with the letters dispersed but in correct order is "selv[E shall Lyke to thIS decay, | And eek my name BEe wiped ouT]". And more condensed anagrams with the letters scrambled include "[And Eek my name BEe wyped ouT LykewIZE]" (ABETLIZE: ELIZABET).[72]

Shakespeare's many anagrams in the *Sonnets* (1609) were lost from view for centuries, until R. H. Winnick's closely argued article (published in 2009) startled the scholarly world.[73] Winnick's finds—embedded letter anagrams on WRIOTHESLEY—are not in themselves conclusively proved. Taken together with their self-referring contexts, however, they are so persuasive as to be beyond reasonable doubt. They have, as Winnick himself puts it, a "cumulative plausibility". For example, the fourth line of Sonnet 126—"Thy louers withering, as thy sweet selfe grow'st."— has all the letters needed to make WRIOTHESLEY twice over: a remarkable fact whose extraordinary rarity is brought out by cogent statistical argument. And this is by no means the only such instance in the *Sonnets*. In Sonnet 55 the self-referring couplet again has two anagrams of WRIOTHESLEY. In the fourth line of Sonnet 17, "Which hides your life, and shewes not halfe your partes:", an imperfect anagram of WRIOTHESLEY, is itself "hidden". Sometimes the aptness of the context is so close that substitution of the name for the anagram is syntactically possible, as in Sonnet 39, lines 9–10: "Oh absence what a torment wouldst thou proue, | Were it not thy soure leisure gaue sweet leaue,"—"Were it not WRIOTHESLEY gaue sweet leaue". In the fifth line of Sonnet 1 ("But thou contracted [collected] to thine owne bright eyes,") ten of the eleven letters of WRIOTHESLEY are "collected".[74] Here, the example is more telling than Winnick seems to realize, for "thine owne bright eyes" is an anagram not only of WRIOTHESLEY but of HENRY WRIOTHESLEY.

All this means much more than identifying Shakespeare's fair youth as Southampton. As Winnick shows again and again, recognizing the presence of the anagrams improves the sense of many individual passages, even of whole sonnets. If one had to select a single line to sum the sequence, it would be "Your name from hence immortall life shall haue" (Sonnet 81). Shakespeare, the greatest poet of his age, may prove also the greatest anagrammatist.

Anagrams, however, went quite out of fashion by the end of the seventeenth century. Indeed, they became unworkable as a result of profound changes to the language and to the literary artefact. These changes sprang partly from developments in print technology and the decline of manuscript publication. In part, they reflected the change in philosophy known as the Enlightenment. And in part they responded to the increasing rigour of Method. At all events, English spelling and grammar were so regularized that anagrams became impossibly difficult to compose. Meanwhile the graphemic interface became more transparent, and less noticeable. Much that Mary Hazard has written about in *Elizabethan Silent Language* disappeared from view, at least so far as ordinary readers were concerned. In future, anagrams would be in the main a matter for specialists such as the mathematician Charles Lutwidge Dodgson (Lewis Carroll).

In the nineteenth century there was a resurgence of interest in acrostics, and to a lesser extent in anagrams. But these never recovered their previous status: they were now only amusing puzzles. Besides books of mathematical puzzles, Dodgson composed poems with initial acrostics, notably "A boat beneath a sunny sky" with the 21-letter acrostic read down, ALICE PLEASANCE LIDDELL) and "Is all our life, then, but a dream" (ISA BOWMAN).[75]

Key names

Livres à clef or *romans à clef* (German *Schlüsselromane*) may be defined as fictional works whose characters are actual people under invented names. Although sometimes said to originate with Mme de Scudéry's *Le Grand Cyrus* (1649–53), earlier exemplars abound, notably Honoré d'Urfé's *L'Astrée* (1607), Lady Mary Wroth's *Urania* (1621), and John Barclay's popular *Argenis* (1621). The latter went through more than thirty editions in the seventeenth century alone. Many of Barclay's invented names are simple anagrams, such as DEREFICUS for FREDERICUS (Frederick Count Palatine, son-in-law of James I); DUNALBIUS for UBALDINUS (Roberto Ubaldini, cousin of Pope Leo XI); and HIEROLEANDER for HIERONYMUS ALEANDER.[76]

Critics have come to agree that the narrative of Sidney's *Arcadia* in all three versions reflects contemporary historical situations and personages, and they have made many attempts to establish the details of the reflection. Of these the most successful are A. C. Hamilton's, Katherine Duncan-Jones', and Blair Worden's.[77] Worden, a historian by profession, offers the most valuable historical analysis; although his attunement to literature is less assured. Duncan-Jones offers the most valuable biographical information. But none of the three identifies many of the characters. Indeed, it is not clear how far they regard the *Arcadia* as a *livre à clef*. Yet it is highly probable that as a pastoral it would have aroused some such expectation in Renaissance readers.

The probability is increased by the existence of a seventeenth-century "Key of Pembroke's Arcadia", preserved among John Aubrey's papers.[78] Aubrey had asked one D. Tyndale "conversant amongst his [Sidney's] relations" for the key. Tyndale modestly insists that "all I know of it is not worth anything"—and certainly the key does not rate very highly as literary criticism. But it is priceless as evidence of real-life associations with the *Arcadia* names, less than a century after publication and probably drawing on Sidney family tradition. The most obvious association is with "Philisides", which indeed can hardly be in doubt. It contains Sidney's name: PHILI(p) SID(n)E(y) and is also equivalent to Astrophil, "star-lover" (*sidus* and *astrum* being Latin for star, and *phil-* being Greek for love).[79] According to Tyndale, "it was thought he meant himself by Amphi[alus]"; which agrees with Hamilton's association of Amphialus with Sidney's unlucky side.[80] It is noteworthy how Tyndale sees that the same real-life person may be reflected in several different characters—as indeed happens in Spenser's *The Faerie Queene*. So he might have accepted Duncan-Jones' perception of Sidney's "incautious irascibility" in Pyrocles[81]—except that he identified Pyrocles (misspelt "Pericles") as Lord Rich. Similarly, Pyrocles and Musidorus may both reflect Sidney, as Gabriel Harvey and Worden agree. For the rest, Tyndale is confident that Pamela is Dorothy Devereux (daughter of Walter Devereux, and who married Henry Percy to become Lady Northumberland); that Philoclea is Penelope Devereux (Lady Rich); that Miso is Lady Cox and Mopse Lady Lucy "persons altogether unknown now"; and that Musid[orus] is Dorothy Devereux's husband (Northumberland). He is less certain whether Gynecia is Lettice Devereux, mother of Dorothy and Penelope.[82]

In verse, key names go back much further. Already in the fourth century AD Servius regarded Vergil's Tityrus as figuring the poet's persona. Pastoral was often allegorical in this way: as we saw, the location name Meliboeus typifies the dispossessed farmers. Petrarch did more in the same direction, writing bucolics that criticized prelates at the papal court. Details of his difficult allegories may have baffled Elizabethan poets and critics; but they saw well enough that pastoral eclogues were miniature *livres à clef.* As Puttenham has it, pastoral was devised not to "represent the rustical manner of loves and communication, but under the veil of homely persons and in rude speeches to insinuate and glance at greater matters".[83] Thus, in Spenser's *The Shepheardes Calender* (1579), as we have seen, Piers is a type of the reformer or *vox populi.*

Some resist treating Spenser's characters as real-life individuals. But key names were a persistent feature of Renaissance eclogue: who can deny that Sannazaro's Meliseus refers to Giovanni Pontano's elegy of that name? And Thomas Watson, always a willing cicerone, hands his reader the keys to his *Meliboeus* (1590) in a Preface:

> my pastorall discourse to the unlearned may seeme obscure: which to prevent, I have thought good, here to advertise you, that I figure Englande in Arcadia; Her Majestie in Diana; Sir Francis Walsingham in Meliboeus, and his Ladie in Dryas; Sir Phillippe Sidney in Astrophill, and his Ladie in Hyale, Master Thomas Walsingham in Tyterus, and my selfe in Corydon.

The Shepheardes Calender must be among the most trenchant works in this mode.[84] The March Argument tells us "in the person of Thomalin is meant some secret friend"—misinformation disguising, as we shall see, a highly public figure. And the January Gloss hints that the "feigned name" Rosalinde is an anagram "which being well ordered wil bewray [betray] the very name of hys love and mistresse". (ROSALINDE is a near anagram of IRELONDE.) The editor "E. K." compares famous key names such as Ovid's Corinna and Aruntius Stella's Asteris and Ianthis: there is a "common custome of counterfeicting [inventing] the names of secret Personages".

Among those averse to political allegorizing of *The Shepheardes Calender*, Helen Cooper refuses to envisage Pan as Henry VIII or Syrinx as Anne Boleyn: "This is not an historical statement, and the use by Marot and others of 'Pan' for the French king is beside the point."[85] But Spenser's frequent imitation of Marot is beyond doubt; and the magic of Elisa's mythological generation need not be dispelled by uncovering historical references. Most of Paul McLane's identifications are now agreed, E. K.'s obfuscations notwithstanding. The January Gloss shifts attention away from ecclesiastical politics by hinting at sexual scandal: under the fictional country name Hobbinol seemeth to be hidden the person of some his very speciall and most familiar freend, whom he entirely and extraordinarily beloved, as peradventure shall be more largely declared hereafter. In thys place seemeth to be some savour of disorderly love, which the learned call paederastice.

E. K. insists, however, that only love of the soul is meant.[86] The identity of Hobbinol, hinted at in the January and April Arguments and Glosses, is clinched, as we saw, by Spenser's acrostic sonnet to Harvey.[87]

Other key names in *The Shepheardes Calender* depend on syllabic anagrams like those of Petrarch's satiric eclogues.[88] So ALGRIND stands for Edmund GRINDAL, Archbishop of Canterbury, and MORRELL for John AYLMER, Bishop of London. Sometimes the bishops' sees may be alluded to: THOMALIN is THOMAS Cooper, Bishop of LIN-coln; and DIGGON [Welsh, "Richard"] DAVY is RICHARD DAVIes, Bishop of St DAVI-d's. The most deviously witty is ROFFY for John Young, Bishop of Rochester (Latin ROFFensis), alluding to Marot's shepherd Roffy into the bargain.[89]

Key names in The Faerie Queene

From the time of John Upton, *The Faerie Queene* has been recognized as a *roman à clef*. Spenser's Letter to Ralegh says as much, explaining that Queen Elizabeth "beareth two persons, the one of a most royall Queene and Empresse, the other of a most virtuous and beautifull Lady", expressed in Gloriana and Belphoebe. And some of the other characters, too, bear key names. "Arthegall", besides obvious romance associations,[90] clearly glances at the contemporary Lord Grey of Wilton, Lord Deputy of Ireland and Spenser's superior. The dependable Upton notes that the first syllable of "Arthegall" corresponds to Grey's given name Arthur. Then, "the arms [...] seem devised in allusion to his name, Gray: such bearings [...] are called *Rebusses*. For Griseum in the barbarous Latin age signified fine fur or ermin [...] Gris". Upton assumes we know that medieval Latin for a greyhound was *canis de grecia*. Besides the pun on *grey/gris*, Arthegall's crest is a "grey-hound" and his shield bears "a crowned little Ermilin [ermine]" (*FQ* 3.2.25). Spenser mentions only a "couchant Hound": he doubtless relied on heraldically informed readers catching this hint—and perhaps another, in the last segment of "Arthegall" to (γαλῆ, *gale*), "ermine", as well as to *egall*, "equal").[91]

The wordplays on "Arthegall" extend to appearances of Grey's crest in the narrative. According to Camden, the barons Grey of Wilton held the manor of Eaton "by the service of keeping one gerfalcon of the King's; whence that family bears for their crest *a falcon sitting on a glove*".[92] Hence both Arthegall and his squire Talus are imaged as falcons: "As when a Faulcon hath with nimble flight" (*FQ* 5.2.54); "A gentle Faulcon sitting on a hill" (*FQ* 5.5.15). That the falcon is *sitting* puts the reference beyond doubt.

Arthegall's motto (not the same as Grey's) is SALVAGESSE SANS FINESSE (*FQ* 4.4.39), which has been construed as "wildness without art" or "savagery without refinement". But Spenser flags the motto as "showing secret wit"; which emboldens the reader to treat the motto anagrammatically. SANS FINESSE suggests that FINESSE ("shrewdness, prudence, *sagesse*") should be removed from SA-LVA-GESSE. This procedure leaves LVA or LUA—no meaningless syllables but the name of a Roman goddess, cult partner of Saturn. To Saturn and Lua, captured arms were dedicated: Arthegall's motto well befits a victorious military commander.[93]

The minor characters bear simpler key names, depending on rebuses or anagrams. They have been treated as mere romance wallpaper; but they are probably all identifiable as historical figures. Consider Marinell's six co-challengers at the Tournament for Florimell's spousals:

> The first of them was hight [named] Sir Orimont,
> A noble Knight, and tride in hard assayes [trials]:
> The second had to name Sir Bellisont,
> But second unto none in prowesse prayse;
> The third was Brunell, famous in his dayes;
> The fourth Ecastor, of exceeding might;
> The fift Armeddan, skild in louely layes;
> The sixt was Lansack, a redoubted Knight:
> All sixe well seene in armes, and prov'd in many a fight.
>
> (*FQ* 5.3.5)

The key name ORIMONT surely masks Thomas Butler, tenth earl of ORMOND (1531–1614), addressed in Dedicatory Sonnet 7. The thin disguise of ORIMONT consists of a gliding vowel *i* and the substitution of *t* for *d*, the same indication of Irishness as Jonson uses in *The Irish Masque*.[94]

"BELLISONT" probably shadows Sir Warham St Leger (1525?–97), Provost Marshall of Munster.[95] The first component BELLI- (Latin, "war") translates the first component of his given name WAR-ham. "BRUNELL" might be Sir Valentine Browne (d. 1589), another key player in the settlement of Munster. In "ECASTOR", Upton reasonably saw Arthurian and classical associations; but the Latin element *castor* ("beaver") more obviously indicates George BEVERley,Victualler of Ireland. Similarly "ARMEDDAN" imperfectly anagrams EDWARD DENNY, another Munster undertaker. And "LANSACK" must be a rebus for Sir Henry BAGNAL (c. 1556–98), LAN backwards and SACK for BAG.

At least two of these men (Ormond and St Leger) were, like Spenser, "undertakers" in the Munster plantation. All were actors in the Munster scene.[96] Ormond, of old English Catholic descent but reared a Protestant, was a powerful, turbulent grandee, an administrator not specially friendly to new English like Spenser or Baron Grey of Wilton. Ormond's loyalty to his regal cousin Queen Elizabeth was questioned more than once: Grey eventually dismissed him from his Lieutenancy of Munster. As for St Leger, one of Lodovic Bryskett's friends, he was an unprincipled adventurer without the resources to realize his ambitions. As custodian of the rebel Earl of Desmond he cheated him out of his daily allowance. St Leger's nomination as Lord President of Munster was opposed by Ormond, under whom he served, however, during the second Desmond rebellion. Yet he figures, with Spenser, as an interlocutor in Ludowick Bryskett's *A Treatise of Civill Life* (1606). Bryskett was an Irish Civil Service friend of Spenser, with whom he shared philosophical interests. Bagnal, another greedy adventurer, notoriously quarrelled with the earl of Tyrone (with whom his sister eloped). Marshall of the army, Bagnal was often at loggerheads with Grey. A house divided, then.

As usual, alternative identifications beset the interpreter. Perhaps anagrammatists, mindful of repercussions, valued escape clauses. Here, ARMEDDAN might also be ROBERT NEEDHAM, a successful cavalry officer and dedicatee of Spenser's *Amoretti*.[97] BRUNELL suggests Henry BURNELL, Recorder of Dublin, of old English Catholic descent. Burnell was certainly "famous in his day": in the 1580s he had organized opposition to taxes on recusants. He went to London to negotiate, and the composition reached was of his framing. He won the grudging respect of Sir Henry Sidney as "the least unhonest of the three [representatives], and yet he trusted to see the English Government withdrawn". Burnell as Brunell would imply a wider Irish setting.

All six descriptions in *FQ* 5.3.5 are respectful and complimentary but not without sharper overtones: "Second unto none" is only too apt for the overambitious St Leger. MARINELL (MAL-ERIN, "troubled Ireland")

and the six "challenge all in right of Florimell", that is, of the ideal state. Marinell shows great prowess, but is taken prisoner and has to be res-cued by the sovereign power of Arthegall (*FQ* 5.3.10–11): together they defeat the rebel "crew" opposing Elizabeth's sovereignty. Marinell's knights, helpless without Arthegall, seem to represent discordant cadres of old and new English. As often in *The Faerie Queene*, the meaning of Marinell himself is implied by his genealogy: he is the "warlike sonne unto an earthly peare [peer], | The famous Dumarin".

DUMARIN ("Of the Sea") anagrammatizes RAIMUND, that is, Ray-mond Fitzgerald (Raymond le Gros, d. 1182), in Giraldus Cambrensis a pillar of the Anglo-Norman conquest of Ireland. Marinell must then be of old English descent. His opposition to Britomart on the Rich Stronde and his capture in the tournament suggest that loyal inde-pendence seems to Spenser impracticable for the old English without the assistance of Elizabeth's representative. Indeed, Marinell's capture in *FQ* 5.3 tropes captivation—assimilation into the rebel crew. St Leger was accused, perhaps wrongly, of Roman Catholicism; and even Ormond with his English upbringing was suspected of double loyal-ties. Spenser's allegory is far removed from any simple confrontation of rebels and loyalists.

Satiric key names

A chief ancient source of satiric key names was Martial: about half of his names belong to this type. In Elizabethan poetry, Sir John Haring-ton (1561–1612) was the seminal figure to explore the potential of key names: before Jonson he widened the emotional range of satire beyond Martial's limits. Harington used key names to disguise fierce attacks on powerful courtiers, refusing the relative safety that membership of one or another of the main factions might have offered. He called himself "neither Papist, Protestant, nor Puritan, but "a protesting Catholicke Puritan". While not taking up an extreme position, he became one of the most subversive satirists of the period. Among his targets was Sir Walter Raleigh, which he disguised by inappropriately calling him Paulus ("Short"), a name he and Sir John Davies took over from Mar-tial.[98] Harington's targets can sometimes be inferred from the context or from hints in the name itself, as when "Lelia" disguises the acknowl-edged mistress of Elizabeth's Champion Sir Henry Lee. With more difficulty, "Lynus" can be identified as Thomas Nashe.[99] Others remain unidentified; perhaps these were so dangerous as to call for specially impenetrable disguises. Harington's fear of discovery shows in the way he distributed presentation copies of his epigrams: the revealing manuscript annotations went to safe recipients only, such as Lady Rogers, his mother-in-law.[100]

The system of key names may seem riskily transparent as a disguise. Like a simple transposition cipher, it cannot have presented insuperable difficulty to a determined enquirer. Perhaps Harington felt this, for he developed additional means of concealment. He generalized the keys by sharing them both with Martial and with contemporary satirists. And he multiplied the names for a single individual, referring to himself, for example, both as Lepidus and as Misacmos.

Alexander Pope used a similar system. But he added a brilliant new device: simulated annotation of the key names. In *The Rape of the Lock*, "Belinda" might suggest the "gentlewoman" in Etherege's *Man of Mode* (1676) or the "affected lady" in Congreve's *Old Bachelor* (1693), among others. It was a fashionable name, as well as being one that resembled the actual name of his target, Ara*bella* Fermor. When the Fermors took offence at Pope's publication of the 1712 *Rape of the Lock*, he had to work hard to convince Arabella that "the Character of Belinda" resembled her "in nothing but in Beauty".[101] Within the close-knit community of the much-intermarried Catholic families, key names were a transparent disguise. But Sir George Browne, the original of Sir Plume, did not wish a wider circle to know him as a fop with "round unthinking Face" (4.125): he "blustered" and threatened. Nevertheless Pope felt himself in the right and, far from leaving the matter, he published (pseudonymously) *A Key to the Lock* (1715).[102]

A Key generated smokescreens of irrelevant political allegorizing. Prefaced by an elaborate paratext of encomia of the pretended author Esdras Barnivelt and attacks on Pope himself, it constituted a new invention, a creation in its own right. The Dedication to the 1714 *Rape of the Lock* explicitly identifies Belinda as Mrs Arabella Fermor, but *A Key* now interprets her as a representation of Great Britain. Her lock of hair is the Barrier Treaty, and Shock the lapdog is Dr Sacheverell.[103] To allow Sir George Browne to save face, *A Key* pretends that more than one gentleman has claimed to be the original of the fashionable Sir Plume: not only "a Roman Catholick Knight" at the Cocoa Tree, but also "a Roman Catholick Lord" at Will's. Besides drawing attention away from Arabella's morals, *A Key* has the effect of uniting the Catholic community against the wild, humourousless notions of the ignorant sectarian Barnivelt. To the satirist, everything is grist to the satiric mill, even the system of key names itself. Yet Pope never allows the relations of real and fictional names to be oversimplified.

In *Gulliver's Travels*, Jonathan Swift (1667–1745) describes the methods of interpretation practised "in the kingdom of TRIBNIA, by the natives called LANGDEN [BRITAIN, ENGLAND] to discover plots. Two of these "the learned among them call acrostics and anagrams" (book 3, chapter 6). Thus Swift uses anagrams to satirize the anagrammatic method itself. His own key names do not always offer such easy clues to the interpreter.

Nineteenth-century fiction offers many instances of characters recognizable as representing real individuals. Skimpole in *Bleak House* (1852–3) clearly glances at James Henry Leigh Hunt (1784–1859); although Dickens denied representing more than Leigh Hunt's mannerisms of speech. For a thorough-going *livre à clef* one needs to turn to Thomas Love Peacock's satiric *Nightmare Abbey* (1818), in which Scythrop ("sullen-faced") represents Shelley, and Flosky Coleridge. An authorial note indicates that Flosky is a corruption of *Φιλοσκίος*, *Philoskios* ("Lover of shadows"), suggesting Coleridge's love of abstraction. But the name may also suggest Floscule ("flower", "embellishment of speech"), a characteristic of the Flosky who claims "I never gave a plain answer to a question in my life."[104] In the same period Mary Shelley's *The Last Man* (1826), although it is hardly a typical *roman à clef*, has several fictionalized real people, such as Adrian (Percy Bysshe Shelley), Lord Raymond (Byron), and Ryland (William Cobbett).

The *livre à clef* flourished well into the twentieth century, especially in satire. Aldous Huxley's *Point Counter Point* (1928), which owes much to Peacock, is an essayistic novel of conversation between thinly disguised real people such as D. H. Lawrence ("Mark Rampion") and himself ("Philip Quarles"). And Somerset Maugham's *Cakes and Ale* (1930) satirizes the novelist Hugh Walpole as "Alroy Kear". One should perhaps distinguish instances with no consistent system of key names from thorough-going exemplars of the *roman à clef*. A recent example of the latter is Joe Klein's *Primary Colours* (1996), an account of Bill Clinton's presidential campaign. Clinton himself appears under the key name Jack Stanton; Orlando Ozio disguises Mario Cuomo; and Henry Burton is George Stephanopoulos. In another direction, the non-fictional novel, or faction, is easily distinguished. Truman Capote's *In Cold Blood* (1965), for example, has no disguises: his real people are presented under their own names.

Notes

1. *De Divinatione* 2. 111; see Knox 1924: 3.
2. Laȝamon 1963: 2; see Burrow 1984: 164–5.
3. Kane 1965: 65; Burrow 1984: 167–8.
4. B-Text 15. 152, Langland 1988: 543; cf. C-Text *passus* 6. See Burrow 1984: 162; Kane 1965: 32–3. Cf. Kane's Langland entry in *ODNB*: "a cryptogrammatic signature in the convention of the genre"; McKinley 1940: 30–1; Kastan 2007: 98–101. The signature is confirmed by a marginal note in Trinity College, Dublin, MS 212: "willielmi de Langlond". See Middleton 1990; Wallace 1999: 513.
5. *The Flower and the Leaf* 24, Skeat 1897: 362; see Seaton 1961: 318–19.
6. *The House of Fame* 729; *The Legend of Good Women* Prologue G 234–460; *The Man of Law's Tale* Intro. 45–50.
7. See Burrow 1984: 174.
8. *Confessio Amantis* 8. 2316–22, Gower 1980: 469. For the adverbial phrase "halvinge a game" cf. OE *healfunga*; for the verb, see *OED* s.v. *halve* 4.
9. Lines 1318–19; see Williams 2006: 150; Trigg 2006: 301–2.
10. Davies 1935: No. 240 (alluding to James 1: 21, "receive the engrafted word"); see de Vinne 1902: 34–6; Davies 1935: 665; McKerrow 1949 *passim*; Williams 1954: 314.
11. Douglas 1874: 4. 167.
12. Matt. 27: 34, Mark 15: 23, and Deut. 32: 32.
13. See Reid Baxter 2008: 87.
14. "IHS" was wrongly taken as a Latin abbreviation of *Iesus Hominum Salvator*. This acrostic name appears e.g. in Langland, *Piers Plowman* B-text 3. 154 and 16. 144; see *OED* s.v. *IHS*.
15. Vendler 1975: 68–9 compares Herbert's "Love Joy" and its divine initials J. C.
16. See Wright 1998: 272.
17. For other exs. see Turville-Petre 1988: 264–9, esp. 264 on *The Destruction of Troy* with the acrostic signature "MAISTUR IOHANNES CLERK DE WHALELE".
18. 1. 19–24; see Minnis 1984: 170, 274 nn. 34, 35. Cf. Osbern Bokenham, who states that he has given his name in acrostic form; see Horstmann 1887: 34; Minnis 1984: 193.
19. E.g. D'Assigny 1697, drawing on Guglielmo Grataroli, *De Memoria Reparanda* (Zürich, 1553).
20. Imitating Pierre Gringore; see Coldiron 2009: 158–61.
21. See Skeat 1897: xix–xx; cf. Burrow 1984: 166, citing Dobson 1976: 327–68 on the practice of locating an author's name next to a petition for readers' prayers.
22. In compliment to Maria D'Aquino; see Fowler 2007: 36.
23. See Seaton 1961: 112 *et passim*.
24. Parry 2005: 167; for biographical context see pp. 2–3, 10–13; Honigmann 1985; Brown 1914.
25. Davies 1975: 71–86. See Fowler 1964: 198–9; Fowler 1996: 101.
26. Moseley 1989: 110–13, 116, 118. An interesting and influential complimentary acrostic is James VI's to his second cousin: ESMESTEWARTDVIKE. See James 1955: 40–1.
27. *Characters*, Butler 1908: 53. For other 16C and 17C complimentary acrostics, see Marotti 1995: 174.

28. Addison: *Spectator* 60 (9 May 1711); Cambridge: *Scribleriad* (1751).

29. For literary anagrams and acrostics ancient and modern, see Williams 1954: 315; Clauss 1997; Knox 1924; Augarde 1984; Ricks 2003; Fowler 2007. Ferdinand de Saussure (*PrincetonEnc* 69–70) and Ahl 1985 treat the broader topic of words within words; see Starobinski 1971.

30. On Elizabethan consciousness of words as sequences of letters, see Hazard 2000: 47–9; Potter 1989: 50–1; and Ferry 1989: 19–21, 128–33, 195 *et passim*.

31. Baratella defines the device as *compositio nominis divisim et per sillabas in metris ponendi in capi versibus uel alibi*. See Da Tempo: 1869: 172–3 and 230–31 where Baratella and Da Tempo are both printed. I owe this reference to Thomas P. Roche.

32. Du Bellay 1948: 154: "cette inversion de lettres en un propre nom, qui porte quelque devise convenable à la personne".

33. Included in Eusebius, *Life of Constantine*; tr. by St Augustine into Latin; see du Bellay 1948: 156. Cicero, *De Divinatione* 2. 54. 110–12.

34. E.g. Jonson, *Epicoene* 4. 3. 48, "Make *anagrammes* of our names, and invite us to the cock-pit"; Shirley 1646: 36, "Anagram upon her Name".

35. *The Arte of English Poesie* (1589) 2. 8, STC 20519.5, known from at least five copies (not only from Jonson's copy as Frank Whigham and Wayne Rebhorn assert, Puttenham 2007: 198). See Puttenham 1936: cviii–ix; Puttenham 2007: 71.

36. Puttenham 2007: 197.

37. Puttenham 2007: 198–200.

38. Camden 1984: 143.30–144.16.

39. Camden 1984: 143.25. About the rebus he is somewhat contemptuous; e.g. Camden 1984: 139, "they which lackt wit to expresse their conceit in speech".

40. Camden 1984: 142.16–21.

41. Camden 1984: 142. Licences not mentioned by Camden but considered valid by others are *I* and *IE* for *Y*, *J* for *I*, *CS* for *X*, and *S* for *X* (and vice versa).

42. "Character of a perfect Anagram", Drummond 1711: 230–1. On Drummond's own anagrams, see Masson 1969: 116–17. For other rules or licences, see Puttenham 2007; Knox 1924: 19; Friedman and Friedman 1957: 162 *et passim*; Augarde 1984: 74; Winnick 2009: 262–3. The Friedmans' draconian rules would exclude most well-attested anagram acrostics.

43. Camden 1984: 144–54.

44. Ibid. 147, 148.

45. Ibid. 144.

46. Ibid. 150.

47. Ibid. 151.

48. Ibid. 150.

49. Ibid. 152 (my capitals).

50. Ibid. 145: Jonson 1925–52: 7.223; see 10.514. At the central point of *Barriers* Jonson conceals another encomium: lines 213–14 name two British heroes, King Richard and King Edward, precedents for Henry since he too showed heroism while "being but prince".

51. See Augarde 1984: 75.

52. Hamilton-Paterson 2008.

53. Translation adapted from Robert Durling's, Petrarch 1976.

54. See Roche 1989: 13, 19–25.

55. Du Bellay 1993: 1.18; xxiv.

56. See *SEnc* 495 col. c; Rigolot 1977: 129–54; Katz 1985.

57. Murray 1823, Klein 1984: 1.448, 2.242–4.

58. For William Fowler, see Sarah Dunnigan in *ODNB*; Jack 1972; Jack 1986; Petrina 2009; Elliott 2010.

59. Miscellaneous Poems, Fowler 1914–40: 1.316.
60. Sonnet 2, Fowler 1914–40: 1.216, signalled "anagramme" in margin. Cf. *Tarantula of Love* 33 and 67 ("no Fouler cachting bot a Fouler caught"), Fowler 1914–40: 1.162 and 198.
61. Miscellaneous Sonnets 13, "Uppon a Horologe" (1603), Fowler 1914–40: 1.260.
62. Miscellaneous Sonnets 23, Fowler 1914–40: 1.269.
63. Sonnets 26, 48; cf. Sonnet 88, "When Sun is hid, can starres such beames display?", Sidney 1962: 177–8, 188–9, 223.
64. And probably for that reason omitted from the Briton-Houghton MS.
65. Hughey 1960: 1.254, 2.354.
66. Cf. Song 10: "When I blessed shall DEVOWER"; and the similar wordplay in *Prothalamion* 153–4: "endlesse happinesse of thine owne name | That promiseth the same" (DEVEREUX: DEVENIR HEUREUX, "become happy").
67. Eustathius, comm. on *Odyssey* 1.130; cf. Browne 1964: 1.188, "the Proci or Prodigall Paramours disposed their men, when they played at Penelope. For being themselves an hundred and eight, they set fifty four stones on either side, and one in the middle, which they called Penelope, which he that hit was master of the game." See Fowler 1970: 174–80. The compositional number 108 is given to a different, musicological interpretation in Parker 1998 *passim*; but the two explanations are not mutually exclusive.
68. Davies 1975: 299. Cf. J. Weever's syllabic anagram "In Elizabetham", Weever 1599: B1b, Weever 1987.
69. See Fowler 2007: 38–40.
70. See, e.g., Bungus 1591: 358.
71. In Friedman 1957 they reject all short anagram acrostics as too easily invented by a discoverer. See further in Fowler 2007: 37, 40.
72. With *H* silent, a common licence. The anagram is signalled by the unusual *z* spelling. On a possible wordplay on Elizabeth Peace ("Is there no means to purchase Peace"), see Spenser 1929: 198.
73. Winnick 2009.
74. Winnick 2009: 267–9.
75. See Knox 1924; Crystal 1998: 58–9; Humez and Humez 2008: 23; Augarde 1984: 36.
76. Barclay 2004: 46–7.
77. Hamilton 1977; Duncan-Jones 1991; Worden 1996.
78. Aubrey 1898: 2.250–2.
79. Tyndale: "they sayd Philisides was himself to[o], but it was all a guesse." This confirms Duncan-Jones' sense (pp. 42–3) of "self-projection" in Philisides. Hamilton 1977: 125, Duncan-Jones 1991: 42–3, and Worden 1996: 5, 297, 313 all agree on the identification.
80. Hamilton 1877: 139.
81. Duncan-Jones 1991: 21–2, 42–3; Worden 1996: 297, 313, 328.
82. See Aubrey 1898: 2.250–1. Lettice, daughter of Sir Francis Knollys, married Walter Devereux.
83. Puttenham 2007: 128.
84. See McLane 1961; Johnson 1990.
85. Cooper 1977: 155.
86. See Johnson 1990: 110.
87. See Fowler 2007: 39–40. "Hob" was a form of Robin; cf. "Robin Goodfellow"; "Hob-goblin".
88. E.g. NEREUS for NERO; EPY for the papal court, EPISCOPATUS. See Cooper 1977: 41–2.
89. See *SEnc*, Hamilton 1990: 648–9.

90. See Yonge 1884: 266. Geoffrey of Monmouth writes of a historical "Arthgallo", a consul attending Arthur; John Hardyng's 1543 *Chronicle of England* makes him a knight of the Round Table. As half-brother of King Arthur his name can be taken as Arth-egall, "peer or equal of Arthur". In the pre-Shakespearean drama *Artegal and Elidure*, Elidure's generosity converts his brother Arthgallo from an early cruelty, much as Spenser's Arthegall changes from his initial savagery. Legally, *egall* meant "equal"; see OED s.v. *Egall*, a., quotation of 1594: "Ministers of Justice [...] frame their judgments after the square and rule of good and egall".

91. Leslie 1983: 52, 57, 63.

92. Camden 1970: 280.

93. For Lua, see Servius on *Aen.* 3.139; *Pauly Real-Encyclopädie* 13 (2). 1534; Grimal 1987: 262.

94. See, e.g., line 18, "ant" for "and". See further in Fowler 2007: 40–43.

95. In State Papers sometimes given as "Sentleger", *sent* and *sont* being archaic forms of *saint*.

96. Satyrane is probably another Munster figure, Lord Justice Sir William Drury, President of Munster 1576–8.

97. See McCabe 2005: 247.

98. See Gerard Kilroy in Harington 2009: 44, 47.

99. See Fowler 2009: 10.

100. See Kilroy in Harington 2009: 74, 71.

101. Dedication to *The Rape of the Lock* (1714).

102. In the genre of *A Key to the Rehearsal* (1704), produced by a well-informed member of the Duke of Buckingham's circle: see Buckingham 2007: 2.334–40.

103. Pope 1936: 185.

104. Peacock 1948: 397; see OED s.v. *Floscule* 1, 1b.

5

Shakespeare's Names

In *Munera Pulveris* (1872), John Ruskin famously remarked, in a monster footnote to a discussion of government,

Shakespeare's names [...] are curiously—often barbarously—much by Providence,—but assuredly not without Shakespeare's cunning purpose—mixed out of the various traditions he confusedly adopted, and languages which he imperfectly knew. Three of the clearest in meaning have been already noticed [Perdita, Cordelia, and Portia]. Desdemona, δυσδαιμονία, "miserable fortune", is also plain enough. Othello is, I believe, "the careful"; all the calamity of the tragedy arising from the single flaw and error in his magnificently collected strength. Ophelia, "serviceableness", the true lost wife of Hamlet, is marked as having a Greek name by that of her brother, Laertes; and its signification is once exquisitely alluded to in that brother's last word of her, where her gentle preciousness is opposed to the uselessness of the churlish clergy—"A *ministering* angel shall my sister be, when thou liest howling". Hamlet is, I believe, connected in some way with "homely", the entire event of the tragedy turning on betrayal of home duty. Hermione (ἕρμα), "pillar-like" [...] Titania (τιτήνη, "the queen"); Benedict and Beatrice, "blessed and blessing"; Valentine and Proteus, enduring (or strong), (*valens*), and changeful. Iago and Iachimo have evidently the same root—probably the Spanish Iago, Jacob, "the supplanter".[1]

Every name is meaningful, some "plain enough", others requiring etymological clarification. Ruskin's approach seems at times simplistic, for the root of a name is often less important than its associations. Still, his grasp of the various aptnesses of names—through their contrasts, multilingual meanings, and components—can be impressive.

Etymologies

Matthew Arnold, however, rejects the whole substance of Ruskin's digression (for that is what the footnote amounts to):

> Now, really, what a piece of extravagance all that is! I will not say that the meaning of Shakespeare's names (I put aside the question as to the correctness of Mr Ruskin's etymologies) has no effect at all, may be entirely lost sight of; but to give it that degree of prominence is to throw the reins to one's whim, to forget all moderation and proportion, to lose the balance of one's mind altogether. It is to show in one's criticism, to the highest excess, the note of provinciality.[2]

Arnold concedes Ruskin's genius, but dismisses the idea of a special significance in names. Ruskin's character was "too febrile irritable and weak to allow him to possess the *ordo concatenatioque veri* [order and connectedness of truth]".[3] Arnold takes fright at the notion of an onomastic method, as if Ruskin had proposed names as the key to all literature. In hinting Ruskin's etymologies might be questioned, moreover, Arnold betrays not only emulousness but also a provinciality of his own. Ruskin better understood the importance of names in Shakespeare's world. And his superior historical sense told him the correctness of Elizabethan etymologies was irrelevant.

In fact, many of Ruskin's etymologies are sound enough, so far as they go. The derivation of Desdemona ("miserable fortune") from δυσδαιμονία, "misery" and δυσδαιμονέω, "be wretched, unlucky" is accepted by modern scholars as preferable to that from δεισιδαίμων, "superstitious". In any case it is wrong to assume, as Arnold does, that etymologies must correct by the standards of modern philology. Modern etymologies generally have little to do with Shakespeare's meanings. He would have drawn his meanings from the contemporary etymologies of such as Richard Verstegan, William Camden, and John Florio.[4] "Edgar" in *King Lear* might now be derived from Old English *ead* ("prosperity") and *gar* ("spear"). But Camden's derivation ("happy or blessed honour") is far more relevant to Shakespeare's use of the name. In any case, Shakespeare knew enough to form his names from ancient words, like Sir Philip Sidney and Edmund Spenser before him. Exaggerated inferences have been drawn from Ben Jonson's remark about Shakespeare's "small Latine, and lesse Greeke" (a learned quotation from the Italian theorist Sebastiano Minturno).[5] "Miranda" in *The*

Tempest is a Latin tag name, as 3.1.37 makes explicit: "Admir'd Miranda". Moreover, she continually admires Ferdinand and others: "It carries a brave form" (1.2.414), "O brave new world" (5.1.183).

Variety of meaning

Root meanings belong only to one sort of aptness. Another is direct description of a personal attribute, as with "Aguecheek", which indicates gaunt cheeks. Or the point may lie in associations with previous bearers of the name in history, literature, or the stage. Corin in *As You Like It* had already been a shepherd in *Clyomon and Chlamydes* (1570, printed 1599). A further aptness of this name, in a play featuring wrestling, is that legend made Corin the first wrestler.[6]

Many of Shakespeare's names convey meaning through their form. There may be a relevant association or encapsulated word, as with "Caliban", an anagram of "cannibal". Words embedded in names are common, and sometimes relevant, as perhaps with *demon* in "Desdemona", *hell* in "Othello", and *ass* in "Cassio" (said to fit his "ingenuous nature").[7] But Murray Levith sees a different embedding in "Othello": *Oth*, the first syllable of Othoman (founder of the Ottoman empire).[8] More obvious in Shakespeare's day would have been the anagram of Thorello, the jealous husband in the early version of *Every Man in his Humor* (1598, printed 1601), in which Shakespeare himself acted.[9] Other names are puns, like Jacques and Ajax, both suggesting "jakes", a dark place then supposed to induce melancholy; or Mistress Quickly (who comes quickly, or offers a quick lay). In *Merry Wives*, Master Ford's assumed name Brook is not exactly a pun, but its riverine sense is activated by the ford–brook association, as Harry Levin shows ("Such Brooks are welcome to me, that o'erflows such liquor").[10] In *Henry VI Part 2* the puns are black: "Suffolk's duke" will not "be suffocate" but take his death by "water" (Walter Whitmore, his assassin).[11] Sometimes Shakespeare's given and family names contradict each other with ludicrous effect, as with the timorous Sir Andrew Aguecheek. As Camden notes, Andrew is from Greek meaning "warrior, manly".[12]

Specially characteristic of Shakespeare are formal resemblances between the names of principal characters. Thus "Viola", "Olivia", and "Malvolio", as near anagrams, invite formal comparison and contradistinction;[13] and so do "Rowland", "Orlando", and "Oliver" in *As You*

Like It. Sometimes, as with "Edgar" and "Edmund" in *King Lear*, like-ness underlines the direct moral contrast.[14] Also characteristic is the large group of names—large enough to call for separate treatment—that have mythological associations. Autolycus in *The Winter's Tale* is "litter'd under Mercury" and "a snapper-up of unconsidered trifles" (4.3.24–6). The geniture implies a Child of Mercury, likely to be involved in business or theft. Some would recall, in this connection, that Mercury, who stole Apollo's cattle, was the father of Autolycus. Shakespeare has also key names, covertly referring to real individuals. "Polonius" in *Hamlet* may be one example, and *Cymbeline* certainly offers another, for Richard du Champ (4.2.377) is a witty, rebus-like disguise for Richard Field, Shakespeare's friend and publisher. The joke here is that Field liked to play on his own name in this very way: on the title pages of his Spanish publications he called himself Ricardo del Campo.[15]

Shakespeare's penchant for multiple relevance may be exempli-fied in his naming of drunkards. "Borachio" (*Much Ado*) has been associated with Spanish *borracha* or Italian *boraccia*, a leather wine-skin or flask; but even before Shakespeare it may also have been good English as a nickname for a drunkard.[16] Stephano in *The Tempest* has been traced to Florio, where *Stefano* "hath been used in jest for a man's bellie [...] also a garland" (Greek στέφανος, *stephanos* "wreath"), the chaplet used by serious drinkers to cool their heads. The Folio spelling "Stephano" favours the second pos-sibility. "Trinculo", Stephano's companion, suggests Italian *trincare*, "to bib or tipple merily" and *trinci*, "idle ornaments about gar-ments" (both in Florio). Sir Toby Belch in *Twelfth Night* has an equally complicated name. "Belch", a common physical accompa-niment of drinking, goes well with "toby" in the sense of posterior (*OED* sb.[1]), indicating rudeness at both ends; and "toby" in thieves' slang meant "highway robbery", relevant to Toby's fleecing of Sir Andrew.[17] "Toby" has anachronistically been linked with the well-known piece of drinking equipment. "Toby jug" is not attested until the nineteenth century, and the object itself was an eight-eenth-century invention.

Shakespeare scholarship has fortunately taken Ruskin's route as often as Arnold's.[18] Levith, for example, devotes much of *What's in Shake-speare's Names* (1978) to tracing derivations. But he focuses specially on "denotative or 'tag' names": "dealing with minor and especially comic characters and secondary play actions, Shakespeare will single out a vivid attribute and so label a character, either by occupation, physical trait or feature, or some notable aspect of personality".[19] This is a necessary and valuable sort of criticism: tag names need not always be obvious. Polixenes, for example, is plausibly enough explained as taken at random from North's Plutarch to replace the Egistus of Greene's *Pandosto* (1588).[20] More probably, however, it labels the character as πολιός, "grey-haired" and ξένος, "stranger". Prevalent as tag names are, relying on them too much may induce a simplistic approach. Shakespeare more often combines direct with indirect, literal with figurative aptness and association.

Changes of name

Characters who appear in disguise often adopt false names: Portia becomes Bellario; Master Ford, Master Brook; King Henry, Harry Leroy; Florizel, Doricles; Viola, Cesario; Sebastian, Rodorigo; and Feste, Sir Topas.[21] (The last example alludes to Chaucer's mock-knight, but perhaps also to the jewel topaz, considered a cure for lunacy.)[22] As Levin points out, assumed names are sometimes semi-allegorical, adding moral commentary. Thus, Tamora in *Titus Andronicus* becomes "Revenge", and faithful Imogen in *Cymbeline* becomes "Fidele".[23] Rosalind going into the forest in *As You Like It* declares she will have "no worse a name than Jove's own page, | And therefore look you call me Ganymed" (1.3.120). "Ganymede" may have had ambitious associations, but was also slang for a catamite.[24] Celia maintains her rank by choosing the name Aliena (Latin, "foreigner, stranger" or "estranged").

Changes of name are a feature of Shakespeare's later plays, although disguise was more a speciality of the rival Admiral's Company.[25] The banished Earl of Kent, to continue serving the cause of King Lear, disguises himself as Caius (*probus*, "parents' joy"). Similarly Edgar, Gloucester's true son, takes the name and role of "Poor Tom", type-name for a mad beggar.[26] Edgar's unprepossessing outer appearance as Poor Tom belies a good inner character—the opposite relation of name and nature to that of his half-brother Edmund. Such symbolic changes of name were to become an important device in Victorian novels, especially in those of Charles Dickens.

Social background

At times Shakespeare uses groups of names to adumbrate distinct social milieux. Anne Barton draws attention to how, in the Induction of *The Taming of the Shrew*, Christopher Sly's head

is crammed with incidental proper names, most of them belonging to people who never appear in the play: "Marian Hacket", the fat alewife of Wincot, "Cicely Hacket", her maid, "Stephen Sly and old John Naps of Greece, | And Peter Turph, and Henry Pimpernell, | And twenty more such names and men as these" [...]. Absent presences, they are telling all the same against the elegant, witty, but also somewhat chilly and inhuman world of that anonymous, upper-class milieu to which Sly finds himself so inexplicably translated.[27]

Through Warwickshire associations the names strongly evoke a rural society of the time. Another example is Falstaff's gang—Peto, Nym, Bardolph, and Ancient Pistol—whose names are all linked with aspects of thievery. Besides being a Warwickshire family name, "Peto" suggests both Latin *peto*, "attack, strike, seek to get",[28] and English *petard*. "Nim" or "Nym" ("steal") is a tag name, punned on in *Henry V* 5.2.1 ("I'll live by Nym"); stealing eventually causes his death, when he is hanged for looting churches.[29] Pistol is named after another tool of their trade. And "Bardolph" is close to "bardo" which Florio explains as "light, nimble, saucy, bould". The whole gang is labelled as bent on a life of crime, violence, and robbery with menaces.

In *A Midsummer Night's Dream*, the names of the "rude mechanicals" relate to their trades and evoke an entire artisan world.[30] Thus "Quince" brings to mind quines or quoins, carpenter's wedges (*OED* 2); and Snug's joinery makes all close-fitting (*OED Snug* 1). "Snout" suggests the spout of a kettle or the nozzle of a pipe or bellows (*OED* 4a): as Wall in the playlet he is well qualified to provide its "orifice". Flute the bellows-mender would repair flute organ stops (worked then with bellows).[31] Forms of address reflect their social rankings. So it is "Francis Flute, the bellows-mender" and "Tom Snout the tinker" (never just "Tom Snout"). Contrast "Peter Quince" or, if Bottom is speaking, "good Peter Quince" (a courteous form of address to inferiors or superiors).[32]

Although Puck lumps the six artisans together as "rude mechanicals", some are more mechanical than others. They form pairs, with each pair ranked according to their trades' degrees of dependence on *disegno* or intellectual thought. Bottom weaves mechanically, but Starveling the tailor shapes woven cloth into garments. Similarly with Flute and Snout: bellows were indispensable in furnaces and church organs, whereas tinkers mostly repaired kettles (unless called in to help with the occasional organ pipe).[33] Again, Quince and Snug both work in wood, but Quince's skills have wider scope. For carpentry and joinery have radically altered in status since Shakespeare's time: carpenters then practised every sort of woodcraft, from housebuilding to fine carving.[34] In wooden building carpenters outranked joiners, whose work was limited to decorative fitting. It is Quince's experience in coordinating many such crafts harmoniously that qualifies him to be bookholder (in modern terms, director) of the inset play. The three pairs make up a comprehensive representation of the rag trade, building trade, and maintenance workers.

Patricia Parker's able essay on "Shakespeare's Joinery" finds classism implied by the term "mechanicals": "references to mechanicals in Shakespeare are thus most often the embodiment of a distinct class voice, tied to the attempt to 'singulate' or distinguish high from low".[35] But lumping the six artisans together like this misses something of Shakespeare's subtlety. The "mechanicals" are individuals, and by no means of equal rank. In fact, they compose together a *mis-en-abyme* of the play's social hierarchy.

Some of the mechanicals' metaphorical joinery may indeed lay bare "the joints and seams of theatrical spectacle",[36] and show up the "suspect joinery and the ending of this marriage play". But Quince as carpenter is above maladroit joinery. The play he directs may forfeit theatrical illusion through obsessive anxiety about frightening the ladies, but in Shakespeare's play it works effectively enough to satirize the aristocratic spectators. The attentiveness of the players contrasts tellingly with their audience's cruel wit. And the dimmer players' difficulties with mythological names can sometimes have satiric edge. Flute simply cannot get his tongue round "Ninus' tomb": his "Ninny's tomb", taken up by Bottom and repeatedly corrected by Quince, becomes a running joke. Similarly with "Shafalus" for Cephalus, and "Prorus" for Procris, both faithfully followed by Flute. Again, Flute substitutes "paramour" for "paragon" (4.2.112) and Bottom puts "Lemander" for Leander: their minds run on the courtiers' paramours and lemans ("lovers").

Nick or Nicholas is no longer thought to have been a type-name for a weaver;[37] but "Bottom" obviously refers to the spool or nucleus a weaver's thread is wound on.[38] The surname, obfuscated by scholarly errors, has been taken to crack a vulgar joke. But in Shakespeare's time "bottom" did not mean "posterior". Your arse could be your bum, butt, cheeks, croup, prat, rump, seat, stern, tail, toute, backside, buttocks, hurdies, fundament, or sitting-place; but before about 1794 it was not your bottom.[39] Was Bottom not translated to an arse-head, then? No; for "arse" was not yet rude and so never needed to be euphemized to "ass". That euphemism came after 1860, and mostly in the USA, for example in Morris Palmer Tilley's invaluable *A Dictionary of Proverbs in England in the Sixteenth and Seventeenth Centuries* (1950). Tilley was a prissy scholar who couldn't spell "arse" and consistently replaced it by "ass" in his influential dictionary.[40] His primness has seriously distorted modern understanding of Elizabethan literature.

So in the present instance we must give up (however reluctantly) the notion of Bottom with his arse where his head should be. Instead, his transformed "scalp" is to be explained in terms of Elizabethan proverbial usage whereby "ass-head" meant "fool".[41] In the play, Bottom applies this very insult to Snout: "You see an ass-head of your own, do you?"[42] And he uses "ass" again in the same sense when he awakes restored to ordinary humanity: "man is but an ass if he go about to expound his dream", for the dream has "no bottom".[43]

Besides occupational tags the mechanicals' names present further congruencies. "Snug", meaning "quiet, secret",[44] suits a player who has no surname, has no speaking part (he confesses he is "slow of study"), and who even roars mildly. The Elizabethan idiom "snug's the word" resembles our "mum's the word".[45] Starveling is emaciated for lack of nourishment, as was proverbial of tailors whose bills remained unpaid by courtiers like those who form his audience. And his forename Robin suits too: in Britain the robin is a small bird. Clearly a "thin man part for Sinklo".[46] "Flute" fits a youth with "a beard coming" and a high, unbroken voice.[47] Snout, as Levith suggests, may have a large nose. And, for a carpenter and bookholder holding all together, "Quince" is doubly apt: "quoin" could mean "keystone" as well as "wedge"(*OED* 2 d).

Other groupings

Groups of names need not always serve to evoke social backgrounds: they may be more directly thematic. A striking instance is *Twelfth Night*, where many of the names have calendrical relevance. Toby, Orsino, Feste, Cesario, Antonio, Fabian, Sebastian, Curio, Maria, Andrew, Antonio's nephew Titus, Valentine: all share the property of being named after a saint whose day falls in the festive season or immediately after. Thus, St Tobias is 2 November; St Ursinus 9 November; Sts John and Festus 21 December; St Caesaria 12 January; St Antony Abbot 17 January; Sts Fabian and Sebastian 20 January; Sts Cyrus and John 31 January; Purification of the Virgin Mary 2 February; St Andrew Corsini 4 February; St Titus 6 February; St Valentine 14 February. In view of the prominence of twins in the play, it may be worth mentioning that four of the saints' days are of paired saints (Festus, Fabian, Sebastian, Cyrus).

What are we to make of this? Should we conclude that Shakespeare used the liturgy as a source of names, as Henry Fielding used a subscription list and Henry James *The Times*? By no means. Saints' days are more relevant than that to Shakespeare's themes. They must have been important to him, because not all were easily accessible. True, Maria, Titus, Antony, Andrew, Valentine, Fabian, and Sebastian were familiar from the General Calendar of the Catholic church. But for lesser-known saints such as Festus Shakespeare must have gone to such compilations as the *Roman Martyrology* (from 1584), *Sanctorum Priscorum Patrum Vitae* (1551–60), or *De Probatis Sanctorum Historiis* (1570–5).[48]

Many of Shakespeare's plays were written for particular occasions.[49] Their actions were then not only generated by individual motivation but also emerged from associations with the appropriate festal customs or institutional conventions. Leslie Hotson and C. L. Barber have connected many topics in *Twelfth Night* with customs of the Elizabethan festive season, such as riddles; practical jokes; formal praise of folly; and saturnalian revelry.[50] "Fabian" was a type-name, almost a common noun, for a roisterer;[51] and "Feste" (from Latin *festus*) was a tag name meaning "festive, merry". There can be little doubt that *Twelfth Night* was meant for an Epiphany occasion.

The names' liturgical associations lend support to religious interpretations of the play such as Barbara Kiefer Lewalski's and Marion

Bodwell Smith's.[52] Twelfth Night marked the end of a festive season with several other feasts, notably the *Festum Stultorum* or Feast of Fools (26 December or sometimes New Year's Day). But Shakespeare's main focus is on Twelfth Night. The play's melancholy and its atmosphere of transience fit the end of festivity. The following day, St Distaff's Day, was supposed to mark a return to ordinary life:

> Then bid Christmas sport good-night.
> And next morrow, every one
> To his own vocation.[53]

Sir Toby's untimely revelling puts off this return, and so meets with sharp correction in the denouement. He is brought to his senses so completely that he censures Dick Surgeon as a "drunken rogue". Viola's assumed name Cesario is particularly appropriate to the time of transition to normality: St Caesaria's day, 12 January, in 1601 fell on Plough Monday (the first after Epiphany), when work was officially resumed.[54]

Epiphany celebrated a divine revelation in Jesus' humble birth. The First Lesson for Epiphany, Isaiah 60 ("Arise, be enlightened [...] ") has been related to Malvolio's incarceration. When he complains of his dark prison, Sir Topas (Feste) replies "Madman, thou errest. I say there is no darkness but ignorance, in which thou art more puzzled than the Egyptians in their fog".[55] Feste refers to the plague of palpable darkness in Exodus 10:21, then interpreted as a type of sin: imagery of illumination was ubiquitous in Christmas and Epiphany sermons.[56] Moreover, Feste repeatedly invokes Pythagoras ("Thou shalt hold th'opinion of Pythagoras ere I will allow of thy wits").[57] For, in the so-called Minor Epiphany, the journey of the Magi was interpreted as a spiritual pilgrimage, a *preparatio evangelii*. Syncretists speculated on an oral tradition whereby "Pythagoras had managed to reach the Jews and their doctrines in Egypt, and knowledge of their sacred mysteries."[58]

Names could also be grouped according to any of the traditional schemes of thought that still made up a large part of Elizabethan literature. These were often ridiculed: to Shakespeare himself they were *vieux jeu*, "right painted cloth"[59]—opportunities for finesses now no longer appreciated. An example is the Nine Worthies scheme that provides the culmination of *Love's Labour's Lost* (printed 1598). Properly, the Nine Worthies or Nobles consisted of three gentiles (Hector of Troy, Alexander the Great, and Julius Caesar); three Jews (Joshua, David, and Judas Maccabeus); and three Christians (King Arthur, Charle-magne, and Guy of Warwick or Godfrey of Bouillon).[60] This scheme was almost invariable, except that a modern name would occasionally be substituted in compliment to a local patron.[61]

As entertainment for the Princess of France, the schoolmaster Holofernes proposes a pageant of the Nine Worthies (5.1.119). Initially, the curate Sir Nathaniel is to represent Joshua; Don Armado, Judas Maccabeus; the page Moth, the infant Hercules; and the clown Cos-tard, Pompey the Great. Already this cast departs from the time-hon-oured scheme. Pompey has displaced his enemy Julius Caesar; Hercules has come from nowhere; and neither is Jewish. Moreover, Holofernes proposes to address the shortage of worthy actors by taking on three parts himself.

The pageant itself (5.2.518–660) is prefaced with witty repartee about arithmetic. Costard asks if the "three Worthies" should enter; whereupon the courtier Berowne makes difficulties: "are there but three?" Costard explains that "every one pursents [presents] three"; which leads to quibbles about whether "three times thrice is nine" (487–98). This repartee, amusing in itself, has the serious purpose of reminding the audience about the traditional scheme of 3 × 3 Wor-thies. Next, the King of Navarre is given a cast list, and announces that Don Armado will present Hector; Costard, Pompey; Sir Nathaniel, Alexander; Moth, Hercules; and Holofernes, Judas Maccabeus: "And if these four Worthies in their first show thrive, | These four will change habits, and present the other five" (523–4). This provokes further objec-tions by Berowne, who sees five Worthies, not four. By the time the much-delayed pageant begins, the audience is well primed to expect the familiar grouping of "three times thrice" Worthies (5.2.488, 491).

It never eventuates. The sequence actually presented—until the pageant breaks up amid accusations, counter-accusations, and a quarrel fomented by the courtiers—is Pompey; Alexander; Judas Maccabeus; Hercules. Despite careful discrimination between the loyal Judas Mac-cabeus and the treacherous Judas Iscariot, the provincials have forgot-ten the whole point of the Nine Worthies scheme. They begin with two out of three pagan Worthies (unless a trace of Julius Caesar remains in his enemy Pompey). But they never get to the three Christian Wor-thies before the pageant breaks up. Despite Costard's repeated boasts that he is "deemed worthy" to perform Pompion [Pumpkin] the Great, none of the actors represents a Christian champion.[62]

Mythological names

In Shakespeare's time, textual allusion was relatively new. The textual
stability made possible by print was too recent an achievement. Besides,
a familiar vernacular canon hardly yet existed.[63] Verbal allusion in popular drama was therefore scarcely practical, except for a few passages in
the Bible, or in the Latin classics read at school. Allusion may be said to
begin with names, especially the great names of romance. Chaucer's
extensive use of biblical, legendary, and mythological names had opened
up important avenues of possibility. And now Shakespeare's *oeuvre*
explored these further, exploiting the names' complex associations. In
The Merchant of Venice the names of Shylock's circle are all biblical and
Hebraic: Tubal, Chus, Leah, and Shylock himself, *Shalach* ("cormorant")
or *Sa'lah*. "Jessica" may seem invented but is probably from the genealogy in Genesis 11:29. In the King James version she is "Iscah", in the
Bishops' Bible (1568) "Jischa", and in Douay (1609) "Jescha".

Mythological names figure so extensively in *A Midsummer Night's
Dream* that it calls for particular attention.[64] How much does Shakespeare mean "Theseus" to mean? How much narrative do allusions to
Theseus necessarily imply? Peter Holland answers this boldly: "the
mere presence of Theseus in [*A*] *Midsummer Night's Dream* makes the
whole of the Theseus myth available".[65] Holland does not explain how
Shakespeare could have known "the whole of the Theseus myth". Yet
this is a strategic question with decisive bearing on Theseus' reputation, to say nothing of the chances of his marriage with Hippolyta.
According to Holland, the play

> leaves entirely open the question of what the [...] outcome of this marriage
> of Athenian and Amazon will be, describing and blessing the future without
> directly stating what might or rather *will* happen (*will* because it is already
> accomplished, already fixed unalterably in the Theseus mythography). In any
> version of the Theseus story Theseus does not stay with his Amazon bride.[66]

The outcome of the marriage is "entirely open"—except that it is
"already fixed unalterably" in the myth.

Holland does what he can to resolve what seems a stark contradiction:

> the triumphant ending of the play, the overwhelming celebration of marriage
> and blessing that the end of *A Midsummer Night's Dream* so fully evokes is set
> in relation to an individual for whom marriage-vows are transient devices for

satisfying lust and whose career of broken marriage is a pattern of male dominance and oppression carried to [an] extreme.

To amplify this, Holland blackens Theseus' character far beyond anything in Shakespeare, writing of "Theseus' promiscuity and his brutality towards his lovers"—on the authority of accusations made during
Oberon's quarrel with Titania.

In this scene (2.1.65–80) Titania casts up Oberon's amours with
Phillida[67] and with his "mistress" Hippolyta "the bouncing Ama-
zon". Oberon counters by accusing Titania of desire for Theseus. It
was she who occasioned Theseus' infidelity to Aegles, Ariadne, and
Antiopa. Holland says Theseus has no excuse for his betrayals; yet
Oberon specifically supplies one, and so exonerates him. The
betrayals were Titania's fault: did she not "lead him" away from
Perigouna and "make him [...] break his faith" with the others?
Titania dismisses these charges as "forgeries [lies] of jealousy" on
Oberon's part; but in Holland's view the accusations once made
cannot be dismissed. Instead, he exaggerates them: "the rapes and
seductions [...] are not the product of warlike conquest, as with
Hippolyta, won by the sword, but of something creeping, deceitful
and thief-like". This false Theseus is "substantially different from
the one seen in the play",[68] yet is somehow entailed by the use of
his name: "the name cannot choose whether to be allusive".

This position seems to me based on misconceptions about Renaissance mythology. To write of *the* myth of Theseus is misleading:
no single, universal myth exists, far less a deep structure or system
of global mythology. Myths are known from diverse narrative, visual, and other embodiments, all different and some mutually incompatible.[69] Lilio Gregorio Gyraldi (1479–1552), for example, collected
the names of hundreds of distinct Venuses in *De Diis Gentium Varia
et Multiplex Historia* (Basel, 1548). Certain myths tell how Theseus
killed the Cretan bull, sire of the Minotaur; certain others tell how,
with Ariadne's help, he killed the Minotaur itself. Some myths give
Theseus' father as Aegeus, others as Poseidon (who visited his
mother Aethra on the same night as Aegeus). Thus, in Seneca's *Hip-
polytus* Theseus' father is Poseidon : "Neptune great | My Syre".[70]
"Everywhere else," writes Holland striving for system, "Theseus'
father is named Egeus".[71] Not so. Many other poets and mythographers make Poseidon the father: notably Hyginus, and Ovid (for
whom Theseus is *Neptunius heros*).[72] These myths were so familiar

that Natale Conti (1520–82) calls them the traditional version: *ut traditum est in fabulis*.[73] In sum, Holland's portrait of a false, vicious Theseus is far from Shakespeare's. To authenticate it, irrelevant myths have to be enlisted, such as those about Theseus' son Hippolytus, who never figures in the play.[74]

Anthony Nuttall, similarly, regards Theseus as a "brutal womanizer".[75] He calls it "a mistake to suppose that the darker side of the mythical material has been excluded from the play". Nuttall writes of Shakespeare "retaining in his happy comedy reference to Theseus' rape of Perigenia (Perigoune)" and reminds us "Shakespeare's smiling duke has in fact ravished Perigenia".[76] He contrasts Theseus "the ravisher of Perigenia" with Berowne in *Love's Labour's Lost*, who is "intent upon the cognitive power of love, its tender sensitivity". But the idea of Theseus as ravisher is probably anachronistic. In Elizabethan English "ravish" and "rape" referred to abduction rather than violation.[77] Even North's Plutarch, a hostile witness, says only that Theseus "stale away Ariadne, Antiope, and Anaxo".[78] As for Perigouna, North (Nuttall's and Bate's supposed authority for "brutal rape" and "notorious rapist"[79]) tells how Theseus found her hiding, and "sware by his faith he would use her gently, and do her no hurt, nor displeasure at all. Upon which promise she came out of the bush, and lay with him".[80] Is this brutality? In modern terms such sex would be called consensual. Throughout, Nuttall's treatment of Theseus is unhistorical.[81]

In the opening scene of *A Midsummer Night's Dream*, Nuttall suggests, a properly sensitive Theseus would have said "But I will wed thee in another key, | And humbly sue to earn thy love at last". Shakespeare's Theseus, however, has recently been at war with Hippolyta and her Amazons: is he to apologize for defeating her? In the play he comes near to doing just that: "I woo'd thee with my sword, | And won thy love doing thee injuries" (1.1.16–17). Nuttall hears a "domineering tone" in Theseus' talk of pomp and triumph: others may hear a promise to make amends by giving her a big wedding. Shakespeare's Theseus is a soldierly leader: even his Master of Revels is Philostrate ("Lover of Armies").[82] Yet he is also generous and considerate to the "mechanicals" quite beyond expectation. Against Philostrate's advice he insists on hearing their play:

> I will hear that play;
> For never anything can be amiss
> When simpleness and duty tender it. . . .

> Love, therefore, and tongue-tied simplicity
> In least speak most, to my capacity.   (5.1.81–105)

Unlike the jeering Berowne, Theseus is an ideal patron. Yet Nuttall makes him out to be "ungenerous".

In some ways Laurie Maguire's portrayal of Theseus is even more adverse. To her, Theseus in Chaucer's Knight's Tale is "ambiguously presented",[83] although even Holland concedes that "Chaucer suppresses this [vicious] Theseus in the Knight's Tale".[84] Since The Knight's Tale makes Theseus a protector of women—not to say a Boethian sage—Maguire turns instead to Chaucer's shorter poems, where Theseus is invariably "traitorous, pitiless and false". (She passes over *Anelida and Arcite*, which is wholly favourable to Theseus.) It makes most sense, however, to focus on The Knight's Tale, which is a "clearly defined adequate narrative source" of *A Midsummer Night's Dream*.[85]

Maguire brings in Chaucer's minor poems to make a case against Theseus. Hoping to cite Shakespeare for the prosecution, she accepts Oberon's lies despite Titania's denials, and ignores the charge against Hippolyta that she is Oberon's mistress. Despite Shakespeare's casting doubt on Hippolyta's virtue, all these critics fault Theseus instead.

What associations did "Theseus" call up in the early modern period? Some idea of this can be arrived at from seventeenth-century reference books such as Paul Aler's *Gradus ad Parnassum*.[86] Aler's recommended epithets for Theseus are *fortis, superbus, ferox, bellator, perfidus, peijurus, inclytus, horridus, fidus, profugus, crudelis, armiger, ingratus* (bold, proud, fierce, warlike, false, forsworn, renowned, severe, trustworthy, fugitive, cruel, unpleasant, unacceptable). *Perfidus* yet *fidus*: a complex reputation, then. But nothing about brutality.

How much fire are we to find in Oberon's smoky lies? Perhaps only that Theseus had been sexually active in the past.[87] Mythological and fairy modes were often resorted to by Elizabethan poets when touching on dangerous court matters, so that Shakespeare may be glancing at the perennial problem of political leaders with uninhibited sex lives. Even so, Oberon promises to bless Hippolyta's bride-bed so that "the issue there create | Ever shall be fortunate". Maguire thinks this offset by the dramatic irony of Hippolytus' violent end. But Hippolytus was the son not of Theseus and Hippolyta but of Theseus and Antiope. And that is a different myth altogether.

Short of Greek names for *A Midsummer Night's Dream*, Shakespeare
took several from North's Plutarch, already his source for several myths
of Theseus. Plutarch has a Life of Demetrius, who "only of all the kings
in his time, was most detected with this vice of lechery".[88] This may
find reflection in the accusations of Lysander (the subject of another of
Plutarch's *Lives*): "Demetrius [...] that vile name" and "spotted and
inconstant man".[89] Theseus' reply to the last speech ("I must confess
that I have heard so much") suggests Demetrius' lechery is notorious,
just as Plutarch reported it to be.

Helena and Hermia have equally thematic names. "Hermia", from
Hermes, is almost a charactonym: she early shows the rhetorical skill
one might expect from a child of the eloquent god. Helena is intrigu-
ingly referred to as the daughter of Nedar—an anagram of Arden,
Shakespeare's mother's name.[90]

Helen, Ἑλένη, had ominous associations for the ancients, notably the
tragedians:[91] "etymology" made it imply destruction. In *Agamemnon*
Aeschylus calls her ἐλέναυς, *helenaus* ("ship-destroying"), inverted by
Christopher Marlowe in "the face that launch'd a thousand ships".[92] In
homiletic mode, "Helen" could even be connected with "hell", an
association remembered in George Peele's *Edward I* 1097: "Hell in thy
name, but heaven is in thy looks".[93] For Florio, Helena was "the name
of a cursed, dreadfull, and threatening Meteor".[94] Indeed, "Helen" has
such bad associations in the sixteenth century as to be, in Maguire's
view, an "onomastic straitjacket from which Shakespeare tries to liber-
ate his Helens".[95] There is much in this. Both Maguire and D'Orsay
Pearson collect many unfavourable appearances of Helen in English
writers.[96] And the pedagogic view was no different: Aler's recommended epithets for Helen were *formosa, decora, venusta, adultera, infamis,
iniqua, perfida, lasciva, impudica, rapta, superba, exitiosa, perniciosa* ("beautiful, charming, attractive, adulterous, ill-famed, discontented, false, unin-
hibited, shameless, abducted, proud, fatal, destructive").

But less ominous meanings were possible. Some medieval authors
even exonerated Helen as not to be blamed for man's wickedness.[97]
Ἑλένη, *Helene* meant "torch", a common emblem for love or passion;[98] which may contribute to the name's associations here. In *A
Midsummer Night's Dream* Helena experiences passion more than once.
First she suffers the passion of unreturned love, then (after Robin's
ministrations) she provokes unreturned love in others. As an object of
compassion she recalls Camden's derivation of "Helen" from Ἐλεεινή,

Eleeine ("pitiful").[99] Shakespeare was always ready to depart from a name's prevailing interpretation.

Deploying a mythological name called for nice judgement. When Philostrate lists possible entertainments for Theseus' approval—much as the Elizabethan Master of Revels did—the first item is "The battle with the Centaurs, to be sung | By an Athenian eunuch to the harp". The reference is to the battle of Lapiths and Centaurs at the wedding of Theseus' friend Perithous the Lapith king, a battle Theseus himself had fought in. But he now rejects the recitation: "We'll none of that; that have I told my love | In glory of my kinsman Hercules". Doubtless he has boasted about his family connection with the great Hercules more than once, and fears Hippolyta would be bored to hear the story yet again.[100] This plausible addition to a Theseus myth is as sophisticated as any by Apollonius Rhodius.

Elsewhere Shakespeare introduces fleeting hints of motifs from the Theseus cycle, naturalizing and localizing them. The Minotaur's labyrinth is echoed in the "nine-men's-morris [...] fill'd up with mud", and echoed again in the winding tracks of the forest around Athens. And perhaps, as Nuttall and others have suggested, the Minotaur itself is recalled in Bottom's metamorphosis to ass-man.

Names in tragedy

The tragedies and history plays gave Shakespeare less freedom to invent names. As Aristotle put it in *Poetics* 9.6, "tragedians keep to actual, historical names" (γενομένων ὀνομάτων). Following ancient tragedy Shakespeare names protagonists and their famous families according to the *mythos* or history. Thus, in the Henry IV cycle, the principal names come from Holinshed's *Historie of England*, as does the characterization of Hotspur as an impetuous, honour-seeking individual. His age is reduced, however, perhaps to encourage direct contrast with Prince Hal.[101] *King Lear* is like the other tragedies, in that "Lear", "Goneril", "Regan", and "Cordelia" all come from historical sources—in this case Geoffrey of Monmouth's *Historia Regum Britanniae*, Holinshed's *Historie*, the historians handed down in Spenser's *The Faerie Queene*, and the anonymous *The True Chronicle Historie of King Leir* (1605).[102] With the closely interwoven plot of Gloucester, Edgar, and Edmund, Shakespeare had more freedom. He drew much

of its narrative from *The Mirror for Magistrates* (1574) and Sidney's
Arcadia (1590), replacing Latinate names (Leonatus, Plexirtus) by
English (Edgar, Edmund). Or else he used bare titles, as with the
Duke of Cornwall (formerly Coridagus) and the King of France
(formerly Aganippus). A remarkable moment of problematic titling
occurs in *Hamlet* at 1.4.44–5, where the prince hesitates over the
right form of address to use: "I'll call thee Hamlet, | King, father,
royal Dane", hoping to induce the ghost to speak.[103]

Although names in the tragedies were largely determined, history
or legend sometimes left room for nuances. As we have seen, Camden
explains the Old English derivation of "Edgar".[104] But there is more to
naming than etymology. From Holinshed Shakespeare would know of
the tenth-century King Edgar's imperial and maritime aspirations.[105]
Again, when Camden comments on "Edmund" as auspicious (Saxon
Eadmund, "Happy, or Blessed Peace") he adds "some translate *Mund* by
Mouth". This may suggest that whereas the words of Edmund's mouth
are peaceful, his nature is anything but. Such ironies are not infrequent
in Shakespeare's naming.

Several characters in the tragedies and history plays are identified
by title only. Even Cleopatra is addressed as "great Egypt", "royal
Egypt", and with the strangely intimate formality of "I am dying,
Egypt". A title, visually confirmed by costume and heraldic accoutre-
ments, was then sufficient identification. (Internal evidence suggests
that crests were used for this purpose in the history plays.[106]) The historical associations of a title would convey almost as much as the full
name. Thus, in the sources of *King Lear* the Duke of Albany (ancient
Scotland) is "Maglaunus" (Geoffrey of Monmouth), "Maglanus"
(Holinshed), and "Maglan" (Spenser); whereas Shakespeare avoids
burdening audiences with the unnecessary personal name. The title of
Albany had passed from Darnley to King James himself; perhaps for
this reason he turns out well.[107] The Earl of Kent is "banish'd Kent",
"good Kent", or simply "Kent"—in contrast to "Perillus" in *King Leir*.
He is simple, honest, and free from excessive ambition: the last a quality appropriate perhaps for a county where succession was by gavel-
kind, not primogeniture. As for the kings, they have representative
characters, the King of France being relatively poor and the Duke of
Burgundy rich, like their domains.

The minor figures in *King Lear* have tag names or none at all. Thus
"Oswald" is explained by Camden as derived from Old English

"House-ruler" or "Steward". The unnamed herald, fool, doctor, and gentleman would be identified by tabard, motley, or other costume. "Curan", long a puzzle, may not name a character at all, but an actor.

The names in *Hamlet* are as little appreciated as those in any of Shakespeare's tragedies.[108] "Hamlet" and "Gertrude" are from the sources, direct or indirect: Saxo Grammaticus, François Belleforest, and a lost Hamlet play. Already Saxo's Amleth married Gerutha, daughter of the King of Denmark. Shakespeare probably knew nothing about the Old Norse meaning of "Amleth" ("dim-witted"). But Camden's derivation of *Gertrud* from German "All True, and Amiable" may give an idea of how her name would initially have been understood.[109]

Claudius, named only in his first entry-direction and speech-heading, replaces Saxo's and Belleforest's "Feng" and alludes to a Roman emperor closely associated with corruption. Erasmus refers to Claudius in *Institutio Principis Christiani* (1515) as a typical bad ruler. The Roman Claudius married his niece Julia Agrippina, who (as Harold Jenkins notes) poisoned him and was put to death by Nero (3.2.384–5). For Andrew Fitzmaurice, too, the parallel with Tacitus' account of Claudius is "unmistakable".[110] Polonius, another invented name, is an obvious tag, *Polonia* being Latin for Poland. It may also be a key name, referring to the Polish ambassador rebuked by Queen Elizabeth in 1597; or to the Polish statesman Wawrzyniec Goślicki (Laurentius Grimalius Goslicius); or to the loquacious counsellor in Goslicius' *De Optimo Senatore*, recently translated as *The Counsellor* (1598); or to Henrik Ramel (Ramelius), a Danish diplomat who headed an embassy to England.[111]

Several names seem designed to suggest a Danish setting. Rosencrantz and Guildenstern bear the names of influential Danish families: at the coronation of Christian IV (King James' brother-in-law) a tenth of the 160 nobles in a procession bore one or another of the two names.[112] Similarly with the ambassadors to Norway (1.2.34): "Voltemand" is a corruption of "Valdemar", a name of Danish kings; and "Cornelius" was the name of Dutch incomers settled in Denmark.[113] Laertes (Q1 "Leartes"), invented from Odysseus' father, seems to Jenkins an odd choice for the son of a famous father. But Laertes is after all the son of the wily and sententious Polonius: the association with *polytropos* Odysseus is there, even if the roles are reversed. Laertes' sister Ophelia also has a Greek name, generally taken as from ὠφέλεια (*opheleia*, "succour")—hence

Ruskin's "Ministering Angel". But how are "succour" or "ministering angel" relevant to the themes of *Hamlet*?[114] It seems more likely that "Ophelia" is from ὀφείλω, *opheilo* ("owe") and ὀφείλεια, *opheileia* ("indebtedness"), a common Greek word. This is just what Ophelia represents to Hamlet: an obligation he rejects. Hamlet denies it and precipitates her suicide.[115]

"Horatio" was a fairly common name in contemporary drama, probably from its use for a loyal friend in *The Spanish Tragedy* (1587). Levith relates it to the Latin "Horatius", citing *Hamlet* 5.2.341, "more an antique Roman than a Dane". Camden suggests ὅρατος, *horatos* ("of good eyesight").[116] More simply, ὁρατής, *horates* means "beholder", which exactly describes Horatio's role. Hamlet calls on him to witness the Ghost, and again to witness Claudius' reaction to the Gonzago play: "observe my uncle" (3.2.80). In fact, Horatio is a *beschouwer* figure: a viewer whose looking directs our own.[117]

The names of the minor characters in *Hamlet* are mostly labels, like the gravedigger, called Delver at 5.1.14. The agent sent by Polonius to spy on Laertes is "Reynaldo", a variant of "Reynard", a quasi-proper name given to a fox.[118] Jenkins compares Spenser's *Mother Hubbard's Tale* 917–8, "a Reynold". And Fortinbras, replacing Saxo's Coller, is French, *fort-en-bras* ("Strong arm").[119] But "Osric" is more puzzling. It was Anglo-Saxon, not Danish, and had been used in the recent plays *A Knack to Know a Knave* (1594) and *Osric* (1597).[120] Jenkins asks why Shakespeare should give such a prominent name to "one who inspires contempt". The answer may lie in the Q2 spelling "Ostricke", which is close to "ostrich", a word then subject to a great many spellings and misspellings. The ostrich was the subject of a familiar emblem, based on its inability to fly: Geoffrey Whitney's *Nil penna, sed usus* ("Not the quill, but its use") with the epigram "As the ostrich spreads its wings but rarely flies, so the hypocrite makes great show of his religion but merely dissembles." P. S.'s ostrich "makes great ostentation with its feathers and wings"; and George Wither applies it to "men of high birth who do nothing of worth".[121] In short, "Osric" is a tag name for an aristocrat given to idle display.

Spenser realized the manifold possibilities of naming; but it was Shakespeare who made name after name icons of the great works they dominate. Hamlet, Cleopatra, Othello, and scores of others: no other English writer save perhaps Dickens has so many evocative names that have become current in the popular imagination.

Notes

1. Ruskin, *Munera Pulveris* ch. 5: Ruskin 1902–12: 17.257–8.
2. Arnold 1968: 47. Cf. Frye 1957: 9–10, "it is Arnold who is the provincial".
3. Letter to Jane Martha Arnold Forster, 31 March 1856: Arnold 1996: 336.
4. Verstegan, *A restitution of decayed intelligence*, 1605; Camden, *Remains concerning Britain*, 1605, Camden 1984; John Florio, *Queen Anna's new world of words*, 1611, Florio 1968.
5. Jonson 1925–52: 8.391, 11.145; see Jones 1977: 4 *et passim*.
6. Drayton, *Poly-Olbion* (1612) 1.479, Drayton 1931–41: 4.13.
7. See Levith 1978: 53.
8. F. N. Lees, cit. Levith 1978: 53.
9. Where Thorello corresponds to the Kitely of the 1616 version.
10. *MWW* 1.1.124; 1.4.33; see Levin 1976: 59. "Brook" was changed to "Broome" in the Folio to avoid offending Lord Cobham; see Levith 1978: 22–3.
11. Levin 1976: 59; Levith 1978: 30.
12. Camden 1984: 58.
13. Cf. Cave 1988: 280.
14. Cf. Levith 1978: 21, 24.
15. See Pitcher 1993: 1–16; Maguire 2007: 35.
16. *OED*, *borachio*, citing Florio on *boraccia*, "a boracho or bottle made of a goates skin such as they use in Spaine." Florio 1611 also has *boracchiare*, "to gluttonize", comparing *crapulare*, "to surfet or commit excesse in meate and drinke".
17. See Farmer and Henley; *OED* s.v. *toby* sb.[2].
18. Among extensive literature on Shakespeare's names may be mentioned Stokes 1970; Levin 1976; Levith 1978; Calderwood 1979; Barton 1990; Pitcher 1993; Spevack 1993; Davis and Frankforter 1995; Fleissner 2001; Litt 2001; Lucking 2007; and Maguire 2007.
19. Levith 1978: 19.
20. Davis and Frankforter 2004: 391.
21. See Levin 1976: 59–61, 72.
22. See Levin 1976: 60; Levith 1978: 93 citing Leslie Hotson.
23. Levin 1976: 61. On names in *Cymbeline*, see Pitcher 1993.
24. *OED* 2, 1603 quotation: "a young beardlesse Ganymede whome he loved". On Ganymede as a type-name, see Saslow 1986.
25. Gurr 2009: Index, s.v. *Disguise*.
26. See Davis and Frankforter 2004: 394.
27. See Barton 1990: 103.
28. See *OLD* s.v. *Peto* 2, 3, 7.
29. 4.4.70–4; see Levith 1978: 19, 21.
30. Cf. Levith 1978: 77: "Bottom's gang are named for their trades".
31. *OED*, s.v. *Flute* 2.
32. See *OED*, s.v. *Good* A2 and C; Abbott 1883: 26; Onions 1986: 119.
33. See *OED*, s.v. *Bellows* 1 b, quotation of 1566 (an organ lacking a piece of lead belonging to the bellows). Both trades are represented in Jonson's *Pan's Anniversarie* (1620, ptd 1641).
34. Salzmann 1952: 32, 259.
35. Parker 1996: 86.
36. Parker 1996: 94.
37. See Shakespeare 1994: 147.
38. Questioned by Stroup 1978: 79–82 but reasserted by Willson 1979: 407–8.
39. See *HTOED* s.v. *Buttock(s)*. The earliest example of "ass" in this sense is 1860. See Montagu 1967: 316.

40. E.g. Tilley 1950: A 387, "You would lose your Ass if it were loose".
41. See Tilley 1950: A 388, "An asshead of your own"; F 519, A fool's head of your own".
    See *OED*, s.v. *Ass-head*, examples from 1550; cf. Tilley 1950: A 373–9, in all of which
    "ass" means "numbskull"; Tilley A 348 (As dull as an Ass); Whiting 1968: A 218 (As dull
    as an Ass); Carroll 1954: 75, 79; Salisbury 1994: 131, 153–4.
42. 3.1.111; cf. 114, "make an ass of me".
43. 4.1.203–12, from 1 Cor. 2: 9–10 (Geneva version).
44. Cf. *OED* 6, 7, not attested however before 1687.
45. *OED* 7, not attested however before 1700.
46. Shakespeare 1994: lxxxii citing Gaw 1926.
47. Harold Brooks takes the "fluty tones" to indicate sexual defectiveness; see Shakespeare
    1979: 22.
48. Most likely to Baronius' scholarly and controversial *Annales Ecclesiastici* (1588–1607) or
    his edition of *Martyrologium Romanum* (1586, 1589). Knowledge of Baronius need not
    have had any recusant implication. For Sts Titus, Caesaria, Cyrus, Festus, and Ursinus
    see the Bollandists' great collection, Bollandus and Henschenius 1643–1867: 1.163;
    1.729; 2.769; 2.1080. For Tobias and Ursinus, see Millard 1989. Both Fabian and Val-
    entine were rare names in the 16C; see *ODECN*: xxix. On the aptness of the names
    Shakespeare gives to Franciscans, see Salter 2004.
49. See Nosworthy 1965; Hassel 1979.
50. See Hotson 1954; Barber 1959.
51. *OED*, s.v. *Fabian* B 1. From the Fabian priests of Pan at the Lupercalia (15
    February).
52. See Lewalski 1965; Smith 1966.
53. Robert Herrick, "Saint Distaffs day, or the morrow after Twelfth Day", Herrick 1963:
    416.
54. See Blackburn 1999: 601–2.
55. 4.2.43–5. See Hassel 1979; Lewalski 1965: 168–81, esp. 176–7; Smith 1966: 112.
56. E.g. Lancelot Andrewes' Christmas sermon, 1622, Andrewes 1967: 101.
57. *12 N* 4.2.58–60.
58. So Pico della Mirandola; see Walker 1972: 50.
59. *AYLI* 3.2.275. See Carroll 1976: 233–4.
60. *OED*, s.v. *Worthy* C. 1. c. For the scheme's history, see Carroll 1976: 229–41.
61. See Carroll 1976: 233.
62. Carroll 1976: 236 misses the joke: "I have been unable to find any other instance in
    which Hercules is one of the Nine Worthies".
63. See Fowler 1994: 3–6.
64. E.g. Shakespeare 1994; Maguire 2007; Nuttall 2007: 23, 121–6, *et passim*.
65. Shakespeare 1994: 151.
66. Shakespeare 1994: 143.
67. Phillida may recall the Phyllis betrayed by Demophon, a son of Theseus, in Ovid,
    Heroides 2.
68. Holland, Shakespeare 1994: 144.
69. On this point see Morales 2007: 23 *et passim*.
70. Tr. John Studley, 1581.
71. Holland, Shakespeare 1994: 145.
72. Ovid, *Metamorphoses* 9.1; cf. Hyginus, *Fabulae* ch. 37.
73. *Mythologiae* 7.9, Conti 1979: 386.
74. Holland regards Hippolyta as a "backformation" from Hippolytus; cf. Maguire
    2007: 79.
75. Nuttall 1994: 121, 128.
76. Nuttall 1994: 23, 122.

77. *OED*, s.v. *Ravish* 1a, 2a, 4b. Maguire 2007: 91 sees that "the categories of rape, abduction,and consensual adulterous sex were not distinct" in Renaissance culture. On the complex semiotics of rape, see Donaldson 1982; Ritscher 2009; Morales 2007: 85–6 and ch. 6 *passim*.

78. Bullough 1966–75: 1.388. On Shakespeare's closeness to Plutarch, see now Gillespie 2011: ch. 4.

79. Bate 1993: 136–7.

80. Plutarch 1898–9: 1.42. Plutarch puts it more succinctly but just as favourably: "When Theseus called upon her and promised he would take care of her honourably and do her no wrong (πίστιν διδόντος ὡς ἐπιμελήσεται καλῶς αὐτῆς καὶ οὐδὲν ἀδικήσει) she came out and had sexual intercourse with Theseus, and bore him Melanippus (τῷ μὲν Θησεῖ συγγενομένη Μελάνιππον ἔτεκε), and afterwards lived with Deioneus [...] to whom Theseus gave her" (*Theseus* 1.8).

81. Cf. the critique of Nuttall's approach in Wootton 2008: 10–11.

82. "Philostrate" comes from The Knight's Tale, where it is Arcite's assumed name.

83. Maguire 2007: 82.

84. Holland, in Shakespeare 1994: 144.

85. Holland, in Shakespeare 1994: 139.

86. This immensely popular word list by "one of the Society of Jesus" went through at least twelve editions from 1680 to 1749, and another nineteen editions of later revisions by Pedro de Ville, Thomas Morell, and others up to 1832; see Stray 2010, minimizing Aler's role in the early development of the *Gradus*. Poole 1677: 197 also gives a mixed view of Theseus: "valiant, magnanimous, couragious, cruel, victorious, undaunted, valorous, attemptive, perjured, perfidious, disloyal, faith-breaking, faithless, unfaithful, ingrateful".

87. Cf. Gillespie 2004: 397 on Shakespeare's use of Ovidian materials: "With Theseus and Hippolyta... Shakespeare avoids the considerable body of negative associations surrounding the figures, or else presents the characters as having been educated out of such attitudes towards love".

88. Plutarch 1898–9: 8.277; cf. 8.289 on Demetrius' whores and abominable practices.

89. *MND* 2.2.105–6; 1.1.110.

90. *MND* 1.1.107, 4.1.130. See Holland, in Shakespeare 1994: 138–9; Hawkes 1992: 11–13, 15, 27.

91. See *OCD*.

92. *Agamemnon* 66, "ship-destroying, man-destroying, city-destroying; *Doctor Faustus* 12.81. Cf. Maguire 2007: 32, 77.

93. Maguire 2007: 77 citing Roberts 1991: 145–7.

94. Cf. *OLD*: "a form of St Elmo's fire"; cf. Pliny, *Nat. Hist.* 2.101, "[stellam] diram illam ac minacem appellatamque Helenam".

95. Maguire 2007: 119; Maguire 2009 *passim*.

96. Maguire 2007: ch. 3; Maguire 2009: ch. 4; Pearson 1974: 276–98.

97. See, e.g., Bliss 2008: 70. On the rehabilitation of Helen, see also Maguire 2009: 92, and cf. my review in *TLS* (6 June, 2008) 22.

98. See Diehl 1986: 208–9 citing Philip Ayres, Otto van Veen, and Claudius Paradin from among many instances; cf. Chapman, *Bussy D'Ambois* 5.4.209–10.

99. Camden 1984: 84.

100. Hercules was his cousin on the mother's side; see Plutarch 1898–9: 8.40.

101. See Stokes 1970: 250. The familiar form "Hal" is dropped on Prince Henry's succession, except by Falstaff, who presumes on previous intimacy; see Maguire 2007: 29–30.

102. See Bullough 1966–75: 7.269–308; Muir 1977: 196–208. The form "Cordelia" is from *FQ* 2.10.29. On possible puns with *cor*, "heart", however, see Musgrove 1956, Fleissner 2001: 43–5.

103. See Jenkins, Shakespeare 1982: 211–12; cf. *Paradise Lost* 7.1–2: "Descend from heav'n Urania, by that name | If rightly thou art called", using a convention of ancient hymns.
104. Camden 1984: 63.
105. See Pugh 2010: 127 on King Edgar's imperial rule. On the maritime aspect, see Pepys 1970–83: 6.81.
106. E.g. *2 Henry VI* 5.1.202–4 (the wrong crest for Nevil, however; see Barron 1916: 2.90.
107. Cf. Davis and Frankforter 1995: 10.
108. Despite Jenkins' Herculean efforts.
109. Camden 1984: 84. See p. xxi for his Continental sources, potentially accessible to Shakespeare.
110. Fitzmaurice 2009: 145; cf. Bullough 1966–75: 7.34–6.
111. See Jenkins, Shakespeare 1982: 421–2 on these possibilities and on the change of name to *Corambis* in Q1.
112. See Jenkins, Shakespeare 1982: 422.
113. See Jenkins, Shakespeare 1982: 163.
114. Jenkins sees the difficulty, and suggests confusion with Ἀφέλεια ("Simplicity", "Innocence"), which, however, is not much better.
115. Cf. 3.2.187–8, "Most necessary 'tis that we forget | To pay ourselves what to ourselves is debt".
116. Camden 1984: 69.
117. On this visual art convention, see Melion 1991: 8–10; Fowler 2003: 76, 210; Fowler 2010: 343.
118. See *OED*, s.v. *Reynard*.
119. On Shakespeare's multilingual puns, see Levin 1976: 65–8.
120. Also in Thomas Heywood's *Marshal Osric* (1602); see Gurr 2009: 104, 227.
121. Whitney (1586) 1969: 51; P. S. 1591: 55; Wither 1635: 36. See Diehl 1986: 157.

6

Milton's Changing Names

On one count, Milton performs 2,662 acts of naming in *Paradise Lost*.[1] Larry Isitt's catalogue may be too generously inclusive— counting place names and circumlocutions as well as personal names— but it certainly reveals a major concern of the poem.[2] During Milton's lifetime naming was a significant focus of philosophical and scientific thought.[3] It figured in the various artificial languages of the time, in the "true names" of Adamic discourse, and in natural history. The assigning and classifying of terms for vast numbers of newly discovered species was a major enterprise that engrossed the efforts of Caspar Bauhin (1560–1624), John Ray (1627–1705), and many others. *Paradise Lost* reflects this in several ways, most obviously in Adam and Eve's naming of animals and plants.[4] Important though they are, such acts are not our present concern. They gave rise to common nouns, not proper names. So far as personal names go, Milton's naming is simpler than Spenser's or Shakespeare's. In *Paradise Lost* Milton represents only very few aspects of naming. He always focuses on the Fall and the changes it led to. Besides, he opts to use biblical names as much as possible, believing the Bible to be in some sense literally true.

Milton's sources

The considerations weighing with Milton in naming the angels of *Paradise Lost* are illuminated by comparison with those of Cowley in his contemporary epic *Davideis* (1668). In his notes to book 1, Cowley explains that the Book of Tobias speaks of Seven Angels superior to all the rest; and this has been constantly believed according to the letter, by the ancient Jews and Christians. He cites Clement of Alexandria on "the Seven that have the greatest power, the First-born Angels". Among Cowley's chief texts are Tobit 12: 15 ("I am Raphael, one of the Seven holy Angels, which…go in and out before the glory of the Holy one") and Daniel 10: 13 ("Lo Michael, one of the chief Princes came to help me"). On the question of hierarchy, he reasons

that some Angels were under the command of others, may be collected out of Zecharius 2: 3 where one Angel commands another "Run, speak to this young man etc." and out of Rev. 12: 7, where Michael and his Angels fought with the Dragon and his Angels. [...] Three names of these seven the Scripture affords, Michael, Gabriel, and Raphael; but for the other four, Oriphiel, Zachariel, Samael, and Anael, let the Authours of them answer, as likewise for their presiding over the *Seven Planets*.[5]

Cowley notes that in Luke 1: 19 "Gabriel is called [...] he that stands before the face of God." On *Davideis* book 2, Cowley explains "Gabriel" as signifying "The Power of God":

I have seen in some Magical Books, where they give barbarous names to the Guardian Angels of great persons, as that of Mathattron to the Angel of Moses, that they assign one Cerviel to David, and this Gabriel to Joseph, Joshua and Daniel. But I rather use this than that Diabolical Name (for aught I know) of an Angel, which the Scripture makes no mention of. Especially because Gabriel is employed particularly in things that belong to the manifestation of Christ, as to the Prophet Daniel, Zacharia, and to Mary. The Rabbis account Michael the Minister of God's Justice, and Gabriel of his Mercies, and they call the former Fire, and the latter Water.[6]

Cowley prefers to rely on the Bible where he can, but, failing this, on Rabbinic tradition and "the Magical Books". He is anxious, we should note, in case he uses a "diabolical" name not in Scripture.

Milton, like Cowley, drew most of his angel names from the Hebrew Bible or the Apocrypha. As we saw in chapter 1, the meanings of these names were mostly common knowledge, since a standard feature of Latin Bibles was an alphabetic list of personal names glossing their Hebrew meanings. This "Interpretation of Hebrew Names", begun as a separate work, later took its place as an appendix to the Latin Bible and for centuries was a regular feature.[7] After the Reformation, the Geneva version (often used by Milton) similarly included "A Brief Table of the Interpretation of the propre [sic] names [...] chiefly found in the olde Testament [...]". In this glossary Milton may have found several angel names, for example Michael ("who is like God?" 1 Chron. 7: 3), Gabriel ("man of God, strength of God", Dan. 8: 16), and Uriel ("light or fire of God", 2 Chron. 13: 2).

Naming of angels was not to be lightly undertaken. In 745 the Council of Rome recognized only Michael, Gabriel, and Raphael as authentic angel names. Indeed, Zacharias the then Pope explicitly prohibited names not in the Bible to be used for angels.[8] Such prohibitions were meant to restrain speculative multiplication of angels by the cabbalists, who took any mention of a spiritual work or office in the Bible as an occasion for generating by anagram yet another angel name. On the authority of these occultists, Henricus Cornelius Agrippa (1486–1535) included dozens of angels in his magical system. He notices that good angels' names usually end in *el, on, jah*, or *jod* (signifying the divine name). The only angels named as such in the Old Testament are glossed accordingly: GabriEL (Dan. 8: 16, "a man of God" or "the strength of God"), RaphaEL (Tob. 3: 17, 5: 4, "healing of God"), and MichaEL (Dan. 10: 13–21, 12: 1, "who is like God?").

The four Archangels Michael, Gabriel, Raphael, and Uriel traditionally ruled the four corners of the world. But Milton, who applies hierarchic titles elusively, calls only Michael, Raphael, and Uriel Archangels—and Satan.[9] Gabriel, although "Chief of the angelic guards" (4.550) is not titled Archangel. "Archangel" sometimes seems to imply mission or office, sometimes a leading role.[10] Thus Uriel "rules in the power of the meridian sun".[11] Milton accepts the common pre-eminence of four chief angels, and the preference for biblical names. But he needed far more than four Archangels or even seven "eyes of the Lord" (Rev. 1: 4). So for minor characters he quarried the cabbalists and occultists, still using biblical names, but names of men, not angels. The faithful Abdiel, although biblical, occurs there only in human genealogies (1 Chronicles) and in the form "Abdeél, servant of God" (Jeremiah 36: 26).[12] He occurs as an angel, however, in *The Book of the Angel Raziel*.[13] Even Uriel ("Light or Fire of God"), the Archangel of 2 Esdras 4, is also Uriel of Gibea, father of Michaiah in 2 Chron. 13: 2. Such angel names of human origin are in effect charactonyms. Milton's wordplays on such etymological meanings have been commented on at least since Thomas Newton (1704–82). The more recent notion that Milton was a thorough-going Cratylist stems from misunderstanding of Plato's dialogue. And Herbert Marks rightly characterizes as "naïve" the accusation that Milton was an "essentialist". Marks'

magisterial note on the history of this false idea traces the various attitudes to it of Arnold Williams, Christopher Ricks, Stanley Fish, and
William Kerrigan.[14]

Milton names most of the good angels in this way, and some of the
rebels too. Abdiel overthrows "Ariel and Arioc, and the violence | Of
Ramiel" (*PL* 6.371–2, all biblical or from the Apocrypha). Here Ariel
("Lion of God" or "Divine light") comes from the pseudepigraphical
Book of Enoch or from Esdras. But other devils are named differently.
Some are called after heathen gods such as the Syrian Beelzebub
("Lord of the flies"). This "fallen Cherub" is discovered weltering by
Satan's side, and next him also in power: "Long after known in Pales-
tine, and named | Beelzebub" (*PL* 1.78–81). He is "prince of the dev-
ils" (Matt. 12: 24). Milton may here allude to St Jerome's allegorization
of Beelzebub as "Pertinacity". Thus, Milton's Beelzebub "*never ceases* to
infect the human race [...], to lay now this snare, now that for our
destruction".[15] Other devils bear overtly allegorical names. Mammon
(*PL* 1.678–9, 2.228, 291) comes from the New Testament, where his
name is an Aramaic abstract noun, "Wealth": "Ye cannot serve God
and Mammon" (Matt. 6: 24, Luke 16: 13). In John 12: 31 Mammon is
"prince of this world". In the Middle Ages Mammon was a Syrian
deity, prince of the ninth order of devils;[16] but Milton's devil owes
more to Spenser's Mammon in *The Faerie Queene* 2.7. From various
sources Milton's Satan collects a band of twelve parodic devil-disciples:
Moloch, Chemos, Baal, Ashtaroth, Astarte, Thammuz, Dagon, Rim-
mon, Osiris, Isis, Horus, and Belial (*PL* 1.392–490). The minor devils,
being identified with the pagan gods of classical antiquity, have drawn
the latter with them down to hell.

Old and new names

Milton learned from *The Faerie Queene* how naming might be made
thematic. He took over from Spenser the device of doubled names
(Fidessa, Duessa) as well as the idea of true and false genealogies. For
example, a false genealogy, immediately corrected, is advanced in *PL*
1.508–10:

> The Ionian gods, of Javan's issue held
> Gods, yet confessed later than Heaven and Earth
> Their boasted parents...

This self-deluding inconsistency recalls those that undercut Spenser's Night and Mutability. But Milton the historical poet applies the device of paired names on a more diachronic plan. He imagines the Fall as deforming the rebel angels so profoundly that they lose not only their original characters but even their very names. In fact he conceives naming to be a fundamental part of his great argument, the Fall.

The naming of Milton's protagonist goes through three stages. Latterly he is Satan, as Raphael instructs us: "So call him now, his former name |Is heard no more in heaven".[17] What was that former name? Before his fall, Satan had been Lucifer:

> Lucifer from Heav'n
> (So call him, brighter once amidst the Host
> Of Angels, then that Starr the Starrs among)
> Fell with his flaming Legions through the Deep
> Into his place.
>
> (*Paradise Lost* 7.131–5)

"Lucifer" is here almost reduced to an astronomical trope for the angel's brightness. But in the earlier, infernal books the diminished devil has lost his old bright name without yet having acquired the new name Satan ("Antagonist"). There, the narrator uses the name Satan, but the devils do not. After all, Satan is not their enemy. He himself first hears his fallen name when he is brought to Gabriel as an intruder in Paradise: "Why hast thou, Satan, broke the bounds prescribed [...]?" (*PL* 4.478) Later, he exults in the bad name: "I glory in the name, | Antagonist of heaven's almighty king" (*PL* 10.386–7). Here the location of "Antagonist", beginning the line, gives it a momentary ambiguity. Is it a capitalized proper name, translating "Satan"?

Other devils are named analogously. Beelzebub has at first no name at all: to Satan he is merely "one next himself in power" (*PL* 1.79). As Raphael explains in his narration of the war in heaven, the fallen angels were

> Cancelled from heaven and sacred memory,
> Nameless in dark oblivion let them dwell.
> For strength from truth divided and from just,
> Illaudable, naught merits but dispraise
> And ignominy...
>
> (*Paradise Lost* 6.379–83)

The very word "ignominy", derived from *in-* + *nomen*, meant "nameless".

Yet Satan's companion, the narrator of book 1 tells us, was "long
after known in Palestine, and named | Beelzebub".The fallen angels as
a group acquired new names from their postlapsarian experience:

> Princely Dignities,
> And Powers that earst in Heaven sat on Thrones;
> Though of their Names in heavenly Records now
> Be no memorial, blotted out and ras'd
> By their Rebellion, from the Books of Life.
> Nor had they yet among the Sons of Eve
> Got them new Names [. . .]
>
> (*Paradise Lost* 1.359–65)

Milton subscribes to St Augustine's identification of fallen angels with
pagan gods.[18] At first the devils all had innocent, original names match-
ing their uncorrupted identities—lost names like "Lucifer". The loss
of these names was more than titular, for they meant reputation and
standing in the angelic community.To lose them implied loss of honour and integrity, loss of character and nature. What the devils had
been was gone, forgotten even.

No longer knowing his friend Beelzebub's name, Satan must resort
to circumlocution: "Fallen Cherub" (*PL* 1.157). And for his part Beelzebub cannot say "Lucifer" but must address the superior fiend as
"Leader of those armies bright" (*PL* 1.272)—"bright" being a remain-
ing trace of the former "Lucifer". This difficulty of missing names,
repeatedly encountered, partly explains Milton's "adjectival" style, often
remarked by critics. In hell as in the House of Commons—although
partly for different reasons—circumlocutory naming is the rule.

John Leonard studies Milton's naming in an incisive book, *Naming
in Paradise* (1990). There he traces the ideological method whereby
Milton withholds, assigns, and changes names. Writing on the avoid-
ance of "Beelzebub" in *Paradise Lost* book 5, Leonard draws attention
to a great difficulty facing Milton: namely, that at the time of Raphael's
narrative the fallen angels had yet to acquire their postlapsarian names.
They were not yet "known to men by various names, | And various
idols through the heathen world" (*PL* 1.374–5). Leonard notices the
fine decorum whereby in narrating the rebellion Raphael avoids referring to Satan's "next subordinate" by name (*PL* 5.670), since that subordinate still enjoys (if only just) "unspoiled innocence".[19] On the
other hand, in the history of the war in heaven, Raphael makes free use
of the devils' fallen names: Moloc, Adramelec, Asmadai, Ariel, Arioc,

Ramiel. Here, Leonard detects a danger of anachronism: "how can Raphael know these 'new Names' when they have not yet been 'Got' by their owners?"[20] He suggests that Raphael speaks from foreknowledge:"Things by their names I call, though yet unnamed" (*PL* 12.140). Perhaps. But it is simpler to suppose that Raphael's angelic intelligence intuits the fallen names of the devils from their present, corrupt natures. After all, unfallen Adam can apprehend the names of the animals.

Why then does Satan fail to recognize, in the portress of hell, his own daughter Sin? Is it because she presents a different, postlapsarian aspect of sin from what he has previously known? At her "birth", Sin "pleased, and with attractive graces won | The most averse" (*PL* 2.762–3). But now she is "abhorred" by Satan, ending "foul in many a scaly fold" (2.650–1). In other words, sin seems attractive in prospect—"tempting" in fact—but once committed becomes utterly different. Guilt and consequences make it repellent. So Sin asks Satan "Hast thou forgot me then, and do I seem | Now in thine eye so foul, once deemed so fair[?]" (2.747–8). Much has been said about "Sin" as a new name, a new word or sign.[21] But the naming of Sin seems to me much like the unproblematic naming of the animals. Unfallen angels know about evil as a theoretic possibility, and so can intuit Sin's nature and name. When Satan in heaven sins, "back they recoiled afraid | At first, and called me Sin" (2.759–60): a rational response. With familiarity, however, sin became temptingly attractive—so long as it remained uncommitted.

Titles

Milton's God usually refers to the angels by their titles, collectively:

> Thrones, Princedoms, Powers, Dominions I reduce:
>> (*Paradise Lost* 3.320)

> Hear all ye Angels, Progenie of Light,
> Thrones, Dominations, Princedoms, Vertues, Powers…
>> (*Paradise Lost* 5.600–1)

Faithful Abdiel repeats this roster exactly at *Paradise Lost* 5.840, and Satan, although sardonically, follows it too, at 5.772 and 10.460, on the earlier occasion adding a qualification:

> If these magnific Titles yet remain
> Not meerly titular, since by Decree
> Another now hath to himself ingross't
> All Power, and us eclipst under the name
> Of King anointed...[22]

(Paradise Lost 5.773–7)

All these titles, with one apparent exception, are authorized by familiar biblical passages: "For by him were all things created, which are in heaven, and which are in earth, things visible and invisible: whether they be Thrones, or Dominions, or Principalities, or Powers..." (Col. 1: 16, Geneva).[23] And the Virtues are biblical too, although authorized by different texts: "Vertues that be in heuvenes schulen be movyd" (Mark 13: 25 Wyclif); "*Virtutes, quae in caelis sunt, movebuntur*" (Vulgate). (In other versions *Virtutes* is rendered as "Powers".)

The seven angels of the presence are also biblical: the "eyes of the lord" (Zech. 4: 10), "the seven spirits which are before his throne" (Rev. 1: 4, 5: 6, 8: 2). Only one of these eyes or spirits, however, is named in the Bible: Raphael. In Tobit 12: 15 he declares "I am Raphael, one of the seven holy angels, which present the prayers of the saints, and which go in and out before the glory of the Holy One". And Milton identifies Uriel ("Light of God") as another angel of the presence:

> Th'Arch-Angel Uriel, one of the seav'n
> Who in Gods presence, nearest to his Throne
> Stand ready at command, and are his Eyes
> That run through all the Heav'ns, or down to th'Earth
> Bear his swift errands over moist and dry,
> O're Sea and Land: him Satan thus accostes:
> "Uriel, for thou of those seav'n Spirits that stand
> In sight of God's high Throne, gloriously bright,
> The first art wont his great authentic will
> Interpreter through highest Heav'n to bring..."

(Paradise Lost 3.648–56)

Robert West regards the idea of Uriel's being "Regent of the sun" (3.690) as arcane. But he is named Angel in 4 Esdras 4:1 Vulgate (2 Esdras Geneva) and Archangel (under the form Ieremiel) at 4: 36. And his solar role was standard enough to appear in Pierio Valeriano's *Hieroglyphica*, a school textbook.[24] In Valeriano's roster, on the authority of "Greek theology", Sol is assigned to Uriel and Adonis. The cabalists gave Uriel prominence as ruling "in the power of the meridian sun" and as one of the four Archangels ruling the corners of the world.[25]

Elsewhere in *Paradise Lost* a different roster is to be found. Raphael narrates the journey of Satan with his yet unfallen host:

> Regions they pass'd, the mightie Regencies
> Of Seraphim and Potentates and Thrones
> In their triple Degrees...

(Paradise Lost 5.748–50)

This refers to the nine orders of angels in Pseudo-Dionysius' *Celestial Hierarchy*.[26] Dionysius' nine fixed orders were commonly considered as three groups of three, the "trinal triplicities" of *The Faerie Queene* 1.12.39. Agrippa's *Scala Novenarii* gives the complete list of nine orders: Seraphim, Cherubim, Throni, Dominationes, Potestates, Virtutes, Principatus, Archangeli, Angeli.[27] A similar roster is found at *Paradise Lost* 7.198–9, this time adding Cherubim to the orders attending Messiah's chariot: "Cherub and Seraph, Potentates and Thrones, | And Virtues". Other authorities, Rabbinical or later, add individual names.[28] Robert Fludd in *Philosophia Sacra* (1626) 163 gives *Zaphkiel seu Oriphiel, angelus Saturni, Zadkiel seu Zachariel Iouis, Samael Martis, Michael Solis, Anael Veneris, Raphael Mercurii, atque Gabriel Lunae.* And Petrus Bungus, while agreeing on the others, gives Zaphkiel as Hariphiel, citing his authority as Charles de Bovelles or Bovillus (c.1480–1533).[29]

Milton seems little concerned to define the angelic caste system in detail; although some apparent vagueness arises from the ambiguity of "Angel" used both for a particular Order and for a member of any Order. He may have thought, as Andrew Willet did, that it was ungodly curiosity to enquire too far into such matters;[30] he certainly believed that mystifying "names, | Places and titles" (*PL* 12.515–16) was wrong. Rather than a fixed hierarchy of being, he imagines an upwardly mobile hierarchy of office and merit.[31] And he shares Thomas Heywood's view that "the name of Angell is a word of Office, not of nature". In *Paradise Lost* book 3, when the "heavenly choir" remains silent, only Messiah volunteers to ransom mankind by becoming mortal. Whereupon God gives him "all power" (217, 317): "under thee as Head Supream | Thrones, Princedoms, Powers, Dominions I reduce:" (319–20). The hierarchy of Milton's God is mobile and meritocratic. No single, fixed system of angelic titles such as Pseudo-Dionysius' ever emerges in *Paradise Lost*. On the other hand, Milton's angelic titles are more than a species of sonorous music.

The many schemes of thought that Milton drew on often authorize features of his angels. Thus Raphael, the most individually characterized, is Adam's spiritual guide and counsellor, just as he is Tobias'. And when Milton describes Raphael alighting on the eastern cliff of Paradise –

> Like Maia's son he stood,
> And shook his Plumes, that Heav'nly fragrance filld
> The circuit wide.

> *(Paradise Lost* 5.285–7)

—the comparison to Maia's son Mercury probably alludes to two angelo-logical schemes. One scheme is found in Charles de Bouelles, Petrus Bun-gus, and Reginald Scot's *The Discovery of Witchcraft* (1584),[32] the other in Robert Fludd's *Philosophia Sacra et Vere Christiana seu Meteorologia Cosmica* (1626).[33] In both, Mercury is the planet assigned to Raphael.[34] Similarly with the description of Michael's equipment: "by his side | As in a glister-ing Zodiac hung the Sword, | Satans dire dread" (11.246–7). His wearing the zodiac befits his correlation with the sun in many schemes.[35]

In the angelological schemes, Gabriel ("Strength of God") was associated with war, making him a suitable choice for captain of the important guard on Paradise, "Chief of the angelic guards" (*PL* 4.550). When this "warrior angel" (4.946) confronts Satan, his "angelic squadron bright | Turned fiery red, sharpening in moonèd horns | Their phalanx". Here again the phrase "moonèd horns", vividly descriptive of the squad-ron's crescent formation, may well allude to the angel schemes, in which the moon is invariably assigned to Gabriel.[36]

Threatened by Gabriel, an enraged Satan replies in Homeric fashion with insults: "Then when I am thy captive talk of chains, | Proud limitary Cherub" (*PL* 4.970–1). "Limitary" (*OED* s.v. *Limitary* 2) accurately reflects Gabriel's office of border guard at the limits of Paradise (4.549); but Satan also implies Gabriel's responsibilities are subject to limits (*OED* s.v. *Limi-tary* 1). Both Gabriel and Lucifer-Satan are Seraphs and Archangels, so that "Cherub" is insulting:[37] Cherubs are of a lower rank than Seraphs in the most usual ordering, that of Pseudo-Dionysius.[38] Perhaps, too, the Cherubs' contemplative role would seem to Satan an insignificant one.[39]

Hidden names

As we saw in chapter 4, it was still common in Milton's time for poets to sustain a covert level of meaning distinct from the more or less obvi-ous rhetorical sense. On this hidden level, a poem could be given topical applications, and real-life names could be specified through acrostics, rebuses, and anagrams. Such devices were governed by conventions going back to classical antiquity. Even in the longest poems acrostics might be used to emphasize or signpost specially significant passages. When the gates of Mars are opened at *Aeneid* 7.601–4, Vergil makes the initial letters of the lines form the acrostic MARS.[40]

This tradition continued through the Middle Ages and enjoyed a renewed vogue in early modern England and Scotland. So one finds Milton, almost at the end of the tradition, inserting the initial-letter acrostic SATANVS in *Paradise Lost* at the crucial juncture when Satan disguised as a serpent first attracts Eve's attention:

> **S**cipio the highth of Rome. With tract oblique
> **A**t first, as one who sought access, but feard
> **T**o interrupt, side-long he works his way.
> **A**s when a Ship by skilful Stearsman wrought
> **N**igh Rivers mouth or Foreland, where the Wind
> **V**eres oft, as oft so steers, and shifts her Saile;
> **S**o varied hee [...]
>
> (*Paradise Lost* 9.510–16)

Mark Vaughn has noticed other instances of acrostic words closely relevant to their immediate contexts.[41] Most of these, however, do not involve names, which were more often hidden in anagrams.

When Raphael addresses Eve with the greeting "Hail" (*PL* 5.385–92) Milton alludes to a familiar Latin conceit based on Gabriel's salutation of the Virgin Mary in Luke's gospel. *Ave gratia plena* (Vulgate Luke 1:28) was taken to allude to Mary's role as the antitype of Eve—AVE : EVA.[42] This conceit has not usually been regarded as an anagram; but it is one—and a palindrome at that.[43] This clearly foregrounded anagram is obvious enough. But some of the anagrams in *Paradise Lost* are much less so. Once a common device, the embedded anagram was already obsolescent. Soon it was to become deeply unfashionable and almost forgotten.

Earlier, Ben Jonson had embedded name anagrams, notably in *The Speeches at Prince Henries Barriers* (1610). There the phrase "CLAIMES ARTHURS SEAT"—a celebrated anagram for CHARLES JAMES STEUART—occurs without any signposting.[44] In the same entertainment Prince Henry bears his preferred chivalric name Meliadus, alluding to Rusticier de Pisa's romance *Meliadus de Leonnoys* (1528). But in *Teares on the Death of Meliades* (1613), William Drummond—a poet Milton admired—gives Henry's name as Mœliades, which "in *Anagramme*

maketh *Miles a Deo*".[45] Despite such high-profile examples, the popularity of anagram was waning. Already in 1619, indeed, Jonson told
Drummond he was quite uninterested in anagrams and acrostics. He
denied having "pomp'd [laboured] for those hard trifles, Anagrams" or
having "*Acrostichs* and *Telestichs* on jumpe [exactly coinciding] names".[46]
According to Drummond, Jonson "scorned Anagrams and had ever in
his mouth" Martial's lines about the degrading labour of puerile trifles.[47] This was possibly disingenuous on Jonson's part: he was an
aggressive talker, and Drummond was an authority on anagrams.[48]
Besides, Jonson would not want to admit to the laboriousness entailed
by his secret work. In any event, the exchange may be a straw in the
wind of change away from hidden meanings.

Milton was the last great English poet to engage seriously with
anagrams. In the Enlightenment, discourse would triumph over pattern, as syntax and rhetoric triumphed over schemes. A greater gulf
than politics separated Milton and Dryden: namely, their attitudes to
hidden orders of letters. Milton still concealed words within words,
whereas to Dryden, "mild anagram" was no better than a "peaceful
province in acrostic land", fit for Mac Flecknoe. The older set of mind
was on the way out; before long the rules governing embedded anagram would be lost.

Milton's circumstances were such as to make disguise of the political
content of *Paradise Lost* a necessity. After the Restoration, when he was
finishing his poem, transparent political allegory would have been sui-
cidal for a regicide. (His books were burned on 27 August 1660, and he
was released from the Tower only on 15 December.) Nor would an
obvious *roman à clef* have served his purpose best. His plan in *Paradise
Lost* seems to be one of difficult tests of discrimination between complex analogies. Hence his use of embedded anagrams.

Today, these are obscured by misconceptions about the Civil War.
Many modern readers, influenced by the Romantic radicals, imagine
Milton's Satan as a hero rebelling against the tyranny of Charles I.[49]
But seventeenth-century Parliamentarians considered Charles to be
the rebel. It was Charles I, they thought, who rebelled against the
Crown. Both sides in the Civil War claimed to fight for the Crown,
that is, the state. So, when Milton's Satan orders the standard moved to
the north (*Paradise Lost* 5.683–701), the obvious analogy is with the
real-life raising of the royal standard at Nottingham on 22 August 1642,
not by the rebel Oliver Cromwell but by Charles I. Similarly, Satan is

compared to an eastern tyrant (10.431–59), just as Charles is, in *Eikono-klastes*.[50] At first Milton shared this Parliamentarian view. Later, however, after Cromwell's imperialist ambitions became evident, and after the Commonwealth failed, Milton's political views changed. He now came to oppose rule by any "single person", Cromwell included.[51]

It is hardly surprising to find anagrams of the names of Charles I (or Charles II) in a Satanic context at salient points in his epic. But when Satan reviews his model army in *Paradise Lost* 1.535–89, the political figure anagrammatized is one whose ambition Milton had come to distrust almost as much as Charles I: namely, Oliver Cromwell. Thus, in the passage "Of dreadful length and dazling Arms, in guise | Of War-riers old with order'd SpeaR [...]" (1.564–5), prompted by the initial *O* and the final *R*, it is not hard to see anagrams of OLIVER. An anagram with letters dispersed but correctly ordered is "[<u>O</u>f dreadful <u>L</u>ength and dazling Arms, <u>I</u>n guise | Of <u>V</u>variers old with ord<u>ER</u>]'d", that is, OLIVER. And a condensed but scrambled anagram can be found in "<u>OL</u>d <u>VVI</u>th ord<u>ER</u>]'d", that is, OLVIER: OLIVER.

At *Paradise Lost* 5.703–5, a crucial passage where the tempter is about to corrupt the angels under his command, anagrams of OLIVER also occur:

> To sound
> [Or taint integritie; but all obey'd
> The wonted signal, and superioR]...

Within the frame indicated by square brackets "[*Or*...superio*R*] may be seen an anagram with letters dispersed but correctly ordered: "[Or taint integritie; but al<u>L</u> obe<u>Y</u>'d | The <u>V</u>vont-<u>E</u>d signal, and superio<u>R</u>]". And a condensed, scrambled anagram may be found in "[<u>V</u>vonted signa<u>L</u>, and sup<u>ERIOR</u>]", that is, VLERIOR: OLIVER. (Only one *R* is used, a common licence.)

These and similar anagrams, throwing unexpected light on Milton's political stance, raise new questions. Were they hidden from all but a like-minded inner circle? Or were they obvious to any well-educated reader of poetry? In either case, *Paradise Lost* appears to have been an even more incautious poem than has been thought—quite on a par with the fearless tract *A Ready and Easy Way*. But perhaps Milton cal-culated (as Robert Herrick must have done in 1648 when he published his royalist poems) that governments pay little attention to poetry. Poems pose little political threat to a state.

Notes

1. Isitt 2002.
2. Milton's angels and their names have attracted a considerable but intermittent literature. Ignored in the eighteenth century (e.g. by his editor Richard Bentley) and in
   recent Milton handbooks, the names have received valuable treatments in Masson
   1890, Verity 1910: 680–2, West 1955, Davidson 1971, Leonard 1990, Isitt 2002, and
   Raymond 2010.
3. On Adamic language and universal or "perfect" languages, see Wilkins 1668; Urquhart 1983: 23; Jones 1951; Fish 1971: 107–30; Salmon 1972; Knowlson 1975; Fraser 1977;
   Donawerth 1984; Leonard 1990: 17; Eco 1995; Poole 2008: 536, 539, with further
   refs.
4. 7.385–549; 11.273–9. Cf. Donne 1984: 2.78: "Adam was able to decipher the nature of
   every creature in the name thereof". See Gallagher 1990: 39, 57. Ray, e.g., classified
   16,100 species of plants (Scott Mandelbrote's estimate) or even 18,000 (A. C. Crombie's
   estimate); see Fowler 1998: 447. Adam's own name was sometimes thought Cratylic,
   implying the universality of the four regions of the world; see Evans 1995: 17–18.
5. *Davideis* book 1, note 28, Cowley 1905: 273–4.
6. *Davideis* book 2, note 94, Cowley 1905: 321.
7. See De Hamel 2001: 112–13, 123.
8. See West 1955: 67, 195 n.15.
9. See West 1955: 133–4; Davidson 1971.
10. E.g. "The summoning Arch-Angels" (*PL* 3.325); see Raymond 2010: 262–3.
11. West 1955: 208 citing Henry More, *Psychozoia* 3.1.
12. Cf. William Patten, *The Calender of Scripture* (1575), where Abdiel is glossed "serving
    God".
13. See Raymond 2010: 271.
14. See Marks 1988: 212–13, 231.
15. My italics; see Fowler 1998: 65.
16. See West 1955: 157; Fowler 1998: 101.
17. *PL* 5.658–9; 5.760, 10.425. Cf. Leonard 1990: 86–7, 149.
18. *Confessions* 1.17: St Augustine 1991: 20; see Fowler 1998: 83.
19. See Leonard 1990: 155–6.
20. Leonard 1990: 80.
21. See Leonard 1990: 120–1, 166–7.
22. On the context of republican titles and on Messiah's inheritance of power through
    merit, see Fowler 1998: 332.
23. Cf. Vulgate, *sive throni, sive dominationes, sive principatus, sive potestates*; King James Ver-
    sion, "whether they be thrones, or dominions, or principalities, or powers".
24. Valeriano 1613: 549; see Fowler 1998: 209.
25. See West 1955: 208; Henry More *Psychozoia* 3.1.5n; Fowler 1998: 209.
26. Pseudo-Dionysius wrote as Dionysius the Areopagite; his *De Caelesti Hierarchia*, trans-
    lated from Greek in 860 AD by John Scotus Eriugena, attracted commentaries in the
    12th century. But to Francis Bacon he was "that supposed Dionysius"; see Ellrodt
    1980: 165.
27. Agrippa 1992: 285–6.
28. Agrippa's *Scala Septenarii* names the seven angels who attend before the face of God
    (*septem angeli qui adstant ante faciem Dei*) as Zaphkiel, Zadkiel, Camael, Raphael,
    Hamiel, Michael, and Gabriel; see Agrippa 1992: 282.
29. Bungus 1591: 290.
30. Cf. Raymond 2010: 49.
31. Cf. Raymond 2010: 79.

32. Bungus 1591: 289–90; Scot 1584: 400.
33. See Heninger 1977: 156–8 and fig. 92.
34. See Scot 1584: 400.
35. See e.g. Bungus 1591: 290, Fludd 1991: 40.
36. See Agrippa 1992: 286; Bungus 1591: 290; and Godwin 1991: 40. For the crescent formation as a martial tactic, see Fowler 1998: 276.
37. Lucifer was replaced after the Fall by the Seraph and Archangel Michael; see Raymond 2010: 49, 79, 262 quoting *PL* 1.593, 1.600, 2.750, 6.579, 6.604. Cf. *OED* s.v. *seraphim* 2 c.
38. Agrippa 1992: 286; cf. Raymond 2010: 262.
39. Contrast Satan's deferential address to the Archangel Uriel as "Brighter Seraph" at *PL* 3.636, 648, 667.
40. Cf. FONS in Vergil, *Eclogues* 1.5–8; see Clauss 1977: 267–87; Klemp 1977: 91–2; Ahl 1985.
41. Notably STARS at 3.552–6; WHY at 9.704–6; WOE at 9.1004–6 (when Adam eats); and BOAT at 12.249–52 (the ark). See Vaughn 1982: 5–8.
42. See Austin, *Haec Homo* (1637) 182: "Others [...] anagrammatize it from Eva into *væ*, because (they say) she was the cause of our woe." See also Willet 1608: 54; Leonard 1990: 49–50; Fowler 1998: 305.
43. See Ricks 2003: 132 citing Robert Southwell: "Spell *Eva* backe and *Ave* shall you find".
44. Cf. Jonson, *For the Honour of Wales*: "EVAN: [...] his Madestees Anagrams of *Charles James Stuart*. JENKIN: I [Aye], that is *Claimes Arthurs Seate*, which is as much as to say, your Madestee sud be the first King of gread *Prittan*, and sit in *Cadier Arthur*, which is Arthurs Chaire [...] And then your Sonne Master *S'hrles* his, how doe yow caull him? Is *Charles Stuart, cals true hearts*, that is, he cals us, the Welse Nation [...]" (Jonson 1925–52: 7.323, 509; see Ricks 2003: 113–14). The second embedded anagram CHARLES STUART : CALS TRUE HEARTS, although slightly imperfect, is significantly acknowledged by Jonson.
45. See Jonson 1925–52: 10.515.
46. "An Execration upon Vulcan", *Under-wood* 43, lines 35, 39, Jonson 1925–52: 8.204. For "pomp'd" see *OED*, s.v. *Pump* v. intr.
47. *Conversations* 437–9, Jonson 1925–52: 1.144. See Martial 2.86.9–10.
48. See e.g. his *Character of a Perfect Anagram* (1711), Drummond 1970: 230. In 1620, entertaining an exiled friend with anagrams yet dispraising the practice, he cites the same passage in Martial: either he has taken Jonson's negative view on board or else he too is keeping his secret.
49. E.g. Hill 1977: 367.
50. Cf. Hill 1977: 366, 371; Fowler 1998: 42. For a comparison between the proportion of the angelic host that fell and the proportion of royalist MPs, see Hill 1977: 372.
51. See *The Readie and Easie Way* (1660), Milton 1953–82: 7.361–2 and n. 23. Cf. Hill 1977: 418.

7

Assumed and Imposed Names

One of the earliest name plays in literature—and one of the earliest pseudonyms—is found in Homer's *Odyssey*. Odysseus, trapped in the Cyclops' cave, offers to tell his famous name in return for a guest-gift. "Noman—that's my name. Noman— | So my mother and father call me, all my friends".[1] Or, in Alexander Pope's version,

> Thy promis'd boon, O *Cyclop*! now I claim,
> And plead my title: *Noman* is my name.
> By that distinguish'd from my tender years,
> 'Tis what my parents call me, and my peers.[2]
>
> (*Odyssey* 9.431–4)

When the neighbours hear the screams of the blinded Polyphemus, they ask if anyone is oppressing him "by fraud or power", but he answers "Friends, *Noman* kills me; *Noman* in the hour | Of sleep, oppresses me with fraudful pow'r". They reply that if no man is hurting him but a divine hand has inflicted disease, he should resign himself. They advise prayer, and leave (9.485–8).

The joke disappears in translation. When Polyphemus says *Outis* (οὖτις, "no man"), he means the name assumed by Odysseus—Οὖτις (changing the accent makes it a proper name). But his friends take him to be saying the common noun οὔτις, (*outis*, "no one"). Pope disapproves of "this piece of pleasantry": he thinks "the whole to be nothing but a collusion of words, and fitter to have place in a Farce or Comedy, than in Epic Poetry." In Pope's view "the whole wit or jest lies in the ambiguity of οὔτις (*outis*), which Ulysses imposes upon Polyphemus as his own name, which in reality signifies *No Man*".[3] Pope, a man of the

Enlightenment, has turned his back on secret anagrams and unsuitable puns. He studiously ignores Homer's thematic, self-referring word-plays when Odysseus exults in the cleverness of the name trick: "my heart laughed that my name and flawless device (μῆτις ἀμύμων, *metis amumon*) had so deceived him" (9.414). Here *metis* puns on the repeated phrase *me tis*, "surely no one", a few lines earlier[4]—"surely no one is driving off your flocks?"

It has been assumed that when Odysseus claims to be Noman (*outis*) he is giving a false name. But the device is cleverer than that. Odysseus is divided between the necessity of saving his life and the desire to claim responsibility by leaving a boast for posterity. (It is much the same later, when, still within range, he taunts Polyphemus from ship-board.[5]) Such was Odysseus' reputation that to reveal his name openly would have alerted even the befuddled Polyphemus. So he hints it in a way too subtle for the Cyclops. He calls himself *Outis*, "Noman", a near synonym of *Oudeis*. For ancient Greek had two ways of saying "nobody". The one Homer normally prefers is *outis* (ὄυτις, "not any-one"); the other way is to say *oudeis* (οὐδείς, "not one"). Now, *Oudeis* is an "anagram" of *Odysseus*.

—Or rather an *analegomenon* of Odysseus, since the *Odyssey* is oral poetry. We do not know whether Homer was illiterate and dictated his poem, or whether (as Barry Powell holds) the Greek alphabet was invented to record Homeric song.[6] If, however, Homer was literate, he almost certainly meant *Oudeis* as more than a phonetic hint of *Odys-seus*. Taking into account the spelling *Odusseus* or *Oduseus* (24.398), the phonetic equivalence of iota and upsilon, and the dialectal forms that led to Latin *Ulysses* rather than *Ulusses*, we can hear the puns and see *Oudeis* as an anagram of *Oduseus*.[7] In short, Odysseus told his true name. He really was Noman, only with the letters rearranged.

Romances

Homer's naming is very different from that of medieval and later romances; but they have at least one feature in common: distrust of anyone without a name. It is better to know who you are dealing with. In literature namelessness has often been mysterious and frightening. It is certainly so in Lewis Carroll's *The Hunting of the Snark*, where the Baker, who has forgotten his true name, dreads he will be annihilated:

that he will "softly and suddenly vanish away"—as if a name were essential for existence.[8]

We noticed in chapter 3 the tendency of romances to delay disclosing names. This concern with names and naming was ubiquitous throughout the genre. Jane Bliss, indeed, goes so far as to say that "a large number of medieval romances are explicitly about name, naming, or namelessness".[9] A knight's namelessness, whether voluntary or not, very often led to a provisional name, as did disguise. Throughout the romances there may be as many pseudonyms—names adopted or arbitrarily imposed by others—as real names. The nicknames might be speculative, tautological (like "Le Bel Inconnu"), or aptly descriptive.[10] Or anagrammatic, like "Tramtris" in the Auchinleck manuscript of *Tristram*.

The motives of pseudonymity are various. Lancelot takes the name Le Shyvalere Ill Mafeete when he is rejected by Guinevere after discovery of his affair with Elaine.[11] And Amadis de Gaul assumes the name Beltenebros when he receives a cruel letter from his mistress Oriana and retires to a hermitage. Very different is the naming process in the fourteenth-century *Libeaus Desconus* (corrupted from *Le Bel Inconnu*, "the Fair Unknown"). Here, the real name of Ginglein (Gawain's son) is unknown, so he is knighted as "Li Beaus Desconus".[12] Ginglein's mother gives him the more descriptive byname *Beau-fyz*, "handsome face". Again, a true name may emerge through recognition of moral characteristics, through questioning, or after a decisive passage of arms.

Bliss' remarkable book brings out very well the implications of romance naming, both Cratylic and Hermogenean, and the many literary name games they give rise to. She shows romance to be both philosophical and enquiring, even if it is not quite so theoretical a genre as she believes. Central to its concerns are the social functions of naming. Name generally meant reputation. Thus a nameless knight might have to "make a name for himself". Or he might secretly bear a great name but choose to conceal it. In an age when kinship was of paramount importance, anonymity could temporarily confer power, or open a way to discover the attitudes of others. An inoffensive pseudonym like "The Knight of the Black Shield" might be a useful protective device.

In Malory's *Sir Garethis Tale*, when Arthur asks Gareth his name he replies, ambiguously, "Sir, I can nat tell you". This surprises Arthur, since

Gareth looks "goodly". Initially, Gareth asks only one boon: his keep for
a year. Arthur gives him the best of the doubt: he is to have "all manner
of finding as though he were a lordys son". But Sir Kay concludes
Gareth's aspirations are low: he didn't think to ask for horse and armour
because he is basely born. Or illegitimate. (Having no identifiable father
naturally implies illegitimacy, although commentators seldom draw this
inference.) Questioning might lead to the name withheld. So there are
many questions. Who is your father? Where are you from? What is your
name? These are not only attempts to discover how famous the unnamed
knight is. They are also questions about kin.

Kay bestows on Gareth the ambiguous nickname "Bewmaynes"
("Fine Hands"). Are Bewmaynes' fine large hands apt for stealing in
the kitchen, or the result of laziness, or a sign of his largesse? Malory
indicates that Kay's scornful jesting is not the way to learn about reality: the unknown's true name, Gareth, has nothing to do with hands.[13]
Sir Garethis Tale explores the topics of reputation: contributions of
nature and nurture, values of titular nobility and noble deeds, and
requirements for social advancement. Gareth goes incognito not so
much to test others as to pursue an ideal of his own. His aspiration is
never to claim respect he has not earned by merit. Thus, in face of
Lyonett's scorn of a mere kitchen boy, he treats her courteously and
continues to perform noble deeds.

A romance pseudonym may be foregrounded by puns and other
wordplays, as in *The Romance of Horn*. Horn's evasive self-descriptions
keep clear of revealing his family name. So, for example, he says he is
called "Y-comen ut of the bote" (lines 201–7).[14]

Romances reached the zenith of their popularity in the seventeenth
century, when romance names, as we have seen, were fashionable in
real life. Later still they provided convenient pseudonyms for amorous
correspondence. Richard Steele's lover writing of his affair says: "this
Lady has corresponded with me under Names of Love, she my Belinda
I her Cleanthes".[15] Here, "Belinda" is what Cleanthes calls a "bor-
rowed name", a pseudonym. In contrast, the malicious Mrs Jane in the
same essay merits no such concealment. Romantic pseudonyms were
common in the Restoration and the eighteenth century, when a few
personas did service for many actual names. Another romantic mask
was the initial letter (or letters) with a long dash of omission, a form of
blank name not so clearly recognizable before the introduction of
printing.

Anonymity

The anonymity of much medieval literature may in part have been accidental. Readers may simply have failed to discover assertions of authorship too well hidden in difficult acrostics or anagrams. But this is not very likely so far as the educated elite was concerned: especially in the fifteenth century, the skill of reading sub-verbal patterns seems to have been highly developed.[16]

Coming to printed literature, one cannot doubt that a large proportion was deliberately anonymous on first publication. John Mullan draws attention to the vast catalogue of anonymous titles compiled by Samuel Halkett and Rev. John Laing in no fewer than eight volumes.[17] Anonymity might be secured by omitting the author's name altogether or by substituting a reticent descriptive phrase such as "By a lady".[18] Or the anonymity itself might be concealed under a false name, such as the conventional "N.H." (*nat hwilc*, "know not what"). The motives of such anonymity are various, and sometimes unsearchable. Mullan's thoughtful study suggests several main possibilities, such as shame, diffidence, and fear of consequences. To these he adds motives of mischief, and of gender disguise.[19] The desire to hoax, not to speak of the satirist's fondness for pen names, hardly fits his category of mischief. Admittedly, Pope and Swift must have had fun devising personas such as "Scriblerus". And in *A Key to the Lock* (1715) Pope clearly enjoyed the complicated invention of a Dutch author with political motives. But were these devices only *mischievous*? Surely a fear of consequences entered in too: Pope more than once received threats, and was rumoured to have been actually beaten.[20]

Literary hoaxes have been going a long time. Indeed, K. K. Ruthven is tempted to regard literature itself as fake.[21] Hoaxes often call for false names, as for example in Pope's manoeuvrings in *A Key to the Lock*. The author of this spurious work purports to be "Esdras Barnivelt", a plausible combination of a biblical given name (suggesting Puritan provenance) and a surname with Dutch associations (for example, the statesman Jan van Olden Barneveldt). Swift had occasion to write from behind a number of masks, or "impersonations" as his biographer Irvin Ehrenpreis calls them. Not all of these involved names, but of those that did, Lemuel Gulliver and M. B. Drapier both suggest plain men.[22] In *The Drapier Letters*, written against Walpole and Wood, Drapier's initials probably gesture to Marcus Brutus the tyrannicide.[23] "Martinus Scriblerus" served as a mask for half a dozen writers of very different character. This group resulted from the merger of two literary sets: a younger, comprising Pope and John Gay, and an older, more experienced association of pronounced Tory affiliation, namely Swift, Arbuthnot, Parnell, and the Earl of Oxford.[24] The Scriblerus project generated many disparate works, including the *Dunciad Variorum*, *A Key to the Lock*, and *Peri Bathous, or the Art of Sinking in Poetry*.

Another consortium—including Congreve, Swift, Gay, Pope, and Steele—wrote the Partridge–Bickerstaff papers, under the assumed names of John Partridge and Isaac Bickerstaff.[25] The real Partridge was a cobbler who had set up as a serious astrologer and become successful. Swift as Bickerstaff predicted Partridge's death on 29 March 1708, and followed this with *An Elegy on the Supposed Death of Mr Partridge, the Almanac Maker* (April 1708), *An Account of the Death of Partridge*, and *A Vindication of Isaac Bickerstaff* (April 1709), in which he proves Partridge dead, despite Partridge's protestation that he is "now alive, and was so on that day".[26] Irvin Ehrenpreis analyses the shades of fictitiousness Swift generated, with some impersonations "flaunting his identity", others concealing it under deceptive personae:

All these acts of mockery only strengthen our sense that the essential person behind them is different from the objects of his satire. Besides being stable where they are changeable, he is impartial where they are prejudiced, rational where they are capricious.[27]

In the same century the gothic vogue saw several instances of deceptive authorship, notably James Macpherson's *Fingal* (1762), by an "early" Gaelic bard, the legendary Ossian or Oisin. *Fingal* was accepted as genuine by Hugh Blair, the Edinburgh Regius Professor of Rhetoric and Belles Lettres, and at first by David Hume, not to speak of Schiller and Goethe. Dr Johnson meanwhile remained sceptical. It is now thought Macpherson did translate original "texts", but very freely, supplying much from his own invention. His atmospheric pastiche inhabits a vague province on the distant boundaries of heroic literature.

Horace Walpole's *The Castle of Otranto*, more completely fictive, was at first published (in 1764) as by "William Marshall, Gent. From the Original Italian of Onuphrio Muralto, Canon of the Church of St Nicholas at Otranto", an imaginary original "printed at Naples, in the black letter, in the year 1529". Walpole's *Otranto* has remained a brilliant enigma, resembling a monumental fragment saved from some other-wise unknown culture. In 1769 the same Walpole was sent by Thomas Chatterton (1752–70) a "medieval" work allegedly written by a fif-teenth-century monk, Thomas Rowley. The authenticity of Rowley's poems (mostly published in 1777 after Chatterton's death) was soon challenged by Thomas Warton and Edmond Malone. But Chatterton's medieval world is vividly enough imagined to be enjoyed as a gothic fantasia.

In the twentieth century the Crabtree hoax had a similarly back-handed success. Joseph Crabtree (1754–1854) is a fictitious poet Sir James Sutherland conjured up in 1954 out of period clichés. The hoax worked so well that it led to a Crabtree Foundation: annual Crabtree lectures were delivered and eventually gathered as *The Crabtree Orations 1954–1994*.[28] Sutherland's invention was for fun (and perhaps to test the alertness of colleagues); but other hoaxes have had a sharper edge. In 1914 the US poet Witter Bynner and his friend Arthur Davison Ficke wrote and published a volume of quasi-imagist poems purportedly by Emmanuel Morgan and Anne Knish. Bynner himself reviewed this bogus collec-tion in *New Republic*, describing its authors as members of a "Spectric School"; but he clearly had Ezra Pound's imagism in his sights. Such spurious reviewing is common enough. David Foster Wallace's *Obliv-ion*, for example, was reviewed in *Modernism/Modernity* (2004) by "Jay Murray Siskind". Siskind, "Professor at Blacksmith College", is better known as a character in Don de Lillo's *White Noise* (1985).

A characteristic of entrapment hoaxes is that they usually depend on being revealed in some dramatic fashion. Yet in the classic example, Kipling's "Dayspring Mishandled" (1932), exposure never quite takes place.[29] This hoax is designed by James Manallace to pay out Castorley, an unpleasant man of letters setting himself up as a Chaucer authority. Manallace wants to revenge an unspecified offence committed against the woman he loves. So he forges a Chaucer manuscript, contriving to have Castorley "discover" it and believe it to be "the work of Abraham Mentzius, better known as Mentzel of Antwerp (1388–1438/9)". Ment-zel's distinguishing characteristics include "a tendency to spell English words on Dutch lines", as in "Daiespringe mishandeelt". The 107 new lines at the end of The Parson's Tale are accepted as genuine by Castorley, who hopes it will bring him inevitable "recognition". To trap the shallow scholar, Manallace means to reveal exactly how the manuscript was faked. As clinching proof he hides his own name as an acrostic in the "Monkish Hymn": *ILla |ALma |MAter | ECca |SEcum |AFferens | ME | ACceptum | NIcolaus |ATrib.*[30] "Read down the first and second letters of 'em; and see what you get". What you get is IAMES A MANALLACE FECIT. In the event, Castorley dies before the trap can be sprung, leaving Manallace with complex problems of guilt and complicity in Castorley's tainted success. The hoax has been too good.[31]

Several features of Kipling's story were realized in a real-life hoax by Bevis Hillier.[32] In 2006, when Hillier had spent more than twenty-five years on a magisterial three-volume biography of John Betjeman, the second volume was harshly reviewed by A. N. Wilson. And now Wilson himself was to bring out a rival biography of Betjeman. Hillier carried out a devious revenge. He sent Wilson a letter from France signed "Eve de Harben", enclosing a love letter allegedly written in 1944 by the married Betjeman to a colleague, Honor Tracy. When the unsuspecting Wilson used the letter in his biography it was time to spring the trap. Hillier revealed "Eve de Harben" to be no more than an anagram of EVER BEEN HAD. And the sentence initials of her love letter made the acrostic A N WILSON IS A SHIT. The hoax is strikingly similar to Manallace's, with Wilson resembling (at least in Hillier's view) the villain Castorley.

A name was also central to the Botul hoax in 1999. The French journalist Frédéric Pages invented an imaginary philosopher called Jean-Baptiste Botul, supposedly the author of a critique of Immanuel Kant; whereupon the fashionable *penseur* Bernard-Henri Lévy cited the "School of Botulism" as allies against Kant. Lévy failed to notice the play on "botulism", and when the trap was sprung he brazened it out: he claimed it made no difference whether the arguments against Kant were Botul's or Pages'.[33]

Although Hillier's amusing deception partly aimed to uphold literary standards, it cannot be called literature of a very high order. But some other hoaxes have had purely literary purposes. An instance is the Bynner–Ficke hoax, which as we saw implied criticism of imagist poetry. Another is the McAuley–Stewart hoax, again aimed at a difficult, innovative poetry movement. In 1944 Max Harris, the Australian poetry editor, published *The Darkening Ecliptic*, a volume of modernist poems supposedly by Ern Malley but in fact put together by James McAuley and Harold Stewart. They meant to show that difficult poetry is easy to write. The disclosure was sensational: the hoax was taken so seriously, indeed, that it gave rise to talk of a national identity crisis.[34]

In general, literary hoaxes are aggressive, like other practical jokes. As Kipling's "Dayspring Mishandled" brings out, they are cruel in themselves and likely to corrupt the perpetrators.[35] But sometimes that doesn't prevent them from being irresistibly funny to all except the victims.

Sobriquets

"Bewmaynes" is almost what we now call a nickname, "an eke name". Bynames and nicknames are not given ceremonially, and may change and change again during life. I have had four: Ala and Skinz as a child, Slasher and Al as a medical student. Of these, Skinz and Slasher are nicknames. Given instead of, or in addition to, a proper name,[36] nicknames reflect a salient aspect of appearance, personality, or achievement.[37] So "Monk Lewis" refers to *The Monk* (1796), a gothic novel that made the reputation of Matthew Gregory Lewis (1775–1818). A nickname may become better known than the proper name and even displace it. So the categories of name and byname overlap.

Nevertheless, nicknames fall into fairly distinct groups. Thus Emperor Tiberius (Claudius Tiberius Nero, 42 BC–AD 37) was known for his excesses as Caldius Biberius Mero ("Mulled Wine Drunkard"); and Robert Baden-Powell (1857–1941) was Bathing Towel, from his enthusiasm for cleanliness. Some nicknames are personally descriptive (Ginger, Four-Eyes); others describe a moral characteristic, as with Jack Dawkins in *Oliver Twist* ("The Artful Dodger"). Since the nineteenth century, if not earlier, King Ethelred ("Noble Counsel") has been called "Ethelred the Unready" (*redeless*, "lacking in good advice"). Descriptive nicknames are as often as not derogatory; hence Steele's view of them as vulgar "disgraceful Appellations".[38]

A surprising number of nicknames are plays on real names—"given in sport" as Puttenham says. So "Chalky" is anyone with the surname White; Chuck goes with Charles; and Nobby goes with Clark (hinting perhaps at the social pretensions of clerks). The protagonist of William Golding's *Pincher Martin*, Christopher Hadley Martin, is naval and therefore inevitably nicknamed "Pincher". Here the association is historical: William Fanshawe Martin (1801–95) was a British admiral, notorious for his strictness in having ratings arrested ("pinched") for trivial offences. Golding's Pincher Martin—quite unlike Taffrail's

Pincher Martin—is just the sort of man who would have been pinched
by his namesake the admiral. Nicknames of British noblemen are often
taken from their courtesy titles (used during their father's lifetime).
Thus Victor Pasmore's pupil George Alexander Eugene Douglas Haig,
second Earl Haig (b. 1918) was known as Dawyck (pronounced Doik):
his courtesy title until his father's death in 1928 had been Viscount
Dawick.[39] A familiar literary example is "Bridey" in Evelyn Waugh's
Brideshead Revisited (1945) chapter 4. Lord Brideshead is the courtesy
title of Sebastian Flyte's elder brother during the lifetime of their tru-
ant father, Lord Marchmain.

   Nicknames of literary characters are so numerous as to call for separate treatment. A few examples may stand for many. Shakespeare's plays
are distinguished by their intimate characterization: no other writer of
his time makes more use of nicknames. This applies even to his royals.
Thus, Prince Henry is Hal; and Henry VI addresses his queen as Meg
(*2 Henry VI* 3.2.26). For the less exalted ranks in *Merry Wives of Windsor*,
nicknames are still more frequent: Mrs Page is Meg; Ford is Frank (an
Elizabethan abbreviation of Francis); Falstaff's page is Robin—aptly a
diminutive of Rob, from Robert; and the Queen of the Fairies is "sweet
Nan". Caius is apt for a gynaecologist: pronounced as a monosyllable
it puns on "keys", slang for "penis".[40]

   Dickens knew more than Shakespeare about names and their history. But his nicknames and pet names are often too conspicuous for
subtlety. Thus the anti-hero of *Great Expectations* (1860–61) is Philip
Pirrip, nicknamed Pip. The uncommon name alerts the reader to
notice the familiar form "Pip". Once meaning "a very small degree",[41]
it may indicate a theme of the book: social mobility. Dickens' own
family environment teemed with associative names: his seventh son,
Edward Bulwer Lytton Dickens, had the evolving nickname "Plorn",
"the Plornishgenter", "Plornishmaroon Tigunter". Nicknames in
modern literature are even more often allusive, sometimes quite
obscurely so. The official code name of Ian Fleming's James Bond, for
example, probably alludes to Kipling's story, ".007".[42]

Authorial nicknames

Writers' sobriquets go back to the Middle Ages: St Thomas Aquinas
(1225–74) was known as *Doctor Angelicus* and Roger Bacon (c. 1214–94)

was *Doctor Mirabilis*. But *noms de plume* (French *noms de guerre*) used by the writers themselves only became common with the growth of neo-Latin. A chief occasion for Latin pen names was the printed title page: decorum suggested the author's name should be in the same language as the title. Familiar Continental examples include "Carolus Stephanus" for Charles Étienne and "Nolano" (a location name) for Giordano Bruno.[43] Many British names were Latinized by translation, rebus, similarity of sound, or simply by a change of ending: for example "Boethius" (Hector Boece), "Camerarius" (David Chambers), and the ugly "Sevenochensis" (William Painter).[44] The circle of John Donne ("Johannes Factus") included "Christopherus Torrens"; "Henricus Bonum-Annum"; and "Ignatius Architectus".[45] Other British writers followed the French fashion for anagram disguise: "Rolihayton" (John Taylor), "Ryhen Pameach" (Henry Peacham), and "Salochin Trebon" (Nicholas Breton).[46] A slightly wittier sobriquet was "Voy Sire Saluste" for Joshua Sylvester, translator of Saluste Sieur du Bartas.

Many Renaissance poets were known by poetic names. These might allude to their inspirational models, and so help fashion a literary persona. Thus Pierre de Ronsard could boast the anagram "Rose de Pindare".[47] On the common model of Virgil's Tityrus, Clément Marot's "Colin" and "Thenot" shadow poets; John Skelton's "Collyn Cloute" is an outspoken satirist;[48] and Spenser has another Colin Cloute "under whose person the Author selfe is shadowed".[49] (Helen Cooper suggests Colin may have been a type-name for shepherds— like Robin, Marot's own pen name.[50]) Other poets followed suit: Thomas Watson with "Corydon", Michael Drayton with "Rowland", and Alexander Pope with "Alexis". The pastoral names of Skelton, Marot, and Spenser implied political stances, even literary manifestos. And so, perhaps, did Spenser's other sobriquet, *Immerito*. This is usually translated "Undeserving"; but besides the modest Italian adjective Spenser may intend the Latin adverb, as in Terence, *Phormio* 290—"Unjustly (accused)". It was common for writers to have two poetic names, one simple and the other grandiloquently periphrastic. So Walter Raleigh was "Water" (punning on Walter) and "The Shepherd of the Ocean" (Spenser's invention, later adopted by Raleigh himself).[51]

Names such as Immerito and Sidney's Astrophil ("Stella-Lover") sometimes distanced the poet, establishing a fictive persona to ward off crude biographical inferences. But in other instances the disguise is so transparent that the pen name suggests witty display rather than concealment. The poet Sydney Dobell reversed himself as "Sydney Yendys". Much has been made of writers' fear of the "stigma of print" as a motive for disguising their names. More often, perhaps, their vulnerability made them welcome the protection a pen name gave. Supporting this point is the special fondness of pen names among satirists, from John Marston ("Kinsayder"[52]), Jean Baptiste Poquelin ("Moliere"), and François-Marie Arouet ("Voltaire", anagram of "Arouet l[e] j[eune]") to Thomas Carlyle ("Teufelsdröckh", "Devil's dust").[53]

Literary groups naturally went in for proliferating nicknames. Dr Johnson called Topham Beauclerk "Beau", Boswell "Bozzy", Bennet Langton "Lanky", and Thomas Sheridan "Sherry". Johnson himself was "The Great Cham of literature" and "Ursa Major".[54] He also came to be known as "Dictionary Johnson", on the model of "Scipio Africanus", just as William Melmoth the younger was "Pliny Melmoth"; Richard Glover, "*Leonidas* Glover"; and Boswell, "Corsica Boswell".[55]

In the nineteenth century, male as well as female writers still sometimes valued pen names. Although Jane Austen's literary identity was known to her family circle, she communicated with the publisher Thomas Cadell through her father and brother, and wrote to Crosby and Co. as Mrs Ashton Dennis. Like Scott, she enjoyed the pleasures of notorious anonymity. Elizabeth Gaskell first published under the name of Cotton Mather Mills, alluding to the satanic cotton mills of Manchester. She may have felt the need for a male pen name in view of the political stance of *Mary Barton*: its social protest called for a good deal of documentary evidence. A few decades ago feminist critics taught that women had to take male names to get their novels published. Almost the reverse was true. The publisher William Howlitt told Gaskell it would be advantageous if her works "were known as the works of a lady".[56] Nevertheless she tried, too late, for the pen name Stephen Berwick, and in the event the novel was published anonymously.

Gender disguises were so common as to be almost the norm.[57] Women writers' modest wish for anonymity may have been one motive; another, surely, was the desire to compete with male writers on equal terms. Charlotte Brontë published *Jane Eyre* as by Currer Bell. And the Brontës published *Poems* (1846) as by Currer, Ellis, and Acton Bell, retaining each their own initials. All three pen names could be taken as masculine. Mary Ann Evans published the first of her *Scenes of Clerical Life* (1857) anonymously, but later used the pen name George Eliot. She explained the "George" as from Lewes' given name, and

"Eliot" as a "mouth-filling easily pronounced word". Ambitious for
the "prestige" of anonymity, she was also defensive: to call herself Cross
would have announced she was living with a man not her husband.

Female names for male writers are less common.[58] But John Keats
planned to use the pen name Lucy Vaughan for "The Cap and Bells"
(left unfinished at his death); William Sharp (1855–1905) used the pseudonym Fiona Macleod; Victor Purcell's "The Sweeniad", a T. S. Eliot
parody, was published as by "Myra Buttle"; and Charles Hamilton
(1876–1961) published his Bessie Bunter stories as "Hilda Richards".

In the nineteenth century, writers' pen names and nicknames proliferated. Sir Walter Scott (1771–1832) had four, corresponding to
phases of his career. His poetry made him "The Ariosto of the North"
(Byron's invention); as the author of *Waverley* he was "The Great
Unknown" (James Ballantyne's invention); later he became "The Great
Magician" (John Wilson's invention) and "The Wizard of the North".[59]
Thackeray, as a satirist, found a need for many names. At first he wore
a footman's disguise, "Charles Yellowplush". For *Catherine* (1839–40),
satirizing the vogue for criminal biographies, he wrote as "Ikey Solo-
mons", a real-life fence (and model of Dickens' Fagin). For a review of
a National Gallery exhibition he became "Michael Angelo Titmarsh",
an alias he used again for *The Paris Sketch Book* (1840). Among other
acknowledged pen names he used Bashi-Bazouk, Folkestone Canterbury, George Savage Fitz-Boodle, Dr Solomon Pacigico, and Launcelot Wagstaffe.[60]

Dickens was more sparing with names. For contractual reasons he
might publish anonymously; and he was "Tibbs" for the twelve
sketches "Scenes and Characters" in *Bell's Life in London* (1835–6).
But for other sketches as early as 1834, for *The Pickwick Papers* (1837),
and for the first two issues of *Oliver Twist* (1838) he was "Boz". Boz
originated as "Moses", a pet name of Dickens' youngest brother
Augustus, whom he called Moses "in honour of the Vicar of Wakefield; which being facetiously pronounced through the nose, became
Boses, and, being shortened, became Boz. 'Boz' was a very familiar
household word to me long before I was an author; and so I came to
adopt it".[61]

Pen names are sometimes selected for their associative value. Samuel
Clemens chose "Mark Twain" for its river association, the call of the
leadsman. And in Anthony Powell's *Casanova's Chinese Restaurant* (1960)
the violinist's real name "is Wilson or Wilkinson or Parker [...] something

rather practical and healthy like that. A surname felt to ring too much of plain common sense."[62]

In the Bloomsbury circle, nicknames were both abundant and polymorphous. Virginia Woolf was "the Goat", "Billy [goat]", and later "Miss Jan":

Every relationship was defined by her animal-name for herself—Sparroy or Wallaby for Violet Dickinson, Billy or Ape for Vanessa, Goat for Thoby and Emma Vaughan, and, later, Mandril or Marmoset for Leonard. And everyone she knew would be reinvented and taken possession of by a nickname: Vanessa was Tawny or Maria or Marmot, or, more lastingly, Dolphin; Thoby was Gribbs or Grim or Cresty or Thobs; Stella (a nickname apparently originating with Julia) was "The Old Cow". These nicknames would then in turn be nicknamed, and the animals would reproduce by a literary parthenogenesis into yet more beasts. So "Goat" or "the Goat" becomes Goatus Esq, Capra, Il Giotto; Emma Vaughan's "Toad" would be "dearest Reptile", or "Todkins, Toadlebinks, or Todelcrancz; the Ape might be the Apes, or Singe, or the Singes.[63]

Many modern writers have used pen names: notably the "George Orwell" of Eric Arthur Blair (1903–50), the "James Aston" of T. H. White, the "Rebecca West" of Cecily Fairfield, and the "Victoria Lucas" of Sylvia Plath for *The Bell Jar* (1963). The "Saki" of Hector Hugh Munro (1870–1916) is from the "Minister of Wine" in *The Rubáiyát of Omar Khayyám*, or from the name of a species of monkey, an animal congenial to Munro. In the later twentieth century, however, complete anonymity became less feasible: publishers increasingly obliged writers to participate in selling their books. So pen names held less mystery. They were now no more than labels, in John Mullan's view, and often indicated the less ambitious part of a writer's output—romances, crime fiction, or science fiction.[64] Julian Barnes uses "Dan Kavanagh" for his detective stories, just as Edith Pargeter uses "Ellis Peters" and Ruth Rendell "Barbara Vine". Mullan finds nothing shamefaced in this "gesture", and he may be right. But in the 1950s, when academics and schoolmasters used pen names for their detective stories, they certainly wished to keep their popular writing low profile, in case their salaries were held frozen at the "efficiency bar". Thus C. Day Lewis wrote poetry under his own name, but detective stories as "Nicholas Blake". Bruce Montgomery wrote as "Edmund Crispin"; Glyn Daniel as "Dilwyn Rees"; and J. I. M. Stewart as "Michael Innes" (a pen name not used for his more serious novels). Academic authors did not go in for anagrammatic pen names. But among other writers, anagrams—retaining at least the letters of their own name—seem to have had a strong appeal. Marguerite Yourcenar, for example, was baptized de Crayencour.[65]

Multiple pen names are convenient for prolific writers as well as those thought scandalous or subversive. Pornography teems with disguised names: "Count Palmiro Vicarion" (Christopher Logue); "Marcus van Heller" (John Stevenson); "Greta X" and "Angela Pearson" (John Millington-Ward); "Frances Lengel" (Alex Trocchi); "Henry Crannach" (Marilyn Meestie); "Pauline Réage" (Dominique Aury); and "Felix Salten" (Siegmund Salzmann, who wrote both *Bambi* and the anonymous *Josefine Mutzenbacher*, the memoir of a prostitute).[66] Mullan attributes pornographers' use of disguises to motives of shame; but they may as often have been motivated by fear. Before (and even after) the *Lady Chatterley's Lover* case in 1960, pornographic fiction was liable to prosecution.

Type-names

Names for social, ethnic, or geographical types include: Jack and Jill (low class), Joan, Jenny, and Hodge (rustic), Geordie (northeast English), Biddy, Mick, Paddy (Irish), Jock, Jimmy, Mac, Mack (Scottish), Taffy or Davy (Welsh). Occupational names include Sparks (electrician), Chips (joiner or carpenter), Bobby (policeman), Charlie (night watchman), Thomas (tapster), and Nan, Nancy, Moll, Doll, Jenny, and Kate (prostitute). Scots "Cuddy", from Cuthbert, means a donkey or stupid person, as in *Shepheardes Calender* February. And Robin was once a name for a fool.

Such generic, sometimes allusive names may have quite ordinary beginnings. An early instance is Vergil, *Eclogue* 3, satirizing the jealous minor poets Bavius and Maevius.[67] Apparently real-life individuals, these two became proverbially hypercritical. In *The Baviad: A Paraphrastic Imitation of the First Satire of Persius* (1791, 1793) and *The Maeviad* (1795), William Gifford (1756–1826) could still use these names in writing against the *Della Cruscans*, a late-eighteenth-century coterie producing sentimental poetry. (Their leader Robert Merry had adopted the pseudonym "Della Crusca" after the Florentine academy.)

A similarly allusive type is "Farmer Giles", probably alluding (as we saw in chapter 2) to *The Maid of the Mill* (1765) by Isaac Bickerstaff

(1733–?1808). The name is obsolescent but survives in J. R. R. Tolkien's *Farmer Giles of Ham* (1949). Another such type, John Bull the generic Englishman, was popularized by Pope's friend Dr John Arbuthnot (1667–1735) in his satire *Law is a Bottomless Pit* (1712), republished as *The History of John Bull*, and by George Colman the Younger in *John Bull* (1805). Its meaning, however, shifts according to the writer's views. Dickens writes "By some he was called 'a thorough-bred Englishman', by some 'a genuine John Bull'" (*Barnaby Rudge* ch. 47). J. H. Newman's meaning is sharper: "Anglo-maniacs or John Bullists, as they are popularly termed".[68] And in 1904 George Bernard Shaw explores Irish implications in his *John Bull's Other Island*, its title probably modelled on Leon Paul Blouet's *John Bull and His Island*.

As a common first name, John has many representative applications. It is generic for a footman, butler or waiter (*OED* 1 b). In Jonson's *A Tale of a Tub* (1633) John is the type-name for an official: "All Constables are truly Johns for the King, | What ere their names are; be they Tony, or Roger".[69] But John can also be a ponce, or a prostitute's client (*OED* 1 c, f). And "Sir John" in the sixteenth century was a disrespectful term for a priest. In legal terminology, John is used for legal fictions: Ronald Rubinstein dedicates *John Citizen and the Law* (1948) to John Doe and Richard Roe.[70]

Similarly with Jack, a familiar form of John. As early as 1362 Jack was the ordinary, common man, a usage underlying "Iacke the iogelour" in *Piers Plowman* (A 7.65) and surviving in the idiom "every man Jack" (*OED* 2c). To Dickens Jack means a serving man or labourer: "Having a chat with the 'jack', who [...] seems to be wholly incapable of doing anything but lounging about."[71]

The generic Jone or Joan (later Jane) as a female equivalent of John is readily documented. In the early Middle Ages Joan (contracted from Old French *Jo(h)anne* and Latin *Joanna*) could be a queen's name; but in the sixteenth century it was applied to female rustics, ordinary or coarse country maids: "many a countrie Jone"; "a homely Joan, a Coarse Ord'nary Woman"; "such a dowdy, such a country Joan".[72] Proverbially, Joan was someone at the opposite end of the social spectrum from a lady. So Shakespeare (1595), "Some men must love my Lady, and some Ione"; Shakespeare (1596), "Now can I make any Ione a Lady"; Anthony Munday (1599), "Joan as good as my Lady"; Arthur Dent (1601) and John Day (1606), "Ile teach him to put a difference betwixt Ione and my Ladie".[73] Often the emphasis falls on a common humanity or sexuality, as in Munday and Henry Chettle (1601), "He is our Ladies Chaplaine, but serves Ione"; Thomas Heywood (1606), "Joan's as good as this French lady"; John Davies of Hereford (1611), "Ioan in the darke is as good as my lady"; Francis Beaumont and John Fletcher (1616), "When they are drunk, e'ne then, when Jone and my Lady are all one"; Thomas Shelton (1620), "in the night Joan is as good as my lady"; Robert Herrick (1648), "Jone as my Lady is as good i' th' dark"; James Howell (1659), "in the dark, Joan is as good as my Lady"; Giovanni Torriano (1666), "Jone is as good as my Lady, in the dark".[74]

The stereotype shows up everywhere in character names. In Henry Medwall's *Fulgens and Lucres* (1497) Joan is a handmaid to Lucres; in Shakespeare's *1 Henry VI* Joan of Arc is Joan de Pucelle, and Talbot puns on pucelle/puzzel ("maid", "whore"); in Robert Greene's *Friar Bacon and Friar Bungay* (1594) Joan is "a Country Wench"; in Jonson's *Bartholomew Fair* (1614) Joane Trash is a gingerbread woman; in Heywood's *A Woman Killed with Kindness* (1607) Joan Miniver is a country wench; and in William Cartwright's *The Ordinary* (1634–5) Joane Potlucke is a vintner's widow, vulgarly genteel. The name was not fully rehabilitated until the twentieth century—as a result, apparently, of Shaw's *St Joan* (1924).

Slave and servant names

From ancient times, slaves and servants usually had single names, perhaps with the addition of their master's name in adjectival or genitive form: *Eros Aurelius* ("Eros of the Aurelii"), "Walker's Ned".[75] Booker Washington claimed not to know his own second name (it was Taliaferro).[76] And the slaves' single names were more often than not used in shortened, familiar forms: Bob, Tom, and the like. These hypocoristic, diminutive, or pet names took intimacy for granted, without at all negating hierarchy. Servile names seem usually to have been arrived at by one or another of two routes: occupational type-names, or the arbitrary names often assigned to slaves.

By the seventeenth century the class implication of type-names was fairly distinct: William Gouge observed in 1622 that, for gentles, diminutives such as Jack were "unseemly: servants are usually so called".[77] Laurie Maguire, exploring the links between familiar forms and female domesticity, concludes that "Kate" was "downmarket".[78] That may be too sweeping: allowance needs to be made for the intimacy of the early modern household. Besides, servant status did not necessarily imply a low rank. Many retainers were gentle: some had houses and servants of their own.[79] Besides, status might be sunk, as in *1 Henry IV* 2.4, where Prince Henry is "sworn brother to a leash of drawers, and can call them all by their christen names, as Tom, Dick, and Francis". Diminutives expressed familiarity: they could sometimes be used within the household regardless of rank.

Early-seventeenth-century great households were still predominantly male. Except for a few, such as Anne Clifford Countess of Dorset's, the only female servants were likely to be a lady's maid, laundry maids, and occasionally a kitchen maid.[80] Later, as the aristocracy and landed gentry declined financially, these proportions changed radically, until female servants eventually made up the larger part of a household. Simultaneously, the spread of paid service meant that servants lost status and even individuality. Regulations for the household of the Earl of Cork at Stalbridge (built 1630), specify that "all the Women Servants under the Degree of Chambermaids be certainly known by their names to the Steward, and not altered or changed upon every Occasion without the consent of the Steward".[81] In 1669, Samuel Pepys did not know his new middle maid's name.[82]

Simultaneously, the names of servants lost status and became less fashionable. As we have seen, Joan had become a rustic name by the sixteenth century. Except as a servant name, it was replaced in the seventeenth century by Jane. Servants' names sometimes came to be linked to particular household functions or spheres of activity. Thus the Bedford household had an "Alice-about-the-house" and a "Thomas-in-the-kitchen".[83] Joan may have been generic for a kitchen maid, as in Shakespeare's line "While greasy Joan doth keel [cool by stirring] the pot.[84] And a type-name for messengers was "How'd'ye" or "Howd'ee", from the use of the greeting for the message itself.[85] More bluntly, the function could be used as a name, as in the summons "Page!" (any page would do). Several characters use this summons successfully in George Etherege's *The Man of Mode* (1676). The practice disburdened employers' memories so conveniently that it survived until quite recently—for example in the "Boots" employed in some hotels.[86] (Dickens has a Boots in "The Holly-Tree".) One should not exaggerate the regularity of system. Some type-names were customary; others reflected the preference of a particular employer (as the head of the household should by now perhaps be regarded).

The household roster

"Jeames", an obsolete form of "James", was fashionable until the late eighteenth century, when it became common. Eventually it served as a name for liveried footmen, as in Thackeray's *The Diary of C. Jeames de la Pluche* (1846). Lady Clavering's footman in *Pendennis* (1848–50) is also Jeames, and so is Lady Pocklington's huge footman in *Our Street* (1848)—not to mention the assumed name of the Earl of Bagnigge in *Lords and Liveries* (1847). In *The Virginians* (1857–9) the footman's doomed race is "passing out of the world where they once walked in glory". Even so, in 1875 James Grant still writes of "a tall 'Jeames' in plush".[87]

"James", however, without the slightly jocular associations of "Jeames", is Viscount Castlewood's coachman in *Henry Esmond* (1852),[88] a novel often credited with establishing James as the typical coachman's name. But that may not be right: Austen uses James for a groom or coachman three times. Exactly when James became the name for a coachman is uncertain. In 1641 the Earl of Bedford's coachman was Rolles for example, and in 1653 Whitelocke's coachmen were Edward Ellis and Robert Ash.[89] The type-name has outlasted the coach itself in the idiom "Home, James, and don't spare the horses [more recently 'horse power']", from Fred Hillebrand's 1934 song.

Even in the coaching era, the typecasting of James was never uniform. None of Dickens' ten coachmen is a James. To infer that Dickens' servants are more individualized than Thackeray's, though, would be unfair: Thackeray uses naming in many different ways—including satire of arbitrary naming. In any case Thackeray too rings the changes: his footmen can be Charles or Jack or John.[90] Carey calls "Yellow-plush" stereotypic; but as a surrogate of Thackeray himself Yellowplush is much more. A servant who knows all that goes on, he figures an amusingly avoided, yet utilized, omniscient author.[91]

At first butlers and stewards (often superior individuals) went by their full names. In 1613 Anne Clifford's steward was Edward Legge. The Earl of Kent's steward was John Selden the jurist. Selden was

perhaps the Countess' lover and secret husband, certainly her heir. Bulstrode Whitelocke's swanky travelling household in 1653 included two
butlers, Thomas Thoroughton and Christopher Hen; his steward, John
Walker, was a barrister. In 1681 the Earl of Bedford's steward was Ran-
dolph Bingley. Later, butlers and housekeepers were both regularly
called by their surnames (a mark of status rather than distance). In the
1660s the resident housekeeper at Bedford House was "Mrs Bruce". In
fiction, the formidable *Mansfield Park* butler, for example, is "Badde-
ley".[92] Sir Leicester Dedlock's housekeeper in *Bleak House* (1852–3) is
"Mrs Rouncewell". And the housekeeper in Thackeray's *Bluebeard's
Ghost* (1843) is Mrs Baggs. To upper servants Austen gives convincingly
plain names (Bingley's housekeeper is "Nicholls", the Bennets' "Mrs
Hill", and the housekeeper of Pemberley "Mrs Reynolds");[93] although
several servants in her real-life circle had unusual names (Sackree,
Richis, Bigion).[94] Exceptionally, the butler in *The Alchemist* (1610),
Face's persona, goes by Jeremy—perhaps as the familiar first name of
an accomplice, perhaps as a frequent Puritan name. The butler to the
Pendennis family, too, is simply John.

Among female names, Abigail was early established as suitable for a
waiting-woman or lady's maid. There was biblical authority at 1 Samuel 25: 24–31 and theatrical precedent in the lecherous waiting-woman
in *The Scornful Lady* (1613), Beaumont and Fletcher's popular play. In
the Earl of Bedford's household "Mistress" Abigail (no surname) was
the housekeeper—not yet a housekeeper in the superior sense, since
she buys, or sews, shirts for the pages.[95] "Abigail" could be used as a
common noun: in Congreve's *The Old Bachelor* (1693) the pimp Setter
says "Thou art some forsaken Abigail we have dallied with heretofore"
(3.1.192); and Smollett's *Humphrey Clinker* (1771) has "an antiquated
Abigail, dressed in her lady's cast clothes". In 1849, Bulwer Lytton
could still write "the woman was dressed with a quiet neatness that
seemed to stamp her profession as that of an Abigail—black cloak with
long cape, of that peculiar silk which seems spun on purpose for ladies'
maids".[96]

Sally Lunn was a famous pastry cook in Bath in the eighteenth century; but in the next century the name lost status. Among the hundred
or so servants in her novels, Austen uses Sally for a lower servant
four times. "Old Sally" was a workhouse nurse in *Oliver Twist* (1838),
and Sally in our alley was the daughter of a cabbage-net maker and a
shoelace seller.[97] In the same way Betsy, fashionable in the eighteenth

century,[98] became common, and relegated to chamber-maid status, before being rehabilitated in the twentieth century. Austen has Betty or Betsy for a maid or kitchen-maid, and Thackeray as many as eight. Betsy is also Mrs Raddle's maid in *Pickwick Papers* (1837) and a prostitute in *Oliver Twist* (1837–8). Another common maid-servant name was Mary: a Mary is housemaid to Nupkins in *Pickwick Papers* (1836–7); to the Copperfields (1850); to Wemmick in *Great Expectations* (1860–1); and to Mrs Brandon in Thackeray's *Adventures of Philip* (1861–2).

Servant names sometimes offered the resources of literary allusion and finessed expectations. Thus, "Valentine" (from *valens*, "healthy, strong"), a name from romance (*Valentine and Orson*), was given in Elizabethan drama to knights' sons, foolish gallants, gentlemen, gentlemen attendants, and servants.[99] In a high-profile instance, Jonson's *The Case is Altered* (1597), Valentine is Colonnia's stupid servant, a man without skill at cudgels and given to repeating people's words. Yet in *Love for Love* (1695) William Congreve makes Valentine the master and his witty valet Jeremy (probably after Jeremy in *The Alchemist*). This inversion, glancing back at the resourceful slaves of Greek New Comedy, foreshadows P. G. Wodehouse's omniscient Jeeves and brainless Bertie Wooster.

Arbitrary naming

Ambitious gentry keen to make a good showing have generally wished their servants to have impressive, or at least not inappropriate, names. In Tudor times, this might be achieved by attracting retainers of good name: in the seventeenth century, when servants came and went more quickly, it was not so easy. (To have someone like John Selden as steward—a celebrated jurist with a mother of knightly family—was then fortunate indeed.) But there was apparently no thought as yet of assigning names to servants as if they were slaves.

There were many slaves in Britain then—more than most history books indicate.[100] And since Roman times slaves had been named at their masters' will—almost necessarily so, since African slaves often had names difficult for Western tongues to learn. Most often slaves were given ordinary English names such as servants had. But sometimes they were called Quashee or Quashie, Ashantee or Fantee *Kwasi*, the name of a Sunday's child, extended as a type-name for any black. And sometimes celebrated Republican names like Brutus and Cassius were imposed. Ancient Roman custom forbade slaves to be named after great captains;[101] but this was ignored or flouted in Renaissance England. "Pompey" in *Measure for Measure* has been regarded as pretentious classicizing, made comical by juxtaposition with the low surname "Bum". But the tapster was possibly a black slave. Such high-flown names reflected a master's ambition and gave rise to terribly amusing jokes at the slave's expense. It would be a long time before William Cowper's slaver reflected "I must no more | Carry Caesars and Pompeys to Sugar-cane shore".[102] The tradition continued, and is referred to by Derek Walcott in *Omeros* (1990), where Achille and Hector are descendants of slave ancestors. Shakespeare several times used "Balthasar" for an attendant:[103] an exotic name that would have had special aptness for a black. In iconography from the late Middle Ages to the baroque the second Magus, Balthasar, was commonly represented as African.[104] Similarly, perhaps, with other ostentatious servant names.

The connection between slave and servant naming comes out clearly in *Robinson Crusoe*. When Crusoe saw a savage pursued by cannibals, "it came now very warmly upon my Thoughts [...] that now was my Time to get me a Servant, and perhaps a Companion, or Assistant; and that I was call'd plainly by Providence to save this poor Creature's Life". When, however, the rescued savage abased himself, this is taken as a "Token of swearing to be my Slave for ever". Servant, or slave? This ambiguity continues in the naming: "his Name should be *Friday*, which was the Day I sav'd his Life; I call'd him so for the Memory of the Time; I likewise taught him to say *Master*, and then let him know, that was to be my Name".[105] Friday, the day of his liberation and salvation, is the first day of his new life of service (religious overtones can be heard). "Friday" suggests arbitrary naming, and has a jocular ring to the European reader. Crusoe may also have been aware, however, of the West African custom of giving "day-names", whereby "Friday" was a serious name, quite "suitable" for a servant.[106]

Defoe's names have historical implications that anticipate more recent fiction. A novelist who outstandingly realizes the literary possibilities of slave naming is Toni Morrison. In *Beloved: A Novel* (1987), for example, she uses names in a special way to allude to the characters' racial history. Cynthia Lyles-Scott gives a telling instance: "the *D* at the end of Paul's name denotes his being fourth in a succession of male slaves all named Paul. [...] the characters' names are as much a part of the novel as is the plot".[107] She cites Genevieve Fabre: "Names are an essential part of the legacy (of black people) [...] Blacks receive dead patronyms from whites [...] names are disguises, jokes, or brand names—from yearnings, gestures, flaws, events, mistakes, weaknesses. Names endure like marks or have secrets they do not easily yield".[108]

Servant names

During the seventeenth century, in a largely new development, names began to be imposed on servants almost as if they were slaves. For nearly three centuries this custom prevailed: servants might have to relinquish their own names and take instead those associated with their household office. They made a sort of altruistic identification with the family, in particular with a predecessor in office. The existence of arbitrary naming offers strong evidence in support of Ragussis' "family plot" theory. The arbitrary names imposed on successive incumbents overwrote individual identity, just as happened with children. Indeed, seventeenth-century servants often were relatives, as with Pepys' sister.

Exactly when arbitrary naming began is hard to determine. The names themselves are but equivocal evidence. In 1653, for example, Bulstrode Whitelocke had a postilion called Aurelius ("Golden") Newman. The Roman name is clearly an example of fashionable classicizing.[109] But was it a nickname, a name given at baptism, or a name imposed on a black slave? Or is this an early instance of arbitrary servant naming? I have found few signs of the practice before the Restoration. There is no obvious evidence of it in Bedford household records, for example, although the accounts are full and list many servants' names, including those of seven or eight women.

Arbitrary naming seems to be topical in 1676, the probable date of the first performance of Etherege's *The Man of Mode*. Sir Fopling Flutter does not know (or pretends not to know) the name of his only English footman, and this exchange follows:

MRS LOVEIT. What's your name?
FOOTMAN. John Trott, madam!
SIR FOPLING. Oh unsufferable! Trott, Trott, Trott! there's nothing so barbarous as the names of our English servants. What countryman are you sirrah?

FOOTMAN. Hampshire, sir?
SIR FOPLING. Then Hampshire be your name. Hey, Hampshire!

(*The Man of Mode*, 3.3.304–11)

Etherege's precise target here is not immediately obvious. Servants in Sir Fopling's social circle seem to be treated as mere instruments and summoned accordingly by a call of "Page!" But replacing "Trott" (the ordinary occupational name for a messenger) by "Hampshire" is presented as a particular affectation. Sir Fopling's other footmen are all French, with French names—"Champagne, Norman, La Rose, La Fleur, La Tour, La Verdure"—apparently in imitation of Moliere's servant names in *Les Précieuses Ridicules* (1659), Scene 11. Congreve's comment suggests he thought Etherege's target to be the aping of French customs: "The Ancients us'd to call their Servants by the names of the Countries [counties] from whence they came [...] The French to this Day do the same, and call their Footmen *Champagne le Picard, le Gascon, le Bourgignon, &c.*"[110]

At any rate, arbitrary naming continued in the eighteenth century, and was still a target in 1853–5, when Miss Honeyman in *The Newcomes* "called all her young persons Sally; and a great number of Sallies were consumed at her house".[111] Thackeray's satire is sharp. Martha Honeyman is charitable, and each "Sally" comes from the workhouse. But the fact that the Sallys do not last long tells against their employer.

Henry James seems to give mature consideration to arbitrary naming in "A Bundle of Letters" (1879). There Evelyn Vane writes that "Lady Battledown makes all her governesses take the same name; she gives £5 more a year for the purpose. I forget what it is she calls them; I think it's Johnson (which to me always suggests a lady's maid). Governesses shouldn't have too pretty a name; they shouldn't have a nicer name than the family".[112] At first this may be taken as yet another instance of James using a traveller as a device to introduce "objective" observations on European mores. But apparently he had in fact newly discovered the institution of arbitrary naming. For in the very same year he explains to his sister Alice (as a new discovery) that "it is part of the British code that you can call a servant any name you like, and many people have a fixed name for their butler, which all the successive occupants of the place are obliged to assume, so that the family needn't change its habits".[113]

James relates here the very conversation from which he divined the code (perhaps not current then in the parts of the USA he knew well):

When she [the chamber-maid] came I said—"You had better tell me your name, please." *She.* "Well sir, it might be Maria." "It *might* be?" "Well, sir, they calls me Maria." "Isn't it your name?" "My name is Annie, sir, but Missus (Miss Balls) says that's too familiar." So I have compromised and call her Annie-Maria."

Apparently in Miss Balls' view, servants' names should not risk suggesting the degree of intimacy that had obtained in, say, Elizabethan times.

By the end of the nineteenth century more than Henry James were feeling the oppressiveness of the code. Lady Battledown's £5 suggests as much; and so does the delicacy shown towards renaming by Evelyn Vane's parents. Mrs Vane had perfect confidence in the new governess Miss Turnover: "it is only a pity she has such an odd name. Mamma thought of asking her if she would mind taking another when she came; but papa thought she might object." The problem was solved by leaving the governess behind at Eastbourne.

Saki's story "The Secret Sin of Septimus Brope" (1911) brings out the full enormity of imposing names on servants. When Mrs Riversedge accidentally overhears a servant being called "Florrie", this sharp exchange follows:

"Is your maid called Florence?"
"Her name is Florinda."
"What an extraordinary name to give a maid!"
"I did not give it to her; she arrived in my service already christened."
"What I mean is," said Mrs Riversedge, "that when I get maids with unsuitable names I call them Jane; they soon get used to it."
"An excellent plan," said the aunt of Clovis coldly; "unfortunately I have got used to being called Jane myself. It happens to be my name."

As late as 1920, L. M. Montgomery attempted a sentimentalized version of the renamed servant in *Anne of Avonlea.* The lonely Miss Lavendar Lewis, unable "to pay the wages of a grown-up girl" employs successive sisters of the Bowman family as companions, from the ages of thirteen to sixteen. For convenience she names them Charlotta the First, Second, Third, and Fourth. Perhaps Montgomery means gentle satire of the vaunted democracy of the USA, belied by its dynasties of wealth. In Canada, by contrast, it is the servants, not the rich, who are named like royalty. Unfortunately the numbering of servant generations also recalls the names imposed on slaves. And Miss Lavendar's make-believe "tea-parties" cannot make up for the suppression, almost eradication, of the Charlottas' true names: "they all look so much alike there's no telling them apart".[114]

Later, the memory of imposed names blurs into "aristocratic" stereotypes. In Frank Richards' story "My Lord Bunter", Bunter writes "I've got a valet here named James. I usually call him George, because I can't remember that his name is James…I can't be expected to remember servants' names, being accustomed to such immense numbers of them".[115]

Notes

1. *Odyssey* 9.364–7, Homer 1996: 151.
2. Homer 1967: 323–4.
3. Pope's n. to 9.432, Homer 1967: 323–4.
4. *Metis* could mean a poet's craft. Other wordplays include the description of the drunken Polyphemus as *krateros*, "strong", punning on *krater*, "wine-bowl".
5. "If anyone asks who blinded you, say it was Odysseus son of Laertes" (*Odyssey* 9.502–5).
6. See Powell 1991. The case for Homer being literate is put in Rutherford 1996.
7. A perfect anagram, given the usual licence of treating multiple letters as single. Chronograms and anagrams were used by Euripides in the fifth century BC: see Margoliouth 1915.
8. Fit the Third, line 55, Carroll 1939: 687.
9. Bliss 2008: 105; see Parker 1979: Index s.v. *Naming*; Cooper 2004: Index s.v. *Naming*.
10. See Bliss 2008: 23, 36, 48–9.
11. See Bliss 2008: 66; Vinaver 1971: Index s.v. *Lancelot*. More usually Lancelot du Lac, almost a full name.
12. Chaucer's Lybeux; see Bliss 2008: 48–9, 115; Cooper 2004: Index s.v. *Lybeaus Desconus*.
13. See Bliss 2008: 16, 93.
14. See Bliss 2008: 89–90, 179–80; Cooper 2004: Index s.v. *King Horn*.
15. *Spectator* 272 (11 January 1712).
16. See Seaton 1961: App. C.
17. Halkett and Laing 1926–34; see Mullan 2007: 5, Starner and Traister 2011.
18. See Mullan 2007: 55. Although "pseudonym" is not recorded before 1833, the adjective "pseudonymous" already warrants definition ("that has a counterfeit name") in the 1706 edition of Edward Phillips' *The New World of English Words*. Earlier still, *pseudonymal* is in Blount's *Glossographia* of 1656 and *pseudonymus* ("he that hath a counterfayte name") in Cooper 1578 and *pseudonimo* in Florio 1611.
19. Mullan 2007: 6.
20. See Mullan 2007: 167–8; Mack 1985: 490, 555.

21. See Ruthven 2001; Mullan 2003; Morton 2011 ("Authorship is always, in some sense, a hoax, an adoption of voices and personalities, sometimes indicated by a pseudonym [...] but always with a little tremor of ambiguity.")

22. The two are compared in Ehrenpreis 1962–83: 3.240.

23. See Ehrenpreis 1962–83: 3.207–8, 291–4.

24. See Scriblerus 1988: 1–22. For other group pseudonyms, such as Smectymnuus and Cabal, see Wilson 1998: 288.

25. See Ehrenpreis 1962–83: Index s.v. *Bickerstaff*.

26. See Ehrenpreis 1962: 2.197–209; Mayhew 1964.

27. Ehrenpreis 1962–83: 2.417; cf. 2.279, 407.

28. Bennett and Harte 1997.

29. Kipling 1932: 3–33.

30. Kipling 1932: 11–12, 22.

31. Robson 1964: 277 persuasively brings out how the hoax has a corrupting effect on Manallace.

32. See Libby Purves in *The Times*, 29 August 2006; Valerie Grove, *The Times*, 9 September 2006; and Katsoulis 2010, a lively but not very accurate general account of literary hoaxes.

33. See Charles Bremner, in *The Times* (9 February 2010) 21.

34. See Nolan and Dawson 2004. *The Darkening Ecliptic* is reprinted in *The Penguin Book of Modern Australian Poetry*.

35. Cf. Katsoulis 2010: 327–8 on William Boyd's confession of remorse for his Nat Tate hoax of 1998. "The subject's name alone should have rung bells for anyone familiar with the two most famous art galleries in Britain".

36. See *ODECN* vii; Crystal 1995: 145, 149, 152, 306; Adams 2009 (a critique of Kripke's causal theory).

37. See Crystal 2010: 180–1.

38. *Spectator* 244 (10 December 1711).

39. See Trevor-Roper 2006: 28 n. 4.

40. *MWW* 2.2.142; 2.1.144; 4.4.71; see Levith 1978: 84; Kökeritz 1966: 20.

41. *OED* 1. b; cf. Middleton, *A Chaste Maid in Cheapside* (1611) 1.2.63, "He's but one pip above a serving-man", not attested after 1693.

42. *The Day's Work* (1898).

43. For others see Williams 1954.

44. Others include De Insulis (Lisle); De Fluctibus (Robert Fludd); Junius (Patrick Young); Benevolus (Edward Benlowes); and Faeni-Lignum (Thomas Heywood).

45. I.e. Christopher Brooke; Henry Goodyear; and Inigo Jones. For others, see Aubrey 1898: 2.50–51.

46. Also FIDE HONOR for IOHN FORD, a perfect anagram.

47. Attributed to Jean Dorat or Daurat (1508–88); see du Bellay 1948: 154 n.

48. See Griffiths 2006: 13–14 *et passim*.

49. E. K., Prefatory Epistle to Gabriell Harvey before *The Shepheardes Calender* (1579).

50. For his wordplays on Marot/Maro, identifying with Vergil, see Paterson 1987: 110; Rigolot 1977: 66–7.

51. *CCCHA* 358; he was also Paulus ("Shorty"): see Harington 2009: Index.

52. Probably a rebus-like cryptogram for Mar-stone; see Marston 1961: 265; *OED* s.v. *kinsing*.

53. *Carlyle Newsletter* 9: 31.

54. Coined by Smollett and Boswell's father Lord Auchinleck respectively; see *ODECN*.

55. See Boswell 1934: 1.385. William Melmoth (1710–99) is not to be confused with Courtney Melmoth (the pseudonym of Samuel Jackson Pratt), nor with Sebastian Melmoth, Oscar Wilde's pseudonym after 1895 (Charles Maturin, author of *Melmoth the Wanderer*, was Wilde's great-uncle).

56. Mullan 2007: 76.

57. See Mullan 2007: chs 2–4.

58. But see correspondence in *TLS* (2 March 2007) 17.

59. See *ODECN*.

60. Mullan 2007: 248–50.

61. Pierce and Wheeler 1878: 1; Moses is Dr Primrose's son in Goldsmith's *The Vicar of Wakefield*.

62. Wilson 1998: 289.

63. Lee 1996: 111.

64. Mullan 2007: 287–8.

65. See Harrison 2009: 82.

66. See Meeske 1965; Campbell 1992: 17; Kearney 2008.

67. *Eclogues* 3.90–1: "Qui Bavium non odit, amet tua carmina, Maevi, | atque idem iungat vulpes et mulgeat hircos" ("Let him who hates not Bavius love your songs, Maevius; and let him also yoke foxes and milk he-goats"); see Knox 1961: 114 citing Richard Sherry, *Rhetorike* (1555) on the Vergilian lines as an example of astysmus; Minnis and Scott 1988: 39–40.

68. *Lectures on the Present Position of Catholics in England* (1851) 25. On John Bull generally, see Miles Taylor's *ODNB* entry.

69. *A Tale of a Tub* 4.1.57–8.

70. Rubinstein 1948.

71. OED 4a; *Sketches by Boz* (1850) 59. Cf. the use of "jack" for various machines.

72. William Warner, *Albion's England* 1586, 1606) 14.91; B.E. 1698; Mary Martha Sherwood, *The History of Susan Grey* (1801).

73. *Love's Labour's Lost* (1595) 3.1.207; *King John* (1596) 1.1.184; Wilson 1970: 412; Tilley 1950: J57; see Barton 1990: 60.

74. Tilley 1950: J57.

75. See Wilson 1998: 25, 311. Occasionally two names are found, e.g. "Dido Belle", a black slave in the Kenwood household: see Musson 2009: 120; Heller 1987.

76. See Hall 1981: 140.

77. Gouge 1622: 283.

78. Maguire 2007: 123–4.

79. See Mertes 1988: 59; Woolgar 1999; Thomson 1937; Hecht 1980; Heal 1990.

80. In 1653, Bulstrode Whitelocke had three laundry maids. Complete lists of servants have survived for several households; see, e.g., Clifford 1923.

81. Musson 2009: 65.

82. Pepys, *Diary*, 5–6 April 1669.

83. Thomson 1923: 120–1.

84. *LLL* (1595) 5.2.919.

85. See e.g. Steele, *The Funeral* 3.2.5; *Tatler* 245; Brome, *Northern Lass*.

86. See *OED* s.v. *Boots*. The usage perhaps originated in John O'Keefe's *Jack Boots* (1798).

87. *One of the Six Hundred* (1875) ch. 15.

88. 1.4; also a servant in *The Book of Snobs* (1846–8) and *The Newcomes* (1853–55) ch. 58; and a waiter at the "Cave of Harmony" and "A Night's Pleasure" in *Sketches and Travels in London* (1847–50). See *OED*, s.v. James; Pierce and Wheeler 1878; Mudge and Sears 1910: xxiii.

89. Thomson 1923: 52; Whitelocke 1990: 296.

90. *The Newcomes* (1853–5) ch. 10; *The Great Hoggarty Diamond* (1841) ch. 13; *The Book of Snobs* (1846–8); and *Mrs Perkins' Ball* (1837). Austen too has a manservant called John; see Austen 2010: 253.

91. *Vanity Fair*, ed. John Carey (2001), p. xv; Mudge and Sears 1910: 298.

92. For a list of respected housekeepers fictional and real, see Musson 2009: 150.

93. *Pride and Prejudice* (1813) vol. 1, chs. 11 and 13; *Mansfield Park* (1814) vol. 2, ch. 1.
94. Richis was a Rowling servant; Sackree was Elizabeth's maid, and Mme Bigeon was Henry's Eliza's maid; see Hodge 1972: 47, 91, 100, 199; Le Faye 2004: 200, 248, 259.
95. See Thomson 1923: 119.
96. *The Caxtons* (1850) 14.6.
97. Carey 1800? Black Sal was a black-face doll popular in nineteenth-century London, named after Black Sal in Pierce Egan's *Life in London* (1821), probably the original of our Aunt Sally.
98. E.g. Pope, "Epistle to Cobham" 247, "Betty—give this Cheek a little Red." For other instances see Pope 1961: 36–7 n.
99. Berger et al. 1998 lists thirteen examples.
100. See Edwards 1990.
101. For the rule, see Camden 1984: 49.
102. "Sweet Meat Has Sour Sauce", lines 34–5, Cowper 1934: 375. In *Tatler* 245 (2 November 1710), "a Black-moor Boy" signing himself "Pompey" complains of his treatment. The Earl of Suffolk had a black running footman called "Scipio Africanus"; see Musson 2009: 121.
103. *Much Ado* 2.3 (attendant); *Romeo* 5.1 (servant); *Merchant* 3.4 (servant). See Levith 1978: 80–1; cf. Barton 1990: 96–7. On the presence of blacks in Britain, see Edwards 1990.
104. Schiller 1971: 1.96.
105. Defoe 1972: 202, 206.
106. E.g. in Akan. Thus Kofi Annan's forename means "Boy born on Friday". See Wilson 1998: 310; Harrison 2006: 53, "Man Friday is taken on as a servant, not a partner. Crusoe also renames him, that most potent form of possession". An Italian Appeal Court recently ordered parents to name their son Gregorio instead of Venerdi (Friday): see *The Times* (19 December 2007) p. 34.
107. Lyles-Scott 2008: 23.
108. Fabre 1988: 108–9.
109. See Wilson 1998: 202–4.
110. Etherege 1982: 281.
111. *The Newcomes* (1853) ch. 9; cf. ch. 15.
112. James 1999: 507.
113. Letter of 26 March 1879, James 1974–84: 2.224–5.
114. Montgomery 1909: 249.
115. *Magnet* (11 December 1937) 9.

8

Thackeray, Dickens, and James

In the opening chapter of *Waverley* (1814) Walter Scott expatiates on his hero's name, writing about its art to conceal it. He has avoided the chivalrous associations of "Howard, Mordaunt, Mortimer, or Stanley", being too diffident of "unnecessary opposition to preconceived associations".[1] So he has chosen for his hero "an uncontaminated name, bearing with its sound little of good or evil, excepting what the reader shall be hereafter pleased to affix to it".[2] By "uncontaminated" Scott seems to mean it bears none of the conventional associations of existing genres of fiction. His examples of sentimental romance names—"Belmour, Belville, Belfield and Belgrave"—had many such associations, besides suggesting other similar names. David Garrick has a "Belville" in *Country Girl* (1766) and Fanny Burney a "Belfield" in *Cecilia* (1782): these suggest the "Belford" in *Clarissa* (1748) and Maria Edgeworth's *Belinda* (1801). Scott means to inaugurate a new genre, the historical novel, in which the associations of a hero's name will not be generically determined but supplied by the reader.

Unobtrusive naming

Nevertheless "Waverley" is notably Cratylic: it already hints at Waverley's wavering allegiance (made explicit in chapter 25) as he decides where honour lies. Its innovation lies elsewhere, in associations of a new sort, associations of historical context. The name had already been used in Charlotte Smith's *Desmond* (1792), which Scott himself describes as written while she had "caught the contagion" of violent revolutionary ideas. Scott's Waverley makes an analogous mental journey from the Jacobite sympathizers at Waverley Honour, through the Enlightenment progressivism and Protestantism of Lowland associates, to realization of the cost of progress when he visits the ancient feudal society of the Highlands. "Waverley" epitomizes all this, in that its salient association is with Waverley Abbey in Surrey, familiar as the first Cistercian house in England.[3] This association, one notices, is historical rather than literary. Scott's influential example was to turn fictional naming towards similarly unobtrusive associations.

Meanwhile Jane Austen was following a similar method of naming, without writing about it. The names in her novels seldom stand out: far from claiming attention, they are almost self-effacing. The majority are Hermogenean in their ordinary plausibility, as we found with her servants' names in chapter 7. Only a very few, such as "Mr Knightley", display anything like moral Cratylism. Austen was attuned, however, like other novelists after Scott, to the possibility of less obvious congruences. In *Northanger Abbey* (1818), she *may* have associated General Tilney with General Tilly the cruel victor of Magdeburg. And she *may* mean Colonel Brandon to be associated with the Charles Brandon who is an agent of justice in Shakespeare's *Henry VIII*. But such fleeting associations are hardly, for her, the focus of attention. A little more substantially, George Eliot returned to history and to Isaac Casaubon (1559–1614) for the name of her dry, over-ambitious scholar in *Middlemarch* (1871–2).[4] Equally uncertain is the naming of Lord Cumnor's agent "Sheepshanks" in Elizabeth Gaskell's *Wives and Daughters* (1866). It might be thought the duty of Sheepshanks to take up slack in the indulgent Cumnor's dealings; which would make his name Cratylic. For that is what a sheepshank knot does. Perhaps. But Sheepshanks happens also to be the family name of the Earls of Southdown in *Vanity Fair* (1847–8). In such instances, one almost hankers after the simpler aptness of Smollett's "Bramble" for the prickly protagonist of *Humphry Clinker* (1771). Anthony Trollope (1815–82) sometimes went back to Fielding for validation of his tag names;[5] but he also has names in the newer, unobvious mode. And with Dickens the shift in naming is decisive.

Victorian interest in names

Many Victorians seem to have had the impulse to explore the history of names. Several substantial articles and even book-length studies informed a widespread interest in this development. Little progress had been made in onomastics during the two centuries after Camden. Writers such as the antiquary Richard Rowlands (alias Richard Verstegan) (fl. 1565–1620) supplemented Camden's lists of names, but often with speculative etymologies less scholarly than his.[6] The eighteenth century, however, brought gradual advances in lexicography and studies of contextual associations. In *A Classsical Dictionary of the Vulgar Tongue* (1785), Francis Grose (1731?–91) explains eponymous terms like Brown George ("munition bread"), Brown Bess ("firelock"), and Black Jack ("jug"). Particularly relevant here are studies of slang and thieves' argot such as those of Grose and John Camden Hotten (1859). They were to prove useful to Victorian novelists as quarries for criminal language and names.[7]

Nineteenth-century onomastics put less emphasis on etymology and more on putative origins in national mythologies. The most ambitious contribution since Camden was *Christian Names* (1863), a lifelong labour of the novelist Charlotte M. Yonge (1823–1901). Drawing on specialists such as the Anglo-Saxon historians Sharon Turner and John Mitchell Kemble, Yonge ranged over a field impossibly wide both historically and geographically. She was no very precise scholar, conflating Martin Luther and Petrus Dasypodius, for example, when she supposes Camden's etymologies came from "the German author Luther Dasipodius".[8] Nevertheless Yonge made a significant contribution, especially by relating first names to the ethnic literatures in which they had their origins. She begins with the usual glossary listing perfunctory meanings. But she goes on to explore the cultural associations of patriarchal, Israelite, Persian, and ancient Greek names, both mythological and abstract. On Roman naming, as might be expected, her treatment is fullest: she explains in detail the system of nomenclature—*praenomina, gens* names, and *cognomina*—together with origins in pagan cults and Christian festivals. Under Celtic and Cymric romance she focuses on the names in legends of King Lear and his daughters. Tracing stories of Leir and Cordelia through "old ballads", Shakespeare, and Spenser to Geoffrey of Monmouth, she speculates about possible origins earlier still.

Yonge boldly ventures into Celtic, Teutonic, and Scandinavian literatures, taking up anthropological themes of "summer gods and frost powers" in the sagas. A writer's interests show in her arrangement by genres, distinguishing the heroic Nibelung cycle from the "Karling

romances". Yonge has most to say about the romances. To take just one
example, she relates Astolfo to Orlando, Ottone, Rinaldo, and the Four
Sons of Aymon, not forgetting his magic lance in Boiardo nor his visit
to the Palace of Lost Things in Ariosto (p. 400). In short, she understands "Astolfo" as carrying associations not only with the lexical
meaning ("swift wolf") but with the literature of romance, with historical connections, and with contemporary survivals in the names of
modern Lombardy. Similarly, she follows up the Roman *gens* names
through their reapplication as surnames or nicknames "familiar to the
readers of Dante" (p. 451). She loves to trace a migrating name such as
the Norman-French Drogo, "brought to England by Dru de Baladon"
and found again "in Sir Drew Drury, the Keeper of Mary Queen of
Scots". And she detects the consequences of literary fashion: "Romance
had some influence—Orlando, Oliviero, Rinaldo, Ruggiero—and the
more remote Lancilotto, Ginevra, Isolda, Tristano, all became popular
through literature; and the great manufacture of Italian novels, no
doubt, tended to keep others in vogue" (p. 452). The range of Yonge's
interests stands out as almost unique. Most other nineteenth-century
writers focused on names that struck them as unusual or "quaint"; or
else they had a specialism, like Charles Bardsley in his *Curiosities of
Puritan Nomenclature* (1880).

   Some of the best general essays on naming appeared in *Household
Words*, the weekly periodical Dickens started in 1850. Thomas Colley
Grattan (1792–1864), an Irishman who served as British consul at
Boston from 1839 to 1846, met Dickens there and corresponded with
him. Grattan's lead essay, "American Changes of Names", exposes the
frequent practice whereby "the commonest persons" thrust themselves
into well-considered families. Grattan cites examples from the records
of the Massachusetts legislature, in which undesirable names were
modified; as when Diodate G. Coon became "Diodate Calhoun"
(Calhoun being a famous name in politics). Some inventions lacked
even the excuse of resembling the discarded name: Caleb C. Woodman
quite arbitrarily took the name Emerson Mortimer.[9] Grattan also
notices the fashion for given names with romantic associations
(Sophronia,[10] Almira, etc.) as well as the taste for jocular or stupid
names ("And", "Nevertheless", etc.[11]).

   The Rev. James White continued the theme of US name changing
in "Family Names" (1857).[12] He drew much of his material from
Nathaniel Ingersoll Bowditch's *Suffolk Surnames* (1857, enlarged 1858),

a gathering of curious, and in some cases grotesque, names such as Aldebarontiphoscofornia, an actual given name.[13] Bowditch, son of the celebrated translator, lived in Boston, met Dickens, and sent him copies of his books.

In the twentieth century onomastics has developed as a recognized specialism.[14] Many historical studies of personal and place names have appeared, together with general essays on literary naming, essays on individual authors, even essays on particular works.[15]

Henry James

Directly and indirectly Henry James benefited from Victorian studies of naming. As William Veeder impressively shows, James' character names "derive often from the literary tradition": "'Roderick', for example, is highly romantic—with Scott's gloomy and passionate Roderick Dhu, his 'The Song of Roderick', Southey's *Roderick, the Last of the Goths*, Poe's Roderick Usher, and Hawthorne's Roderick Elliston."[16] And "there are at least six names in *The Portrait* that derive directly from traditions which James knows." Gilbert Osmond provides a characteristic instance. Veeder traces "Osmond" from *Osmond, the Great Turk*, through Monk Lewis' *The Castle Spectre* (with an Osmond, a Gilbert, and a "Portrait of a Lady"); Maria Edgeworth; Charles Brockden Brown; and Alicia Lefanu's *Lucy Osmond* (popular in America); besides Osmond the betrayer of Lucy Leslie in the play of that name. "Gilbert", similarly, has a lineage extending from Scott to artists such as Gilbert Stuart and the painter Gilbert in *The Wide, Wide World*.[17] To these one might add the well-known architect Gilbert Scott (1811–78).

James cultivated an exquisite sense of the associations character names might activate in readers. So as to name his characters appropriately, he kept extensive lists of potential names, which can be tracked through his *Notebooks*. These he collected from many sources, including *The Times* newspaper. A typical day's gathering (for 27 July 1891, when he was forty-seven) is as follows:

Names. Pickerel–Chafer–Bullet–Whitethorne–Dash–Elsinore (place)–Douce–Doveridge (person or place)–Adney–Twentyman (butler)–Firminger–Wayward (place)–Wayworth–Greyswood (place)–Nona (girl's name)–Runting–Scruby–Mellifont (a place, or still better, title. Ld. Mellifont)–Undertone (for a countryhouse)–Gentry–Butterton–Vallance–Ashbury–Alsager–Bosco (person or place)–Isherwood–Loder–Garnet–Antram–Antrim–Cubit–Ambler–Urban (Xtian name)–Windle–Trivet–Middleship–Keep–Vigors–Film–Philmor–Champ–Cramp–Rosewood–Rosin–Littlewood–Esdaile–Galleon–Bray–Nurse–Nourse–Reul–Prestige–Poland–Cornice–Gosselin–Roseabel (Xtian name)–Shorting–Sire–Airey–Doubleday–Conduit–Tress–Gallup–Farrington–Bland–Arrand–Ferrand–Dominick–Heatherfield–Teagle–Pam–Locket–Brickwood–Boston-Cribb–Trend–Aryles–Hoyle–Flake–Jury–Porches (place)–Morrish–Gole.[18]

The names (only partly related to current projects) had to satisfy several requirements: they should be authentic ("of the shade of the real"); they should be slightly unusual (but not too odd); and they should be perceptibly meaningful although not crassly so. James spent much effort collecting names that might never be used, and when used spent more giving them plausible life. The name, for him, "was a character's foothold on life, and therefore had to come first. Seemingly random, a name was the first fact from which other details could be elaborated, the germ of all possibilities".[19]

James' notes for *The Ivory Tower* (1914) give an unparalleled sense of the sort of deliberation he thought it worth recording, about the connections of a single name:

My Girl, in the relinquished thing, was Cissy Foy; and this was all right for the figure there intended, but the girl here is a very different one, and everything is altered. I want her name moreover, her Christian one, to be Moyra, and must have some bright combination with that; the essence of which is a surname of two syllables and ending in a consonant—also beginning with one. I am thinking of Moyra Grabham, the latter excellent thing was in the Times of two or three days ago; its only fault is a little too much meaning, but the sense here wouldn't be thrown into undue relief, and I don't want anything pretty or conventionally "pleasing". Everything of the shade of the real. Remain thus important the big, the heavy Daughter of the billionaire, with her father; in connection with whom I think I give up Betterman. That must stand over, and I want, above all, a single syllable. All the other names have two or three; and this makes an objection to the Shimple, which I originally thought of as about odd and ugly enough without being more so than I want it. But that also will keep, and while I see that I have the monosyllable Hench put down; only put down for another connection.[20]

Considerations, qualifications, and counter-qualifications follow, seemingly without any early conclusion in sight:

On the other hand I am not content with Hench, though a monosyllable, for the dear Billionaire girl, in the light of whom it is alone important to consider the question, her father so little mattering after she becomes by his death the great Heiress of the time. And I kind of want to make *her* Moyra; with which I just spy in the Times a wonderful and admirable "Chown"; which makes me think that Moyra Chown may do. Besides which if I keep Grabham for my "heroine" I feel the Christian name should there be of one syllable. All my others are of two; and I shall presently make the case right for this, finding the good thing.

(Notes for *The Ivory Tower*, summer 1914)

How conscious and momentous naming was for James. Dickens spent perhaps just as much time finding the right names for his characters; but one cannot imagine him writing about it in terms such as these.

Nor Trollope, certainly. James disliked Trollope's less traditional names, particularly the abstract and "fantastic" ones (although he admired "Mrs Proudie" and "the Duke of Omnium"). He reserved his main animus for names such as Pessimist Anticant, Mr Stickatit, and the two physicians Mr Rerechild and Mr Fillgrave: "it would be better to go back to Bunyan at once".[21] James was ready to accept "Quiverful" for the generative rector of Puddingdale in *Barchester Towers*. Fielding's precedent authorized such humorous names in the case of a minor character: "it matters little so long as he is not brought to the front". When, however, Quiverful becomes "an important element", that changes everything: "the primitive character of this satiric note makes the reader unhappy". Besides, "a Mr. Quiverful with fourteen children [...] is too difficult to believe in. We can believe in the name and we can believe in the children; but we cannot manage the combination." James may be right in judging Trollope to be sometimes heavy-handed and over-casual in his naming. "Quiverful" may not be the best example, however: it is considered and apt through allusion.[22] But James rigorously maintained the rule that face cards, regardless of aptness, must be plausibly named. In the main plot every chief character should be realistically named, even if a few minor characters are amusingly denominated, in what amounts to a comic subplot. James made little allowance for the possibility of allusive names in previous writers: allusion was indeed relatively new and its uptake unreliable. When Fielding annotated Princess Huncamunca's speech in *Tom Thumb the Great* 2.4 ("O Tom Thumb! Tom Thumb! Wherefore art thou Tom Thumb?") he referred the reader to Otway's *Marius* ("Oh! Marius, Marius, wherefore art thou Marius?").[23]

William Makepeace Thackeray

From James' viewpoint, "Thackeray's names were perfect; they always had a meaning"; yet "we can imagine, even when they are most figurative, that they should have been borne by real people".[24] By "figurative", James seems to imply metaphorical aptness; and by "meaning", Cratylic associations. These associations are extraordinarily varied in Thackeray. He makes naming a medium of sustained suggestion, almost an ancillary chain of discourse. Sometimes sound effects are the main thing: when a bell tolls at Tinkleton church the name advances the narrative and adds a soundtrack, besides suggesting a certain triviality.[25] Sometimes descriptive details add political implications, as in "Lord Bigwig", Lord Tapeworm's father (*Vanity Fair*, chapter 63). One suggestion is the large wig worn by men of importance; another is "bagwig", the older style of wig part-enclosed in an ornamental bag.[26] Most often Thackeray's names are Cratylic "moral names".[27] The sycophantic Hugby "rose by kindness to the aristocracy"; Guttleton is a "dining-out snob"; Captain Guzzard "has a tremendous bass voice"; Guttlebury is a "student who owes money for dinners"; Gruffanuff a "fierce porter"; and Jawkins "a Club Snob, of great conversational powers". Thackeray excels at names of firms, such as Gann and Blubbery the whale-oil firm.

Elsewhere Thackeray epitomizes (or caricatures) social types, such as the upper-class cadre given family surnames as first names. Double surnaming gave him great scope, both for broad humour and for complex associations. Granby Tufto, a great military snob "too incorrigibly idle and dull for any trade but this", derives his name from "tufts of the university", that is, undergraduates who wore the gold tassel distinguishing noblemen and sons of noblemen.[28] Superficially, Granby is an obvious key-name for John Manners, Marquis of Granby (1721–70), a Lieutenant-General and a well-known target of the satirist Junius. But "Marquis of Granby" was a title of all the Dukes of Rutland: Thackeray's real target is more probably Charles Manners the sixth duke (1815–88), MP 1841–7, a strong protectionist, styled Marquis of Granby until 1857. In Bute Crawley (Rector of Crawley-cum-Snailby) and Sir Pitt Crawley (parsimonious and grovelling in his tastes), Thackeray hits at other aristocratic politicians. Usually such names have moral implications too, as in "Sir Huddleston Fuddleston" with its hint of inebriation.

Thackeray can sketch social panoramas with impressive economy, almost it seems through the mere deployment of iconic names. One instantly knows Mrs Kewsy is a barrister's wife, Lady Kicklebury is aggressive, and Sir Thomas Kicklebury kicks his heels at the gaming tables of Rougetnoirbourg. Thackeray is particularly good at foreign names: Count Towrowski (*Book of Snobs*); Madam la Comtesse de Schlangenbad (*The Newcomes*); and the Schlippenschlopps (*Fitz-Boodle Papers*). Taken at speed, the associations and allusions may pass unnoticed now; but once they would have had immediate effect. If Thackeray had any predecessor in this, it was Shakespeare, who can call up an entire community through a few names of characters who never appear on stage.[29]

Thackeray's unpredictable switching from one semantic field to another can produce wildly funny results. Yet it can also be subtle, particularly when he brings together associations from very remote registers—nursery rhymes, say, and the African mission field. In such instances the mechanism is subliminal: the "Orthodox settlement in Feefawfoo" suggests bloodthirstiness long before one reaches the explicit phrase "most savage of the Cannibal Islands".[30] This flight of fancy, while hardly PC, is too exaggerated to give serious offence. Amusing as they may be, however, such insinuations run the risk of dehumanizing. Perhaps that is what John Carey means when he writes that Thackeray's "people remained types, often with type-cast character-names ('Yellowplush' for a footman, 'Deuceace' for a card-sharper, and so on)".[31] More generally, Thackeray's rapid indirect communication may be achieved at too heavy a cost of ironic distancing: we don't empathize with his characters as much as with Dickens'.

Hyper-conscious naming also runs a different risk. James praised Thackeray's names because they "always had a meaning"; but not every reader enjoys such relentless signification. In our own century, Thackeray's brilliant naming has been emulated, as we saw in chapter 2, by Martin Amis, who specializes in names with multiple associations. *Money* (1984), for example, is full of pretentiously named restaurants like Goliath's or Assisi's.[32]

Charles Dickens: background and preparation

Throughout his career Dickens showed a keen interest in the history and curiosities of names and nicknames. Already in *Pickwick Papers*

(1836–7) Samuel Weller remarks that Job Trotter's name is "only one I know, that ain't got a nickname to it".[33] Thematic in *Great Expectations* (1860–1) is the protagonist's pet name "Pip", his infant attempt at both his father's family name Pirrip and his own given name Philip (chapter 1). Herbert Pocket proposes to call him Handel because he doesn't like the associations of Philip: "we are so harmonious, and you have been a blacksmith [...] Would you mind Handel for a familiar name? There's a charming piece of music by Handel, called the Harmonious Blacksmith" (chapter 22).

Dickens keenly observed naming practices of all kinds. He published in *Household Words* Grattan's essay on the American use of "unmeaning" initials for a first name. And in *Mrs Lirriper's Legacy* (1864, partly by Dickens himself), Rosa Mulholland's story features a handicapped orphan called Teecie Ray. On the important topic of how to address family members, Dickens does full justice to the weightiness of naming. How is Mrs Gradgrind to know what to call her son-in-law?—

"I shall be worrying myself, morning, noon, and night, to know what I am to call him! [...]Whatever I am to call him, Mr Gradgrind, when he is married to Louisa! I must call him something. It's impossible," said Mrs Gradgrind, with a mingled sense of politeness and injury, "to be constantly addressing him and never giving him a name. I cannot call him Josiah, for the name is insupportable to me. You yourself wouldn't hear of Joe, you very well know. Am I to call my own son-in-law, Mister! Not, I believe, unless the time has arrived when, as an invalid, I am to be trampled upon by my relations".

(*Hard Times* (1854), ch. 15)

The social implications of forms of address and choices of name weigh heavily on her.

Choosing names became an especially public procedure in the case of foundlings. Margaret Reynolds describes how this worked at Coram's Hospital in London:

Many parents left their infants with tokens to assist in later recognition and acknowledgement [...] each child was given a new name, his or her previous existence wiped out. To begin with the children were named after the illustrious living. Not surprisingly, this began to cause problems. So the process settled on names drawn from the illustrious dead—Julius Caesar, Edward Plantagenet, Philip Sidney, Oliver Cromwell, Perkin Warbeck. Or they reflected aspirational or moral qualities—Diana Thrifty, Judith Bright, Alice Hope, Eliza Meek, Michael Angel. Otherwise the children were given geographical names, presumably alluding to their beginnings in life—Mary

Islington, Thomas Africa, Frances Ladbrooke. Finally the children were given appropriate names drawn from legend and literature. Of these Moses was immensely popular, but so was Aaron, and there was even an Ishmael and an Epaminondas. There was also a Clarissa Harlowe, a Sophia Western, a John Blifil, a George Allworthy, and—perhaps unsurprisingly—there were several named Tom Jones.[34]

Several contributions to *Household Words*, some by Dickens himself, address this topic, notably "Received, a Blank Child".[35]

Dickens wrote this essay in collaboration with W. H. Wills, a prolific divine he had great affection for. It explains where the names given to foundlings came from, and how, at group baptisms of foundlings, "persons of quality" competed in "honouring the children with their names, and being their sponsors". Hence the early registers of the London Foundling Hospital "swarm with the most aristocratic names in the land". The peerage having been run through, names of historical celebrities were used. Then, "celebrated real names having, in process of time, been exhausted, the authorities had recourse to novels, and sent into the world, as serving-maids, innumerable Sophia Westerns, Clarissa Harlowes, and Flora MacIvors." Finally, the governors were reduced to using their own names, "until some of their namesakes on growing up, occasioned inconvenience (and possibly scandal) by claiming kith and kin with them." Accordingly, "the present practice is for the treasurer to issue lists of names for adoption; in which responsible duty he, no doubt, derives considerable comfort from the Post Office London Directory". Besides reflecting Dickens' interest in the class structure of naming , the essay has a particular bearing on *Oliver Twist* (1837–8). And its focus (p. 464) on the identity of a foundling called Joe suggests the model for a name in *Bleak House*, the novel Dickens was writing at the time.

To Henry James, Dickens seemed an exuberant writer, and so he was. But when it came to choosing character names he was also a writer who relied on long study and preparation. Like many novelists, Dickens needed to determine the names of characters before he could tell their stories. As Harry Stone puts it, Dickens "felt uncomfortable and inhibited, unable to proceed, until he settled on a name—the right name". "He agonized especially over the names of his chief characters [...]. Two of the names in *Martin Chuzzlewit* (1843) went through such intricate changes as Pick, Tick, Flick, Flicks, Fleezer, Sweezer, Sweezleden, Sweezlebach, Sweezlewag, Cottletoe, Sweetletoe, Pottletoe, Spottletoe,

Chuzzletoe, Chuzzlebog, Chubblewig, Chuzzlewig, and Chuzzlewit".[36] He searched always for the "right name"– "the name that conveyed the outward show and inward mystery of a character or a book,
the name which revealed and yet concealed. Part of a name's magic lay
in this latter property, this ability to be open and yet secretive". In the
course of searching for right names, especially during the decade
1855–65, Dickens wrote a great many memoranda of ideas and names
for future use. One list of "Available Names" is divided into the categories: "Girls from Privy Council Education Lists", "Boys", "More
Boys", and "More Girls". Another list begins "Toundling. Mood.
Guff. Treble. Chilby. Spessifer. Wodder", and includes the more productive "Mrs Flinks", "Twemlow", "Rokesmith", "Magwitch", "Podsnap", "Pumblechook", "Boffin", "Wilfer", "Gargery", "Riderhood",
"Wopsell", and "Wegg".[37] In such memoranda David Copperfield
appears variously as "Master Copperfield", "Mr Copperfield",
"Copperfull", "Brooks of Sheffield", "Young Innocent", "Trotwood",
"Trot", "David", "Davy", "Mas'r Davy", "Doady", "Copperstone",
"Stonebury", and "Daisy". Similarly, Stone traces the evolution of
Murdstone from Merdle and Murdle. Some of the variants represent
failed attempts at "rightness"; others succeed in capturing distinct fac-
ets of the character.[38] Dickens' names, like Thackeray's, sometimes
belonged to real people; a well-known Pickwick, for example, kept the
famous White Hart Inn at Bath. But often Dickens drew on lists he
had extracted from institutional records, ticking them off as he used
them.

Books probably also contributed to his name-store. Dickens' Gadshill library seems not to have included Yonge's *Christian Names*; but it
may have been in one or another of his earlier collections. Or his
notorious prejudice against female novelists may explain the omission:
in all his vast correspondence he only once mentions Yonge. James
White's *Household Words* article on "Family Names" drew heavily on
the first edition of Nathaniel Ingersoll Bowditch's *Suffolk Surnames*
(1857), which appeared in the same year.[39] Dickens retained both editions of Bowditch's book in his Gadshill library, and annotated them.[40]
His own name features in Bowditch's category "Names from Ejacula-
tions" ("What the Dickens" etc.). *Suffolk Names* had much to offer
Dickens, since he shared Bowditch's taste for unusual, flavoursome
names. Dickens enjoyed things "misshapen or strangely shapen, uncommon or grotesque";[41] and, as Grattan observed in his 1856 article in

Household Words, American names showed "a curious taste for grotesque".[42] Some critics identify as gothic this taste for bizarre names such as "Quilp".[43] Certainly Dickens' last and most gothic novel has several strikingly medieval names: "Bazzard", "Jasper", and "Drood" itself.[44]

Dickens' meaningful names

Dickens seems to have regarded names as epitomizing individuality. Occasionally he minimizes their significance: a child's funeral can prompt the reflection that in the "same church, the pretty boy received all that will soon be left of him on earth—a name" (*Dombey and Son*, chapter 18). More often, his remarks about names point in the direction of Cratylism.[45] Indeed, he sometimes uses obviously meaningful names such as "Swiveller" or the brand new "Veneerings" (suggesting an upwardly mobile family with a *veneer* of culture) or "Havisham" (combining *have* and *sham*).

Much of the tenth chapter of *Bleak House* amounts to an onomastic theory in miniature. Characteristically indirect in structure, it begins with the enshrining of past history in place names. Thus, "a brook 'as clear as crystal' once ran right down the middle of Holborn [originally a river name], when Turnstile really was a turnstile, slap away into the meadows". The law-stationer's inscription PEFFER AND SNAGSBY has displaced "the time-honoured and not easily to be deciphered legend, PEFFER, only". The once-junior but now sole partner Snagsby "stands behind a desk in his dark shop, with a heavy flat ruler, snipping and slicing at sheepskin". "Sheepskin", the earlier stage of vellum. All things are palimpsests, ancient, overwritten survivals; so that names display the historical process of their own formation. Mrs Snagsby is first heard finding fault with Guster, "a lean young woman from a workhouse (by some supposed to have been christened Augusta)": "This proper name, so used by Mr Snagsby, has before now sharpened the wit of the Cook's-Courtiers to remark that it ought to be the name of Mrs Snagsby; seeing that she might with great force and expression be termed a Guster, in compliment to her stormy character". Not a Cratylic name for Augusta herself, then: the workhouse authorities would have assigned it by a thoroughly Hermogenean, randomized procedure.[46]

In the same chapter, the Writer sought by Tulkinghorn is Nemo. "'Nemo!' repeats Mr Tulkinghorn. 'Nemo is Latin for no one.' 'It must be English for some one, sir, I think,' Mr Snagsby submits, with his deferential cough. 'It is a person's name.'"[47] Tulkinghorn has chambers in a former house of state (modelled on 58 Lincoln's Inn Fields):[48] a building with painted ceilings, where Allegory personified "in Roman helmet and celestial linen, sprawls among balustrades and pillars, flowers, clouds, and big-legged boys". Here, among his many boxes labelled with "transcendent names", lives Tulkinghorn. His name, as Snagsby says it, gradually forms itself from its separate components, syllable by syllable: "Tul-king-horn—rich—in-flu-en-tial".

The chapter pursues allegorical naming through images, such as Vergil's Rumor, "a rumour flying among them" and "the many tongues of Rumour".[49] Later the topic is reprised in Krook's naming of Miss Flite's birds: "Hope, Joy, Youth, Peace, Rest, Life, Dust, Ashes, Waste, Want, Ruin, Despair, Madness, Death, Cunning, Folly, Words, Wigs, Rags, Sheepskin, Plunder, Precedent, Jargon, Gammon, and Spinach" (chapter 14). Miss Flite (Flight?) shrinks from listing the birds herself, perhaps because they epitomize *in abstracto* the sad experience of Chancery litigants. As Gary Watt explains, the "insatiable chancery suit" is named Jarndyce and Jarndyce because this "is obviously a pun on the sickness and attitude of jaundice". Watt finds an allusion to the Grimms' tale "Jorinda and Jorindel", where Miss Flite's birds also figure.[50]

If names are significant, altering them becomes a serious matter. In Judaeo-Christian tradition, every believer had an individual name in heaven.[51] This special name might be revealed or, at some decisive juncture, changed. Thus the name Abram ("High Father", Genesis 11: 31) was changed to Abraham ("father of many nations"),[52] in recognition of his new identity and covenant with God. And in the same way Saul the persecutor of Christians became Paul the Christian Apostle. Renaming became common in medieval Morality plays—a literary device later exploited by Shakespeare, Jonson, and others. By the end of *The New Inn* (1629) most of the characters have changed names.[53] It is almost a generic requirement of romance that the plot should find resolution in discovery of a true name (Spenser's Redcrosse/St George; Shakespeare's Cesario/Viola).

The romance of identity ultimately belongs to a biblical tradition. But Dickens takes it up for his own purposes, renaming characters in accordance with newly discovered potentialities. In *The Old Curiosity Shop* (1840–41) the Marchioness takes on a new identity of class and education when she becomes Sophronia Sphynx (chapter 73). And in *Bleak House* (1852–3) Esther Summers gradually comes to be recognized as Esther Hawdon, daughter of Lady Dedlock and Captain Hawdon. Dickens prepares for this recognition scene by multiplying the pet names Jarndyce devises, to postpone it: "Old Woman, and Little Old Woman, and Cobweb, and Mrs Shipton, and Mother Hubbard, and Dame Durden, and so many names of that sort, that my own name soon became quite lost among them".[54] His nicknames for her allude to "figures who attend to others or foster them, or [...] figures with prophetic ability".[55]

Dickens' theory of naming is not unlike Henry James'; except that he relates his names to real-life originals more often than to previous literature. James, collecting impressions for *Princess Casamassima* (1886), visited a prison (and hated doing so); Dickens, with a similar purpose, consulted his own lifelong memories. John Dickens had been imprisoned for debt in the Marshalsea in 1824, where his twelve-year-old son visited him and became comfortably familiar with low life. Later, Charles Dickens the journalist interviewed criminals and learnt their argot, finding in it a source of suggestion for names that concealed yet revealed appropriate associations. Only familiarity with rhyming slang and similar substitutions, for example, enabled him to hit on such a nickname as "Chops" for the lottery-winning dwarf in "Going into Society". Chops

was wrote up as Major Tpschoffki, of the Imperial Bulgraderian Brigade. Nobody couldn't pronounce the name, and it never was intended anybody should. The public always turned it, as a general rule, into Chopski. In the line he was called Chops; partly on that account, and partly because his real name, if he ever had any real name (which was very dubious), was Stakes.[56]

Similarly, in *Oliver Twist* (1837–8), Bet or Betsy, the companion of Bill Sikes' mistress Nancy, gets her name from "Betty", slang for a jemmy or a pick-lock. These meanings are given by Francis Grose, Dr Johnson, and Pierce Egan, among others, from 1671 onwards; but Dickens would know them without consulting books. "Fagin" was certainly a personal association, for Dickens' mentor in the blacking warehouse "was Bob Fagin, and I took the liberty of using his name long afterwards in *Oliver Twist*.[57]

Thieves' argot provided an invaluable aid to naming in *Oliver Twist*, for Dickens' artistic preferences were such that the more meaningful a character name, the more determinedly he would conceal it. Oliver's name may serve as an example. The duller sort of readers are content, like Mrs Mann, to believe Bumble's boast "I inwented it". Bumble assigned surnames from an alphabetic list, and in Oliver's case it chanced to be Twist's turn, rather than Swubble's. As we have seen, Dickens and Wills gave a full account of how foundlings were named in an article published two years earlier than *Oliver Twist*. According to Michael Ragussis, the narrator in *Oliver Twist* disclaims responsibility for a name "found in the arbitrary order of language"—the social system soon replaced "Oliver" with the offensive class name "orphan". Such naming, Ragussis concludes, lies at the opposite extreme from Cratylism.[58] Dickens' and Wills' mention of Treasurers' lists drawn from the Post Office London Directory might be taken to support this view. Still, Mrs Mann's question to Bumble deserves a fuller answer, taking Dickens' naming practices into account.

Both of Oliver's names turn out to be fully Cratylic in their associations. In the slang of the underworld he would soon enter, "twist" meant "appetite" and "hang by the neck". So when the pangs of "twist" (hunger) make Oliver ask for more, Mr Limkins predicts "that boy will be hung" (will "twist"). To underline the point, Noah Claypole "announced his intention of coming to see him hung".[59] As for his first name Oliver, it meant "sky-lantern", moonlight as a hindrance to crime.[60] And, sure enough, when the alarm is raised at the Maylies', what should Oliver do but drop his eponymous lantern, fatally hindering the burglary. Ragussis would have society bear responsibility through the names it assigns. But Dickens, never a victim historian, makes Oliver resist such determinism. As a romance of identity, *Oliver Twist* comes to resolution through the discovery of Oliver's parentage and his true name, Leeford. Renaming follows, with redistribution of wealth from the haves to the secretly entitled have-nots.

Our Mutual Friend

Many critics of *Our Mutual Friend* (1864–5) have gone along with Henry James' view of it as tired writing, "the poorest of Mr Dickens' works", "intensely *written*, so little seen, known, or felt": its characters eccentric, "creatures of pure fancy", "grotesque creatures" who "have nothing in common with mankind at large".[61] Although James' review was written at the age of twenty-two, his prejudice against Dickens' allegory continued in later life. Yet *Our Mutual Friend* remains in its way one of Dickens' most brilliant novels.

Our present interest is in its highly unusual naming. Some characters bear tag names, like the oily Duke of Linseed; others are identified through thematic associations, such as "Jonathan of the no surname" (chapter 2.3) and "Boffin", a name that only the initial consonant distinguishes from "Coffin"). When Wrayburn introduced "Mr Dolls" he had "no idea what his name was, knowing the little dressmaker's to be assumed, but presented him with easy confidence under the first appellation *that his associations suggested*".[62] To understand how valuable Dickens' names are as guides to interpretation, consider his characterization of Wilfer:

> He was shy, and unwilling to own to the name of Reginald, as being too aspiring and self-assertive a name. In his signature he used only the initial R., and imparted what it really stood for, to none but chosen friends, under the seal of confidence. Out of this, the facetious habit had arisen in the neighbourhood surrounding Mincing Lane of making Christian names for him of adjectives and participles beginning with R. Some of these were more or less appropriate: as Rusty, Retiring, Ruddy, Round, Ripe, Ridiculous, Ruminative; others derived their point from their want of application: as Raging, Rattling, Roaring, Raffish. But, his popular name was Rumty, which in a moment of inspiration had been bestowed upon him by a gentleman of convivial habits connected with the drug market, as the beginning of a social chorus, his leading part in the execution of which had led this gentleman to the Temple of Fame, and of which the whole expressive burden ran: "Rumty iddity, row dow dow, | Sing toodlely, teedlely, bow wow wow."
>
> (*Our Mutual Friend*, chapter 1.4)

The various expansions of the anything-but-meaningless initial *R* attempt to penetrate Wilfer's withdrawn nature with little success: Rumty he is not.[63] Although in *Our Mutual Friend* Dickens has moved away from the novel of Thackeray and James, his writing is far from tired: indeed, it seems inventive and experimental.

Dickens carries renaming to Jonsonian lengths and beyond, risking a confusion of merely kaleidoscopic effects. Boffin, who has inherited the Harmon estate through default of the heir John Harmon, transfers it to his secretary Rokesmith (really Harmon) and keeps only the elder

Harmon's house. This house is ironically called "Harmon's Jail" or "Harmony Jail" (perhaps alluding to New Harmony, the utopian community) because he disagreed with everyone. Mrs Boffin with a different irony calls it "Bella's Bower".

The true heir John Harmon comes to be "John Rokesmith" by way of several changes of name. Travelling to England to inherit, he exchanges clothes and identity with a fellow passenger, George Radfoot, to avoid recognition by the lady his father's will obliges him to marry. On arrival, however, Radfoot drugs Harmon and attempts to drown him in the Thames, before being himself drowned by his accomplice. When Radfoot's corpse is identified as Harmon's, the way lies clear for Harmon himself to take a new alias, Julius Handford, and then yet another, John Rokesmith. Through the sinister wordplays "Chokesmith" and "Artichoke", Dickens glosses "Rokesmith" as death by suffocation.[64] Later, Harmon recapitulates for Bella's enlightenment the entire sequence Harmon–Radfoot–Handford–Rokesmith (chapter 3.15).

At The Six Jolly Fellowship-Porters the solicitor Mortimer Lightwood changes Harmon's name very differently in his half-sleeping fantasy of "having to dine in the Temple with an unknown man who described himself as M.R.F. Eugene Gaffer Harmon" (chapters 1.12, 13). This improbable name combines four elements: (1) "M. R. F.", his friend Wrayburn's usual shorthand for "My Respected Father"; (2) "Eugene", Wrayburn's first name; (3) "Gaffer" for Jesse Hexam, the waterman suspected of murdering Harmon; and (4) "Harmon" himself.

Confusions of relationship resolve themselves when imagined likenesses emerge as full identities. Thus Harmon, perplexed when he tries to recall the circumstances of his near drowning, "became as like that same lost wanted Mr Julius Handford as never man was like another in this world" (chapter 2.13). (Never, because the resemblance springs from identity, not mere likeness.) "Yet in that same moment he was the Secretary also, Mr Boffin's Secretary. For John Rokesmith, too, was as like that same lost wanted Mr Julius Handford as never man was like another in this world". Identity not of this world has a religious sound; and so has Rokesmith's demand that Bella should "put perfect faith" in him, even when he turns out to be the very Julius Handford suspected of murdering Harmon (chapter 3.12). Throughout *Our Mutual Friend* renaming draws so much attention to itself that it could be said to incorporate the entire allegory. It is as if Dickens were reaching for a neo-Spenserian version of allegorical romance: a retrospective mode of fiction, manneristic in its authorial interventions. Each renaming brings Harmon a further abasement. The Radfoot role (assumed to deceive Bella) leads to the more degraded Handford role (suspected murderer); and that, in turn, to the humble role of Rokesmith, a mere secretary.

Three Victorian novelists stand out as especially creative in their naming: Thackeray, Dickens, and James. James himself thought Thackeray's names "perfect" because "they always had a meaning" although the reader can imagine them as "borne by real people". That is, Thackeray conceals his art, adhering to the canons of James' own method of composition: *ars est celare artem*. Thackeray's names are natural and plausible, even when they also suggest relevant associations. His main figures bear relatively low-profile names ("Becky Sharpe", "Rawdon Crawley"): only his minor satiric figures bear the self-defining names of charactonyms.

By contrast Dickens makes no attempt to hide his art. Indeed he often makes acts of naming explicit, and sometimes explains them in inset essays in his own person—the very device James condemns Trollope for, subverting the realistic illusion. Dickens' names are salient, egregious, gothic icons. A name such as "Pumblechook" makes the reader think it could never occur in real life, even if in fact it did. Dickens might satirize the sentimental medievalizing of Mrs Skewton in *Dombey and Son*, but his own naming is thoroughly exotic, gothic, and romantic. As Chesterton puts it, "Dickens was much more mediaeval in his attacks on mediaevalism than they [the pallid mediaevalists] were in their defences of it."

James has similarly complex interests in naming, which he rigorously subdues to the consistency of his art. Gilbert Osmond may have a whole army of medieval and artistic Gilberts behind him; but these associations never become explicit. At times, they seem hardly conscious. James withdraws, so that readers can have confidence in the fictional reality of the characters, names and all.

Notes

1. E.g. *Mortimer Hall* (1811); Edward Mortimer [Edward Montague], *Montoni, or the Confessions of the Monk of St Penedict. A Romance* (1808). See Sadleir 1951, Summers 1938.
2. Scott 1981: 3.
3. Scott 1981: 418–19; see Lascelles 1980: 9–11, 36–41.
4. For the fictional Casaubon's many resemblances to the historical Casaubon's biographer Mark Pattison, see John Considine's *ODNB* entry.
5. Fielding's tag names have come to seem less numerous than they did before changes of meaning intervened. Besides obvious instances such as Square and Thwackum there are others. Mrs Slip-slop is a borderline tag name: "slip-slop" perhaps only later came to mean malapropism such as her confusion of "essence" and "incence" (*Joseph Andrews* ch. 2); see *OED* s.v. *Slip-slop*, a., exs. from 1757.
6. Rowlands (R. Verstegan) 1605; Penkethman 1626; Lyford 1655; Anon. 1689.
7. See Coleman 2004.
8. Yonge 1884: v.
9. Grattan 1856: 434.
10. Possibly a source for Sophronia in *The Old Curiosity Shop*.
11. "Nockemorf" in *Pickwick Papers* ch. 38 comes in this category.
12. White 1857: 525–8.
13. White 1857: 527.
14. See, e.g., the journals *Names* (1953–2008) and *Onoma* (1950–).
15. For some of these, see Rajec 1978, Barton 1990: 188 n. 13. General studies of naming include Wilson 1998; Ragussis 1986. Dictionaries of names include *ONC, ODECN*, and Payton 1991. Dictionaries of fictional characters include Freeman 1963, West 1977, Gillespie 1973, Chandler 1992, and Bruce 1999.
16. Veeder 1975: 120; cf. 187 on the associations of "Sloper" in *Washington Square*.
17. See Veeder 1975: 120–1.
18. James 1987: 60.
19. See Mullan 2006: 277. Plausibility was not without its risks: a person actually called Capadose took offence at James' "The Liar".
20. James 1987: 467–8.
21. James 1984: 1344.
22. Ps. 127: 4–5, "As arrows are in the hand of a mighty man; so are children of the youth. Happy is the man who hath his quiver full of them: they shall not be ashamed, but they shall speak with the enemies in the gate".
23. Gilbert Highet 1962: 265 rightly asks whether Fielding takes the *Romeo and Juliet* original for granted, or fails to recognize it himself.
24. James 1984: 1344. As critics remark, Thackeray's names can be unobtrusive: he has many Browns, Joneses, and Smiths.
25. *Pendennis* ch. 22.
26. *OED* s.v. *Bigwig* and *Bagwig*.
27. The term "moral names" is Geoffrey Tillotson's; see Thackeray 1963: vi.
28. *OED*, s.v. *Tuft* 7 b.
29. Cf. Barton 1990: 104–5.
30. Thackeray 2001: 227. See *OED*, s.v. *Fee faw fum*, with quotations from the nursery tale "Jack the giant killer"; *King Lear*, Dryden's *Amphitryon*; a 1711 chapbook; and Macaulay 1854.
31. See Thackeray 2001: xv.
32. Well characterized in Mullan 2006: 275–8.
33. *Pickwick Papers* ch. 16; see *ODECN*: xxvii. Did Dickens know that "Trotter" was in fact an occupational nickname?

34. Reynolds 2007: 12–14. On Coram, see ibid. 8–9.
35. Dickens and Wills 1853: 49–53.
36. Stone 1985: 191.
37. Dickens 1981. See John Foster, *The Life of Charles Dickens*, bk. 9 ch. 7.
38. Stone 1985: 193–8.
39. White 1857: 525–8.
40. The 1857 and enlarged 1848 editions. See Stonehouse 1935: 14–17.
41. Meynell 1917.
42. Grattan 1856: 435.
43. Speculations about "Quilp"—a dog's name; "quill pen" etc.—are endless.
44. On Jasper as a medieval name, see *ODECN*.
45. See Clarkson 1999.
46. For real-life originals of "Guster", see Shatto 1988: 100.
47. For Nobody, cf. "The Lazy Tour of Two Idle Apprentices" (*Household Words* 3 October 1857) by Dickens (as Francis Goodchild) and Wilkie Collins (as Thomas Idle), an account of their north England tour of 1857: "who wanted to see the country? Nobody. And again, who ever did walk? Nobody." For "Nobody" in *Little Dorrit*, see e.g. the Plan, Number 8, ch. 26, "Nobody's state of mind", Dickens Centenary Catalogue 1970: 90. White 1857: 528 notices a "Personne (that is, nobody)" who changed his name to Pearson, and compares "the Nemos or Nimmos of Scotland". Collins' interest in namelessness is reflected in his novel *No Name* (1862).
48. See Shatto 1988: 101.
49. See Shatto 1988: 99.
50. Watt 2009. The chancery case Dickens probably had in mind was that concerning Peter Thellusson's will; see Nigel Hall, *TLS* 11 September 2009.
51. E.g. Rev. 2: 17, "a new name written, which no man knoweth saving he that receiveth it". Cf. Rev. 3: 1; Luke 10: 20.
52. Gen. 17: 5 Geneva with note, "Not only according to the fleshe, but of a farre greater multitude by faith".
53. See Barton 1984: 170–93 esp. 179; Barton 1990: 78.
54. See Axton 1966.
55. See Shatto 1988: 83.
56. *Christmas Stories* (1871).
57. The altered spelling is probably authorial; see Rowland 2011.
58. Ragussis 1987: 36–7.
59. Dickens 1999: 12; cf. 43. The editor Stephen Gill notes over a hundred other examples of thieves' cant, although not this. See *OED*, *Twist*, 18; cf. Farmer and Henley 1974: 7.244–5; Grose 1963 ; Egan 1823. George Cruikshank claimed Dickens overheard a bus conductor mention an Oliver Twist; for this and other real-life possibilities, see Paroissien 1992: 47–8.
60. *OED*, *Oliver*, sb³; Farmer and Henley 1974: 7.244–5; Egan 1823.
61. James 1984: 853–5.
62. Chapter 3.10, italics mine.
63. On "rumty" see *OED*, s.v. *Rumti*, "commonplace".
64. For the gallows humour, cf. Robert Louis Stevenson's June 1864 letter to Henrietta Traquair: "Bryce's breakfast consisted of an artichoke and oyster (hearty choke and hoister)", Stevenson 1994: 1.104.

9

Arrays of Names

The so-called Catalogue of Ships in Homer's *Iliad* book 2 is one of the most discussed passages of ancient literature; yet until recent decades it has not been much valued by modern scholars. A classic account, T. W. Allen's monograph of 1926, focused on the archaeological contexts of its geography, which seemed to need explanation before addressing the catalogue itself. A similar emphasis has persisted in studies by R. Hope Simpson and J. F. Lazenby, G. S. Kirk, Elizabeth Minchin, and others; and in commentaries by Kirk, Peter Jones, and others—without all this leading to reinterpretation of the Catalogue in relation to the *Iliad* in general.[1] Indeed, so many new place-name problems have been encountered that a Russian scholar, L. S. Klejn, has described the Catalogue's geography as fictitious.[2]

Homer's catalogues

Cedric Whitman's *Homer and the Heroic Tradition* (1958) promised a new approach through oral traditions of memorial literature. Whitman's analysis of the "ring composition" of scenic structures convincingly explains the sequence of parts in book 2:

Deceitful dream sent by Zeus
Council of chiefs
  1 Assembly: deception by Agamemnon
  2 Assembly: deception by Odysseus
Council of chiefs
Sacrifice to Zeus and refusal of the prayer.[3]

Whitman gives a sensitive account of the Catalogue, even if his analysis stops short of a breakthrough:

The *Catalogue* has been most unjustly despised. In its way, it is just as vivid as the famous similes which introduce it. No love is more deeply imbedded in the Greek soul than the love for places in Greece, with their names, the mountains, valleys, nooks, and rivers of the maternal soil. It is more than patriotic; the *Catalogue*, with its recounting of those place names, their leaders and their legends, has a religious love about it, it is a kind of hymnic invocation.

Read aloud, it "seems resistless and inexhaustible, like the movement of an army on the march":

each contingent as it goes by is splendid with the retrospect of home, the continuous surprise of the familiar. At the close of each entry, a stock line gives the number of ships attending the leader, and these lines, varying a little, but all echoing each other, have the incantational validity of a refrain.

He compares the structure to that of hymn: "a hymn to a god recounted his deeds; the hymn to an army recounts its constituents".[4]

Whitman had little to say, however, about the place of the Catalogue of Ships in the *Iliad* at large. No progress could be made towards this until the epic catalogue as a genre came to be better understood. Stratis Kyriakidis, for example, found that epic catalogues often have a "centre of density". This was still very abstract, but it led on to more persuasive accounts.

Elizabeth Minchin's *Homer and the Resources of Memory* (2001) revises the ethnic geography of the *Catalogue* in the light of memorial requirements. Taking up the idea of the geographical order as a *periplous* or circumnavigation of Greece, she finds Homer's review of contingents in geographical sequence suggestive of the "places" in an *ars memorativa*.[5] But how does this memorial form relate to the narrative of the *Iliad*? The same problem arises in Jones' commentary. At *Iliad* 2.576, Agamemnon "finally appears in the catalogue, ninth in the pecking order". He brings a hundred ships; whereas Odysseus is "a major character, but with only a feeble twelve ships". On *Iliad* 2.685 Jones exclaims: "Achilles: at last!" He clearly senses that the Catalogue of Greeks has a structure of its own, distinct from that of the narrative. Perhaps it is not even by Homer? "With Hector heading it up, the Trojan catalogue seems more closely related to the *Iliad* than the Greek [catalogue is]".

Comparison with catalogues in modern literature has brought a clearer sense of the structure.[6] In particular, the "centre of density" (as Kyriakidis calls it) can be seen as central emphasis. And the item at the centre of a catalogue occupies a place of honour, politically or morally. Critics customarily refer to *Iliad* 2.494–759 as the Catalogue of Ships. But this convenient shorthand is misleading. What matters in the passage, after all, is not so much ships as leaders: leaders and their contingents and the regions (richly evoked) that provide them.

In writing "the *Catalogue* is a simple vision of the Acheaean panorama", Whitman underestimated Homer's formal sophistication. For the structured array of names may be set out as in Table 9.1.

The symmetry of this array is striking. The twenty-nine contingents are drawn up not merely as a muster list, but as an army.

Agamemnon and Achilles occupy salient positions; but the most honourable position of all, the central fifteenth place, is reserved for Odysseus, "peer of Zeus in counsel" (*Iliad* 2.636). The central group represents privileged qualities—legal right (Menelaos, husband of Helen the *casus belli*), sagacity (Odysseus), and seniority (Nestor)—that offset the ill-directed political power of Agamemnon and the strength of Achilles. The contingents are symmetrically arranged like this:

8 | *Agamemnon* | 5 | *Odysseus* | 5 | *Achilles* | 8
1–8 | *Mycenaeans* | 10–14 | *Kephallenians* | 16–20 | *Myrmidons* | 22–29

Moreover, the distinct array of forty-four leaders has a similarly balanced arrangement:

1–16 | *Agamemnon* | 18–25 | *Odysseus* | 27–33 | *Achilles* | 35–44
16 | *Agamemnon* | 8 | *Odysseus* | 7 | *Achilles* | 10

– which can also be seen as:

16 | *Agamemnon* | 16 | *Achilles and others.*

In the first part of this array—consisting of thirty-three leaders—Agamemnon holds the sovereign centre place, in accordance with his power. But at *Iliad* 2.681 (which is generally regarded as marking a division[7]) there begins another group of eleven leaders, Achilles and others, who challenge Agamemnon.

The tally of ships, which scholars have found historically implausible or merely conventional, makes sense in literary terms. The ship numbers have a formal value, in that they repeat and so confirm the

Table 9.1 The Catalogue of Ships

Text			Contingent	Leader(s)	Ships
494–510	1.	Bœotians	1–5	Peneleos, Leitos, Arkesilaos, Prothoenor, Klonios	50
511–516	2.	Minyans	6–7	Askalaphos, Ialmenos	30
517–526	3.	Phokians	8–9	Skhedios, Epistrophos	40
527–535	4.	Lokrians	10	Aias the Less	40
536–545	5.	Abantes	11	Elephenor	40
546–556	6.	Athenians	12	Menestheus	50
557–558	7.	Salaminians	13	Aias the Greater	12
559–568	8.	Argives etc.	14–16	Diomedes, Sthenelos, Euryalos	80
569–580	**9.**	Mycenaeans		AGAMEMNON	100 (442)
581–590	10.	Lakedaimonians	1	Menelaos	60
591–602	11.	Pylians	2	Nestor	90
603–614	12.	Arcadians	3	Agapenor	60
615–624	13.	Epeans	4–7	Amphimakhos, Thalpios, Diores, Poluxeinos	40
625–630	14.	Ekhinaians	8	Meges	40
631–637	**15.**	Kephallenians		ODYSSEUS	12 (302)
638–644	16.	Aetolians	1	Thoas	40
645–652	17.	Cretans	2–3	Idomeneus, Meriones	80
653–670	18.	Rhodians	4	Tlepolemos	9
671–675	19.	Sumeans	5	Nireus	3
676–680	20.	Kalydnians	6–7	Pheidippos, Antiphos	30
681–694	**21.**	Myrmidons		ACHILLES	50
695–710	22.	Phulakians	1	Podarkes	40
711–715	23.	Pheraians	2	Eumelos	11
716–728	24.	Meliboians	3	Medon	7
729–733	25.	Oekhalians	4–5	Podaleirios, Makhaon	30
734–737	26.	Eurupulians	6	Eurupulos	40
738–747	27.	Argissans etc.	7–8	Polupoites, Leonteus	40
748–755	28.	Enienes etc.	9	Gouneus	22
756–759	29.	Magnetes	10	Prothous	40 (442)

symmetry of the arrays of leaders and contingents. They form, again, three groups:

Up to Agamemnon 442 | *Menelaus to Odysseus 302* | *Achilles and remainder 442*

In 2010, Klejn independently proposed a Catalogue that is informed with a complex symmetry involving geographical and ethnic groupings. But there is little doubt that early modern readers, at least, would have seen the Catalogue more simply as a centralized array of leaders. Alexander Pope (1688–1744) refers to it indeed as a catalogue of dynasties and "princes", reflecting awareness of Macrobius' comparison of Homer's and Vergil's catalogues.[8] So the symmetry of leaders that I proposed in 1970 still seems to me the salient pattern.[9] Nevertheless, this pattern remains unaddressed by classical scholars. After decades of productive archaeological research, they are understandably more interested in the geography of the Homeric age than in the moral significance of the Catalogue.

In all probability, however, the central emphasis of Homer's Catalogue was still understood in England as late as 1715. George Chapman's translation of *Homer's Iliads* (1598, 1611)[10], for example, although making additions, nevertheless retains Homer's symmetrical design. Moreover, Chapman's description of Agamemnon implies a central emphasis:

> and he in triumph then
> Put on his most resplendent armes, since he did overshine
> The whole heroique host of Greece in power of that designe.
>
> (*Homer's Iliads* 2.504–6)

Homer has nothing about a triumph: Chapman's addition shows his awareness of the Catalogue's symmetry, a regular feature of Renaissance triumphal forms.[11]

Pope's translation also enlarges the geographical and genealogical element of the Catalogue. But again he retains the symmetry, and again he refers to Agamemnon's triumph:

> High on the Deck the King of Men appears,
> And his refulgent Arms in Triumph wears;
> Proud of his Host, unrival'd in his Reign,
> In silent Pomp he moves along the Main.
>
> (*Homer's Iliad* 2.697–700)

In case his additions have obscured the Catalogue's symmetry, Pope makes it explicit by inserting the phrase "in Triumph". He and his collaborators have closely studied Homer's "Catalogue of Greece" (as they call it), for they annotate the geographical descriptions extensively.[12] Pope cites Porphyry and Eustathius as evidence that anciently the youth of some nations had to learn the Catalogue of princes by heart.

Chaucer and Dryden

Much early literature took the form of catalogues, a genre distasteful to many post-Enlightenment critics. Yet it was indispensible in oral literature, and hardly less so in later didactic writing meant to be committed to memory. Kyriakidis has laid the foundation for a history of name catalogues in classical epic.[13] The ancient tradition proved useful still in the Middle Ages, as one may infer from the twelfth-century and later lists of curriculum authors surveyed by E. R. Curtius.[14] Both Latin and vernacular works generally abounded with catalogues on every scale. Boccaccio's *De Mulieribus Claris* (1361–75?) is an ordered series of named *exempla*,[15] and much the same could be said of the *Divina Commedia* (?1307–20) and the *Roman de la Rose* (?1270–8). Naturally the degree of order in the catalogues varied.

Denton Fox describes Chaucer as "a great master of lists",[16] while Charles Muscatine remarks his "predilection for making lists of things":

> In a certain sense the sequence of portraits in Chaucer's *General Prologue* (and even the sequence of *The Canterbury Tales* as a whole) has the form of a catalogue; it is possible that Chaucer's liking for this form is related ultimately to the enumerative, processional, paratactic quality that pervades the structure of *The Canterbury Tales* in large and small. The individual portraits are themselves composed of catalogues of traits.[17]

One of the better accounts of Chaucer's catalogues, Stephen Barney's, emphasizes their origins in oral conventions.[18] As Barney observes, characteristic features of the lists—visual realization, "happenings", and "copious display"—were designed to aid memory.[19] He cites Donald Howard's summary of "the habits of 'artificial' memory—order, association, and visualization".[20] Nevertheless, whatever their interest as relics of the age of oral literature, the catalogues have tended to be dismissed as digressive or even dull. C. S. Lewis was unusual in regarding them as self-effacing evocations of the narrative's moral contexts.[21]

But even this totalizing vindication falls short of doing justice to the catalogues' communicative functions. Far from being "mere lists", the best catalogues were structured images of the narrative, and served as supplementary expositions of the theme: in short, they were instances of what modern critics call *mis-en-abyme*.[22]

The rich description of Venus' oratory in Chaucer's *Knight's Tale* presents such a catalogue of qualities, complex enough for its structure to have become unobvious. As Barney observes, it includes both moral personifications and figures as abstract as "Thought".[23] First, a mural portrays six experiences "that love's servantz in this lyf enduren" (1 A 1918–24). Next, the mural sets out an array of fifteen personified abstractions representing aspects of love:

> Plesaunce and Hope, Desir, Foolhardynesse,
> Beautee and Youthe, Bauderie [gaiety], Richesse,
> Charmes and Force, Lesynges [deceits], Flaterye,
> Despense [expenditure], Bisynesse [attention], and Jalousye.
> (The Knight's Tale 1 A 1925–8)

Of these personifications, Jalousye alone is described in detail: she "wered of yelewe gooldes a garland, | And a cokkow sittynge on hir hand" (lines 1929–30).

A further group of six un-personified "circumstaunces" of love follow: feasts, instruments, carol, dances, lust and array [display] (lines 1931–2). Their number is signalled by the conspicuous, self-referring ambiguity "which that I rekned and rekne shal" (lines 1933–4). Next, the dwelling of Venus herself is portrayed "With al the gardyn and the lustynesse" (line 1939). Her mention here thus comes sixteenth in the array of personifications. Now follow eight more named figures (lines 1940–6), Venus' "servants" who "caught were in hir las": 1 *Ydelnesse* her porter | 2 *Narcisus* | 3 *Salomon* | 4 *Ercules* | 5 *Medea* | 6 *Circes* | 7 *Turnus* | 8 *Cresus*. These are exemplary figures, "ensamples oon or two" (line 1953). The Knight next extracts a generalization: six qualities are listed as unable to "holde champartie" with Venus (1947–9): 1 *wysdom*, 2 *richesse*, 3 *beautee*, 4 *sleighte* [craft], 5 *strength*, 6 *hardynesse*. Finally he portrays in detail a statue or idol of Venus, with before it her son Cupido. In short, the array of names is a symmetrical structure with central emphasis:

15 personifications | *VENUS* | *8 servants* | *6 personifications* | *Cupido*

Or:

15 | Venus | 15.

The symmetry and central emphasis honouring Venus (line 1937) is clear enough, even if she is mentioned elsewhere, and her statue appears behind Cupid (lines 1955–62), ending and incorporating the whole array.[24]

Symmetry is not the only means, however, by which the array honours Venus. Unnamed "circumstances" total six both at lines 1920–4 and 1931–2; as do the qualities at lines 1947–9. These repeated sixes remind the reader that Martianus Capella and others assigned this perfect number to Venus as the product of the first male and the first female numbers.[25] Moreover, the personifications leading to Venus amount to fifteen, the number of steps or degrees of approach to a throne, and by a familiar symbolism especially signifying ascent to heaven.[26] To connect this symbol with a worldly Venus implies a Chaucerian irony of the darkest hue. Whatever Venus' charms, they end in the carnality of Cupido. The only one of her qualities described fully, as we saw, is Jalousye with her cuckoo (1928–30): "the cukkow ever unkynde".[27]

The catalogues of murals in the temple of Mars are simpler. Besides, their ordering is blurred by inclusion of unnamed examples and by division into separate scenes. However, nine named qualities stand out, symmetrically disposed about Meschaunce, "amyddes of the temple":

> *1 Felonye 2 Ire 3 Drede 4 Contek*
> *5 MESCHAUNCE*
> *6 Woodnesse* [madness] *7 Compleint 8 Outhees* [outcries] *9 Outrage.*

As for the oratory of Diana (which has no model in Boccaccio's *Teseide*), its catalogue is also simpler than those in the temple of Venus. The array of Diana's named attendants is as follows:

> *1 Callisto 2 Daphne 3 Actaeon*
> *4 DIANA*
> *5 Atalanta 6 Meleager 7 Lucina.*

As with Venus, the number of exemplary figures is appropriate: seven was associated with Diana and Luna because the moon's phases last seven days, and because seven is a "virginal" number, having no factors.[28]

John Dryden's modernizing *refacimento* of Chaucer in *Palamon and Arcite* (1700) is so freely inventive that it raises questions as to how far the structures of the medieval name arrays have been understood. Dryden's imitation is sometimes close, as with the six experiences of love in *The Knight's Tale*, lines 1918–24. The broken sleeps, cold sighs, sacred tears, lamentations, desiring, and oaths become in *Palamon and Arcite* "broken Slumbers", "Sighs that smoak'd along the Wall" (expanding on "cold"), "Complaints", "hot Desires", exaggerated "scalding tears that wore a Channel where they fell". Dryden adds "Prayers that seemed to call for Pity" and enlarges Chaucer's oaths beyond private "covenants" into "Nuptial Bonds, the Ties | Of love's Assurance, and a Train of Lies, | That, made in Lust, conclude in Perjuries". To expose the falsity of *fin amor*, he enlarges the catalogue from six to eight. Similarly, Chaucer's fifteen personified aspects become sixteen in Dryden.

We may infer that Dryden understood Chaucer's catalogues well enough, but took a different view of Venus and of marriage from that of Chaucer, "the servant of the servants of love". In Chaucer, the heroism of both Palamon and Arcite is qualified by irony,[29] but Dryden goes further in preferring Palamon's amorous devotion to Arcite's mad passion.[30] The Venus Chaucer's Palamon prays to is a genial, generative force almost as in Lucretius. But Dryden, avoiding the implications of the medieval number symbolism of ascent to a divine throne, substitutes catalogues of 8 and 16, suggesting a Renaissance Neoplatonic symbolism of 1:2, the diapason, as the proportion between the rational soul and the concupiscible faculty.[31] Moreover, he adds details of occultism, sorcery, and adulterous passion, darkening the associations of Venus and amplifying her need of Diana's restraint.

The Palice of Honour

Gavin Douglas (1474–1522) used to be called a "Scottish Chaucerian", but has long been thought to have followed Chaucer in a very independent way. *The Palice of Honour* resembles *The Knight's Tale* in relying on arrays of names, although its distinctive structure has a moral emphasis of its own.[32] Dream visions generally abound with symmetrically ordered catalogues of personifications and exemplary figures. Such "mere lists" have often been slighted without being very closely examined. But Fox's account of Douglas is an exception: "The basic

structural device of *The Palice of Honour*, then, is the list: the different
parts of the poem are joined together by simple juxtaposition and
these parts are themselves largely made up of catalogues."[33] Fox sees
that "Douglas' catalogues are something more than a medieval vice
[...] Like Dunbar, who is also addicted to lists, Douglas uses them to
group similar or contrasting elements, to balance entities against each
other and to freeze them into a comprehensive and rigid rhetorical
form" (p. 199). Fox stops short of considering the symmetry of Douglas' catalogues, which is unfortunate, since the arrays of *The Palice of
Honour* relate to the narrative, and reward anyone interested in Douglas' ideas of honour.

When the dreamer comes to Honour's "riche Castell" he sees Cicero strike down three turncoats trying to gain entry: Sinon, Achi-
tophell, and Lucius Catiline. Iugurtha and "tressonebill Tryphon" also
fall.[34] On the wall itself, Lawtie the garitour ("watchman") is the first
of the household. Twenty-eight others follow (lines 1784–1825):

1 Lawtie ["Loyalty"]; *2 Patience (porter), 3 Honour (prince); 4 Charity (master of the
household), 5 Constance (secretary); 6 Liberalite (treasurer); 7,8 Innocence and Devotion (clerks of the closet); 9 Discretion (comptroller); 10,11 Humanity and True Relation
(ushers); 12–14 Peace, Quiet, Rest (marshals of renown); 15 Temperance (cook); 16
HUMILITIE (carver); 17 VERTUOUS DISCIPLINE (master sewer); 18 Mercie
(cupbearer); 19 Conscience (chancellor); 20–23 Science, Prudence, Iustice, Sapience
(assessors and auditors); 24–26 Lauborous diligence, Gude warkis, Clene leuing* [liv-
ing] *(out-stewards and caterers); 27 Gude hope (minstrel); 28 Pietie (almoner); 29
Fortitude (lieutenant); 30 Verite (favourite).*

One might expect Douglas to honour some high-ranking office in the
central place. And indeed he approaches the centre, like Chaucer in
the temple of Venus, by fifteen steps, the number of approach to a
throne.[35] But the central place is surprisingly assigned, in both the London and Edinburgh manuscripts, to the two personifications Humility
and Virtuous Discipline. Honour's porter is Patience, not the Idleness of
the *Roman de la Rose* and Chaucer's temple of Venus. And the household
includes the four Cardinal Virtues and three Theological Virtues. Thus
Douglas, as befits the Bishop of Dunkeld, rejects secular views of
honour and ensures that in his palace of Honour the first shall be last.

Behind Chaucer's and Douglas' name arrays lie Continental models
such as those of Dante, Boccaccio, and Petrarch. Studies by E. H.
Wilkins and others show Petrarch's impact to have operated in three
phases: first through his Latin works, next the *Trionfi*, and only subsequently

the *Canzoniere*. The most seminal work, for English and Scottish literature, was his *Trionfi*.

Petrarch's Trionfi

In the *Trionfo della Pudicizia* the array of names begins with sixteen
virtues. These are not merely listed: Petrarch shows their spatial arrangement by many detailed specifications. Eight virtues go in pairs (*teneansi
per mano a due a due*):

> 79–84 *Onestate e Vergogna*
> *Senno e Modestia*
> *Abito con Diletto in mezzo 'l core*
> *Perseveranza e Gloria*

Around these (*intorno intorno*) are four other pairs:

> 85–90 *Bella Accoglienza, Accorgimento*
> *Cortesia , Puritate*
> *Timor d'infamia, Desio sol d'onore*
> *Castità, Beltate.*

The sixteen (or 4^2) virtues visibly form a virtuous square.[36] Next, Laura
subjugates Love and binds him to a column (line 118). Another virtuous array, ordered symmetrically, follows:

118–38 *1 Laura 2 Love 3 Lucrezia 4 Penelope 5 Verginia 6 Virginio*
140–1   *German women*
142–3   *7 Judith 8 Ippone*
146–7   *TRIUMPH OF LAURA*
148–52 *1 Tucia 2 Ersilia*
152–4   *Sabine Women*
157–93 *3 Dido 4 Piccarda Donati 5 Scipio 6 Spurina 7 Ioseppe 8 Ippolito*

Or:

$$8 \mid LAURA \mid 8$$

Lord Morley's English translation of the *Trionfi* (1554) simplifies
Petrarch's scheme while keeping its central emphasis: Laura follows an
array of virtues and precedes another of exemplary figures. The Scottish poet William Fowler (1560–1612), a good Italianist, wrote a more
ambitiously faithful translation of the *Trionfi* (dedicated in 1587).[37]

Table 9.2 The Triumph of Chastity

Text	Virtues and exemplary figures	
109–10	*Honestie;*	*Shamefastnes*
113	*Witt;*	*Modestie*
114	*Delyte;*	*good Behauiour*
115	*Perseverance;*	*Glorye*
116	*Entreatie;*	*Goode Advys*
118	*Courtesie;*	*Cleneliness*
119	*Feare of Schame;*	*Desyre of Glore*
120	*Chastetie;*	*Beutye*
160–67	*1 Laura; 2 Cupido*	
178–83	*3 Lucretia; 4 Penelope; 5 Virginia; 6 Virginio*	
187	*German dames*	
189–91	*7 Juditha; 8 Hippo*	
195–6	*TRIUMPH OF LAURA OVER LOVE*	
198–201	*1 Thucia; 2 Hersilia*	
203	*(Sabine) countrye maids*	
209–56	*3 Dido; 4 Picardo Donati; 5 Scipio;6 Spurinna;*	
	7 Hippolite;8 Ioseph	

Although stylistically immature, Fowler succeeds in making sense of Petrarch's wittily complex syntax, and arrives at the array shown in Table 9.2.

The positions of the virtues are specified much as in Petrarch. But Fowler introduces military terms appropriate to the martial trope, indicating spatial relations by phrases like "in middle guard" (replacing *fuori*) and "in arire [rear] guard". Fowler's translations of the virtues' names are well considered. "Entreatie fair" (*Bella Accoglienza*) recalls the *Bel Accœil* of the *Roman de la Rose*. And *Senno* ("Good Sense") here becomes simply "Witt". Whatever finesses Fowler attempts, he noticeably adheres to Petrarch's symmetry and number symbolisms.

Milton's satiric arrays

In *Paradise Lost*, that most retrospective of masterpieces, Milton re-enlivens the traditional name array and gives it new directions. After the Fall, Adam guided by Michael ascends "a hill | Of Paradise the highest" (*PL* 11.378–9) where he envisions future empires of the world. The name catalogues here have the central emphasis usual with dream visions—but with a characteristically sharp, satiric difference. For the centres of the arrays are problematic.

First comes an array of Asian empires with their rulers' names or titles. The central position is occupied by "golden Chersonese", the only empire without a ruler. Flanking this are the "great mogul" and "The Persian", each with two capital cities, then the "Sinaean kings" with Paquin (Peiping) and the "Russian czar" with Mosco. In the outermost positions are pairs of places ruled by the "Cathaian khan" (Cambalu and Samarchand) and "the sultan" (Bizance and Turchestan):

RULERS	*khan*	*Sinaean king*	*mogul*	—	*Persian*	*czar*	*sultan*
PLACES	2	1	2	*CHERSONESE*	2	1	2

In the closely similar array of African empires, introduced by the transitional phrase "nor could his eye not ken" (*PL* 11.396), the centre is again problematic. The central fifth of nine empires has no incumbent ruler:

1 Negus	*2 King*	*3 King*	*4 King*	*5* ——	——*6 King*	*7 King*	*8 Almanzor*	*9 Pope*
Ercoco	*Mombasa*	*Quiloa*	*Melind*	*SOFALA*	*Congo*	*Angola*	*Barbary*[38]	*Rome*

"Sofala thought Ophir", like Chersonese in the Asian array, is the source of Solomon's gold and refers to the apocalyptic judge "more precious than the gold wedge of Ophir" prophesied in Isaiah 13: 12.[39] Thus the vacant thrones imply the absence of just human sovereignty in the corrupt world: they point to the invisible, millenarian sovereignty of Christ.[40]

The symmetries of these two arrays correspond to that of *Paradise Lost* as a whole.[41] They have also, however, a satiric thrust. The last of the nine African empires is "where Rome was to sway | The world"; so that its placement matches that of Bizance (Byzantium, New Rome) and Turkestan in the previous arrays (*PL* 11.388–95, 396–406). It thus implies an equivalence between modern Rome and Turkestan, the papal empire and the Saracen. In Milton's view, true sovereignty lies not in secular power ("sway"), but in Christ's headship of the "true church".

Anti-Jesuit prejudice may explain Milton's notorious "error" of treating Cathay and China as two separate empires ruled respectively by "Cathaian khan" and "Sinaean kings" (*PL* 11.388–90). Milton could claim in this the support of Ortelius' 1602 *Atlas*. But the Jesuits Bento de Góis and Martino Martini had since shown conclusively that the two empires were one and the same, and by 1667 their proof of this was widely accepted.[42]

T. S. Eliot had his own reasons for wishing to dislodge *Paradise Lost* from the literary canon: Milton's authority was a serious obstacle to the modernist movement. Consequently Eliot's notorious contribution to *Essays and Studies* in 1936 cannot be regarded as a balanced assessment of *Paradise Lost*. Motivated by rivalry with Robert Bridges, Eliot strains to compare Milton's "rhetorical style" to the "later style of Joyce"—while denying "any close parallel" between them. When he writes on the name array in *Paradise Lost* book 11, Eliot unconvincingly claims to enjoy Milton:

I can enjoy the roll of

> . . . Cambula [sic], seat of Cathaian Can
> And Samarchand by Oxus, Temir's throne,
> To Paquin of Sinaean kings, and thence
> To Agra and Lahor of great Mogul
> Down to the golden Chersonese, or where
> The Persian in Ecbatan sate, or since
> In Hispahan, or where the Russian Ksar
> On [sic] Mosco, or the Sultan in Bizance,
> Turchestan-born . . .

and the rest of it, but I feel that this is not serious poetry, not poetry fully occupied about its business, but rather a solemn game.[43]

What exactly is the "business" of poetry? And didn't Homer and Milton understand it quite as well as young Eliot? The essayist seems little interested in discovering just what solemn game Milton has played: he never considers the catalogue in detail, never works out its repeated structure (the business, surely, of criticism)—never, indeed, pursues its meaning. Had Eliot done so, he would surely have discovered its millenarian and anti-papal context. He might still have dismissed the passage, but could hardly have denied its seriousness.

Other critics and scholars have since gone further down the same road, disparaging not only Milton's name array but also those of Homer, Chaucer, and Spenser. It seems the ability to enjoy the art of arrays has been lost. Perhaps the catalogue's games—effortless variety in repetition, digressions into vivid associations, surprises, and secrets—go against the grain of a modernism that is all too "serious". This is not the same issue as that of Milton's numerical composition. William B. Hunter, for example, accepts that the *Paradise Lost* arrays are structured with central emphasis,[44] but defends Eliot's position on the ground that explanation after the event can never create appropriate associations in reading. This means in effect that Milton's epic catalogues can never now be appreciated. And Hunter is not alone in this view. Other editors—notably Barbara Lewalski and Roy Flannagan—seem to agree with him; for when they annotate the names in the catalogues they ignore the catalogues themselves. In effect they embrace Eliot's view, preferring not to consider the epic catalogue as serious literature. A distinguished exception is Umberto Eco (2009), whose *The Infinity of Lists from Homer to Joyce* shows keen appreciation of the list as an art form.

Pope's Dunciad

Alexander Pope takes up from Milton the satiric application of name arrays. His *Dunciad* (1728–43) may seem to consist largely of a myriad names: the "dunces". These are no mere accumulation of writers Pope disapproved of, the enemy "army of midget barbarians" in the Augustans' literary wars (symptoms, in his view, of cultural decline under the Hanoverians). Some of the duncers are included because they had attacked Pope or otherwise become personal enemies. Many were not at all dunces in our sense. "Tibbald" or Lewis Theobald (1688–1744) was a better textual critic than Pope himself; John Dennis was one of the most formidable critics of the age. It is all too easy to accept the poem's estimates of dunceity. In Pope's century George Wither was regarded as a feeble poet, a view James Sutherland and Valerie Rumbold share, in our own. But Wither had been a keen satirist under James I, and later showed himself to be a deep student of the Psalms. Other "dunces" too had their own excellencies, as Pope well knew: his attitudes to them could be ambivalent, even envious.

The 1728 Dunciad may at first give the impression of an urban throng. It is "crammed with the names of actual persons"[45]—or at least, half-named persons. Most are designated by an initial letter and a blank, leaving many puzzles to be resolved in the 1729 *Variorum Dunciad*, which gives most of the names in full.[46] The poem seems like some Grub Street *Trivia*, but with crowds on such a scale as to defy ordered arrangement. In his Chatterton lecture, Emrys Jones identifies a "formlessness" provoking in Pope both hostility and fascination.[47] Chaos, after all, is one of his subjects. Dulness "beholds the Chaos dark and

deep, | Where nameless somethings in their causes sleep":[48] beholds it
as a Satan intending further chaos but also as a parodic Christ creating
potentialities.[49] The impression of formlessness grows with the changes
and additions in successive editions of the *Dunciad*—changes as salient
as replacing Tibbald as protagonist by Dennis and Cibber. Perhaps
Pope needed a certain looseness of structure to allow room for updating names, whether to keep pace with cultural changes or to respond
to shifts in his personal relationships.

Subsequent readings modify this initial impression. Topics, rituals,
and scraps of narrative emerge: processions, gatherings of books, a sacrifice. This is not to say a fully ordered sequence leaps into view. Nevertheless, central emphases assert themselves, even if less boldly than in
the medieval and Renaissance arrays discussed earlier. In all the versions of the *Dunciad*, for example, Dulness is located near the central
place of a book or grouping of books. Thus, the line centre of 1728
book 1 is 125–6 of 250; but Tibbald's address to the goddess begins at
1.133 and he does not formally name her until 1.135. And in the 1729
Variorum Dunciad this becomes line 143 of 260. Or one might consider
the centre of the 1728 *Dunciad* to be the line centre of all three books
taken together, that is, 2.210 (the 460th of 920 lines). But the result is
little different. Dulness announces the noise-making event at 2.203–4,
near the centre but not precisely at it.

Did Pope use symmetrical structures merely as scaffolding to be
discarded when it had served its purpose? Or did he sense the practice
of numerical composition was obsolescent, and aim at a newer, more
impressionistic poetic? The changes he made to line numbers, as version succeeded version, might well suggest as much.[50] Static (gothic?)
name arrays are abandoned in favour of active processions like those of
The Faerie Queene. Critics from Aubrey Williams onward agree that the
structural basis of 1728 book 1 is a mayoral procession from Guildhall
to Westminster Hall.[51] And since the route was also that of coronation
processions, Pope's targets were as much political as literary: the City
poets colluding with "Whig tyranny".[52]

We may agree in part. Williams convincingly explains the place
names as an organizing principle. But references to a procession hardly
amount to dynamic narrative: Jones is nearer the mark with his *tableau*
of writers.[53] Indeed, Pope entirely omits the mayoral procession itself:
it has happened already. "'Twas on the day, when Tho–d, rich and
grave, | Like Cimon triumph'd both on land and wave" raises expecta-

tion of a narrative, but none follows. Instead, a single vivid couplet evokes the occasion with images of "glad chains" and "broad banners", only to announce "the proud scene was o'er" (1.75–6). True, it lives still "in Settle's numbers, one day more". But that too is past; for what actually follows is a catalogue of City writers and their dull sources. Pope offers no Spenserian narrative with transitions from one processing figure to the next—"Then came those...";"These after, came..."; "Ne thence the Irishe Rivers absent were" (*FQ* 4.11.36–40). Perhaps such minute narrative had come to seem "dulness". At any rate, Pope condenses the procession to an array of names, removing several features of the catalogue—common to Homer, Chaucer, Spenser—until the vestigial narrative becomes one of literary filiations and genealogies of imitation: "She saw in N[orto]n all his father shine, | And E[usde]n eke out Bl[ackmore]'s endless line" (1.91–2). Nevertheless Pope retains symmetry and central emphasis, now expressing them exclusively in the sequence of names. At the risk of incurring a charge of dullness, I list the writers in the 1728a Dunciad 1.78–125 in Table 9.3.

Table 9.3 The 1728 *Dunciad* Array

Text	Name	Comment
1.78	Settle	1
1.86	Heywood	2
1.91	Norton Defoe	3 changed to *Prynne* 1728c–e
1.91	Daniel Defoe	4
1.92	Eusden	5
1.92	Blackmore	6
1.93	Philips	7
1.93	Tate	8
1.94	Dunton	9 changed to *Dennis* 1728c–e
1.94	Whately	10
1.96	TIBBALD	11
1.111	Ogilby	12
1.112	Newcastle	13
1.116	Wesley	14 changed to *Wither* 1728c–e
1.116	Watts	15 changed to *Quarles* 1728c–e
1.116	Blome	16
1.119	Caxton	17
1.119	Wynkyn	18
1.123	de Lyra	19
1.124	Holland	20
1.175	Settle	21

This array of City writers and their sources is framed by double appearances of Elkanah Settle (1648–1724), the time-serving author of City pageants and shows for the Bartholomew Fair. A sometime opponent of Dryden, he was a prominent exclusionist, and organizer of Pope-burnings.[54] Within this frame are nineteen names, of which the central eleventh (no surprise) is that of Tibbald, the protagonist:

> Settle | 9 writers | TIBBALD | 9 writers | Settle.

In the 1729 *Variorum Dunciad*, apart from giving most names in full, Pope made few changes to the array. Norton and Daniel Defoe become Prynne and Daniel; Samuel Wesley is changed to George Wither and Isaac Watts to Francis Quarles.[55] More importantly, Dunton and Whately are replaced by John Dennis (1658–1734), a formidable literary critic and a bitter enemy. This reduces the names to eighteen, and puts Dennis and Tibbald at the centre as joint chief dunces:

> Settle | 7 writers | DENNIS, TIBBALD | 7 writers | Settle.

The net result of these changes is to retain the centralized structure. Evidently the central emphasis mattered to Pope.

Perhaps Pope found the structure of the 1728 arrays was proving obscure to readers. At any rate, he prefaced the main array in the 1729 *Variorum Dunciad* with a brief figure, obviously symmetrical. This miniature array, shown in Table 9.4, is easily graspable in rhetorical terms and prepares readers for the more demanding catalogue to follow.

Here the symmetry of the array is spelt out almost explicitly. Pope gives the broadest of hints, apostrophizing Swift with the formula "whatever Title please thine ear" to alert the reader to the number of Swift's avatars, cuing "Settle's numbers" (1.88), and making much of the centre of the array (1.35–6): "Here stood her Opium, here she nurs'd her Owls, | And destin'd here th' imperial seat of Fools". The

Table 9.4 The Miniature Array

Text	Names	Comment
1.18	*Dean, Drapier, Bickerstaff, Gulliver*	*Swift's four "titles"*
1.19–20	*Cervantes, Rabelais*	*two satiric authors*
1.32	*Poverty, Poetry*	*two shivering sisters*
1.38	*Curl, Lintot*	*two booksellers*
1.44–52	*Fortitude, Temperance, Prudence, Justice*	*"Four . . . Virtues"*

echo of *Paradise Lost* in "imperial seat" makes abundantly clear the significance this central emphasis is to have.

In the 1743 four-book Dunciad, Pope made more radical changes; yet he still preserved the symmetrical structures. Tibbald, although continuing to feature, is displaced as joint chief dunce by Colley Cibber (1671–1757), a Whig and enthusiastic supporter of the Hanoverian dynasty. (Tricked into acting a parody of himself in a play written by Gay, Pope, and Arbuthnot, he had not surprisingly retaliated with attacks on Pope.)[56] The centre of a very different array is now occupied by two writers:

Settle | 7 *writers* | DENNIS, CIBBER |7 *writers* | Settle.

Dennis and "Bays" (Cibber) now share the dubious honour of chief duncehood.

In all the *Dunciads*, the catalogues of writers amplify their moribund dulness. They are no more than their dead, old, dry-as-dust works and sources: "sav'd by spice, like mummies, many a year" (*1728* 1.121). To express their lack of wit they do nothing but sleep: "There *Caxton* slept, with *Wynkin* at his side". And to show their substitution of quantity for quality, Pope reduces their characters to the physical qualia of their huge compilations: "One clasp'd in wood, and one in strong cow-hide" and "*De Lyra* there a dreadful front extends, | And there, the groaning Shelves *Philemon* bends" (1.123–4). Pope is supposed to have confused Nicholas de Lyra with Nicholas Harpsfield; but perhaps this "error" should be seen as yet another delicious insult, associating Harpsfield with gothic dulness. Does not his very name betray that he plays the same tunes as the dreadful de Lyra? In any event, the dull writers are figured in the heaped-up, sheepskin-bound works that are all they have to offer. In 1728 and 1729, the top of the heap is Tibbald's tiny *Ajax*: he adds only what is found in "a jakes": crap.

Notes

1. Simpson and Lazenby 1970; Kirk 1985; Visser 1997; Minchin 2001; Jones 2003.
2. See, e.g., Simpson and Lazenby 1970: 156; Klejn 2000.
3. Whitman 1958: 261.
4. Whitman 1958: 262.
5. Cf. Simpson and Lazenby 1970: 168.
6. See Fowler 1970; Belknap 2004; Kyriakidis 2007.

7. E.g. Kirk 1985: 228, "A fresh start is made".
8. "Observations on the Catalogue", Pope 1967: 7.173–7.
9. See Fowler 1970: 92.
10. Chapman 1957: 1.504.
11. For other examples of coded language cuing central emphasis, see Fowler 1970: Index, *Self-referring passages*.
12. Pope 1967: 7.177–85.
13. Kyriakidis 2007.
14. Curtius 1953: 48–51, 247–51.
15. As is Petrarch's *De Viris Illustribus*.
16. Fox 1966: 198.
17. Muscatine 1966: 95.
18. Barney 1982.
19. Barney 1982: 200–1.
20. Barney 1982: 301 n. 34.
21. Lewis 1964: 198–200.
22. E.g. Caws 1985: 17, 271 n. 3.
23. See Barney 1982: 200.
24. Cf. Boccaccio, *Teseida* 7.50–7, where also fifteen personifications lead to Venus' temple *E 'n mezzo il luogo*.
25. Martianus Capella 1977: 280.
26. See Fowler 1997: 173, citing among others Bernard of Clairvaux, Durandus, and Cardinal Bellarmine. The array is Chaucer's: contrast Boccaccio, *Teseida* 7.
27. *The Parliament of Fowls* 358. Cf. Boccaccio, *Teseida*, 7.59.
28. See Macrobius 1952: 108–15.
29. Reverand 1988: 68.
30. Reverand 1988: 59–60.
31. Pico 1573: 1.79.
32. On Douglas' debt to Petrarch's *Trionfi*, e.g., see Jack 1972: 25.
33. Fox 1966: 198.
34. Douglas 2003, readings from the Edinburgh MS.
35. For the fifteen steps, see notes 24 and 26 above.
36. See Fowler 1970: 39.
37. Fowler 1914: 67–76. Jack 1972: 80 describes Fowler's translation as inexperienced yet inventive. On the virtuous quadrate, see Fowler 1964: Index, *Quadrate*.
38. The five kingdoms of Barbary are "Fez and Sus, Maroco and Algiers, and Tremisen" (11.403–4). See further in Milton 1998: 617–20.
39. The just Solomon merits the fifth position among rulers, since the fifth digit was supposed to divide the other digits justly. The "incorruptible" five in pentagram form is the mystic knot of Solomon; see Fowler 1964: 34; MacQueen 1985: 70.
40. Psalm 45: 9 ("upon thy right hand did stand the queen in gold of Ophir") was believed to prophesy the majesty of Christ's millenarian kingdom); cf. Isaiah 13: 12–13, "I will make a man more precious than fine gold; even a man than the golden wedge of Ophir. Therefore I will shake the heavens, and the earth shall remove." See Loewenstein 1990:117–18 on Adam's vision of Christ's secret lordship through the ages.
41. See Milton 1998: 26–9, 617–20.
42. See Chang 1970: 493–8.
43. "A Note on the Verse of John Milton", rpt. in Eliot 1957: 144. For the details of Eliot's sordid manoeuvres, see Ricks 2003: 5. Milton was to be ousted to bring down Bridges with his Miltonizing scansion and make room for American flat-liners like Pound and Eliot himself.

44. See Hunter 1984: 58–61.
45. Jones 1980: 615.
46. See Pope 2007: 114.
47. Jones 1980: 620.
48. 1728 *Dunciad* 1.43–4.
49. Cf. Battestin 1980: 104.
50. See Fowler 1970: 85–8, 121–2.
51. Jones 1980; Brooks-Davies 1985: 108–10; Erskine-Hill 1972: 20; Pope 2007.
52. As Brooks-Davies 1985; cf. Womersley 1968.
53. Jones 1980: 645.
54. See Rumbold in Pope 2007: 415–16.
55. On these changes, already in 1728c–e, see Rumbold in Pope 2007: 31.
56. See Rumbold in Pope 2007: 401–2.

10

Joyce and Nabokov

Few writers after Pope attempted patterned catalogues like those in *The Dunciad*. The post-Enlightenment poetic shunned such arrays along with the "silent language"[1] of acrostics, anagrams, numerical composition—all the invisible architecture represented by schemes of words. As Thomas De Quincey (1785–1859) put it in an ambitious *Blackwood's* review, "the rhetorician's art in its glory and power has silently faded away before the stern tendencies of the age". He agreed with Richard Whately that Dr Johnson's style was characterized by "the addition of clauses which add little or nothing to the sense, and which have been compared to the false handles and key-holes with which furniture is decorated".[2] By rhetorical style De Quincey's editor David Masson took him to mean "rich or ornate style, the art of conscious playing with a subject intellectually and inventively, and of never leaving it till it has been brocaded with the utmost possible amount of subsidiary thought, humour, fancy, ornamentation, and anecdote".[3] The new rhetoric of the nineteenth century by comparison was more directly declarative, more expressive, more subjective. It pursued "the sense" too seriously to have room for ludic patterns or hidden names.

Modernist naming

Ludic writing returned with a vengeance in the twentieth century, however, when modernists dissociated themselves in various ways from Victorian ideas of realism. They no longer took for granted old

assumptions about how names should function in narrative. This is not
to deny of course that Joyce's and Nabokov's naming (for example)
had antecedents in earlier fiction.

Names had long been used to carry meaning, to embody thematic
associations. As we have seen, the significant names contenting authors
from Chaucer to Pope became enriched but also blurred in the fiction
of Richardson and later of Dickens, Thackeray, and Henry James. Character names gathered complex moral and atmospheric associations;
sometimes they pursued the easy appeal of "great names", sometimes (as
in James) the subtleties of literary allusion. Associations could now qualify, contest, even override, a name's explicit meaning. They had become
elusive in their subjectivity. As a child, the short story writer Shena
Mackay felt "the sound and colour" of "Graham Greene" as "a sort of
lovat"; and she felt "Beryl Bainbridge" as brown, not the "green or yel-
low gemstone that her parents envisaged when they named her".[4]

Modernist naming tended to be unobtrusive: although richly
freighted with allusive associations, these were often muted and multiple. This cultivation of highly charged names could lead to ambiguity
and obscurity. Yet the names are thematic: understanding a modernist
work often depends on grasping the force of its names. Robert Louis
Stevenson, for example, saw from the first the multifarious possibilities
of naming. One possibility was allusion. In *Treasure Island* (1882) the
hypocritical Silver may shine brightly but is not true silver: "reprobate
silver shall men call them, because the Lord hath rejected them" (Jer. 6:
30). In *The Ebb Tide* (1894), however, a less obvious symbolism is the
order of the day. Does the menacing Attwater stand *at* the *water* of
baptism? *Dr Jekyll and Mr Hyde* (1886) is even more polyvalent. Readers
have continued to find new implications in the name Hyde: animal
overtones, Jekyll's attempt to *hide* his shadow side, the spelling with *y*
that unsuccessfully conceals this concealment. Richly suggestive too is
"Utterson", referring to expression of covert matters, but also to the
"uttering" or passing of bad cheques.

A signal instance of modernist naming may be seen in Nostromo,
the ubiquitous agent of Joseph Conrad's *Nostromo* (1904). Nostromo is
so serviceable that we come to take his value for granted. When we
witness his nocturnal crime, how are we to distance ourselves from it
and disown him? After all, he is "our man".

In a broader perspective the rhetoric of the nineteenth century can
be seen to have profound consequences for naming in later fiction.

Narrative has continued, of course, but no longer as before. Already in George Meredith (1828–1909) the pace of narration was slowing, and giving way to prolonged description or elaborate conversation. Then in late James and in Virginia Woolf the element of story became further attenuated and (in the latter) merged with lyrical expression of internal experience. Certainly full names—implying as they did a complete social context—were becoming less uniformly expected. By the late twentieth century, indeed, surnames even in real life no longer had quite the same prominence and inevitability. In 1970, Roland Barthes announced "what can no longer be written is the Proper Name".[5] Several writers, among them Franz Kafka and Thomas Pynchon, used truncated names ("K", "V") without the social implications of a full name.[6] David Porush perhaps goes a little far in identifying this formal development as a paranoid response to societies so corrupt as to threaten apocalypse. But he is credible enough when he compares the Russian formalist poetic of "transfiction" with its confrontation of literary devices in order to shatter the realist illusion of "totalizing novel(s)". Unfortunately, the strategy of subverting full names descended all too readily into disintegration and nihilism; as when John Barth's "Bonaparte Bray" believes his books to be plagiarized by—John Barth.[7]

Nevertheless the change in naming had universal, less deliberately engineered effects on mainstream fiction. Not all writers might think disintegration a valid response to the plausible full names of the past. Not all sought to escape the prison house of Victorian realism. But all found difficulties with naming. As the literary canon enlarged, allusions proliferated and literary associations became unpredictably multifarious, until they threatened to elude the writer's control. The new complexity of associations everywhere put pressure on traditional methods. This need not call, of course, for disintegration. James Joyce (1882–1941), for example, addressed the problem by using names in novel ways. Turning aside from the direct individuation of the Victorians, he made a virtue of the growing burden of association, finding ways to manage associations through overdetermination. He would conflate meanings and archetypes until they acquired a representative, paradigmatic authority.

In *Ulysses* (1922) Joyce interweaves Irish and classical names, sometimes with burlesque effect, sometimes with the weight of monumental generality. The selective realism of Irish names evokes bourgeois

social contexts; but this is offset with Homeric analogues universalizing Bloom's experience. This interweaving, impressively sustained
though it is, seldom, however, achieves full integration. *Ulysses* splits, as
it were, between the matter of Rome and the matter of Ireland. The
local realism of place and personal names succeeds so well in educing
modern society that the half-incorporated ancient names risk seeming
merely ironic, or (worse) improbable:

The work of salvage, removal of *debris*, human remains etc has been entrusted
to Messrs Michael Meade and Son, 159 Great Brunswick street, and Messrs
T. and C. Martin, 77, 78, 79 and 80 North Wall, assisted by the men and officers
of the Duke of Cornwall's light infantry under the general supervision of
H. R. H., rear admiral, the right honourable sir Hercules Hannibal Habeas
Corpus Anderson, K. G., K. P., K. T., P. C., K. C. B., M. P., J. P., M. B., D. S. O.,
S. O. D., M. F. H., M. R. I. A., B. L., Mus. Doc., P. L. G., F. T. C. D., F. R. U. I., F.
R. C. P. I. and F. R. C. S. I.[8]

In such passages, names and titles do most of the satiric work, as well
as carrying the narrative. Thus, a list of wedding guests will abound in
apt associations:

Lady Sylvester Elmshade, Mrs Barbara Lovebirch, Mrs Poll Ash, Mrs Holly
Hazeleyes, Miss Daphne Bays, Miss Dorothy Canebrake, Mrs Clyde Twelvetrees,
Mrs Rowan Greene, Mrs Helen Vinegadding, Miss Virginia Creeper, Miss
Gladys Beech, Miss Olive Garth, Miss Blanche Maple, Mrs Maud Mahogany,
Miss Myra Myrtle, Miss Priscilla Elderflower, Miss Bee Honeysuckle, Miss
Grace Poplar, Miss O Mimosa San, Miss Rachel Cedarfrond, the Misses Lilian
and Viola Lilac, Miss Timidity Aspenall, Mrs Kitty Dewey-Mosse, Miss May
Hawthorne, Mrs Gloriana Palme, Mrs Liana Forrest, Mrs Arabella Blackwood
and Mrs Norma Holyoake of Oakholme Regis graced the ceremony by their
presence.[9]

The names here satisfy multiple criteria: arboreal or horticultural connections (appropriate to the bridegroom's being "grand high chief
ranger of the Irish National Foresters"); class associations; celebrity
(like Mimosa San, of *The Geisha*); nationalist overtones; and erotic
suggestions.[10] As if this were not enough, Joyce adds parody of Spenser's
catalogue of trees in *The Faerie Queene* 1.1.7–9 and of newspaper
accounts of social events. In *Surface and Symbol* (1947) Robert Martin
Adams argues that *Ulysses* offers "no proper fictional reason for some
of the things that are said and done" in it. He thinks to dispose of the
alleged signature acrostic in the list of winners of the Bloomsday bicy-
cle race on 16 June 1904 by showing Joyce copied the names from the

Irish Independent. But Adams fails to allow for the possibility that Joyce copied this particular list precisely because the name "J. A. Jackson" made acrostic allusion to "James A. Joyce".[11]

Without aiming at an elaborate plot, *Ulysses* for the most part retains the sequence of events customary in narrative. Even this continuity goes, however, in Molly Bloom's final soliloquy or stream of consciousness. Here, the nostalgic array of lovers' names is what provides the main continuity: "Mulvey and Mr Stanhope and Hester and father and old captain Groves".[12]

Finnegans Wake

Many readers locate the strength of *Ulysses* in its Irish realism, not its mythic universality. And this realism may be said to reside largely in the Irish names. Joyce told Cyril Connolly "I am more interested, Mr Connolly, in the Dublin street names than in the riddle of the Universe".[13] Joyce's Dublin publisher was reluctant to print actual Dublin names, for fear of lawsuits; which provoked a satiric response from Joyce in "Gas from a Burner", supposedly by G. Roberts the manager of Maunsel & Co.: "I'm damned if I do—I'm damned to blazes! | Talk about Irish Names of Places!"[14] Names were Joyce's way into history and anthropology, into the riddle of his own universe. In *Finnegans Wake* (1939) he carried this onomastic method further: far more than *Ulysses* it sums whole cultures in its names. And now the integration becomes more complete. Yet this is achieved at a cost. The names are often unfamiliar, so that their associations are difficult of access. Readers have to discover the associations through attentive reading, through persistent study, even through research.[15]

In *Finnegans Wake* Joyce abstracts the protagonist far beyond the moral and spiritual generality of the medieval Everyman. Earwicker's universal significance is throughout extended through wordplays— sustained ludic devices such as acrostics, acronyms, anagrams, ambiguous spellings and invented idioms. The famous opening sentence begins the game:

riverrun, past Eve and Adam's, from swerve of shore to bend of bay, brings us by a commodius vicus of recirculation back to Howth Castle and Environs.

"Howth Castle and Environs", a geographical and historical expansion of "HCE", serves as a chorographic exordium to the epic. Embodying the universal male, and being a publican, H. C. Earwicker combines hospitable host with Eucharistic Host. As General Man, his initials can be referred to as a *siglum*, and Joyce can write of "a pleasant turn of the populace which gave him as sense of those normative letters the nickname Here Comes Everybody".[16] The initials also imply, however, the disease, pollution, and waste of contemporary mankind: HCE can be expanded as "Heinz cans everywhere" (p. 581). Overwritten by such contemporary associations, historical contexts and exotic analogues can be discerned. HCE may, for example, be thought of as Haroun Childeric Eggeberth (p. 4): Childeric, king of the Franks from AD 458, was an ally of Rome against the Saxons, whereas Egbert (d. 839) was King of the West Saxons, and Haroun, as Caliph of Baghdad, came from outside Christendom altogether. As often, HCE takes all sides at once.

A complementary, female principle informs Earwicker's lover ALP, Anna Livia Plurabelle.[17] Young Anna is Isabel, old Anna is Kate, so that Anna unites mother and daughter. Her ages are eternally ALIKE (p. 165), an acrostic acronym of Anna Livia Isabel Kate Earwicker.[18] Among geographical expansions of ALP, Livia becomes the river Liffey, central to Dublin's history.

The acrostic name HCE is the fountainhead and generative origin of Joyce's work. It appears as early as the draft of 15 November 1926 sent to Harriet Weaver, before even the version of the first paragraph published in the journal *transition* (April 1927). In the 1926 draft, the first sentence is already "Howth Castle & Environs!".[19] Throughout *Finnegans Wake* these fateful initials generate, by repeated macrologia, both narrative and discursive expansions. The method recalls the "etymological narrative" of early Irish fiction, where stories were "spun from [...] onomastic speculation".[20] HCE may expand to Henry Childeric Earwicker, or unfold into geography and history, or into Viconian philosophy. Polyphiloprogenitively, it "Haveth Childers Everywhere".[21] HCE produces "Hay Chivychas Eve" (p. 30) as well as "earthside hoist with care" (p. 31), "hod, cement and edifices" (p. 4), "*hic cubat edilis*", and much more.

Similarly ramifying expansions of ALP engender diverse embodiments of the feminine principle Anna Livia Plurabelle. As Anna Livia she personifies the historic River Liffey that meets the tide near

Chapelizod. Her initials ALP, together with the H of HCE, form ALPH, the sacred river. Moreover, the union of ALP and HCE anagrammatizes CHAPEL; and CHAPEL is the first segment of CHAPELIZOD. Again, the sexual union of Anna and Henry produces Isabel, IZzy, or IZOD, the second segment.[22] Throughout *Finnegans Wake* Joyce sustains this method of abbreviation and expansion of representative initials: they provide Ariadne clues on which the reader's understanding and enjoyment largely depend.

In chapter 2 Joyce explains the significance of HCE's original name: "the genesis of Harold or Humphrey Chimpden's occupational agnomen (we are back in the presurnames)" period "discarding once for all those theories from older sources which would link him back with such pivotal ancestors as [...] the Earwickers of Sidlesham in the Hundred of Manhood".[23] Unlike them, HCE is an Earwicker because of a particular event, which Joyce next recounts. A visit by William IV the sailor king having been announced, Humphrey or Harold, "forgetful of all save his vassal's plain fealty to the ethnarch...stumbled out...hasting to the forecourts of his public". His majesty inquired "whether paternoster and silver doctors [dry flies] were not now more fancied bait for lobstertrapping", and "blunt Haromphreyld [conflating "Harold" and "H(u)mphrey" to hedge bets between Saxon and Norman] answered in no uncertain tones very similarly with a fearless forehead: Naw, yer maggers, aw war just a cotchin on thon bluggy earwuggers".[24] The king,[25] turning to two of his retinue, of "a triptychal religious family symbolising puritas of doctrina", remarked how his red brother William Rufus would fume if he knew we had for bailiwick "a turnpiker who is by turns a pikebailer [turnpike guard] no seldomer than an earwigger". What is so bad about being an earwigger? The answer lies in the history of "earwig" (OE *wicga*). In *Acts and Monuments* (1563), John Foxe tells of "the burning of an Herewigge (for so he termed it) at Uxbridge".[26] Foxe puns on "heretic"; but "earwigs of royalty" also meant ear whisperers, flatterers, parasites.[27] So Earwicker's cringing and "surtrusty" flattery disguises his being at heart a heretic. This is clear from "the best authenticated version" of his family history: namely, the DUMLAT, a backward anagram of TALMUD (p. 30).[28]

Earwicker's heretical tendencies are inherited by his son Shem. The twin brothers Shem and Shaun together make a couple of incompatible, contending principles almost as fundamental as the ones represented by HCE and ALP. As William York Tindall characterizes them,

"Shem is outsider, introvert, artist, and failure. Shaun is insider, extrovert, bourgeois, and success".[29] Or, Shaun is conformist, Shem rebellious. But Shem also figures as a dictator and advocate of a new order: ingratiating and duplicitous, he is a clever questioner, devoid of sympathy.[30] He rejects traditional food and drink, preferring "some sort of a rhubarbarous maundarin yellagreen funkleblue windigut diodying applejack squeezed from sour grapefruice".[31] Both Shem and Shaun are writers: Shaun a poet like T. S. Eliot, Shem an unsuccessful man of letters producing unreadable obscurities.[32] By turns they change places, like Castor and Pollux in the stellar myth, so that the "successful Shem becomes Shaun, and failing Shaun, Shem". But this makes the contrast too schematic: each twin has a bit of the other within him.[33]

Analogously with Shem and Shaun, other complementary couples can be distinguished: twins, conflicted siblings, outright enemies. Reshaping idiom—and alluding to literature or biblical history or ancient mythology—these couples adumbrate far-reaching polarities: Cain and Abel, Jacob and Esau, St Peter and St Paul, St Michael and Satan (Mick and Nick). From classical antiquity emerge Romulus and Remus, as do "castor and porridge" (Castor and Pollux) and "burrous and caseous" (Brutus and Cassius). From modern literature come Swift's Stella and Vanessa,[34] Lewis Carroll's Tweedledum and Tweedlee, and Mark Twain's conformist Tom Sawyer and rebellious Huck Finn.

It would be facile to assume that all this coupling always amounts to profound philosophical dualities. Some pairings merely help to make extreme compression intelligible: "if you're not your bloater's kipper may I never curse again on that pint I took of Jamesons" (p. 305). Here, bloater and kipper, alike yet very different,[35] illuminate as they compress the allusive idiom "am I my brother's keeper?" (Genesis 4: 9). We are our brothers' keepers because, however unlike, we are also like them. Similarly "old Battleshore and Deadleconche", suggesting the game battledore and shuttlecock, frames several wordplays (p. 390). "Battledore", minimally modified, helps with the more extensively morphed and therefore difficult "Deadleconche". No real duality underlies the semantic machinery here—only the association of "-shore" with "-conche" shells and the jingle of "deadle-" with "battle-" (which may leave many "dead"). Pairs based on names, as with "Mick and Nick", are usually the most persuasive.

The diction of *Finnegans Wake* often becomes opaque through over-loading. Joyce compresses together associations, allusions, words, chains of discourse, and names upon names, superimposing them until they are "overlayered" in a way that recalls overdetermination in dream.[36] The excess is deliberate. Over many years Joyce slotted in contributions from others and revisions of his own. These he accommodated not horizontally in the syntax, but rather by adding them paradigmatically or (as it were) vertically. They overlay earlier drafts with a portmanteau effect.[37] And further condensation is brought about by means of acrostics: those already mentioned and many others like them, such as AGSCL, variously expanded as "Arthur Guiness Sons and Company, Limited"; "Awful Grimmest Sunshat Cromwelly, Looted"; etc.[38]

Joyce's acrostics are like—and yet at the same time very unlike—those of medieval and Renaissance literature discussed in chapter 4. They are similar in providing hermeneutic clues, dissimilar in leading to no single expansion. Instead, they generate a great many names whose function is to establish family connections throughout the epic.

Joyce makes great play with a compressive device that I have called modified idiom, whereby a phrase is diverted from its expected completion.[39] This occasions ambiguity and consequently enriches the meaning, as when "man of hod" suggests both "man of God" and "hod carrier". Such morphing need not be confined, of course, to English idioms and collocational norms: Joyce seizes every opportunity to universalize by making new idioms out of foreign imports. Thus, Finnegan's fall is given as "pftjschute", where French *chute* ("fall") enhances the onomatopoeia. Or phonic resemblance will make good a loose association of names, as when "Browne and Nolan" (the Dublin booksellers) is modified to "Bruno of Nola" (the sixteenth-century heretical philosopher, burnt "brown" by the anti-heretics).[40]

Some of Joyce's portmanteaux or composite words are composed entirely of names, as for example "Mamalujo" (p. 397). This may seem rebarbatively foreign. But Joyce gives it in other, mutually illuminating forms: first, "Mat and Mar and Lu and Jo, now happily buried, our four!" (p. 397); then "Marcus" (p. 397) and "M.M.L.J." (p. 397). In context, it is not difficult to make out Matthew, Mark, Luke, and John, the four Christian gospels taken to the four parts of the world. In a feminized version this becomes "Magda, Marthe, Luz and Joan".[41] Similarly exotic, NATHANDJOE anagrams NATHAN AND JOE as well as

"Dean JoNATHAN" [Swift].⁴² Macaronic universalizing operates both centrifugally and centripetally, globally and locally. Thus, Irish "Dublin" is doubled by the Dublin in "Laurens County", Georgia (p. 3) whereas THUART PEATRICK with its rural PEAT and RICK localizes in Ireland the dominical announcement "Thou art Peter" (Matt. 16: 18). Finn Fordham notices more than thirty languages used in compressions, archaisms, and other wordplays. Latin, however, is strategically salient, as in *Hic cubat edilis; apud libertinam parvulum* (p. 7), cloaking "here sleeps the magistrate with the little freed-girl" in the decent obscurity of a learned language.

Finnegans Wake is an immensely onomastic epic. The name of its game, in fact, is names. The short first page explicitly or implicitly refers to forty-four names,⁴³ and the next page has far more. Irish names predominate, although Irishness is less salient here than in *Ulysses*. The names and their hoarded associations reopen entire worlds of Irish and global history and prehistory, to say nothing of contemporary politics. The title *Finnegans Wake* leads one to notice, within the first few pages, "Bygmaster [master builder] Finnegan" (p. 4) and several related names. Most of these—Finnegan and Finnimore and the Scottish Fingal and the diminutive Finucane ("descendant of Finn")—gesture towards Finn the hero of south Irish legend, the third-century champion against Norse invaders, and the supposed father of the poet Ossian.⁴⁴ Joyce's new Ireland will recover Finn's glory: "Hohohoho, Mister Finn, you're going to be Mister Finnagain! [...] Hahahaha, Mister Funn, you're going to be fined again!" (p. 5). Finn (Anglicized from Gaelic *Fionn*, "white") was also leader of the Fianna, predecessors of the Fenians, the anti-British secret society in Joyce's time responsible for bomb outrages and the Phoenix Park murders. The Fenians lurk behind many references to Phoenix Park (p. 3) and to the hill next to Howth:⁴⁵ "Big Méaster Finnykin with Phenician Parkes".⁴⁶ Even the malt brewed by arclight is linked to Finn: McGuiness has a variant McGinnis, and "McGinn" is a patronymic from "Finn".⁴⁷ On the wider, literary stage Finn forms ramifying polarities when Mark Twain's disreputable Huck Finn pairs with the bourgeois Tom Sawyer.

Names, whether explicit or implied, are the seeds from which the forest of *Finnegans Wake* grew in the writing and which appear again in the fruits of reading. Joyce's critics have not much discussed the heuristic function of his names; yet they are obviously the basis of many interpretations and annotations. Both Walt Litz and Christopher

Ricks take for granted the existence of a "basic text" of *Finnegans Wake* that Joyce at first revised and later re- (perhaps over-) revised. His additive method certainly poses problems. And so does his belief that he had discovered a new rhetoric applicable to any topic. As Litz shows, Joyce even boasted his ability to process any material sent him, as if transmuting it by alchemy. He invited Harriet Weaver to order up an episode by sending data to be incorporated in the *Wake*: one such commission led to the Giant image in the third paragraph.[48] Nevertheless, Fordham defends Joyce's accretive revisions against the criticism that they fail the Jamesian touchstone test of selection and discrimination. In Fordham's view the "revisions" must be in continual conflict with the versions they replace: it is in this conflict, this struggle with language, that Joyce works through his problems. Another defence of the revisionary process might be that Joyce's macaronic elaborations and "compressional" arabesques are invariably thematic.[49] Just as the archaisms in *The Faerie Queene* attempt to uncover traces of the Fall of man, so Joyce's composites suggest an earlier wholeness lost by the orthodox and heretical divisions of modern Ireland. Names are strategic agonists in this, acting as nodes that gather, combine, and offset associations reaching back into the country's dark history.

Joyce's use of names has exerted a widespread influence on writers and artists of many countries. This is acknowledged in the case of Joseph Beuys' early work, in which Joyce's examples prompted concepts, methods, and even motifs (such as the use of felt).[50] Eloquent witness here is the annotated copy of *Finnegans Wake* in Beuys' library. In fiction even more, the authority and example of Joyce have powerfully affected many, notably Samuel Beckett, Salman Rushdie, Thomas Pynchon,[51] and Vladimir Nabokov (1899–1977). To Nabokov we may now turn.[52]

Vladimir Nabokov

After Joyce, the most ambitious twentieth-century work based on names is probably Nabokov's *Lolita* (1955). This polynomial masterpiece seems to have no rival in either avant-garde or mainstream fiction, particularly since its names are plausibly incorporated within a narrative. Nabokov's previous interest in onomastic wordplay is evinced in *Bend Sinister* (1947), where Ember suggests that Shakespeare's Ophelia "quite

possibly is an anagram of Alpheius, with the 's' lost in the damp grass—
Alpheus the rivergod, who pursued a long-legged nymph".[53] The
example of *Finnegans Wake* was in various ways decisive for Nabokov.[54]
Echoes and allusions—such as the reuse of Quilty and of MacCoo(l)—
put this beyond doubt.[55] Indeed Nabokov himself acknowledged bor-
rowing the high-school play in *Lolita* from "a passage in James Joyce"
(in fact from *Finnegans Wake* chapter 2).[56]

Nabokov announces the subject of naming in the opening para-
graphs of *Lolita*: "She was Lo, plain Lo, in the morning, standing four
feet ten in one sock. She was Lola in slacks. She was Dolly at school.
She was Dolores on the dotted line. But in my arms she was always
Lolita."[57] At the outset the play on bynames of Lolita encourages readers to consider naming a theme of the novel. They are given plenty of
material to work on. In fact, they are deluged with name after name,
series and groups of names, names real and invented, names allusive
and suggestive. Names crowd the novel: names in a class register, motel
names, names of writers. So prominent are these lists that Michael
Ragussis makes out the subject to be classification—classification as a
means of ordering nature. No accident, then, that the prefatory epistle
of *Lolita* purports to be by John Ray; for Ray was a pre-Enlightenment
naturalist who pioneered scientific classification.[58] In the narrative
itself, however, Humbert finds that the classes of names confusingly
ramify and overlap: he can never quite get sole possession of a uniquely
specified nymphet.

Our understanding of the function of biological associations in
Lolita was quickened by Diana Butler's discovery that the motel names
in Humbert's quest match places where Nabokov the professional
lepidopterist went on expeditions: where, for example, he caught the
first known female of *Lycaeides sublivens Nabokov*, the species that bears
his name.[59] In some sense, Humbert's pursuit of Lolita seems to figure
Nabokov's own search for the rare "nymphet". One can imagine his
excitement at finding the creature subsequently known by his name:
the sublime moment of discovering a new species and so changing the
existent order of nature. In the philosophical context of nomenclature,
that unique event resembled Wittgenstein's irreducible act of unique
reference.

Since *Lolita*, "nymphet" has come to mean a certain sort of fit
pre-woman. But previously it had been a biological term for a transitional stage of butterfly development. That changed when Humbert

the taxonomist of women defined "nymphet" as a species of maiden between nine and fourteen, "who, to certain bewitched travellers, twice or many times older than they, reveal their true nature which is not human, but nymphic".[60] *Lolita*, uniting as it does the human and insect nymphets, has significance for psychologists and entomologists alike, and so links Nabokov's two lives. Both sorts of nymphets are rare because of the transitoriness of their defining state. Since the phase passes in months the insect state is a telling symbol of human evanescence. The theme of mutability accordingly runs through many of the novel's names and allusions, for example Quilty's "To borrow and to borrow and to borrow". And needless to say it appears in the many instances of "nymphets", "nymphage", and the like.[61]

Nabokov's intertwining of biology with human sexuality must be deliberate, since "nymphet" had almost exclusively entomological senses until he gave it human meanings.[62] It is probably no exaggeration to say that for Nabokov much of the interest in writing *Lolita* lay in the possibility of sustained double entendres and endless, ever subtler yet ever more intimate sexual wordplays.

Even if biological classification were seen as pursuit of a higher order of being, however, one could hardly agree with Eric Naiman's view that anatomical allegory is the sole substance of *Lolita*. Its names also point in other directions: pursuit of the romantic sublime, for example, and aspiration to aesthetic heights in art and nature. "Lull" in Lolita's class alludes to Ramon Lull (c. 1232–1315), another authority on classification certainly, but here, significantly, the author of *The Book of the Lover and the Beloved*. And other names on the class register suggest movements away from classification altogether, to singularity of experience. Some undeniably suggest Neoplatonic aspiration: "Stella Fantasia", "Anthony Miranda", and "Viola Miranda". The repeated "Miranda" surely alludes to Prospero's innocent daughter in *The Tempest*. And the motel name "Mirandola" calls up Pico della Mirandola, author of the *De Dignitate Hominis*.[63]

Again, the Ramsdale register includes a strong representation of writers, among them (Richard) Sheridan, (Thomas) Campbell, George Fox, (Washington) Irving, Edgar (Allan Poe), (Lord) Byron, and (Walter) Scott. Moreover, several others are familiar literary characters: Shakespeare's "Viola", Dickens' "Edwin" (Drood), Hughes' "Flashman", Barrie's "Mary Rose", and Hardy's "Angel Clare" in *Tess*—to say nothing of Gene Stratton-Porter's Angel in *Freckles*. And this is not all: quite apart from the class list, Carl Proffer identifies a further sixty-three writers alluded to.[64] Others might be added: notably Charles Maturin, of *Melmoth* ["sweet moth"] *the Wanderer* (1820), and again Stratton-Porter (*A Girl of the Limberlost*).[65] Such allusions accord well with Alexander Luxemburg's view that *Lolita* symbolizes literature itself with all its delights of form, so that her pursuit would be entirely praiseworthy—indeed, self-justifying for a writer.[66] To a similar suggestion, that *Lolita* recorded the author's "love affair" with the romantic novel,[67] Nabokov responded that "it represented instead his passion for the English language"—a not altogether different idea, since languages are sometimes learned, in part, through their literatures.

Nevertheless, Nabokov's (or Humbert's) allusions are more elusive than either of these views suggests. And some of them are less ideal and abstract. Quite often, too, they concern distinctly underage child lovers. Vanessa and Esther (similarly paired in *Finnegans Wake*) refer to Jonathan Swift's "friend" Vanessa, Esther Vanhomrigh (1688–1723), twenty years younger than Swift himself.[68] And "Harry Bumper, Sheridan, Wyo" reminds the reader of Harry Bumper in Richard Sheridan's *A School for Scandal*, who sings "Here's to the maid of bashful fifteen [...] And here's to the nymph".[69] As Proffer points out (p. 34), the most frequent allusions in *Lolita* are to "Annabel Lee", Poe's ballad of lost childhood love, and "Carmen", Merimée's tale of disastrous passion for a young gypsy.

Without doubt, a great many allusions and wordplays in *Lolita*—how many is debatable—have specifically sexual implications. These are the basis of Naiman's argument that Nabokov transforms Lolita "into nothing but vulva, a feminine and genitalized version" of Gogol's "anatomical magnification" in "The Nose": that Nabokov "effectively genitalizes not only Lolita but the entire landscape of the New World".[70] In Naiman's view virtually every name contains an anatomical wordplay. Thus "Mrs Chatfield" puns on *chatte* (pussy) and so does every mention of chatting.[71] Naiman appropriates Butler's butterfly hunting to support his theory: the "nymphae" become *labia minora*.[72] Thomas Karshan, however, roundly dismisses Naiman's theory: "By reducing Nabokov's perversity to a system of hidden dirty words Naiman replaces one literalism with another and reduces Nabokov's protean textual eroticism to something overt, knowable, fixed."[73]

Nevertheless, the names encountered during the journey of Humbert and Lolita cannot be denied to have sexual meanings: "Lake Climax",

"Conception Park", "D. Orgon", "Miss Redcock", and many others.[74]
So too with the place names that supply much of the narrative. Thus,
Humbert registers at 342 motels, and the Haze house is 342 Lawn Street.
The repetition of 342 serves to link the other locations with room 342
of The Enchanted Hunters (an anagram of "Ted Hunter, Cane, N H"),
where Humbert makes love to Lolita. In such ways, names with anatomical associations recur so often that even a normal reader's responses
become quickened and tantalized.[75] But to what end?

Sustained anatomical and sexual double entendres cannot be said to
offer an adequate key to the novel. The complexity of its naming,
indeed, supports Karshan against Naiman's reductive approach. Most
of the names combine multiple associative strands. For example, the
personal name "Melville" links with the quest for Moby-Dick but also
with the place name "Pierre Point" in Melville Sound: topographical
"nature" here seems to overgo the art of *Pierre: or the Ambiguities*, until
Nabokov reaffirms literature's superiority by his own art.[76] Similarly,
the hunt for Quilty leads not only to Lewis Carroll's *The Hunting of the
Snark* but also to Dodgson's real-life fascination with nymphets like
Alice. And even Naiman concedes that the name "Quilty" is "overde-
termined", associated as it is with the celebrated Cambridge Professor
of English, "Q" (Sir Arthur Quiller-Couch). Humbert's pursuit of
Quilty involves much detective work, naturally calling up Agatha
Christie, Arthur Conan Doyle, Edgar Allan Poe (the last, in turn,
recalling "Annabel Lee", the archetypic poem of lost childhood love).

All this need not lead to a formalist notion of eroticized text—as if
Nabokov's love affair were not with either the literature or the language, but with an art of ambiguity for its own sake. *Lolita* is more than
a series of ambiguities, more than a chain of sexual or anatomical
wordplays. Its wordplays are thematic, and the themes are cultural as
well as individual. Nabokov confessed to Edmund Wilson that his
mind had "always contained more associations than thoughts";[77] but
that need not mean an absence of themes connecting the associations.
One such theme is degeneration: the debasement and corruption of
love and literature, innocence and beauty. Over and over again in *Lolita*, conflicting strands of allusion exemplify this. The names, especially,
continually present contrasts and paradoxes: juxtapositions of high and
low culture, lofty origins and vulgar degradations.

This pattern becomes prominent in the journeys, which occasion
surveys of American society. As we saw, Humbert's sordid, obsessive

hunt from motel to motel is intertwined with Nabokov's quest for his butterfly (a common symbol of Psyche and souls freed from the flesh).[78] His selected place names civilize the American landscape, much as Spenser's or Drayton's mythologize the British. A paradigmatic instance is "Scotty's Castle", built by a Mr Walter Scott of Buffalo Bill's Wild West show, juxtaposed with "R. L. Stevenson's footprint on an extinct volcano" and "Mission Dolores".[79] The Scott is not the Walter Scott of romance and medieval castles, but the Walter Scott of Wild West shows: Buffalo Bill has declined from heroic frontiersman to circus performer. Elsewhere, romantic Petrarchan or Proustian passions are reduced to the vulgar sentiment satirized in Kipling's "The Betrothed"—"And a woman is only a woman, but a good Cigar is a Smoke"—and reduced further by the French translation, "une femme est une femme, mais un caporal est une cigarette".[80]

Lolita is a supreme example of the sort of naming found in fiction of the last century, whereby names are so intimately thematic as to be indispensable to the interpreter of the literary work in which they occur. Nabokov's naming guides us to see the state of the "ruined" Lolita as summing the predicament of innocence in a society of precocious sexuality. His art is one of selection: finding meaningful names in the manner of "found" poetry. He selects, for example, places with coincidental literary associations, places whose names always point in the same conflicting directions. A better linguist than Joyce, Nabokov could see the impossibility of Joyce's quest for a deep structure of anthropological naming. More realistically, Nabokov expects his readers to know as little as his real-life students. So he must repeat the lesson again and again, until repetition puts his satiric meaning beyond doubt.

Notes

1. The convenient term used in Hazard 2000.
2. De Quincey 1896–7: 10.97, 128.
3. De Quincey 1896–7: 13.5.
4. Cit. Leatherbarrow 2010: 86 as part of her general synaesthetic approach to words. Cf. Edith Wharton: "an absurd name like Ruby", Wharton 2007: 84.
5. Barthes 1974: 95, cit. Rimmon-Kenan 1999: 29.
6. See Harder 1987.
7. Porush 1985: 104–5.
8. Joyce 1986: 282.

9. Joyce 1986: 268.
10. See Gifford and Seidman 1974: 289. The Masonic society of Foresters was infiltrated by Fenians.
11. Cf. Brooks 1968: 419–40.
12. Joyce 1986: 643, line 1582.
13. Connolly 1963: 271.
14. Joyce 2006: 202.
15. Wayne Booth claimed to find *Finnegans Wake* unreadable *in extenso* although delightful in short passages; see Booth 1961: 301 n. 26.
16. Joyce 1939: 32 (*Finnegans Wake* page refs. are to this edn). Cf. Tindall 1959: 246.
17. Also "Alma Luvia Pollabelle", etc.
18. Cf. Tindall 1959: 249.
19. See Litz 1961: 84–5.
20. See Scowcroft 1995: 124.
21. See Tindall 1959: 248–52.
22. From *Finnegans Wake Abridged*, read by Jim Norton and Marcella Riordan.
23. Joyce 1939: 30; cf. Kitcher 2007: 74–5.
24. Joyce 1939: 31.
25. Presumably "William the Conk", with whose title Noel-Tod 2008: 85 compares "Alfred the Cake" in *1066*.
26. Foxe 1631: 2.12.988, col. 2.
27. *OED* s.v. *Earwig*, sb, 1 and 2.
28. See Kitcher 2007: 74
29. Tindall 1959: 246–7.
30. Kitcher 2007: 32–3.
31. Joyce 1939: 171; see Kitcher 2007: 34–5.
32. Cf. Tindall 1959: 247 n.
33. Cf. Tindall 1959: 248, 255 n., 256 n.
34. See Tindall 1959: 247; Litz 1961: 87.
35. Bloaters are soft, half-dried herrings; kippers, cured then smoked dry. See *OED* s.v. *Kipper* v¹ , *Bloat* v.
36. Cf. Kitcher 2007: 8, 268.
37. On the revisions, see Litz 1961; Fordham 2007. On contrasting syntagmatic and paradigmatic bases of organization, see Lodge 1966.
38. Joyce 1939: 9; see Tindall 1959: 248.
39. See Crystal 1995: 163.
40. See Fordham 2007: 151; cf. 100 on "eminence [...] ambulance [...] embolism [...]".
41. See Fordham 2007: 194.
42. See Litz 1961: 87.
43. Adam; Eve; Commodus; Howth; Sir Amory Tristram; Irish Sea; Tristan; Cornwall; Isolde; King Mark; Isthmus of Sutton; Topsawyer's Rock; Oconee; Dublin, Laurens County; Peter Sawyer; St Patrick; Moses; Peter; Jacob; Esau; Parnell; Isaac Butt; Jonathan Swift; Nathandjoe; Stella; Vanessa; Esther; Nathan; Willie; Jameson; Guinness; Noah; Jhem; Shem; Wall Street; Old Parr; Christy; Finnegan; W. J. Ashcroft; Phoenix Park; Humpty Dumpty; Castleknock; Chapelizod. See McHugh 1980: 3.
44. Finn's genealogy is treated in drafts of *Finnegans Wake*, including one as early as December 1936, revised and expanded in BL Add MSS 47479 fols. 189v–195r and 199r–206r.
45. See Tindall 1959: 250.
46. Joyce 1939: 576.28; see Kitcher 2007: 16.
47. *ONC* s.v. *Finn, Guiness*.
48. See Litz 1961: 84–5.

49. See Fordham 2007: 56.
50. See Hayes 2001.
51. See Hurley 2008; Harder 1987.
52. On Nabokov's relation to Joyce, see Proffer 1968: 132 n. 12.
53. Cit. Levith 1978: 17–18.
54. See Fordham 2007: 20 on the "symbolic power" of *Finnegans Wake* in contemporary letters "as something to be studiously avoided or surreptitiously drawn on".
55. See Proffer 1968:10 and, for further debts, *Index* s.v. *Joyce*.
56. See Fordham 2007: 237 n.
57. Nabokov 1996: 7.
58. See Ragussis 1987: 256 n. 11. Naiman 2010: 42, however, sees an allusion to John 1: 5–10 with its "emphasis on light".
59. See Butler 1960: 58–84; Appel 2000: 6. Naiman 2010: 30 emphasizes the genital meaning of "nymphae" as *labia minora* in the edition of *Webster's New International Dictionary* used by Nabokov.
60. Nabokov 1996: 14; see *OED* s.v. *Nymphal* adj. and sb.; *Nymphet* sb.
61. See, e.g., Nabokov 1996: 14.10, 30.16, 61.7, and 145 on moths.
62. Cf. Proffer 1968: 133.
63. See Nabokov 1996: 233 n. Nabokov told Alfred Appel that the imaginary Mirandola, NY, "has nothing to do with Pico". But Pico was a patron of the Modena *Commedia dell' arte*, and other motel names—Gratiano and Forbeson—come from the *Commedia*. Nabokov, as often, lied to cover his tracks.
64. See Proffer 1968: 21–3.
65. Nabokov 1996: 162, 264.
66. Cf. Luxemburg 2004–5: 119–34.
67. Haas 2008.
68. See Proffer 1968: 96.
69. *School for Scandal* 3.3; see Proffer 1968: 14, 96.
70. Naiman 2010: 30–1, 34.
71. See Naiman 2010: 31.
72. See *OED* s.v. *Nymphae*, example from 1693: "little pieces of Flesh in a Woman's Secrets".
73. Karshan 2011: 3.
74. See Proffer 1968: 96.
75. Cf. Karshan 2011: 3: Nabokov's "main trait was his passion for tantalization".
76. See Proffer 1968: 6.
77. Cit. Naiman 2010: 41.
78. See, e.g., Charbonneau-Lassay 1940: 847–51; Impelluso 2004: 330; Cirlot 1962:33–4; Ferber 1999: 37–8.
79. Nabokov 1996: 147 nn. 11, 13–14.
80. Cit. Proffer 1968: 136.

Afterword

These pages address texts so various, ranging over so many periods of history, that to summarize them in general conclusions is hardly possible. Nevertheless, some things stand out. One is the inappropriateness of synchronic approaches to literary names. Those who have read the first chapter, or the studies of individual authors from Spenser to Nabokov, will, I hope, understand something of how naming has changed in function throughout history: how names have developed from brief descriptions to "full names" fixing places in the family and the larger community.

Pride in the family name and its real or imagined links with the "great names" of history and romance supported a belief that the "good name" of the family was of overriding importance. Embodying reputation, honour, perhaps *vera nobilitas*, names could motivate moral aspiration. They could also, however, be cruelly oppressive, obliterating the individual claims of children, particularly daughters. Such family oppression took an extreme form when arbitrary names were imposed on slaves and servants.

Corresponding changes in naming present themselves in literature, even with the names traditionally characteristic of genres. At some times names have been displayed proudly, at others concealed (or half-concealed) in acrostics or anagrams disguising the objects of forbidden love. In the Renaissance, when any *nomen* might hide an *omen*, interest in anagrams of destiny became intense. In earlier literature, moreover, names were often treated as things to be arranged in patterned lists. These practices lapsed in the eighteenth and nineteenth centuries, but have returned in contemporary literature, especially in Joyce and Nabokov.

Spenser and Shakespeare explored a special type of name, the mythological, involving well-defined classical associations. In later centuries, with the increase of vernacular literature, the associative content of names has greatly increased. Since character names are usually a matter of authorial decision, these associations make names an important route to the meaning of literary works—for example, with Shakespeare's Osric and Dickens' Oliver Twist. Onomastics, previously neglected, is currently proving a vital part of interpretative criticism. It is hard to escape the conclusion that the study of literary names might well be made more central to literary studies. Besides, are names not among the most fascinating of words?

Glossary

.

Acrostic: a device whereby the letters of a name or other words are dispersed according to a regular pattern, often as the first letters of successive verses (INITIAL ACROSTIC). Other options include the last letters (TELESTICH), first and last letters (DOUBLE ACROSTIC), the first letters after caesuras (MEDIAL ACROSTIC), etc. Acrostics may be thought of as special instances of DISPERSED ANAGRAM: like the anagram, an acrostic may be open—displayed typographically—or hidden.

Anagram: words within words. A device whereby the letters or syllables of a word or phrase are rearranged or else dispersed within a larger text. Used to link a name with satiric or eulogistic comment on it (e.g. MARGARET THATCHER: THAT GREAT CHARMER). Sometimes combined with ACROSTIC or REBUS. Anagrams may be CONDENSED (rearranged within a short text) or DISPERSED among other letters). Anagrams may be openly displayed or concealed (as when embedded in a longer text).

Array: a structured catalogue of names or personifications. Often arranged symmetrically, with central emphasis.

Charactonym: a descriptive name suggesting the physical appearance or moral character of its bearer, as with Ben Jonson's character Surly. Sometimes called TAG NAME.

Cratylic (from the character in Plato's dialogue *Cratylus*): regarding names as meaningful. Contrasted with HERMOGENEAN.

Family Plot: referring to a theory of Michael Ragussis, that novels from the beginning have had naming plots. Most often considerations of family name have constrained the individual freedom of children (particularly daughters) and wives.

Formal Realism: a mode of fiction characterized by the use of full names for the characters. Referring to Ian Watt's theory that from Defoe onwards novels used full names, implying a realistic social context.

Hermogenean (from Hermogenes, the character in Plato's *Cratylus*): regarding names as assigned conventionally or arbitrarily. Contrasted with CRATYLIC.

Key Fiction or *livre à clef, roman à clef, Schlüsselroman*: fiction presenting actual persons under the mask of invented names.

Onomastics: the study of names (from Greek *onoma*, name).

Patronymic: personal or family name constructed from that of a father or ancestor by adding a prefix or suffix to indicate descent. So Anderson implies "descended from Andrew".

Proper Names: words used to refer to particular individual persons, animals, or objects (as in personal names and place names). Contrasted with common nouns.

Pseudonym: a false name assumed by an author or a character. Especially a pen name.

Rebus: representation of a name or word by pictures or their verbal description. The pictures or descriptions suggest syllables of the name through resemblances of sound or meaning. So BECKINTON might be represented by a beacon and a barrel.

Tag Name: see CHARACTONYM.

References

Unless otherwise indicated, the place of publication is London.

Abbott, E. A. *A Shakespearian Grammar*. London, 1883.

Abraham, Lyndy. *A Dictionary of Alchemic Imagery* [1998]. Rpt: Cambridge University Press, 2000.

Adams, Michael. "Power, Politeness, and the Pragmatics of Nicknames". *Names*, 57 (June 2009) 81–91.

Agrippa, Henricus Cornelius. *De Occulta Philosophia Libri Tres*. Ed.V. Perrone Compagni. Leiden: Brill, 1992.

Ahl, Fred. *Metaformations: Soundplay and Wordplay in Ovid and Other Classical Poets*. Ithaca, NY: Cornell University Press, 1985.

Alexander, Peter. "Logic and the Humour of Lewis Carroll". *Proceedings of the Leeds Philosophical Society*, 6 (May, 1951) 551–66.

Allen, Thomas W. *The Homeric Catalogue of Ships*. Oxford University Press, 1921.

Alpers, Paul. *What Is Pastoral?* University of Chicago Press, 1996.

Alvarez-Altman, Grace, and Burelbach, Frederick M. (eds). *Names in Literature: Essays from Literary Onomastics Studies*. Lanham, MD: University Press of America, 1987.

Amis, Kingsley. *The Letters of Kingsley Amis*. Ed. Zachary Leader. HarperCollins, 2000.

Anderson, J. K. "The Geometric Catalogue of Ships". In *The Ages of Homer: A Tribute to Emily Townsend Vermeule*, ed. James B. Carter & Sarah P. Morris. Austin, TX: University of Texas Press, 1995. Pp. 181–92.

Anon. (Richard Hogarth). *Gazophylacium Anglicanum*. 1689.

Appel, Alfred. Introduction and notes to *The Annotated Lolita*. By Vladimir Nabokov [1970]. Penguin, 2000.

Arnold, Matthew. *Essays in Criticism First Series*. Ed. Sister Thomas Marion Hoctor, ssj. University of Chicago Press, 1968.

Arnold, Matthew. *The Letters*. Ed. Cecil Y. Lang. *Vol. 1: 1829–1859*. Charlottesville: The University Press of Virginia, 1996.

Ash, Russell. *Potty, Fartwell and Knob*. Headline, 2007.

Ash, Russell. *Frou-Frou, Frisby and Brick*. Headline, 2010.

Aubrey, John. *Brief Lives*. Ed. Andrew Clark. 2 vols. Oxford: Clarendon Press, 1898.

Auden, W. H. *A Certain World: A Commonplace Book*. Faber, 1971.

Augarde, Tony. *The Oxford Guide to Word Games*. Oxford University Press, 1984.

Augustine, Saint. *Confessions*. Tr. and ed. Henry Chadwick. Oxford University Press, 1991.

Austen, Jane. *Pride and Prejudice: An Annotated Edition*. Ed. Patricia Meyer Spacks. Cambridge, MA: Belknap, 2010.

Axton, William. "Esther's Nicknames: A Study in Relevance". *Dickensian*, 62 (1966) 158–63.

Bagwell, Richard. *Ireland under the Tudors*. 3 vols. London, 1890.

Bann, Stephen. "The Mythical Conception Is the Name: Titles and Names in Modern and Post-modern Painting". *Word and Image,* 1 (1985) 176–90.

Barber, Cesar Lombardi. *Shakespeare's Festive Comedy: A Study of Dramatic Form and Its Relation to Social Custom*. Princeton University Press, 1959.

Barclay, John. *Argenis*. Ed. and tr. Mark Riley and Dorothy Pritchard Huber. 2 vols. Assen: Royal van Gorcum; Tempe, AZ: Arizona Center for Medieval and Renaissance Studies, 2004.

Bardsley, Charles W. *Curiosities of Puritan Nomenclature* [1880]. Rpt: Baltimore MD: Clearfield, 1996.

Barney, Stephen. "Chaucer's Lists". In *The Wisdom of Poetry: Essays in Early English Literature in Honor of Morton W. Bloomfield*, ed. Larry Dean Benson and Siegfried Wenzel. Kalamazoo, MI: West Michigan University Press and Medieval Institute, 1982. Pp. 189–223.

Baronius, Cardinal Caesar (Cesare Barone). *Annales Ecclesiastici*. 12 vols. Rome, 1588–1607.

Baronius, Caesar (ed). *Martyrologium Romanum*. Venice, 1587.

Barron, Oswald. "Heraldry". In *Shakespeare's England*. 2 vols. Oxford: Clarendon Press, 1916.

Barthes, Roland. *S/Z* [1970]. Tr. Richard Miller. Cape, 1975.

Barton, Anne. *Ben Jonson, Dramatist*. Cambridge University Press, 1984.

Barton, Anne. *The Names of Comedy*. Oxford: Clarendon Press, 1990.

Baspoole, William. *The Pilgrime*. Ed. Kathryn Walls. Renaissance English Text Society, 31. Tempe, AZ: Arizona Center for Medieval and Renaissance Studies, 2008.

Bate, Jonathan. *Shakespeare and Ovid*. Oxford: Clarendon Press, 1993.

Battestin, Martin C. "The Transforming Power: Nature and Art in Pope's Pastorals." In *Pope: Recent Essays by Several Hands*, ed. Maynard Mack and James A. Winn. Brighton: Harvester, 1980. Pp. 80–105.

Belgion, Montgomery. "The Poet's Name". *Sewanee Review*, 54 (Autumn 1946) 635–49.

Belknap, Robert E. *The List*. New Haven, CT: Yale University Press, 2004.

Bennett, Bryan and Harte, Negley (eds). *The Crabtree Orations, 1954–1994*. Taylor & Francis, 1997.

Berger, Harry. *Revisionary Play: Studies in the Spenserian Dynamics*. Berkeley: University of California Press, 1988.

Berger, Thomas L., William C. Bradford, and Sidney L. Sondergard, *An Index of Characters in Early Modern English Drama: Printed Plays, 1500–1660* [1975]. Cambridge University Press, 1998.

Bergerson, Howard. *Palindromes and Anagrams.* New York: Dover, 1973.

Bernardus Silvestris, *Cosmographia.* Tr. and ed. Winthrop Wetherbee. New York and London: Columbia University Press, 1973.

Blackburn, Bonnie, and Holford-Strevens, Leofranc. *The Oxford Companion to the Year.* Oxford University Press, 1999.

Bliss, Jane. *Naming and Namelessness in Medieval Romance.* Cambridge: Brewer, 2008.

Boccaccio, Giovanni. *The Latin Eclogues.* Tr. David R. Slavitt. Baltimore, MD: Johns Hopkins University Press, 2010.

Booth, Wayne C. *The Rhetoric of Fiction.* University of Chicago Press, 1961.

Bowditch, Nathaniel Ingersoll. *Suffolk Surnames.* Boston, MA, 1857, 1858.

Bollandus, Joannes, and Henschenius, Godefridus. *Acta Sanctorum* [...] (1643–1867). Rev. edn, ed. Joannes Carnandet et al. 69 vols. Paris, 1863–.

Borris, Kenneth. *Allegory and Epic in English Renaissance Literature: Heroic Form in Sidney, Spenser, and Milton.* Cambridge University Press, 2000.

Braden, Gordon. "Riverrun: An Epic Catalogue in *The Faerie Queene*". *English Literary Renaissance,* 5 (1975) 25–48.

Braden, Gordon. *The Classics and English Renaissance Poetry: Three Case Studies.* New Haven and London: Yale University Press, 1978.

Brahms, Caryl, and S. J. Simon. *No Bed For Bacon.* Michael Joseph, 1941.

Brewer, D. S. *Chaucer and Chaucerians.* Nelson: 1966.

Brewer, Ebenezer Cobham. *The Reader's Handbook of Famous Names in Fiction, Allusions, Reference, Proverbs, Plots, Stories, and Poems* [1898]. Rpt: Detroit: Gale, 1966.

Brooks-Davies, Douglas. *Pope's Dunciad and the Queen of Night: A Study in Emotional Jacobitism.* Manchester University Press, 1985.

Brown, P. W. F. "Name Magic". *Names,* 2 (1554) 21–7.

Browne, Sir Thomas. *The Works.* Ed. Geoffrey Keynes. 4 vols. Faber 1964.

Bruce, Christopher W. *The Arthurian Name Dictionary.* New York: Garland, 1999.

Bull, Malcolm. "Pagan Names in *The Faerie Queene,* I", *N&Q,* 242 (1997) 471–2.

Bullough, Geoffrey. *Narrative and Dramatic Sources of Shakespeare* (1957). 8 vols. London: Routledge & Kegan Paul; New York: Columbia University Press 1966–75.

Bungus, Petrus (Pietro Bongo). *Numerorum Mysteria* [...]. Bergamo, 1591.

Burrow, John A. *Esssays on Medieval Literature.* Oxford: Clarendon Press, 1984.

Butler, Diana. "Lolita Lepidoptera". *New World Writing,* 16 (1960) 58–84.

Butler, Samuel. *Hudibras.* Ed. John Wilders. Oxford: Clarendon Press, 1967.

Butler, Samuel. *Characters and Passages from Note-books.* Cambridge University Press. 1908.

Cairns, Francis. *Generic Composition in Greek and Roman Poetry.* Edinburgh University Press, 1972.

Calderwood, James L. *Metadrama in Shakespeare's Henriad: Richard II to Henry V.* Berkeley and Los Angeles: University of California Press, 1979.

Cambridge, Richard Owen. *Scribleriad.* 1751.

Camden, William. *Britannia* [1607]. Facs. edn: Hildesheim: Olms, 1970.

Camden, William. *Britannia* [1695]. Facs. edn: Stuart Piggott and Gwyn Walters. Newton Abbot: David & Charles, 1971.

Camden, William. *Remains concerning Britain* [1605]. Ed. R. D. Dunn. Toronto: University of Toronto Press, 1984.

Campbell, James. "The Olympia Press". *The Times Literary Supplement* (14 Feb. 1992) 17–18.

[Carey, Henry.] *Pretty Sally's Garland.* [London?, 1800?]

Carroll, Lewis [Charles Lutwidge Dodgson]. *The Complete Works.* Nonesuch, 1939.

Carroll, Lewis. *The Annotated Alice* (1960). Ed. Martin Gardner. Penguin, 1965.

Carroll, William C. *The Great Feast of Language in "Love's Labour's Lost".* Princeton University Press, 1976.

Carroll, William Meredith. *Animal Conventions in English Renaissance Non-Religious Prose (1550–1600).* New York: Bookman, 1954.

Cartigny, Jean. *The Wandering Knight.* Ed. Dorothy Atkinson Evans. Seattle, WA: University of Washington Press, 1951.

Cave, Terence. *Recognitions: A Study in Poetics.* Oxford: Clarendon Press, 1988.

Caws, Mary Ann. *Reading Frames in Modern Fiction.* Princeton University Press, 1985.

Céard, Jean and Margolin, Jean-Claude. *Rébus de la Renaissance: Des Images qui Parlent.* 2 vols. Paris: Maisonneuve et Larose, 1986.

Chandler, Frank W. *A Catalogue of Names of Persons in the German Court Epics.* Ed. Martin H. Jones. King's College, 1992.

Chang, Y. Z. "Why Did Milton Err on Two Chinas?" *Modern Language Review,* 65 (1970) 493–8.

Chapman, George. *Chapman's Homer.* Ed. Allardyce Nicoll. 2 vols. Routledge & Kegan Paul, 1957.

Charbonneau-Lassay, Louis. *The Bestiary of Christ* [1940]. Tr. D. M. Dooling. New York: Viking Penguin, 1991.

Chaudhuri, Sukanta. *Renaissance Pastoral and its English Developments.* Oxford: Clarendon Press, 1989.

Cirlot, J. E. *A Dictionary of Symbols.* Tr. Jack Sage. Routledge & Kegan Paul, 1962.

Clark, George A. "Proper Names in Logic and Literature". *Journal of Philosophy,* 58 (1961) 690–1.

Clarkson, Carol. "Dickens and the *Cratylus*". *British Journal of Aesthetics,* 39 (1999) 53–61.

Clauss, J. J. "An Acrostic in Vergil (*Eclogues* 1.5–8): the Chance that Mimics Choice". *Aevum Antiquum,* 10 (1977) 267–87.

Clifford, Anne. *Diary of Lady Anne Clifford*, ed V. Sackville-West. Heinemann, 1923.

Coldiron, Anne E. B. *English Printing, Verse Translation, and the Battle of the Sexes, 1476–1557*. Farnham: Ashgate, 2009.

Coleman, Julie. *History of Cant and Slang Dictionaries*. Vol. 2: 1785–1858. Oxford University Press, 2005

Colie, Rosalie. *Shakespeare's Living Art*. Princeton University Press, 1974.

Colonna, Francesco. *Hypnerotomachia Poliphili* [...] [Venice, 1499]. Facs. edn: Methuen, 1904.

Colonna, Francesco. *Hypnerotomachia Poliphili* [1499]. Tr. Joscelyn Godwin. Thames & Hudson, 1999.

Connolly, Cyril. *Previous Convictions*. Hamilton, 1963.

Considine, John. *Dictionaries in Early Modern Europe: Lexicography and the Making of Heritage*. Cambridge University Press, 2008.

Conti, Natale. *Mythologiae*. Ed. Stephen Orgel. New York and London: Garland, 1979.

Cook, Eleanor. *Enigmas and Riddles in Literature*. Cambridge University Press, 2006.

Cooper, Helen. *Pastoral: Mediaeval into Renaissance*. Ipswich: Brewer, 1977.

Cooper, Helen. *The English Romance in Time: Transforming Motifs from Geoffrey of Monmouth to the Death of Shakespeare*. Oxford University Press, 2004.

Cooper, Thomas. *Thesaurus Linguae Romanae et Britannicae* [1578]. Hildesheim and New York: Olms, 1975.

Cowie, A. P. *The Oxford History of English Lexicography*. 2 vols. Oxford: Clarendon Press, 2009.

Cowper, William. *The Poetical Works*. Ed. H. S. Milford [1905]. Rev. edn: Oxford University Press, 1934.

Craig, Martha. "The Secret Wit of Spenser's Language". In *Essential Articles for the Study of Edmund Spenser*, ed. A. C. Hamilton. Hamden, CT: Archon, 1972. Pp. 313–33.

Crystal, David. *The Cambridge Encyclopedia of the English Language*. BCA, 1995.

Crystal, David. *A Little Book of Language*. New Haven, CT, and London: Yale University Press, 2010.

Culleton, Claire A. *Names and Naming in Joyce*. Madison, WI: Wisconsin University Press, 1995.

Cummings, Robert. "Sannazaro and the Crisis of English Pastoral Poetry", *Canadian Review of Comparative Literature*, 33 (2006) 194–216.

Curtius, Ernst Robert. *European Literature and the Latin Middle Ages* [Bern, 1948]. Trans. Willard R. Trask. Routledge & Kegan Paul, 1953.

D'Assigny, Marius. *The Art of Memory. A Treatise Useful for Such as Are to Speak in Publick*. 1697.

Davidson, Gustav. *A Dictionary of Angels Including the Fallen Angels*. Rpt: New York: Free Press, 1967.

Davies, Hugh William. *Devices of the Early Printers 1457–1560* [...]. Grafton, 1935.

Davies, Sir John. *The Poems of Sir John Davies.* Ed. Robert Krueger. Oxford: Clarendon Press, 1975.

Davis et al. *A Chaucer Glossary.* Oxford: Clarendon Press, 1979.

Davis, J. Madison, and Frankforter, A. Daniel. *The Shakespeare Name Dictionary* [1995]. Rev. edn: Routledge, 2004.

Deguileville, Guillaume de. *The Pilgrimage of the Life of Man.* Tr. John Lydgate, ed. F. J. Furnivall, *EETS* e. s. 77, 83, 92 (1899–1904).

Dexter, Gary. *Why Not Catch-21?: The Stories Behind the Titles.* Frances Lincoln, 2007.

Diaper, William. *The Complete Works.* Ed. Dorothy Broughton. Routledge & Kegan Paul, 1952 [given as 1951].

Dickens, Charles. Centenary Exhibition Catalogue. Victoria and Albert Museum, 1970.

Dickens, Charles. *Charles Dickens' Book of Memoranda.* Ed. Fred Kaplan. New York: The New York Public Library, 1981.

Dickens, Charles. *Oliver Twist.* Ed. Kathleen Tillotson and Stephen Gill [1998]. Rev. edn: Oxford University Press, 1999.

Dickens, Charles, and Wills, W. H. "Received, a Blank Child". *Household Words*, 7 (19 March, 1853) 49–53.

Diehl, Huston. *An Index of Icons in Engish Emblem Books 1500–1700.* Norman, OK, and London: University of Oklahoma Press, 1986.

Disraeli, Isaac. *Curiosities of Literature* [1791–1817]. 3 vols. Rev. edn: 1881.

Dobson, E. J. *The Origins of Ancrene Wisse.* Oxford University Press, 1976.

Docherty, Thomas. *Reading (Absent) Character.* Oxford: Clarendon Press, 1983.

Donaldson, E. T. *"Piers Plowman": The C Text and Its Poet* [1949]. Rev. edn: Cass, 1966.

Donaldson, Gordon. "Surnames and Ancestry in Scotland". In *Her Majesty's Historiographer: Gordon Donaldson (1913–93)*, ed. James Kirk. Edinburgh: Scottish Academic Press, 1996.

Donaldson, Ian. *The Rapes of Lucretia: A Myth and Its Transformations.* Oxford: Clarendon Press, 1982.

Donawerth, Jane. *Shakespeare and the Sixteenth-Century Study of Language.* Urbana, IL: University of Illinois Press, 1984.

Donne, John. *Sermons.* Ed. George R. Potter and Evelyn M. Simpson. 10 vols. Reissue: Berkeley, Los Angeles, and London: University of California Press, 1953–62.

Douglas, Gavin. *The Poetical Works.* Ed. John Small. 4 vols. Edinburgh, 1874.

Douglas, Gavin. *The Shorter Poems* [1967]. Ed. Priscilla Bawcutt. Rev. edn: STS 5th Series, 2. Edinburgh: STS, 2003.

Drayton, Michael. *Works.* Ed. J. William Hebel, Kathleen Tillotson, and Bernard H. Newdigate. 5 vols. Oxford: Shakespeare Head Press, 1931–41.

Drummond, William. *The Works* [1711]. Facs. edn: Hildesheim and New York: Olms, 1970.

Dryden, John. *The Poems: Vol. II: 1682–1685.* Ed. Paul Hammond. London and New York: Longman, 1995.

Du Bellay, Joachim. *La Deffence et Illustration de la Langue Francoyse*. Ed. Henri Chamard. Paris: Didier, 1948.

Du Bellay, Joachim. *Oeuvres poétiques: Tome 1: Premiers recueils (1549–1553)*. Paris: Bordas, 1993.

Duncan-Jones, Elsie Elizabeth, and Chapman, R.W. "The Naming of Characters". *Review of English Studies*, 1 (1950) 252.

Duncan-Jones, Katherine. *Sir Philip Sidney: Courtier Poet*. Newhaven, CT, and London: Yale University Press, 1991.

Dupriez, Bernard. *A Dictionary of Literary Devices*. Tr. and adapted by Albert W. Halsall. New York: Harvester Wheatsheaf, 1991.

E., B. *A new dictionary of the terms ancient and modern of the canting crew*. c.1699.

E., B. *The First English Dictionary of Slang*. Ed. John Simpson. Oxford: Bodleian Library, 2010.

Eco, Umberto. *The Search for the Perfect Language*. Tr. James Fentress. Oxford: Blackwell, 1995.

Eco, Umberto. *The Infinity of Lists from Homer to Joyce*. Tr. Alastair McEwen. MacLehose Press, 2009.

Edwards, Paul. *The Early African Presence in the British Isles*. Inaugural lecture, Edinburgh University, 1990.

Egan, Pierce. *Grose's Classical Dictionary of the Vulgar Tongue Revised and Corrected [. . .]*. 1823.

Ehrenpreis, Irvin. *Swift: The Man, His Works, and the Age*. 3 vols. Methuen, 1962.

Eliot, T. S. *On Poetry and Poets*. Faber, 1957.

Elliott, Elizabeth. " 'A Memorie Nouriched by Images': Reforming the Art of Memory in William Fowler's *Tarantula of Love*". *Journal of the Northern Renaissance*, 2 (Spring 2010) 36–53.

Ellrodt, Robert. "Angels and the Poetic Imagination from Donne to Traherne". In *English Renaissance Studies Presented to Dame Helen Gardner in Honour of Her 70th Birthday*, ed. John Carey (Oxford: Clarendon Press, 1980). Pp.164–79.

Enciclopedia Virgiliana. 6 vols. Rome: Instituto della Enciclopedia Virgiliana, 1984–91.

Erskine-Hill, Howard. *Pope: The Dunciad*. Arnold, 1972.

Erskine-Hill, Howard. *The Augustan Idea in English Literature*. Arnold, 1983.

Estienne, Robert. *Hebraea, Chaldaea, Graeca, et Latina Nomina Virorum, Mulierum, Populorum [. . .]*. Paris, 1537.

Etherege, Sir George. *The Plays*. Ed. Michael Cordner. Cambridge University Press, 1982.

Evans, Joan. *English Posies and Posy Rings*. Oxford University Press, 1931.

Evans, Michael. *Basic Grammar for Medieval and Renaissance Studies*. Warburg Institute, 1995.

Evans, R. J. W. *Rudolf II and His World. A Study in Intellectual History 1576–1612*. Oxford: Clarendon Press, 1973.

Everett, Barbara. "The End of the Big Names: Milton's Epic Catalogues". In *English Renaissance Studies Presented to Dame Helen Gardner in Honour of Her Seventieth Birthday*, ed. John Carey (Oxford: Clarendon Press, 1980). Pp. 254–70.

Fabre, Genevieve. "Genealogical Archaeology or the Quest for Legacy in Toni Morrison's *Song of Solomon*", in *Critical Essays on Toni Morrison*, ed. Nellie Y. McKay (Boston, MA: G. K. Hall, 1988). Pp. 105–14.

Faral, Edmond. *Les Arts poétiques du 12ᵉ et du 13ᵉ siècle*. Bibliothèque de l'École des Hautes Études, fascicle 238. Paris, 1924.

Farmer, John S., and Henley, W. E. *Slang and its Analogues Past and Present*. 7 vols. 1891–1904. Rpt: Millwood, NY: Kraus, 1974.

Febvre, Lucien, and Martin, Henri-Jean. *The Coming of the Book*. Tr. David Gerard [1976]. Rev. edn: London and New York: Verso, 1990.

Ferber, Michael. *A Dictionary of Literary Symbols*. Cambridge University Press, 1999.

Ferry, Anne. *The Art of Naming*. University of Chicago Press, 1989.

Finley, M. I. *The World of Odysseus* [1954]. Rev. edn: Pimlico, 1999.

Fish, Stanley. *Surprised by Sin: The Reader in Paradise Lost* [1967]. Rpt: Berkeley: University of California Press, 1971.

Fitzmaurice, Andrew. "The Corruption of *Hamlet*". In *Shakespeare and Early Modern Political Thought*, ed. David Armitage, Conal Condren, and Andrew Fitzmaurice. Cambridge University Press, 2009.

Fleissner, Robert F. *Names, Titles, and Characters by Literary Writers – Shakespeare, 19th and 20th Century Authors*. Lewiston, NY: Edwin Mellen Press, 2001.

Fleming, Charles F. "Sans Loy, Sans Foy, and Sans Joy". *Notes and Queries*, ser. 12 (1918) 71.

Fletcher, Giles. *The English Works of Giles Fletcher, the Elder*. Ed. Lloyd E. Berry. Madison, WI: University of Wisconsin Press, 1964.

Florio, John. *Queen Anna's new world of words* [1611]. Facs. edn: Menston: Scolar, 1968.

Fordham, Finn. *Lots of Fun at Finnegans Wake*. Oxford University Press, 2007.

Forster, John. *The Life of Charles Dickens*. 3 vols. 1872–4.

Fowler, Alastair. "Emblems of Temperance in *The Faerie Queene, Book II*". *Review of English Studies*, n.s. 11 (1960) 143–49.

Fowler, Alastair. "The River Guyon". *Modern Language Notes*, 75 (1960a) 289–92.

Fowler, Alastair. *Spenser and the Numbers of Time*. Routledge, 1964.

Fowler, Alastair. *Triumphal Forms: Structural Patterns in Elizabethan Poetry*. Cambridge University Press, 1970.

Fowler, Alastair. "Emanations of Glory: Neoplatonic Order in Spenser's *Faerie Queene*". In *A Theatre for Spenserians*, ed. Judith M. Kennedy and James A. Reither (University of Toronto Press, 1973). Pp. 53–82.

Fowler, Alastair. "The Silva Tradition in Jonson's *The Forrest*". In *Poetic Traditions of the English Renaissance*, ed. Maynard Mack and George de Forest Lord (New Haven and London: Yale University Press, 1982). Pp. 163–80.

Fowler, Alastair. *Pastoral Instruction in "As You Like It"*. John Coffin Memorial Lecture. University of London, 1984.

Fowler, Alastair. *Kinds of Literature* [1982]. Rev. edn: Cambridge, MA: Harvard University Press; Oxford: Oxford University Press, 1985.

Fowler, Alastair. "The Beginnings of English Georgic". In *Renaissance Genres: Essays on Theory, History, and Interpretation*, ed. Barbara Kiefer Lewalski (Cambridge, MA, and London: Harvard University Press, 1986). Pp. 105–25.

Fowler, Alastair. "Spenser's Names". In *Unfolded Tales: Essays on Renaissance Romance*, ed. George M. Logan and Gordon Teskey (Ithaca and London: Cornell University Press, 1989). Pp. 32–48.

Fowler, Alastair. "Georgic and Pastoral: Laws of Genre in the Seventeenth Century". In *Culture and Cultivation in Early Modern England: Writing and the Land*, ed. Michael Leslie and Timothy Raylor (Leicester and London: Leicester University Press, 1992). Pp. 81–8.

Fowler, Alastair. "Two Notes on *Hamlet*". In *New Essays on "Hamlet"*, ed. Mark Thornton Burnett and John Manning (New York: AMS, 1994). Pp. 3–6.

Fowler, Alastair. *Time's Purpled Masquers*. Oxford: Clarendon Press, 1996.

Fowler, Alastair (ed). *John Milton: Paradise Lost* [1968]. Second edn: London and New York: Longman, 1998.

Fowler, Alastair. "The Emblem as a Literary Genre". In *Deviceful Settings: The English Renaissance Emblem and its Contexts*. Selected Papers from the Third International Emblem Conference, Pittsburgh, 1993, ed. Michael Bath and Daniel Russell (New York: AMS, 1999). Pp. 1–31.

Fowler, Alastair. *Renaissance Realism: Narrative Images in Literature and Art*. Oxford University Press, 2003.

Fowler, Alastair. "Anagrams". *Yale Review*, 95 (2007) 33–43.

Fowler, Alastair. "Proper Naming: Personal Names in Literature". *Essays in Criticism*, 58 (April 2008) 97–119.

Fowler, Alastair. "Men of Worth". Review of *The Epigrams of Sir John Harington*, ed. Gerard Kilroy. *The Times Literary Supplement* (11 Dec. 2009) 10.

Fowler, Alastair, and Leslie, Michael. "Drummond's Copy of *The Faerie Queene*". *The Times Literary Supplement* (17 July, 1981) 821–2.

Fowler, Don P. "An Acrostic in Vergil (*Aeneid* 7. 601–4)?" *Classical Quarterly*, 33 (1983) 298.

Fox, Denton. "The Scottish Chaucerians". In *Chaucer and Chaucerians*, ed. D. S. Brewer (Nelson, 1966). Pp. 164–200.

Foxe, John. *Actes and monuments [. . .]* [1563]. 1631.

Fraser, Russell. *The Language of Adam: On the Limits and Systems of Discourse*. New York: Columbia University Press, 1977.

Freeman, William. *Dictionary of Fictional Characters*. Dent, 1963.

French, Peter. *John Dee: The World of an Elizabethan Magus* [1972]. Rev. edn: New York: Dorset Press, 1989.

Friedman, Alice T. *House and Household in Elizabethan England*. Chicago University Press, 1989.

Friedman, William F., and Friedman, Elizebeth S. *The Shakespearean Ciphers Examined*. Cambridge University Press, 1957.

Frye, Northrop. *Anatomy of Criticism*. Princeton University Press, 1957.

Gallagher, Philip J. *Milton, the Bible, and Misogyny*. Ed. E. R. Cunnar and G. L. Mortimer. Columbia, MO, and London: University of Missouri Press, 1990.

Gardiner, Sir Alan. *The Theory of Proper Names: A Controversial Essay* [1940]. Rev. edn: Oxford University Press, 1954.

Gaw, Alison. "John Sincklo as One of Shakespeare's Actors". *Anglia*, 49 (1925) 289–303.

Gay, John. *Poetry and Prose*. Ed. Vinton A. Dearing. 2 vols. Oxford: Clarendon Press, 1974.

Gerritsen, Willem Pieter, and Van Melle, A. *Dictionary of Medieval Heroes*. Woodbridge: Boydell, 2000.

Gifford, Don, and Seidman, Robert J. *Notes for Joyce: An Annotation of James Joyce's* Ulysses. New York: Dutton, 1974.

Gillespie, George T. *A Catalogue of Persons Named in German Heroic Literature, 700–1600*. Oxford University Press.

Gillespie, Stuart. *Shakespeare's Books: A Dictionary of Shakespeare's Sources* [2001]. Continuum, 2004.

Gillespie, Stuart. *English Translation and Classical Reception: Towards a New Literary History*. Chichester: Wiley-Blackwell, 2011.

Giraldi, Lilio Gregorio. *De Diis Gentium Varia et Multiplex Historia*. Basel, 1548.

Godwin, Joscelyn. *Robert Fludd: Hermetic Philosopher and Surveyor of Two Worlds* [1979]. Grand Rapids, MI: Phanes Press, 1991.

Gordon, Elizabeth Hope. *The Naming of Characters in the Works of Dickens*. University of Nebraska Studies in Language, Literature, and Criticism, 1. Lincoln, NE, 1917.

Gosse, Edmund. *Seventeenth Century Studies*. 1897.

Gottfried, Rudolph B. "Spenser and the Italian Myth of Locality". *Studies in Philology*, 34 (1937) 107–25.

Gouge, William. *Of Domestical Duties*. 1622.

Gower, John. *Confessio Amantis*. Ed. Russell A. Peck. Buffalo, NY: University of Toronto Press, 1980.

Goyet, Francis. "La Preuve par l'Anagramme". *Poétique*, 46 (April, 1981) 229–46.

Grant, W. Leonard. *Neo-Latin Literature and the Pastoral*. Chapel Hill, NC: University of North Carolina Press, 1965.

Grattan, Thomas Colley. "American Changes of Names". *Household Words*, 348 (22 November, 1856) 433–6.

Greene, Robert. *Menaphon by Robert Greene and A Margarite of America by Thomas Lodge*. Ed. G. B. Harrison. Oxford: Blackwell, 1927.

Greg, Walter W. *Pastoral Poetry and Pastoral Drama* [1905]. Rpt: New York: Russell & Russell, 1959.

Grey, J. David. *The Jane Austen Handbook with a Dictionary of Jane Austen's Life and Works.* Athlone, 1986.

Griffiths, Jane. *John Skelton and Poetic Authority: Defining the Liberty to Speak.* Oxford: Clarendon Press, 2006.

Grigson, Geoffrey (ed). *The Faber Book of Epigrams and Epitaphs.* Faber & Faber, 1977.

Grimal, Pierre. *The Dictionary of Classical Mythology* [1951]. Tr. A. R. Maxwell-Hyslop [1986]. Rev. edn: Oxford: Blackwell, 1987.

Grogan, Jane (ed). *Celebrating Mutabilitie.* Manchester University Press, 2009.

Grose, Francis. *A Classical Dictionary of the Vulgar Tongue.* Ed. Eric Partridge. New York: Barnes and Noble, 1963.

Grose, Francis: *see also under Pierce Egan.*

Guibbory, Achsah. "*Hesperides*: Eros, Flux, and Stasis". In *"Trust to Good Verses": Herrick Tercentenary Essays,* ed. Roger B. Rollin and J. Max Patrick (University of Pittsburgh Press, 1978). Pp. 78–87.

Gurr, Andrew. *Shakespeare's Opposites: The Admiral's Company 1594–1625.* Cambridge University Press, 2009.

Haas, Lidija. "Taken for a ride". Rev. of Mario Vargas Llosa, *The Bad Girl.* In *The Times Literary Supplement* (25 Jan. 2008) 19.

Hadfield, Andrew. "The Fair Rosalind". *The Times Literary Supplement* (12 Dec. 2008) 13–14.

Halkett, Samuel, and Laing, John (eds). *A Dictionary of the Anonymous and Pseudonymous Literature of Great Britain.* Revised by James Kennedy *et al.* 7 vols. Edinburgh: Oliver & Boyd, 1926–34.

Hall, Donald (ed). *The Oxford Book of American Literary Anecdotes.* Oxford University Press, 1981.

Hamel, Christopher de. *The Book: A History of the Bible.* London and New York: Phaidon, 2001.

Hamilton, A. C. *Sir Philip Sidney: A Study of His Life and Works.* Cambridge University Press, 1977.

Hamilton, A. C. "Elizabethan Romance: The Example of Prose Fiction". *Journal of English Literary History,* 49 (1982) 287–99.

Hamilton, A. C. "Elizabethan Prose Fiction and Some Trends in Recent Criticism". *Renaissance Quarterly,* 37 (1984) 21–33.

Hamilton, A. C. (gen. ed). *The Spenser Encyclopedia.* Toronto and Buffalo: University of Toronto Press; London: Routledge, 1990.

Hamilton, A. C. (ed). *Spenser: The Faerie Queene.* Harlow and London: Pearson, 2001.

Hamilton-Paterson, James. *Rancid Pansies.* Faber, 2008.

Hammond, Paul. *John Oldham and the Renewal of Classical Culture.* Cambridge University Press, 1983.

Hanks, Patrick. "Dictionaries of Personal Names". In *The Oxford History of English Lexicography*. Vol. 2: *Specialized Dictionaries*, ed. A. P. Cowie (Oxford: Clarendon Press, 2009). Pp. 122–48.

Hanks, Patrick, and Hodges, Flavia. *A Dictionary of First Names*. Oxford University Press, 1990. [Rev. edn included in *The Oxford Names Companion* (Oxford University Press, 2002).]

Hanks, Patrick, and Hodges, Flavia. *A Dictionary of Surnames*. Oxford University Press, 1988. [Rev. edn included in *The Oxford Names Companion* (Oxford University Press, 2002).]

Harder, Kelsie B. "Names in Thomas Pynchon's *V*". In *Names in Literature: Essays from Literary Onomastics Studies*, ed. Grace Alvarez-Altman and Frederick M. Burelbach (Lanham, MD: University Press of America, 1987). Pp. 79–88.

Harding, Vanessa, and Wright, Laura (eds). *London Bridge: Selected Accounts and Rentals, 1381–1538*. London Record Soc., 1995.

Hardy, Thomas. *Tess of the d'Urbervilles*. Ed. David Skilton. Penguin, 1978.

Harington, Sir John. *The Epigrams*. Ed. Gerard Kilroy. Farnham: Ashgate, 2009.

Harrison, John. "Big Windies". *Slightly Foxed*, 9 (Spring 2006) 50–4.

Harrison, Pegram. "On the Lost Isle". *Slightly Foxed*, 29 (Spring 2009) 82–6.

Harrison, S. J. *Generic Enrichment in Vergil and Horace*. Oxford University Press, 2007.

Harvey, Gabriel. *Four Letters and Certain Sonnets*. Menston: Scolar, 1992.

Hassel, R. Chris. *Renaissance Drama and the English Church Year*. Lincoln, NE: University of Nebraska Press, 1979.

Hawkes, Terence. *Meaning by Shakespeare*. Routledge, 1992.

Hayes, Christa-Maria Lerm. *James Joyce als Inspirationsquelle für Joseph Beuys*. Hildesheim: Olms, 2001.

Hazard, Mary E. *Elizabethan Silent Language*. Lincoln, NB, and London: University of Nebraska Press, 2000.

Heal, Felicity. *Hospitality in Early Modern England*. Oxford: Clarendon Press, 1990.

Hecht, Jean J. *The Domestic Servant Class in Eighteenth-Century England* [1956]. Rev. edn: Routledge & Kegan Paul, 1980.

Heller, Joseph. *Catch-22*. Cape, 1962.

Heller, Murray. "The Names of Slaves and Masters: Real and Fictional". In *Names in Literature: Essays from Literary Onomastics Studies*, ed. Grace Alvarez-Altman and Frederick M. Burelbach (Lanham, MD: University Press of America, 1987). Pp. 171–82.

Hellinga, Lotte, and Trapp, J. B. *The Cambridge History of the Book in Britain*. Vol. 3: *1400–1557*. Cambridge University Press, 1999.

Heniger, S. K. *The Cosmographical Glass: Renaissance Diagrams of the Universe*. San Marino, CA: Huntington Library, 1977.

Herendeen, Wyman H. *From Landscape to Literature*. Pittsburgh, PA: Duquesne University Press, 1986.

Herrick, Robert. *The Complete Poetry*. Ed. J. Max Patrick [1963]. Rev. edn: New York: Norton, 1968.

Herrick, Robert. *The Poetical Works*. Ed. L. C. Martin. Oxford: Clarendon Press, 1956.

Highet, Gilbert. *The Anatomy of Satire*. Princeton University Press, 1962.

Hill, Christopher. *Milton and the English Revolution*. Faber and Faber, 1977.

Hodge, Jane Aiken. *The Double Life of Jane Austen*. Hodder & Stoughton, 1972.

Holland, Peter. "Theseus' Shadows in *A Midsummer Night's Dream*". *Shakespeare Survey*, 47 (1994) 139–51.

Holland, Peter (ed). *A Midsummer Night's Dream*. Oxford University Press, 1994.

Homer. *The Odyssey*. Tr. Robert Fagles. Penguin, 1996.

Homer. *Poetical Works*. Tr. Alexander Pope. Vol. 9: *Homer's Odyssey Books 1–12*. Eds Maynard Mack et al. London: Methuen; Yale University Press, 1967.

Honigmann, E. A. J. *John Weever [. . .]*. Manchester University Press, 1987.

Honigmann, E. A. J. *Shakespeare: The Lost Years* [1985]. Manchester University Press, 1998.

Horsfall, Nicholas. "The Poetics of Toponymy". *Literary Imagination,* 4 (2002) 305–17.

Hostmann, C. "Mappula angliae von Osbern Bokenham". *Englische Studien*, 10 (1887) 6–34.

Hotson, Leslie. *The First Night of "Twelfth Night"*. London: Hart-Davis; New York: Macmillan, 1954.

Hotten, John Camden. *A Dictionary of Modern Slang, Cant, Vulgar Words [. . .] With Glossaries of Two Secret Languages, Spoken by the Wandering Tribes of London, the Costermongers, and the Patterers*. 1859.

Hubbard, Thomas K. "Exile from Arcadia: Sannazaro's Piscatory Eclogues". In *Pastoral Palimpsests: Essays in the Reception of Theocritus and Virgil*, ed. Michael Paschalis (Herakleion: Crete University Press, 2007). Pp. 59–77.

Hughey, Ruth (ed). *The Arundel Harington Manuscript of Tudor Poetry*. 2 vols. Columbus, OH: Ohio State University Press, 1960.

Hunter, William B. "Milton's Laundry Lists". *Milton Quarterly*, 18 (1984) 58–61.

Hurley, Patrick. *Pynchon Character Names: A Dictionary*. Jefferson, NC: McFarland, 2008.

Impelluso, Lucia. *Nature and Its Symbols*. Tr. Stephen Sartarelli. Los Angeles, CA: J. Paul Getty Museum, 2004.

Isitt, Larry R. *All the Names in Heaven. A Reference Guide to Milton's Supernatural Names and Epic Similes*. Lanham, MD; London: Scarecrow, 2002.

Jack, Albert. *Pop Goes the Weasel*. Allen Lane, 2008.

Jack, R. D. S. *The Italian Influence on Scottish Literature*. Edinburgh University Press, 1972.

Jack, R. D. S. *Scottish Literature's Debt to Italy*. Edinburgh University Press, 1986.

Jack, R. D. S. *The Road to the Never Land: A Reassessment of J. M. Barrie's Dramatic Art*. Aberdeen: Aberdeen University Press, 1991.

James VI of Scotland. *The Poems: Vol. I The Essayes of a Prentice; Poetical Exercises at Vacant Hours*. Ed. James Craigie. STS 3rd ser., 22. Edinburgh and London: Blackwood, 1955.

James, Henry. *Literary Criticism: Essays on Literature: American Writers: English Writers*. The Library of America. Cambridge University Press, 1984.

James, Henry. *The Complete Notebooks of Henry James*. Ed. Leon Edel and Lyall H. Powers. Oxford University Press, 1987.

James, Henry. *Complete Stories. Vol. 2: 1874–1884*. The Library of America. New York: Penguin Putnam, 1999.

James, Henry. *Letters*. Ed. Leon Edel. 4 vols. Cambridge, MA: Belknap; London: Macmillan, 1974–84.

Jefferies, Richard. *Hodge and His Masters* [1880]. 2 vols. Read Books, 2008.

Jensen, Peter. *Secrets of the Sonnets*. Eugene, OR: Walking Bird Press, 2007.

Jespersen, Otto. *The Philosophy of Grammar*. Allen & Unwin, 1924.

Johnson, Lynn Staley. *"The Shepheardes Calender": An Introduction*. University Park, PA, and London: Pennsylvania State University Press, 1990.

Johnson, Samuel. *The Lives of the Most Eminent English Poets...* Ed. Roger Lonsdale. 4 vols. Oxford: Clarendon Press, 2006.

Jones, Emrys. *The Origins of Shakespeare*. Oxford: Clarendon Press, 1977.

Jones, Emrys. "Pope and Dulness". In *Pope: Recent Essays by Several Hands*, ed. Maynard Mack and James A. Winn (Brighton: Harvester, 1980). Pp. 612–51.

Jones, Mike Rodman. *Radical Pastoral, 1381–1594*. Farnham: Ashgate, 2011.

Jones, Peter. *Homer's* Iliad: *A Commentary on Three Translations*. Bristol Classical Press, 2003.

Jones, Richard Foster. "Eclogue Types in English Poetry of the Eighteenth Century". *Journal of English and Germanic Philology*, 24 (1925) 33–60.

Jones, Richard Foster, and others writing in his honour. *The Seventeenth Century: Studies in the History of English Thought and Literature from Bacon to Pope*. Palo Alto, CA: Stamford University Press, 1951.

Jones, Richard Foster. *The Triumph of the English Language*. Oxford University Press, 1951.

Jonson, Ben. *Ben Jonson*. Ed. C. H. Herford and Percy and Evelyn Simpson. 11 vols. Oxford: Clarendon Press, 1925–52.

Jonson, Ben. *Ben Jonson*. Ed. Ian Donaldson. Oxford Authors. Oxford University Press, 1985.

Joyce, James. *Ulysses* [1922]. Students' edn. Penguin, 1986.

Joyce, James. *Finnegans Wake*. Faber & Faber, 1939.

Joyce, James. *Finnegans Wake Abridged*. Read by Jim Norton and Marcella Riordan. Naxos Audiobooks, 1998.

Joyce, James. *Dubliners*. Ed. Margot Norris and Hans Walter Gabler. New York & London: Norton, 2006.

Junius, Adrian. *The Nomenclator, or Remembrancer (Nomenclator Omnium Rerum)*. Tr. John Higins. 1585.

Junius, Franciscus (François du Jon), "F[rancisci] F[ilius]". *Gothicum Glossarium*. Dordrecht, 1665.

Junius, Franciscus. *Etymologicum Anglicanum . . .* Ed. Edward Lye. Oxford, 1743.

Kane, George. *"Piers Plowman": the Evidence for Authorship*. Athlone, 1965.

Kane, Harnett T. *The Bayous of Louisiana*. New York: Bonanza Books, 1943.

Kaplan, Justin, and Bernays, Anne. *The Language of Names*. New York: Simon & Schuster, 1997.

Karshan, Thomas. "Nabokov in Bed". *The Times Literary Supplement* (4 Feb. 2011) 3.

Kastan, Madeleine. *In Search of "Kynde Knowynge"*. Amsterdam: Rodopi, 2007.

Katsoulis, Kate. *Telling Tales: A History of Literary Hoaxes*. Bloomsbury Publishing, 2010.

Katz, Richard A. *The Ordered Text: The Sonnet Sequences of Du Bellay*. New York and Bern: Lang, 1985.

Kearney, Patrick J. *The Paris Olympia Press*. Ed. Angus Carroll. Rev. edn: Liverpool University Press, 2008.

Kermode, Sir Frank. "Literary Criticism: Old and New Styles". F. W. Bateson Memorial Lecture. *Essays in Criticism*, 51 (2001) 191–207.

Kiel, Cornelis (Kieliaen, Kilianus). *Etymologicum teutonicae linguae*. Antwerp, 1599.

Kilvert, Rev. Francis. *Diary*. Selected and ed. William Plomer [1960]. 3 vols. Rev. edn: Cape, 1971.

Kipling, Rudyard. *Limits and Renewals*. Macmillan, 1932.

Kirk, G. S. *The Iliad: A Commentary. Vol. 1: Books 1–4*. Cambridge University Press, 1985.

Kitcher, Philip. *Joyce's Kaleidoscope: An Invitation to* Finnegans Wake. Oxford University Press, 2007.

Klein, Holger M. (ed). *English and Scottish Sonnet Sequences of the Renaissance*. 2 vols. Hildesheim, Zürich, New York: Olms, 1984.

Klejn, L. S. "The Catalogue of Ships: Structure and Stratigraphy". *Stratum Plus*, 3 (2000) 17–51.

Klemp, Paul J. "'Now Hid, Now Seen': an Acrostic in *Paradise Lost*". *Milton Quarterly*, 11 (1977) 91–2.

Knowlson, James. *Universal Language Schemes in England and France 1600–1800*. Buffalo, NY, and Toronto: University of Toronto Press, 1975.

Knox, Ronald A. *A Book of Acrostics*. Methuen, 1924.

Kökeritz, Helge. *Shakespeare's Names: A Pronouncing Dictionary* [1959]. Rev. edn: New Haven, CT, and London: Yale University Press, 1966.

Kripke, Saul A. *Naming and Necessity* [1980]. Rev. edn: Cambridge, MA: Harvard University Press, 1981.

Kyriakidis, Stratis. *Catalogues of Proper Names in Latin Epic Poetry: Lucretius–Virgil–Ovid*. Newcastle: Cambridge Scholars Publishing, 2007.

Laʒamon. *Brut*. Ed. G. L. Brook and R. F. Leslie. EETS o.s. 250, 1963.

Lamarque, Peter, and Olsen, Stein Haugom. *Truth, Fiction, and Literature: A Philosophical Perspective*. Oxford: Clarendon Press, 1994.

Langland, William. *Piers Plowman: The B Version*. Ed. George Kane and E. Talbot Donaldson [1975]. Rev. edn: London: Athlone; Berkeley, CA: University of California, 1988.

Lascelles, Mary. *The Story-teller Retrieves the Past*. Oxford: Clarendon Press, 1980.

Lawson, Edwin D. *Personal Names and Naming: An Annotated Bibliography*. New York: Greenwood; London: Eurospan, 1987.

Leatherbarrow, Linda. "Sunsets and Suburbia". *Slightly Foxed*, 26 (Summer 2010) 86–90.

Lee, Hermione. *Virginia Woolf*. Chatto & Windus, 1996.

Lee, Rensselaer W. *Names on Trees: Ariosto into Art*. Princeton University Press, 1977.

Leonard, John. *Naming in Paradise: Milton and the Language of Adam and Eve*. Oxford: Clarendon Press, 1990.

Lerer, Seth (ed). *The Yale Companion to Chaucer*. New Haven, CT, and London: Yale University Press, 2006.

Leslie, Michael. *Spenser's "Fierce Warres and Faithfull Loves": Martial and Chivalric Symbolism in "The Faerie Queene"*. Woodbridge: Boydell & Brewer; Totowa, NJ: Barnes & Noble, 1983.

Le Faye, Deirdre. *Jane Austen: A Family Record* [1989]. Rev. edn: Cambridge University Press, 2004.

Levin, Harry. *Shakespeare and the Revolution of the Times: Perspectives and Commentaries"*. Oxford University Press, 1976.

Levith, Murray J. *What's in Shakespeare's Names*. Hamden, CT: Archon, 1978.

Lewalski, Barbara Kiefer. "Thematic Patterns in *Twelfth Night*". *Shakespeare Survey*, 1 (1965) 168–81.

Lewis, Clive Staples. *The Discarded Image: An Introduction to Medieval and Renaissance Literature*. Cambridge University Press, 1964.

Litt, Dorothy. *Names in English Renaissance Literature*. Lewiston, NY: Edwin Mellen Press, 2001.

Litz, A. Walton. *The Art of James Joyce*. Oxford University Press, 1961.

Lodge, David. *The Language of Fiction*. Routledge, 1966.

Lodge, David. *The Art of Fiction*. Secker & Warburg, 1992.

Loewenstein, David. *Milton and the Drama of History*. Cambridge University Press, 1990.

Looze, Laurence de. "Signing Off in the Middle Ages: Medieval Textuality and Authorial Strategies of Self-Naming". In *Vox Intexta: Orality and Textuality in the Middle Ages,* ed. A. N. Doane and Carol Braun Pasternack (Madison, WI: University of Wisconsin Press, 1991). Pp. 162–77.

Lucking, David. *The Shakespearean Name: Essays on "Romeo and Juliet", "The Tempest", and Other Plays*. Frankfurt: Peter Lang, 2007.

Luxemburg, Alexander. "The Mystery of Vladimir Nabokov's Sources: Some New Ideas on *Lolita's* Intertextual Links". *Connotations*, 14 (2004–5) 119–34.

Lyford, E. *The True Interpretation and Etymologie of Christian Names*. 1655.

Lyles-Scott, Cynthia. "A Slave by Any Other Name: Names and Identity in Toni Morrison's *Beloved*". *Names*, 56 (March, 2008) 23–8.

MacCarthy-Morrogh, Michael. *The Munster Plantation*. Oxford: Clarendon Press, 1986.

Macdonald, R. H. *The Library of Drummond of Hawthornden*. Edinburgh University Press, 1971.

Mack, Maynard. *Alexander Pope: A Life*. New Haven, CT, and London: Yale University Press; New York and London: Norton, 1985.

Macrobius. *Commentary on the Dream of Scipio*. Tr. and ed. William Harris Stahl. New York and London: Columbia University Press, 1952.

Maguire, Laurie. *Shakespeare's Names*. Oxford University Press, 2007.

Maguire, Laurie. *Helen of Troy: From Homer to Hollywood*. Oxford: Wiley-Blackwell, 2009.

Maier, Michael. *Atalanta Fugiens* [1618]. Tr. and ed. Joscelyn Godwin. Grand Rapids, MI: Phanes Press, 1989.

Mare, Walter de la. *Lewis Carroll*. Faber & Faber, 1932.

Margoliouth, David Samuel. *The Chronograms of the Euripidean Dramas*. Oxford: Blackwell, 1915.

Marks, Herbert. "The Blotted Book". In *Re-Membering Milton*, ed. Mary Nyquist and Margaret W. Ferguson (Methuen, 1988). Pp. 211–33.

Marks, Herbert, and Gross, Kenneth. "Names, Naming". In *The Spenser Encyclopedia*, gen. ed. A. C. Hamilton (Toronto and Buffalo: University of Toronto Press; London: Routledge, 1990). Pp. 494–6.

Marotti, Arthur F. *Manuscript, Print, and the English Renaissance Lyric*. Ithaca and London: Cornell University Press, 1995.

Marston, John. *The Poems of John Marston*. Ed. Arnold Davenport. Liverpool University Press, 1961.

Martianus Capella. *Martianus Capella and the Seven Liberal Arts. Vol. I: The Quadrivium of Martianus Capella*. Ed. William Harris Stahl. New York and London: Columbia University Press, 1971.

Masson, David. *Drummond of Hawthornden: The Story of His Life and Writings* [1873]. Rpt: New York: Greenwood, 1969.

Mayhew, G. P. "Swift's Bickerstaff Hoax", *Modern Philology*, 61 (1964) 270–80.

McCabe, Richard A. *Spenser's Monstrous Regiment* [2002]. Rev. edn: Oxford University Press, 2005.

McGavin, John J. "Performing Communities". In *The Oxford Handbook of Medieval Literature in English*, ed. Elaine Treharne and Greg Walker (Oxford University Press, 2010). Pp. 200–18.

McHugh, Roland. *Annotations to "Finnegans Wake"*. Routledge & Kegan Paul, 1980.

McKerrow, R. B. *Printers' and Publishers' Devices in England and Scotland, 1485–1640* [1913]. Rev. edn: Bibliographical Society, 1949.

McKinley, R. *A History of British Surnames*. Longman, 1990.

McLane, Paul E. *Spenser's "Shepheardes Calender": A Study in Elizabethan Allegory*. Notre Dame, IN: University of Notre Dame Press, 1961.

Meeske, Marilyn. "Memoirs of a Female Pornographer". *Esquire* (April 1965) 112–15.

Mertes, Kate. *The English Noble Household 1250–1600*. Oxford: Blackwell, 1988.

Meynell, Alice. *Hearts of Controversy*. Burns & Oates, 1917.

Middleton, Anne. "William Langland's 'Kynd Name': Authorial Signature and Social Identity in Late Fourteenth-Century England". In *Literary Practice and Social Change in Britain 1380–1530*, ed. Lee Patterson (Berkeley and Los Angeles: University of California Press, 1992). Pp. 15–82.

Middleton, Christopher. *The historie of heaven*. 1596.

Millard, Dom Bede. *The Book of Saints*. A. & C. Black, 1989.

Milton, John. *The Poetical Works of John Milton*. Ed. David Masson. 3 vols. 1890.

Milton, John. *The Complete Prose Works*. Gen. ed. Don M. Wolfe. 8 vols. New Haven, CT, and London: Yale University Press, 1953–82.

Milton, John. *Complete Shorter Poems*. Ed. John Carey [1968]. Second edn: London and New York: Longman, 1997.

Milton, John. *Paradise Lost*. Ed. Alastair Fowler [1968]. Second edn: London and New York: Longman, 1998.

Minchin, Elizabeth. *Homer and the Resources of Memory: Some Applications of Cognitive Theory to the "Iliad" and the "Odyssey"*. Oxford University Press, 2001.

Minnis, A. J. *Medieval Theory of Authorship: Scholastic Literary Attitudes in the Later Middle Ages*. Scolar Press, 1984.

Minnis, A. J., and Scott, A. B. *Medieval Literary Theory and Criticism c.1100–c.1375*. Oxford: Clarendon Press, 1988.

Minsheu, John (Minschaeus). *Ductor in linguas*. 1617.

Minturno, Antonio Sebastiano. *L'Arte poetica*. Facs. edn: Munich: Poetiken des Cinquecento, 1971.

Montagu, Ashley. *The Anatomy of Swearing*. New York: Macmillan, 1967.

Montgomery, Lucy Maud. *Anne of Avonlea* [1909]. Rpt: Penguin, 1975.

Moore Smith, G. C. "Herrick's 'Hesperides'". *Modern Language Review*, 9 (1914) 373–4.

Morales, Helen. *Classical Mythology: A Very Short Introduction*. Oxford University Press, 2007.

More, Thomas. *Utopia*. Ed. Paul Turner. Penguin, 1961.

Morgan, T. J., and Morgan, Prys. *Welsh Surnames*. Cardiff: University of Wales Press, 1985.

Mortimer, Edward [Edward Montague]. *Montoni, or the Confessions of the Monk of Saint Benedict. A Romance.* 1808.

Morton, Brian. "When Deceiving Is Believing". *Scottish Review of Books*, 7 (2011) 20.

Moseley, Charles. *A Century of Emblems.* Aldershot: Scolar, 1989.

Moss, Ann. *Renaissance Truth and the Latin Language Turn.* Oxford University Press, 2003.

Mudge, Isadore Gilbert, and Sears, M. Earl. *A Thackeray Dictionary.* London: Routledge; New York: Dutton; Toronto: Musson, 1910.

Muir, Kenneth. *The Sources of Shakespeare's Plays.* Methuen, 1977.

Mulcaster, Richard. *The First Part of the Elementary* [1582]. Menston: Scolar, 1970.

Mullan, John. "A Short History of Literary Hoaxes". *The Guardian* (6 Sept. 2003).

Mullan, John. *How Novels Work.* Oxford University Press, 2006.

Mullan, John. *Anonymity: A Secret History of English Literature.* Faber and Faber, 2007.

Murray, Sir David. *Poems.* Ed. T. Kinnear. 2 vols. Bannatyne Club, 1823.

Muscatine, Charles. *"The Canterbury Tales: Style of the Man and Style of the Work"*. In *Chaucer and Chaucerians*, ed. D. S. Brewer (Nelson, 1966). Pp. 88–113.

Musgrove, S. "The Nomenclature of *King Lear*". *Review of English Studies*, 32 (1956) 294–8.

Musgrove, S. "Herrick's Alchemical Vocabulary". Melbourne: Australasian Universities Language and Literature Association, 46 (Nov. 1976) 240–65.

Musson, Jeremy. *Up and Down Stairs: The History of the Country House Servant.* John Murray, 2009.

Nabokov, Vladimir. *Novels 1955–1962.* The Library of America. New York: Penguin, 1996.

Naiman, Eric. *Nabokov, Perversely.* Ithaca, NY: Cornell University Press, 2010.

Nalimov, V. V. *In the Labyrinths of Language: A Mathematician's Journey.* Ed. Robert G. Colodny. University Park, PA: ISI Press, 1981.

Names. Vols. 1–56. Berkeley, CA: American Name Society, 1953–2008.

Nashe, Thomas. *The Works.* Ed. Ronald B. McKerrow and F. P. Wilson. 5 vols. Oxford: Blackwell [1957] 1966.

Nelson, William (ed.). *Form and Convention in the Poetry of Edmund Spenser.* New York: Columbia University Press, 1961.

Nelson, William. *The Poetry of Edmund Spenser: A Study.* New York: Columbia University Press, 1963.

Noble, Vernon. *Nicknames – Past and Present.* Hamilton, 1976.

Noel-Tod, Jeremy. "Freudful Myth-Information". *Slightly Foxed*, 20 (Winter 2008) 84–9.

Nohrnberg, James. *The Analogy of The Faerie Queene.* Princeton University Press, 1976.

Nohrnberg, James. "Supplementing Spenser's Supplement, a Masque in Several Scenes: Eight Literary-Critical Meditations on a Renaissance Numen called *Mutabilitie*". In *Celebrating Mutabilitie*, ed. Jane Grogan (Manchester University Press, 2009). Pp. 85–135.

Nolan, Maggie, and Dawson, Carrie. *Who's Who: Hoaxes, Imposture, and Identity Crises in Australian Literature*. Brisbane: University of Queensland Press, 2004.

Nosworthy, J. M. *Shakespeare's Occasional Plays: Their Origin and Transmission*. London: Arnold; New York: Barnes & Noble, 1965.

Nuttall, A. D. *Shakespeare the Thinker*. New Haven, CT and London: Yale University Press, 2007.

Oliver, Raymond. *Poems without Names: The English Lyric, 1200–1500*. Berkeley and Los Angeles: California University Press, 1970.

Onions, C. T. *A Shakespeare Glossary*. Enlarged and revised by Robert D. Eagleson. Oxford: Clarendon Press, 1986.

Onoma. Louvain: International Centre of Onomastics. 1950–

Opie, Iona, and Opie, Peter (eds). *The Oxford Dictionary of Nursery Rhymes* [1951]. Rev. edn: Oxford: Clarendon Press, 1952.

Ostler, Nicholas. *Ad Infinitum: A Biography of Latin and the World it Created*. Harper 2007.

Owst, G. R. *Literature and Pulpit in Medieval England* [1933]. Rev. edn: Oxford: Blackwell, 1961.

P. S. *The Heroicall Devises of M. Claudius Paradin*. 1591.

Parker, Patricia. *Inescapable Romance: Studies in the Poetics of a Mode*. Princeton University Press, 1979.

Parker, Patricia. *Shakespeare from the Margins: Language, Culture, Context*. Chicago and London: University of Chicago Press, 1996.

Parker, Tom W. N. *Proportional Form in the Sonnets of the Sidney Circle*. Oxford: Clarendon Press, 1998.

Parker, William Riley. *Milton: A Biography*. Oxford: Clarendon Press, 1968.

Parker, William Riley. *Milton: A Biographical Commentary: Second Edition. Revised by Gordon Campbell*. 2 vols. Oxford: Clarendon Press, 2003.

Parnassus Illustratus sive Nomina et Elucidatio Historiarum Poeticarum. . . . Cassovia [Kassa], 1728.

Paroissien, David. *The Companion to "Oliver Twist"*. Edinburgh University Press, 1992.

Parry, Robert. *The Poems*. Ed. G. Blakemore Evans. Tempe, AZ: Arizona Center for Medieval and Renaissance Studies with Renaissance English Text Society, 2005.

Patterson, Annabel. *Pastoral and Ideology: Virgil to Valéry*. Berkeley and Los Angeles: University of California Press, 1987.

Pauly, August Friedrich von. *Real-Encyclopädie* [. . .]. Stuttgart: Metzlersche, 1927.

Payton, Geoffrey. *The Penguin Dictionary of Proper Names*. Revised John Paxton. BCA, 1991.

Peacock, Thomas Love. *The Novels*. Ed David Garnet. Rupert Hart-Davis, 1948.

Peake, Mervyn. *Titus Groan* [1946]. Rev. edn: Eyre & Spottiswoode, 1968.

Pearson, D'Orsay W. " 'Unkinde'Theseus: A Study in Renaissance Mythography". *English Literary Renaissance*, 4 (1974) 276–98.

Pellicer, Juan Christian. Rev. of *Pastoral Palimpsests: Essays in the Reception of Theocritus and Virgil*, ed. Michael Paschalis. In *Translation and Literature* 19 (2010) 93–103.

Penkethman, J. *Onomatophylacium; or, The Christian Names of Men and Women, Now Used within this Realme of Great Britaine*. 1626.

Pepys, Samuel. *The Diary*. Ed. Robert Latham and William Matthews. 11 vols. Bell & Hyman, 1970–83.

Petrarch. *Petrarch's Lyric Poems: The "Rime Sparse" and Other Lyrics*. Tr. and ed. Robert M. Durling. Cambridge, MA: Harvard University Press, 1976.

Petrina, Alessandra. "Translation and Ideology in the Scotland of James VI: The Case of William Fowler". *Storia e Politica*, 1 (2009) 228–50.

Pico della Mirandola. *Opera Omnia*. Basel, 1573.

Pierce, Gilbert A., and Wheeler, William A. *The Dickens Dictionary*. 1878.

Pitcher, John. "Names in *Cymbeline*". *Essays in Criticism*, 43 (1993) 1–16.

Plutarch. *Lives*. Tr. Sir Thomas North [1579]. 10 vols. 1898–9.

Poggioli, Renato. *The Oaten Flute: Essays on Pastoral Poetry and the Pastoral Ideal*. Cambridge, MA: Harvard University Press, 1975.

Poliziano, Angelo. *Silvae*. Ed. Charles Fantazzi. Cambridge, MA: Harvard University Press, 2004.

Pontano, Giovanni Gioviano (Ioannes Iovianus Pontanus). *Opera*. Basel, 1531.

Pontano, Giovanni Gioviano. *Carmina*. Ed. J. Oeschger. Scrittori d'Italia. Bari, 1948.

Poole, Joshua. *The English Parnassus [...] Containing [...] The choicest Epithets and Phrases*. 1677.

Poole, Kristen. "Naming, *Paradise Lost*, and the Gendered Discourse of Perfect Language Schemes". *English Literary Renaissance*, 38 (Autumn 2008) 535–9.

Pope, Alexander. *The Prose Works*. Ed. Norman Ault: *Vol. 1: The Earlier Works, 1711–1720*. Oxford: Shakespeare Head Press and Blackwell, 1936.

Pope, Alexander. *The Poems. Vol. 3-2: Epistles to Several Persons*. Ed. F. W. Bateson [1951]. Rev. edn: London: Methuen; New Haven, CT: Yale University Press, 1961.

Pope, Alexander. *The Poems. Vol. 4: Imitations of Horace*. Ed. John Butt [1939]. Rev. edn: London: Methuen; New Haven, CT: Yale University Press, 1961.

Pope, Alexander. *The Poems. Vol. 5: The Dunciad*. Ed. James Sutherland [1943]. Rev. edn: London: Methuen; New Haven, CT: Yale University Press, 1963.

Pope, Alexander. *The Poems. Vol. 7: The Iliad 1–9*. E. Maynard Mack et al. London: Methuen; New Haven, CT: Yale University Press, 1967.

Pope, Alexander. *The Poems: Vol. 3: The Dunciad (1728) & The Dunciad Variorum (1729)*. Ed. Valerie Rumbold. Harlow: Pearson Longman, 2007.

Porush, David. *The Soft Machine: Cybernetic Fiction*. New York and London: Methuen, 1985.

Potter, Lois. *Secret Rites and Secret Writing: Royalist Literature 1641–1660*. Cambridge University Press, 1989.

Powell, Barry. *Homer and the Origin of the Greek Alphabet*. Cambridge University Press, 1991.

Power, William. "Middleton's Way with Names". *Notes and Queries*, 205 (Jan. 1960) 26–9; (Feb. 1960) 56–60; (March 1960) 95–8; (April 1960) 136–40; (May 1960) 175–9.

Preminger, Alex, *et al. The New Princeton Encyclopedia of Poetry and Poetics*. Princeton University Press, 1993.

Pugh, Syrithe. *Herrick, Fanshawe and the Politics of Intertextuality: Classical Literature and Seventeenth-Century Royalism*. Farnham: Ashgate, 2010.

Puttenham, George. *The Art of English Poesie*. Ed. Gladys Doidge Willcock and Alice Walker. Cambridge University Press, 1936.

Puttenham, George. *The Art of English Poesy*. Ed. Frank Whigham and Wayne A. Rebhorn. Ithaca and London: Cornell University Press, 2007.

Quincey, Thomas de. *The Collected Writings*. Ed. David Masson. 14 vols. 1896–7.

Ragussis, Michael. *Acts of Naming: The Family Plot in Fiction*. Oxford University Press, 1986.

Rajec, Elizabeth M. *The Study of Names in Literature: A Bibliography*. New York: Saur, 1978.

Raymond, Joad. *Milton's Angels: The Early-Modern Imagination*. Oxford University Press, 2010.

Reaney, Percy Hilde, and Wilson, R. M., *A Dictionary of British Surnames* [1961]. Rev. edn: Routledge & Kegan Paul, 1976.

Reaney, Percy Hilde. *The Origin of English Surnames*. Routledge & Kegan Paul, 1967.

Reid Baxter, Jamie. "Liminary Verse: the Paratextual Poetry of Renaissance Scotland". *Journal of the Edinburgh Bibliographical Society*, 3 (2008) 70–94.

Revard, Stella P. *Milton and the Tangles of Neaera's Hair: The Making of the 1645 Poems*. Columbia, MO, and London: University of Missouri Press, 1997.

Reverand, Cedric D. *Dryden's Final Poetic Mode: The Fables*. Philadelphia: University of Pennsylvania Press, 1988.

Reynolds, Margaret. "The Child in Poetry". *Proceedings of the British Academy*, 151 (2007) 1–52.

Richardson, R. C. *Household Servants in Early Modern England*. Manchester University Press, 2010.

Ricks, Sir Christopher B. "Shakespeare and the Anagram". *Proceedings of the British Academy*, 121 (2003) 111–46.

Ricks, Sir Christopher B. "Decisions and Revisions in T. S. Eliot". Panizzi Lecture. British Library and Faber & Faber, 2003.

Rigolot, François. *Poétique et Onomastique*. Geneva: Droz, 1977.

Rimmon-Kenan, Shlomith. *Narrative Fiction: Contemporary Poetics* [1983]. Rpt: London and New York: Routledge, 1999.

Ripa, Cesare. *Iconologia* [1611]. Rpt: New York and London: Garland, 1976.

Ritscher, Lee A. *The Semiotics of Rape in Renaissance English Literature.* Berkeley Insights in Linguistics and Semiotics. Frankfurt: Peter Lang, 2009.

Roberts, Jean A. *The Shakespearean Wild: Geography, Genus, and Gender.* Lincoln, NE: University of Nebraska Press, 1991.

Robson, William Wallace. "Kipling's Later Stories". In *Kipling's Mind and Art,* ed. Andrew Rutherford (Edinburgh and London: Oliver & Boyd, 1964). Pp. 255–78.

Roche, Thomas P. *Petrarch and the English Sonnet Sequences.* New York: AMS, 1989.

Room, Adrian. *Brewer's Dictionary of Names.* Cassell, 1992.

Room, Adrian. *Dictionary of Astronomical Names.* London and New York: Routledge, 1988.

Rosenmeyer, Thomas G. *The Green Cabinet: Theocritus and the European Pastoral Lyric.* Berkeley and Los Angeles: University of California Press, 1969.

Rowland, Peter. "No Sich a Person: In Search of the Original Fagin". *The Times Literary Supplement,* Commentary (21 Jan. 2011).

Rowlands, Richard [R. Verstegan]. *A Restitution of Decayed Intelligence.* Antwerp, 1605.

Rubinstein, Ronald. *John Citizen and the Law* [1947]. Rev. edn: West Drayton: Penguin, 1948.

Rudd, Niall. *The Satires of Horace.* Cambridge University Press, 1966.

Ruskin, John. *The Works.* Ed. E. T. Cook and A. D. O. Wedderburn. 39 vols. George Allen, 1903–12.

Russell, William M. "Love, Chaos, and Marvell's Elegy for Cromwell". *English Literary Renaissance,* 40 (2010) 272–97.

Rutherford, R. B. *Homer.* Oxford University Press, 1996.

Ruthven, K. K. *Faking It.* Cambridge University Press, 2001.

Sadleir, Michael [Michael T. Sadler]. *Nineteenth Century Fiction: A Bibliographical Record.* 2 vols. London: Constable; Los Angeles: California University Press, 1951.

Salisbury, Joyce E. *The Beast Within: Animals in the Middle Ages.* New York and London: Routledge, 1994.

Salmon, Vivien. *The Works of Francis Lodwick: A Study of His Writings in the Intellectual Context of the Seventeenth Century.* Longman, 1972.

Salter, David. "Shakespeare and Catholicism: The Franciscan Connection." *Cahiers Élisabethains,* 66 (2004) 9–22.

Salusbury, Sir John. *Poems by Sir John and Robert Chester.* Ed. Carleton Brown. *EETS* e. s. 113, 1914.

Salzmann, L. F. *Building in England Down to 1540: A Documentary History.* Oxford: Clarendon Press, 1997.

Sambrook, James. *English Pastoral Poetry.* Boston, MA: Twayne, 1983.

Sammons, Benjamin. *The Art and Rhetoric of the Homeric Catalogue.* Oxford University Press, 2010.

Sannazaro, Jacopo. *Arcadia and Piscatory Eclogues.* Tr. Ralph Nash. Detroit, MI: Wayne State University Press, 1966.

Saslow, James M. *Ganymede in the Renaissance: Homosexuality in Art and Society.* New Haven, CT, and London: Yale University Press, 1986.

Scafi, Alessandro. *Mapping Paradise: A History of Heaven on Earth.* The British Library, 2006.

Scaliger, Julius Caesar. *Poetices Libri Septem* [1561]. Facs. edn: August Buck. Stuttgart-Bad Cannstatt: Frommann, 1964.

Scève, Maurice. *Délie.* Ed. I. D. McFarlane. Cambridge University Press, 1966.

Schiller, Gertrud. *Iconography of Christian Art.* Tr. Janet Seligman. 2 vols. Lund Humphries, 1971.

Schoenbaum, S. *Shakespeare's Lives.* Oxford: Clarendon Press; New York: Oxford University Press, 1970.

Schoolfield, George. *Janus Secundus.* Boston, MA: Twayne, 1980.

Schwartz, Stephen P. (ed.). *Naming, Necessity and Natural Kinds.* Ithaca, NY, and London: Cornell University Press, 1977.

Scot, Reginald. *The Discovery of Witchcraft.* 1584.

Scott, Sir Walter. *Waverley; or, 'Tis Sixty Years Since.* Ed. Claire Lamont. Oxford: Clarendon Press, 1981.

Scowcroft, R. Mark. "Abstract Narrative in Ireland". *Ériu*, 46 (1995) 121–58.

Screech, Michael. *Rabelais.* Duckworth, 1979.

Scriblerus, Martinus. *Memoirs [...] of Martinus Scriblerus Written in Collaboration by the Members of the Scriblerus Club: John Arbuthnot, Alexander Pope, Jonathan Swift, John Gay, Thomas Parnell, and Robert Harley, Earl of Oxford.* Ed. Charles Kerby-Miller [1950]. Rpt: Oxford University Press, 1988.

Scruton, Roger. "What's in a Name?" *Poetry Nation Review*, 141 (2001) 42–5.

Seaton, Ethel. *Sir Richard Roos c. 1410–1482: Lancastrian Poet.* Hart-Davis, 1961.

Sessions, William A. "Spenser's Georgics". *English Literary Renaissance*, 10 (1980) 202–38.

Seznec, Jean. *The Survival of the Pagan Gods: The Mythological Tradition and its Place in Renaissance Humanism and Art.* Tr. Barbara F. Sessions. New York: Pantheon for the Bollingen Foundation, 1953.

Shakespeare, William. *A Midsummer Night's Dream.* Ed. Harold F. Brooks. Methuen, 1979.

Shakespeare, William. *Hamlet.* Ed. Harold Jenkins. Methuen, 1982.

Shakespeare, William. *A Midsummer Night's Dream.* Ed. Peter Holland. Oxford University Press, 1994.

Sharpe, Kevin, and Zwicker, Steven N. (eds). *Reading, Society and Politics in Early Modern England.* Cambridge University Press, 2003.

Shatto, Susan. *The Companion to "Bleak House".* Unwin Hyman, 1988.

Shawcross, John T. "The Names of Herrick's Mistresses in *Hesperides*". In Roger B. Rollin and J. Max Patrick (eds). *"Trust to Good Verses: Herrick*

Tercentenary Essays (Pittsburgh, PA: University of Pittsburgh Press, 1978). Pp. 89–102.

Sheingorn, Pamela, tr. *The Book of Sainte Foy*. Philadelphia: Pennsylvania University Press, 1955.

Shirley, James. *Poems* [1646]. Facs. edn: Menston: Scolar, 1970.

Sidney, Sir Philip. *The Poems*. Ed. William A. Ringler. Oxford: Clarendon Press, 1962.

Sidney, Sir Philip. *Miscellaneous Prose*. Ed. Katherine Duncan-Jones and Jan van Dorsten. Oxford: Clarendon Press, 1973.

Sidney, Sir Philip. *An Apology for Poetry (or The Defence of Poesy)*. Ed. Geoffrey Shepherd and R. W. Maslen [1965]. Rev. edn: Manchester and New York: Manchester University Press, 2002.

Simpson, R. Hope, and Lazenby, J. F. *The Catalogue of Ships in Homer's Iliad*. Oxford University Press, 1970.

Singerman, Robert. *Jewish and Hebrew Onomastics*. New York: Garland, 1977.

Skeat, Walter W. (ed.). *Chaucerian and Other Pieces* [1897]. Rpt: Oxford University Press, 1963.

Smith, A. J. *The Metaphysics of Love: Studies in Renaissance Love Poetry from Dante to Milton*. Cambridge University Press, 1985.

Smith, Elsdon C. *Treasury of Name Lore*. HarperCollins, 1967.

Smith, Grant. "A Semiotic Theory of Names". *Onoma*, 41 (2008).

Smith, Margaret M. *The Title-page: its early Development 1460–1510*. London: The British Library; Newcastle DE: Oak Knoll Press, 2000.

Smith, Marion Bodwell. *Dualities in Shakespeare*. Toronto: University of Toronto Press, 1966.

Smith-Bannister, Scott. *Names and Naming Patterns in England, 1538–1700*. Oxford: Clarendon Press, 1997.

Spacks, Patricia Meyer. *Novel Beginnings: Experiments in Eighteenth-Century English Fiction*. New Haven, CT, and London: Yale University Press, 2006.

Spevack, Marvin. "Beyond Individualism: Names and Namelessness in Shakespeare". *Huntington Library Quarterly*, 56 (1993) 303–19.

Spenser, Edmund. *Daphnaïda and Other Poems*. Ed. W. L. Renwick. Scholartis Press, 1929.

Spenser, Edmund. *Works: A Variorum Edition*. Ed. E. Greenlaw et al. 11 vols. Baltimore: Johns Hopkins Press, 1932–57, 1966. [*Variorum Spenser*]

Spenser, Edmund. *Spenser's Faerie Queene*. Ed. John Upton with glossary and notes [1758]. Rev. by John G. Radcliffe. 2 vols. New York and London: Garland, 1987.

Spenser, Edmund. *The Faerie Queene*. Ed. A. C. Hamilton. Text ed. Hiroshi Yamashita and Toshiyuki Suzuki. Harlow: Pearson Education, 2001.

Sprat, Thomas. *History of the Royal Society*. 1667.

Spufford, Margaret. *Small Books and Pleasant Histories: Popular Fiction and Its Readership in Seventeenth-Century England*. Athens, GA: University of Georgia Press, 1982.

Starner, Janet Wright, and Traister, Barbara Howard (eds). *Anonymity in Early Modern England: "What's in A Name?"*. Abingdon: Ashgate, 2011.

Starnes, DeWitt T., and Talbert, Ernest William. *Classical Myth and Legend in Renaissance Dictionaries*. Chapel Hill, NC: University of North Carolina Press, 1955.

Starobinski, Jean. *The Anagrams of Ferdinand de Saussure* [1971]. Tr. Olivia Emmet. Yale University Press, 1980.

Stevens, John. *Medieval Romance: Themes and Approaches*. Hutchinson, 1973.

Stevenson, Robert Louis. *Works*. Ed. L. Osbourne. Vailima edn. 26 vols. London: Heinemann with Chatto & Windus, Cassell, Longmans, Green; New York: Scribner's, 1922–3.

Stevenson, Robert Louis. *The Letters*. Ed. Bradford A. Booth and Ernest Mehew. 8 vols. New Haven, CT, and London: Yale University Press, 1994–5.

Stokes, Francis Griffin. *A Dictionary of the Characters and Proper Names in the Works of Shakespeare* [1924]. Rpt: New York: Dover, 1970.

Stokes, Francis Griffin, tr. *Epistulae Obscurorum Virorum*. New York: Harper & Row, 1964.

Stone, Harry. "What's in a Name: Fantasy and Calculation in Dickens". *Dickens Studies Annual*, 14 (New York: AMS, 1985) 191–204.

Stonehouse, J. H., *Catalogue of the Books of Charles Dickens from Gadshill*. Piccadilly Fountain Press, 1935.

Stroup, Thomas B. "Bottom's Name and His Epiphany". *Shakespeare Quarterly*, 29 (1978) 79–82.

Summers, Montague. *The Gothic Quest: A History of the Gothic Novel*. Fortune Press, 1938.

Summers, U. T. Miller. *Hold Tight Sweetheart: A Memoir of the 1920s and the Great Depression*. Lulu Press, 2007.

Swanson, Donald C. *The Names in Roman Verse*. Madison, WI: University of Wisconsin Press, 1967.

Thackeray, William Makepeace. *Vanity Fair*. Ed. Geoffrey and Katherine Tillotson. Methuen, 1963.

Thackeray, William Makepeace. *Vanity Fair*. Ed. John Carey. Penguin, 2001.

Thomson, Gladys Scott. *Life in a Noble Household 1641–1700*. Cape, 1937.

Tilley, Morris Palmer. *A Dictionary of the Proverbs in England in the Sixteenth and Seventeenth Centuries*. Ann Arbor, MI: University of Michigan Press, 1950.

Tindall, William York. *A Reader's Guide to James Joyce*. Thames & Hudson, 1959.

Trevor-Roper, Hugh. *Letters from Oxford*. Ed. Richard Davenport-Hines. Weidenfeld and Nicolson, 2006.

Trig, Stephanie. "Chaucer's Influence and Reception". In *The Yale Companion to Chaucer*, ed. Seth Lerer (New Haven, CT, and London: Yale University Press, 2006). Pp. 297–323.

Trollope, Anthony. *Mr Scarborough's Family*. 1883.

Tse, Grace Y. W. *A Corpus-Based Study of Proper Names in Present-Day English: Aspects of Gradience and Article Usage*. Frankfurt am Main: Lang, 2005.

Turville-Petre, Thorlac. "The Author of the Destruction of Troy". *Medium Aevum*, 57 (1988) 264–9.

Upton, John: *see* Spenser 1758.

Urquhart, Sir Thomas. *The Jewel* [1652]. Ed. R. D. S. Jack and R. J. Lyall. Edinburgh: Scottish Academic Press, 1983.

Valeriano, Pierio. *Hieroglyphica [. . .] Accesserunt Loco Auctarii, Hieroglyphicorum Collectanea*. Frankfurt, 1613.

Van Langendonck, Willy. *Theory and Typology of Proper Names*. Berlin and New York: Mouton de Gruyter, 2008.

Vaughn, Mark. "More than Meets the Eye: Milton's Acrostics in *Paradise Lost*". *Milton Quarterly*, 16 (1982) 6–8.

Veeder, William. *Henry James – The Lessons of the Master: Popular Fiction and Personal Style in the Nineteenth Century*. Chicago and London: University of Chicago Press, 1975.

Verity, A. W. (ed.). *Milton: Paradise Lost*. Cambridge University Press, 1910.

Vickers, Brian. *Occult Scientific Mentalities in the Renaissance*. Cambridge University Press, 1984.

Villiers, George, Duke of Buckingham. *Plays, Poems, and Miscellaneous Writings*. Ed. Robert D. Hume and Harold Love. 2 vols. Oxford University Press, 2007.

Vinaver, Eugène. *The Rise of Romance*. Oxford: Clarendon Press, 1971.

Vinne, Theodore Low de. *A Treatise on Title-Pages*. New York: The Century Co., 1902.

Visser, Edzard. *Homers Katalog der Schiffe*. Stuttgart & Leipzig: Teubner, 1997.

Walker, Daniel Pickering. *The Ancient Theology: Studies in Christian Platonism from the Fifteenth to the Eighteenth Century*. London: Duckworth; Ithaca, NY: Cornell University Press, 1972.

Wallace, David (ed). *The Cambridge History of Medieval English Literature*. Cambridge University Press, 1999.

Watson, Thomas. *Poems*. Ed. Edward Arber. 1895.

Watson, Thomas. *The Hekatompathia or Passionate Centurie of Love* [1582]. Ed. S. K. Heninger. Delmar, NY: Scholars' Facsimiles & Reprints, 1977.

Watt, Gary. "The origin of Jarndyce and Jarndyce". *The Times Literary Supplement*, Commentary (4 Sept. 2009).

Watt, Ian P. "The Naming of Characters in Defoe, Richardson, and Fielding". *Review of English Studies*, 25 (1949) 322–38.

Watt, Ian P. *The Rise of the Novel: Studies in Defoe, Richardson and Fielding*. Chatto and Windus, 1957.

Watt, Ian P. "The First Paragraph of *The Ambassadors*: an Explication". *Essays in Criticism*, 10 (1960) 250–74.

Waugh, Evelyn. *Decline and Fall* [1928]. Rpt: Penguin, 1979.

Weatherby, Harold L. *Mirrors of Celestial Grace: Patristic Theology in Spenser's Allegory*. Toronto: University of Toronto Press, 1994.

Wedeck, Harry Ezekiel. "The Catalogue in Latin and Medieval Latin Poetry". *Mediaevalia & Humanistica*, 13 (1960) 3–16.

Weekley, Ernest. *The Romance of Names*. John Murray, 1914.

Weever, Jacqueline de. *Chaucer Name Dictionary: A Guide to Astrological, Biblical, Historical, Literary, and Mythological Names in the Works of Geoffrey Chaucer.* New York and London: Garland, 1988.

Weever, John. *Epigrammes* [1599]. [Facs. edn included in Honigmann 1987.]

West, G. D. *An Index of Proper Names in French Arthurian Prose Romances 1150–1300.* Toronto: University of Toronto Press, 1978.

West, Robert H. *Milton and the Angels*. Athens, GA: University of Georgia Press, 1955.

West, William. *Symbolaeography*. 1594.

Wetherby, Harold L. "The True St George". *English Literary Renaissance*, 17 (1987) 119–41.

Wharton, Edith. *The New York Stories*. Ed. Roxana Robinson. New York: New York Review Books, 2007.

Wheatley, H. B. *Of Anagrams*. Hertford, 1862.

Wheeler, William Adolphus. *A Dictionary of the Noted Names of Fiction* [1866]. Rev. edn: 1880.

White, James. "Family Names". *Household Words*, 15 (30 May 1857) 525–8.

White, Patti. *Gatsby's Party: The System and the List in Contemporary Narrative.* Purdue, IN: Purdue University Press, 1992.

Whitelocke, Bulstrode. *The Diary of Bulstrode Whitelocke 1605–1675.* Ed. Ruth Spalding. Oxford University Press for The British Academy, 1990.

Whiting, Bartlett Jere, and Whiting, Helen Westcott. *Proverbs, Sentences, and Proverbial Phrases from English Writings Mainly before 1500.* Cambridge, MA: Harvard University Press, 1968.

Whitman, Charles Huntington. *A Subject-Index to the Poems of Edmund Spenser* [1919]. Rpt: New York: Russell & Russell, 1966.

Whitman, Cedric H. *Homer and the Heroic Tradition*. Cambridge, MA: Harvard University Press, 1958.

Whitman, Jon. *Allegory: The Dynamics of an Ancient and Medieval Technique.* Cambridge, MA: Harvard University Press, 1987.

Whitney, Geoffrey. *A Choice of Emblemes* [1586]. Hildesheim and New York: Olms, 1971.

Wilkins, John. *An Essay towards a Real Character and a Philosophical Language.* 1668.

Willet, Andrew. *Hexapla [. . .] Sixfold Commentary upon Genesis*. 1608.

Williams, Deanne. "The Dream Visions". In *The Yale Companion to Chaucer*, ed. Seth Lerer (New Haven, CT, and London: Yale University Press, 2006). Pp. 147–78.

Williams, Franklin B. "An Invitation into Initials". *Studies in Bibliography*, 9 (1957) 163–78.

Williams, Franklin B. "Renaissance Names in Masquerade". *PMLA*, 69 (1954) 314–23.

Williams, Franklin B. "Those Careless Elizabethans: Names Bewitched". *Proceedings of the Bibliographical Society of America*, 54 (1960) 115–19.

Willson, Robert F. "God's Secrets and Bottom's Name: A Reply". *Shakespeare Quarterly*, 30 (1979) 407–8.

Wilson, Elkin Calhoun. *England's Eliza*. Cass, 1966.

Wilson, F. P. *The Oxford Dictionary of English Proverbs* [1935]. Third edition: Oxford: Clarendon Press, 1970.

Wilson, Stephen. *The Means of Naming: A Social and Cultural History of Personal Naming in Western Europe*. Routledge, 1998.

Winnick, R. H. "'Loe, here in one line is his name twice writ': Anagrams, Shakespeare's Sonnets, and the Identity of the Fair Friend". *Literary Imagination*, 11 (2009): 254–77.

Wither, George. *A Collection of Emblemes* [1635]. Ed. John Horden. Menston: Scolar, 1968.

Withycombe, E. G. *The Oxford Dictionary of English Christian Names*. Oxford: Clarendon Press, 1945.

Wolcot, John [Peter Pindar]. *Poems*. Ed. P. M. Zall. Bath: Adams & Dart, 1972.

Womersley, David. "Dulness and Pope". *Proceedings of the British Academy*, 54 (1968) 231–63.

Woodcock, Thomas, and Robinson, John Martin. *The Oxford Guide to Heraldry*. Oxford University Press, 1988.

Woolgar, C. M. *The Great Household in Late Medieval England*. New Haven and London: Yale University Press, 1999.

Wooton, David. "The Vibes of Marx". *The Times Literary Supplement* (4 Feb. 2008) 10–11.

Worden, Blair. *The Sound of Virtue: Philip Sidney's* Arcadia *and Elizabethan Politics*. New Haven, CT, and London: Yale University Press, 1996.

Wright, Gillian. "A Pattern Poem by William Browne of Tavistock: 'Behold O God in Rivers of my Tears'". *English Manuscript Studies*, 7 (1998) 264–74.

Yates, Frances A. *Astraea: The Imperial Theme in the Sixteenth Century*. London and Boston: Routledge & Kegan Paul, 1975.

Yonge, Charlotte M. *History of Christian Names* [1863]. Rev. edn: 1884.

Ziff, Paul. *Semantic Analysis*. Ithaca, NY: Cornell University Press, 1960.

Index

Balthasar 162
baptism 12
Barber, C. L. 109
Barclay, Alexander 34
Barclay, John 88
Bardolph 106
Bardsley, Charles 14, 174
Barebone, Praisegod 14
Barney, Stephen 198–9
Barnivelt, Esdras (Alexander Pope) 95, 145–6, 197
Barrie, James 21
Barton, Anne 2, 17, 106
Bauhin, Caspar 125
Beatrice 101
Beelzebub 128–30
Belch, Sir Toby 104, 110
Belinda 95–6
Belleforest, François 119
Bellisont (Warham St Leger) 92, 93
Benedict 101
Berger, Harry 59
Berners, Lord 12
Berowne 114–15
Bersuire, Pierre 83
Betsy 160–1
Betty 185
Bickerstaff, Isaac 146
Bigwig 178
Blair, Tony 82
Bleak House 18
Bliss, Jane 143–4
Blount, Charles, Earl of Devon 81
Boccaccio, Giovanni 15–16, 198
    acrostics 77–8
Boiardo, Matteo Maria 61, 69
Boileau, Nicolas 35–6
Bonfont 60
Boots 158
Borachio 104
Bottom 107–8
    not posterior 108
Botul, Jean-Baptiste 148
Bovelles, Charles de 133
Bowditch, Nathaniel Ingersoll 174–5, 182

Boyle, Elizabeth 86–7
Braden, Gordon 63
Braggadocchio 59
Brahms, Caryl 7
Bramble 172
Brandon, Colonel 172
Britomart 65
Brook 103
Brown, George Mackay 13
Brunell (Valentine Browne, Henry Burnell) 92–3
Bryskett, Lodovic 93
Budé, Guillaume 56
Bum, Pompey 162
Bungus, Petrus 134
Burgess, Anthony 42
Butler, Samuel 5, 78
    "false wit" 78–9
Bynner, Witter, and Ficke, Arthur Davison 147
Byron, Lord 96

Cade, Jack 12
Caius (Kent) 105, 118
Calepino, Ambrogio 59
Caliban 103
Calvin, John 82
Cambridge, Richard 78–9
Camden, William 4, 7–8, 20, 23, 91–2, 101
    anagrams 80–1
    etymological explanations 24, 116, 118, 119–20
    on Puritan names 13–14, 55
Capote, Truman 97
Carey, John 159, 179
Carleton, Dudley 20
Carroll, Lewis (C. L. Dodgson) 2, 8, 21, 88, 142, 229
Cary, Joyce 4
Casaubon 172
Casio 103
Castorley 147
Catalogue of Ships 193–8
catalogues 193–8
    as genre 195

Fage, Mary 82
Fagin 185
Faith 14
Fals-Semblent 15
family plot 18–19, 235
Farmer George 31
Feefawfoo 179
Feng 119
Feste 109
fictional names: difficult to find 4
  collected from official lists 4,
    181–2, 186
Fidessa 58
Fielding, Henry 4, 16, 42, 177
fifteen steps to a throne 200, 202
Filelfo, Francesco 83
Finnegans Wake 7, 219–25
  compression 223
  dualities 222
  Dublin doubled 224
  Fenians 224
  macaronic universalizing 224
  modified idiom 223
  names of, strategic 225
  onomastic epic 224
  portmanteau effects 223
  Adams, Robert Martin 218
  Bloom, Molly 219
  Browne and Nolan 223
  Chimpden, Harold or
    Humphrey 221
  Connolly, Cyril 219
  Earwicker 219–25
  Eggeberth, Harun Childeric 220
  Everyman 219
  Finnegan 224
  Fordham, Finn 224–5
  Foxe, John 221
  Litz, Walt 224
  McGuiness 224
  Mick and Nick 222
  Peatrick 224
  Plurabelle, Anna Livia 220–5
  Ricks, Sir Christopher 224–5
  Shem and Shaun 221–2
  Tindall, William York 221

Weaver, Harriet 220, 225
  see also acrostics, anagrams
First names, paucity of Welsh 15
Fitzmaurice, Andrew 119
Fletcher, Giles 45
Fletcher, Phineas 33
Flite 184
Flannagan, Roy 207
Florimell 92, 94
Florio, John 102
Flosky (Coleridge) 96
Fludd, Robert 133–4
Flute 106–8
Forsyte Saga 5
Fortinbras 120
Fortitude 14
Fowler, William 84, 203–4
Fox, Denton 198, 201–2
Franciscus Junius 24
Fraunce, Abraham 69
Free-gift 14
Friday 162
Friedman, W. F. and E. S. 86
Froissart, Jean 12
From Above 14
Fuddleston, Sir Huddleston 178
full names 11–15
  individuating function 16
  of butlers, stewards,
    housekeepers 159–60
  of writers 12

Gabriel 126–7
  guardian of moon 134
Galathea 31
Gamage, Barbara 81
Gammer Gurton's Needle 16
Ganymed 105
Gardiner, Sir Alan 3
Gaskell, Elizabeth 152, 172
  Wives and Daughters 172
Gay, John 35, 146
gematria 80
Gemma 20
Geoffrey of Monmouth 5,
  117–118

naming (*cont.*)
  unobtrusive 171–2, 216
  upper servants 159–60
  withheld in romances 43, 142–4
Napoleon 1
Nature 68
Nedar (Arden) 116
Nelson, William 57
Nemo 184
Nessus 15
Newton, Thomas 127
Nicholas 14, 108
nicknames 3, 11, 13, 149–57
  Latinizations 151
  playing on real names 149
  poetic 151
  used by Bloomsbury circle 154
  "007" 150
  Ariosto of the north 153
  Dickens's 150
  Esther Summers's 185
  Scott's 153
  Shakespeare's 150
  Bathing Towel 149
  Beau 152
  Bozzy 152
  Bridey 150
  Caldius Biberius Mero 149
  Chops 185
  Corsica Boswell 152
  Dictionary Johnson 152
  Dilwyn Rees 154
  Doctor Angelicus 150
  Doctor Mirabilis 150–1
  Lanky 152
  Leonidas Glover 152
  Monk Lewis 149
  Pincher Martin 149–50
  Pip 150
  Sherry 152
  The Great Cham of
    literature 152
  The Great Magician 153
  The Great Unknown 153
  Ursa Major 152
  Wizard of the north 153

Nicola 20
Night 67
Nine Worthies 110–11
Noah 16
Nobody 191 n. 47
Nohrnberg, James 59, 66–7
nominative determinism 6
Norman Conquest 11
North, Thomas 105, 116
Nostromo 216
number symbolisms:
  diapason 201
  fifteen 200, 202
  seven 200
  six 200
  sixteen 203
Nuttall, Anthony 114
Nym 106

Oberon 113, 115
Odysseus 141–2, 195
Oldham, John 39–40
Oliver 186
Olsen, Stein 6
onomastics, interest in 172–5
Ophelia 101, 119–20
Original 14
Orimont (Ormond) 92, 93, 94
Orlando Ozio 96
Osmond 175
Osric 120
Ossian 146
Oswald 118
Othello 101, 103
Ovid 113
Owl and the Nightingale, The 75

Palice of Honour 201–3
  throne approached by fifteen
    steps 200, 202
  Humility and Discipline
    central 202
Palingenius 77
Pamela 17, 89
Pan 90
Pandar 3